# TOIL AND TROUBLE

A HISTORY OF AMERICAN LABOR

# TOIL

## A HISTORY

SECOND EDITION,
REVISED AND ENLARGED

# AND TROUBLE

## OF AMERICAN LABOR

### BY THOMAS R. BROOKS

FOREWORD BY A. H. RASKIN

## A DELTA BOOK

To Sergeant John F. Doyle
Killed February 22, 1945
Mte. Della Torraccia, Italy

A DELTA BOOK

Published by
DELL PUBLISHING CO., INC.
1 Dag Hammarskjold Plaza
New York, N.Y. 10017

ISBN: 0-440-59016-7

THIS EDITION PUBLISHED BY ARRANGEMENT
WITH DELACORTE PRESS, NEW YORK, NEW YORK 10017
MANUFACTURED IN THE UNITED STATES OF AMERICA

Eleventh printing—April 1982

VB

# ACKNOWLEDGMENTS

THE DRAWING UP OF A BIBLIOGRAPHY IS A PAYMENT OF AN INTELLECTUAL DEBT. This one is by no means complete; it is a list of those books I have found most helpful in my journey through labor history. It will, I believe, serve as a good beginning for those who would like to pursue further the story of American labor.

While acknowledgments are in order I would like to express my gratitude to Daniel Bell for bringing about a meeting between author and publisher; to the editor of *Challenge* for permission to use "The Old Guard in Retreat" (July, 1961), which appears here as Chapter XVIII in revised form; to the editor of *Commentary* for use of "The New Administration and Labor" (March, 1961), as Chapter XXII, and "Negro Militants, Jewish Liberals and the Unions" (September, 1961), which in altered form is the basis of Chapter XIX; to the editor of *Dissent* for "Black Upsurge in the Unions" (March–April, 1970), now Chapter XXIV; to the editor of *Dun's Review* for "Bleaching the Blue Collar" (January, 1962), now Chapter XXI; and to the editor of *Kiwanis Magazine* for the use of "Labor Looks at Automation" (December, 1961–January, 1962), as Chapter XX; to the editor of the *Commonweal* for the use of "Settlement in Steel" (July 26, 1963) as the basis for my introductory chapter; to my editors Mrs. Elizabeth Shepherd, Harold J. Blum, and Richard Kennedy, whose patience is exemplary; and to my wife, whose help is beyond reckoning.

Adamic, Louis. *Dynamite*. New York: The Viking Press, 1931.

Bell, Daniel. *The End of Ideology*. Glencoe (Ill.) : The Free Press, 1960.

———, *Work and Its Discontents*. New York: League for Industrial Democracy, 1970.

Bernstein, Irving. *The Lean Years: A History of the American Worker 1920–1933*. Boston: Houghton Mifflin Company, 1960.

Brissenden, Paul Frederick. *The IWW: A Study of American Syndicalism*. New York: Columbia University Press, 1920.

Brooks, John Graham. *American Syndicalism*. New York: The Macmillan Company, 1913.

Buchanan, Joseph R. *The Story of a Labor Agitator*. New York: The Outlook Company, 1903.

Christie, Robert A. *Empire in Wood*. Ithaca (N.Y.) : Cornell University Press, 1956.

Coleman, McAlister. *Men and Coal*. New York: Farrar & Rinehart, Inc., 1943.

Commons, John R., and others. *History of Labour in the United States*. 4 vols. New York: The Macmillan Company, 1918.

Dubofsky, Melvyn. *We Shall Be All: A History of the Industrial Workers of the World*. Chicago: Quadrangle Books, 1969.

Galenson, Walter. *The CIO Challenge to the AFL*. Cambridge (Mass.) : Harvard University Press, 1960.

Gompers, Samuel. *Seventy Years of Life and Labor*. 2 vols. New York: E. P. Dutton & Co., 1934.

Gregory, Charles O. *Labor and the Law*. New York: W. W. Norton & Company, Inc., 1946.

Howe, Irving, and B. J. Widick. *The UAW and Walter Reuther*. New York: Random House, 1949.

Hutchinson, John. *The Imperfect Union: A History of Corruption in American Trade Unions*. New York: E. P. Dutton Co., Inc., 1970.

Karson, Marc. *American Labor Unions & Politics, 1900–18*. Carbondale (Ill.) : Southern Illinois University Press, 1958.

Kempton, Murray. *Part of Our Time*. New York: Simon & Schuster, Inc., 1955.

Leiter, Robert D. *The Teamsters Union*. New York: Bookman Associates, Inc., 1957.

Lens, Sidney. *Left, Right & Center, Conflicting Forces in American Labor*. Hinsdale (Ill.) : Henry Regnery Company, 1949.

Levenstein, Aaron. *Labor Today and Tomorrow*. New York: Alfred A. Knopf, 1945.

Levinson, Edward. *Labor on the March*. New York: Harper & Brothers, 1938.

Lieberman, Elias. *Unions Before the Bar*. New York: Oxford Book Company, 1960.

Lipset, Seymour Martin, Martin A. Trow and James S. Coleman. *Union Democracy*. New York: Doubleday & Company, Inc., 1962.

Mills, C. Wright. *The New Men of Power*. New York: Harcourt, Brace and Company, 1948.

Perlman, Selig. *A Theory of the Labor Movement*. New York: The Macmillan Company, 1928.

Seidman, Joel. *American Labor from Defense to Reconversion*. Chicago: The University of Chicago Press, 1953.

Taft, Philip. *The AF of L in the Time of Gompers*. New York: Harper & Brothers Publishers, 1957.

———. *The AF of L from the Death of Gompers to the Merger*. New York: Harper & Brothers, 1959.

Todes, Charlotte. *William H. Sylvis and the National Labor Union*. New York: International Publishers, 1942.

Vorse, Mary Heaton. *Labor's New Millions*. New York: Modern Age Books, Inc., 1938.

Wagstaff, Thomas, *et al.* "The Negro and the American Labor Movement: Some Selected Chapters." *Labor History*, Vol. 10, No. 3. New York: The Tamiment Institute, Summer, 1969.

Ware, Norman J. *The Industrial Worker, 1840 to 1860*. New York: D. Appleton and Company, 1924.

———. *The Labor Movement in the United States, 1860 to 1895*. New York: D. Appleton and Company, 1929.

Yellen, Samuel. *American Labor Struggles*. New York: Russell & Russell, Inc., 1956.

# FOREWORD

ORGANIZED LABOR, AT THE ZENITH OF ITS ECONOMIC AND
political strength, peers timorously into an automated future that
may leave it an impotent pigmy. The proud boast of the American
union movement is still: *Labor Omnia Vincit.* But no sense of
triumph buoys the leaders of labor as they struggle to adapt the
techniques of collective bargaining to the dizzying new challenges
of an era of rapid technological change.

The nature of work is changing; the frustrations of work are
changing; the need for work is changing. Out of these changes
comes the ironic likelihood that, in a period when unions are
turning most of their attention to easing the impact of automation
on their members, the labor movement itself may become technology's most spectacular victim.

Much of the effectiveness is being drained out of the economic
weapons on which unions have relied to make American wages
the highest in the world, to create a unique system of industry-
financed social security under the union label, and to bring into
being a structure of industrial democracy that has added much to
the dignity of work and the self-esteem of the worker. The slo-
gans that brought millions of men and women trooping into union

ranks in the early years of the New Deal have little appeal in computerized industries—even those in which the principal effect of progress has not been a sharp reduction in the number of organizable workers.

Worse still in its impact on union strength, the protective devices that can be erected at the bargaining table against the onslaught of new technology on jobs are essentially negative, no matter how much ingenuity the negotiators carry to their task. The central mission is to construct an ever stronger umbrella over a shrinking total number of jobs. That means the union's function becomes to do more and more for fewer and fewer workers at a time when the population is expanding at a record pace. The extension of this process can mean union atrophy or social explosion unless the nation—through a combination of public and private effort—does a better job than it has up to now of assuring a full-employment economy, or of providing constructive alternatives to work as we move toward a workless world.

If the historians of American institutions are obliged to record the next decade as a time in which labor was innovating itself into the grave, the fabric of our democracy will have been greatly damaged. Dynamic unions are an indispensable element in maintaining some small measure of restraint on the centralization of authority in government and in giant corporations. If the sole basis on which they can cling to life is as supine wards of government or as glorified company unions, their worth as instruments of human freedom and social justice will be almost as negligible as if they crumbled into nothingness.

The bulwarks against such degeneration lie not in the monumentality of union headquarters or the piling of additional billions of dollars in labor-management welfare funds or the multiplication of invitations to ranking unionists to dine at the White House, but in the rediscovery of the roots of union growth and in the rekindling of a sense of crusade in labor's torpid, stagnant legions.

This may seem strange advice when it is so plain that a large part of the explanation for the sterility of labor's response to the challenges of change is the extent to which its thought patterns and strategy are mired in memories of the brave campaigns of the 1930s. The ideas for translating automation's promise into a society of equitably shared abundance will not come by looking backward to a redistillation of policies developed in a decade of depression and mass unemployment.

But a recognition that one of labor's most conspicuous lags is in social inventiveness in no way negates the need to discover afresh the wellsprings of unionism and to draw from them a clearer consciousness of what unions are for and how they can best serve both their members and the community. Without that awareness, community responsibility can itself be perverted into an avenue for separating union leaders from their rank and file to the ultimate detriment of community as well as workers.

In this book Thomas R. Brooks, long a perceptive evaluator of the labor scene both as a union activist and as an independent commentator, illuminates the long sweep of labor history in a manner that will help to point toward a new forward surge. Clearly, the United States will never move into an era of plenty, democratically shared, without a great deal more planning for the effective use of our manpower and material resources.

Equally clearly, the disposition in Congress and in much of America is to fight anything that smacks of planning. Labor's big task, for its own survival and the country's good, is to mobilize grassroots political sentiment in favor of greater Federal responsibility for full production, full distribution, and full employment.

If workers are to give ungrudging acceptance to the idea that the total welfare requires maximum mechanization, they will want assurance that the country knows what to do with the fruits of this increased efficiency. Such assurance demands an economic general staff representing all elements in the population and administering a program aimed at the sustained development of high levels of public and private economic activity. The chances for eradicating poverty and unemployment would be vastly better with such a program than they can be if we continue to rely on the notion that tens of thousands of corporate and individual decisions, each predicated on what is best for the business, will automatically add up to full protection for the American economy.

Labor has no more urgent task in the '60s than the focusing of its political energies on the conquest of want, illiteracy, and intolerance; the building up of health and decent housing; the realization of the limitless promise of this scientific Golden Age. These undertakings are not only imperative for a better America, but they would be vastly more inspiriting to union membership and leadership alike than the present ever more routine, even self-canceling, function in the policing of day-to-day plant grievances, the writing of mechanized contracts, and the drafting of funeral arrangements for thousands upon thousands of jobs. Ours is a nonideological labor movement, but politics may soon become its chief business. If not, as Tom Brooks suggests, it may soon be presiding at its own funeral.

—*A. H. Raskin*

# CONTENTS

# INTRODUCTION

COLLECTIVE BARGAINING, AS MALCOLM L. DENISE OF FORD MOTOR
Company reminds us, "is a continuous, never-ending, enormously
complicated process." It is also, as the Ford labor relations vice-
president goes on to say, many things to many men. For some of
us, however, it is important because it is an instrument, imperfect
though it may be, of industrial democracy. It is one aspect of
man's struggle against those who would take the meaning out of
work. Collective bargaining gives laboring men and women some
say about the conditions of their employment. More than that, the
pitting of the countervailing power of the unions against that of
the corporations sometimes opens a crack in the institutionalism
that engulfs us, affording the individual worker an additional
measure of freedom. But this is a by-product of a process considered by many to be central to the opening up of democracy in
industry.

Unions are essential to that process. How they came to be is the
subject of this book. But unions too can become bureaucratic,
impediments to the freedom of man to act and create. As bureaucratic institutions they "police the agreement," a phrase meaning
that the enforcement of a labor contract rests with the unions.
Management wants a docile and productive labor force; recog-

nition of a union is one way to achieve it. Paradoxically, however, the unions frequently are destructive of docility; they stir
up workers over issues management would rather see lie dead.
Sometimes this action is negative: the rail unions, for example,
delayed rail managements' outright dumping of some 40,000
firemen and brakemen from their jobs. Sometimes the action is
positive: unions have challenged management's right to make
unilateral decisions over automation. And, as institutions in our
society, the unions often act to extend freedom by backing movements to protect or increase civil rights, education, housing, employment, and like issues.

Compared to the time when workingmen had little or nothing
to say about the conditions of their employment, the unions have
achieved much. In the 1961 auto negotiations, for example,
elected representatives of the industry's workers discussed with
management issues that ranged from the procedure through
which a man can file a grievance against his foreman to the
control of investment policies for a nine-figure pension fund, from
the rules governing personal leaves of absence to the right of
management to locate plants and introduce new methods, from
safety glasses to profit sharing, and from toilet time to placing
hourly workers on a salaried basis. Yet, though American industry plans on a scale few governments match, the unions prefer to
skirt the issue of worker participation in the planning process.
Management initiates action; the individual worker is confined to
a carefully circumscribed challenge—through grievances—of the
effect any such action may have on himself. The same holds for
workers collectively. Management alone can close down a plant or
move its operations. The union cannot challenge such decisions
although it can make them costly by insisting on severance pay,
the carryover of seniority and job rights from the old to the new
plant, transfer pay, and so on.

Worse yet, the workers' struggle to get ahead of production
pressures is unending—and one-sided. No victory is final. Production standards are set by engineers for management; the

workers can challenge these only after they have been put into effect. If the worker and/or his union manages to score a point, management remains free to introduce still another set of production standards. Since the workers are not privy to the planning processes, they are, as Harvey Swados has pointed out, continually off balance when it comes to protecting their interests. "You can strike one week over standards," Swados reports a leader of the United Auto Workers as saying, "and next week they'll introduce new standards." As a result, though unions are stronger today than ever before, they are ultimately powerless when faced with a management determined to cut costs. "What good," asks Swados in a perceptive study of the UAW published in *Dissent*, "does it do to win a battle for yourself or for your fellow workers if you discover after victory not only that the war goes on, but that the rules of war have been changed all over again, unilaterally, by your opponent?"

Whenever the unions have gone beyond this limited role—that of challenging decisions already made—they have been defeated. When the United Auto Workers, for instance, in 1945 demanded that the industry open its books, pegging a proposed wage increase to stable prices and a reasonable profit, industry, government and other unions ganged up, knocked the proposal on the head, and proceeded to tie wages to an inflationary spiral that lasted a decade. The setback of the UAW served to place the unions outside the pale of post World War II planning.

The 1963 steel settlement, with its promise of industrial peace at last, is, to say the least, a very good one indeed. The extended vacation plan is an imaginative innovation in an area generally gone stale. Once every five years, one-half of the industry's employees with the longest seniority will get 13 weeks' vacation at a stretch. This will give added zest to steel workers' lives and save jobs, though the union's estimate of 20–25,000 may turn out too high. The strife-free settlement extends for another two years the industrial peace that has prevailed within the steel industry since the 116-day strike in 1959. After January 1, 1965, either party can reopen the agreement on a 120-day notice—an open-end arrangement that seems to promise continued peace in steel labor relations. Yet, the way it was done casts doubt upon the future of collective bargaining as a viable form of industrial democracy. The steel talks were conducted in a secrecy reminiscent of John L. Lewis's locked-room sessions with the coal barons, a secrecy incompatible with our notion of unions as democratic institutions— a notion, incidentally, incorporated into the nation's labor law by the Landrum-Griffin amendments to the Taft-Hartley Act in 1959. Initially Lewis's conferences were successful. They brought high wages, hospitals, and other welfare benefits for the miners, a free hand on automation for the coal operators. But today hungry miners haunt the hills of Kentucky and Tennessee with guns at the ready. Union hospitals are shut down along with the marginal coal pits. This grim outcome of "pressure free" bargaining ought to give pause to our praise of year-round, "continuously" negotiating labor-management committees, the latest development in collective bargaining.

Automation, with its far-reaching potential for change in our lives, brought on a crisis in collective bargaining, a crisis now receding before a wave of "study" committees set up to discover "bases for agreement" between labor and management. Periodic bargaining, hitched to a two-three contract cycle, is giving way to the new committee system of continual bargaining. The bargaining crisis now fading from the scene was marked by a series of strikes—from the 116-day 1959 steel strike to the 114-day New York newspaper strike and lockout—that posed issues that get to the guts of any real attempt at industrial democracy. Who owns the job? Are workers to participate in the decisions on when and how to automate? Who is to determine work practices, the size of crews, and who is to do what work? How are the gains from automation to be split? What role, if any, are workers (and possibly the public) to have in industrial planning? The answers are implicit in recent collective-bargaining developments and these developments throw into question, or at least raise serious doubts about, the future of industrial democracy.

Unions, as this history shows, have never succeeded in quite breaking through into full participation in American economic life. But though unions do not directly participate in corporate planning, our major form of planning, they were "used" in planning by management. As Daniel Bell has demonstrated, each major postwar strike and concomitant wage increase served as an excuse to jack up prices and as a means of lowering corporate break-even points (the lowest percentage of operating capacity needed to make a profit). In return for this "service," the giant unions won high wages and still greater fringe benefits. But such a development was only possible in the "Fat Fifties," years when demand—consumer and government—ran high. During these years the unions, with a few exceptions, were given their head. The slackening of demand toward the end of the decade cramped management's free-hand style.

The 1959 steel strike signaled a management effort to curtail the unions. Significantly, nearly every major industry or corporation has had "to take" a strike in order to drive the lesson of restraint home to the unions. The 33-day Atlantic and Gulf Coast longshoremen's strike and the New York newspaper shutdown are the latest—if not the last—in this strike series. For the first time since 1945, when the UAW raised the question of a possible role for the unions in economic planning, issues of industrial democracy were at the center of labor-management controversy. Ownership and control of the job, who and what determines the rate of automation, the contracting out of work, plant investment, all kinds of work practices—all these and more were open to debate.

Much of this debate took place outside the hotel suites where management and union men whiled away their time as strikes dragged on. The public interest was aroused, and the government began to intervene. Even the Eisenhower Administration looked askance at the collective-bargaining crisis developing under its aegis; the Kennedy Administration actively fostered third-party intervention. Here was an opportunity for an industrial "opening to the left" by an imaginative Administration. A third party, whether a governmental or lay figure, could pry planning, or important aspects of planning, out of management's selfish solitary grasp. To a limited degree, this did happen in Kaiser Steel, which made a separate settlement with the steel union following the 1959 strike. Of all the current rash of "study" or permanent "human relations" collective-bargaining committees, the Kaiser committee is the only one with public members. The Kaiser "Long-Range" committee came up with the so-far successful "shared-savings" plan. Oddly enough, the plan gives the union at least a glimpse of company books (how else can "savings" be determined?), which is something of an opening in corporate workings—enough of one to say that third-party intervention in the automation-centered crisis could have been leverage for more, not less, industrial democracy. Or, so one would hope.

But the Kennedy Administration just as clearly placed a greater value on industrial peace than on industrial democracy, however mild. The pressure of intervention was pressure for peace no matter how obtained with the only ceiling being one of cost. "We cannot afford strikes affecting the national interest," was the New Frontier line—a line, incidentally, at variance with the facts. We have not had any strikes seriously affecting the national interest in over a decade. Sam Romer, the able labor correspondent for the *Minneapolis Tribune*, has pointed out that all during the longshoremen's strike, ships arrived daily on the West Coast, trains ran and trucks rolled. America's vast heartland, in his opinion, was scarcely affected by the dock walkout. Still, the myth is effective in newspaper editorials and in Washington.

Under pressure from the government, desirous of avoiding attention-getting strikes, labor and management have evolved a new technique, the so-called prebargaining "study" committees on which technicians from both sides either search for a basis for agreement or seek to define the areas of disagreement away from the heat of the bargaining table. Note that in most cases the parties engaged in "study" are also the ones who will bargain contract terms later. This is the ultimate in professionalism in collective bargaining. Union leaders now are true "brokers" of the labor of union members.

Strike deadlines do, of course, intensify conflict. But the process traditionally has also called for a kind of active consultation between the rank and file and the union leadership. This is the guts of democratic unionism. Union demands, true enough, are frequently formulated at the top. Nonetheless, with a contract expiration in the cards, carrying with it the possibility of a strike, these demands must be put to the members, argued, clarified and discussed at countless union meetings that bring out a greater number of participating members than all other union meetings. During this process, the union member does get at least the chance to test union demands against his own needs and wants. If the union demands are found wanting, there is a chance to make them over if enough wish it. As the union prepares for its periodic confrontation with corporate management, the union member is usually well aware of the issues, which ones he is willing to fight for and how much of a fight he would like to put up.

This process no doubt contributes to the "heat" of what Secretary of Labor W. Willard Wirtz calls "countdown bargaining." Hence, the attractiveness of continual "secret" committee bargaining to New Frontiersmen. It also appealed to the professionalism of the Kennedy Administration. What disturbed so many about the New York newspaper strike was this lack of professionalism on the printers' side; the International Typographer's Union is a democratic union, and its negotiators were printers, not full-time professionals. Their officers when defeated go back to the linotype machines. The solution for the unruliness of collective bargaining is typical of the New Frontier: throw the question into committee. Negotiators are to be isolated from the passions of deadline bargaining, and, incidentally, from those of rank-and-file union members.

"We have found," says Ford's Denise of continual, informal exchange between labor and management professionals, "that this kind of communication flourishes best when no one is trying to overreach or to make a production out of it, or to score public relations points." For management to observe these guidelines is no strain. Management is not democratically representative nor responsible to anyone outside of itself. For union bureaucracies, autocratic by inclination, the new way is also an escape from the bother of consultation with union members. But the new way, especially in its secrecy and isolation from union members, is a contradiction to any vision of the unions as democratic countervailing power to the autocracy of the corporate world. It is not in keeping with any notion of industrial democracy. But the new joint committees also can be said to work. For most Americans, this apparently is enough. But is it? When one looks at American labor history one wonders and hopes.

For there is a thin, uncertain line that runs from the early journeymen cordwainers, who struck to save their craft, to Goldfield, Arizona, where the Wobblies defiantly posted the terms of work on the union hall bulletin board for employers to come, read and observe, down to the New York City schoolteachers, who recently threatened to strike to win a reduction in class size. Each of these events had to do with a worker's dignity, his pride in the quality of his work. On this slender thread rests whatever there is of lasting value in the struggles of American labor. This book is an attempt to trace that thin line and its ramifications.

# INTRODUCTION TO THE SECOND EDITION

THREE NEW DEVELOPMENTS RISING OUT OF THE 1960s PROMISE profoundly to affect the labor movement: the unionization of the public sector, the black upsurge within the unions and the coming of a new generation. Each is likely to come to a head in the 1970s and, together, are sure to have a major impact on the essential character of the labor movement, collective bargaining and organized labor's role in the social and political arena. In the new material added to this edition of *Toil and Trouble*, I have discussed the first two developments, but have touched upon the third only indirectly. Since the young are often agents of change, perhaps some speculation about the possible impact of the changeover in generations will serve as an appropriate introduction to this edition.

Unhappily, not nearly enough is known about the lives and attitudes of young blue-collar workers in the United States. As Tom Kahn, executive director of the League for Industrial Democracy, to whom I owe much for whatever insights that follow, put it, the blue-collar young are our "invisible youth." We know a good deal about the alienated middle-class youth; the dissatisfactions of the college student enliven the mass media each spring. As a consequence, we tend to view youth as a homogeneous class and see in the unrest among college students and junior faculty a universal youth rebellion. But, as Kahn reminds us, "there are gaps within the generations as well as between them. Indeed, one youth's discontent may be another's privilege." We overlook such distinctions because we like to believe we live in a classless society.

The truth is clearly otherwise. There are 45 million Americans between the ages of 15 and 29. About seven million of them are in college, 14 million in high school, and possibly another two to three million have graduated from college. But the remaining 21 million are neither students nor college graduates. True, more youth than ever before go on to college, about one out of every three high-school graduates. But that is to overlook the obverse figure: two out of three do not. And their experience is very much determined by their class. For instance, even though the greater economic growth of the late 1960s reduced unemployed rates below four percent, the rate for youth hovered around 15 percent. While it appears that some blue-collar youth, in a tight labor market, have taken to dropping in and out of jobs pretty much as middle-class youngsters do school, that is not the whole story. Young workers, as an instance, often start families earlier, and unemployment for them may take on the fearful cast it has for their depression-experienced fathers, or at least touch a tender nerve. Last hired, young workers are the first fired and the blue slip in the pay envelope may arrive along with a new baby. Add to this the uncertainties created by automation and cybernetics, not to speak of the dissensions of a divided country, and then, I think, one can get a sense of the underlying edginess of working-class life in an allegedly affluent society. The young blue-collar worker's father, or perhaps we ought to talk of grandfathers, wanted "steady work" and "good money." Can the same be said of the new generation now entering the workaday world? Bayard Rustin reminds us of the "instant gratification" syndrome among the slum-bred, who want all that stuff being sold on television *now!* What of the blue-collar young, who may be getting a chunk of it now—on time payments?

The mass media exert a tremendous influence, as they do on all of us. Fifty-eight percent of the union members surveyed by the John Kraft polling organization in early 1967 (reported in the August, 1967, issue of *The American Federationist*) said they spent ten or more hours a week in front of the tube, and 49 percent said television was their most reliable source of information. Thirty-one percent look to the daily newspapers and about nine percent to the weekly news magazines. Significantly two-thirds of unionists over 30 said they paid a fair amount of attention to their union publications, while only half of those under 30 did. So it appears the McLuhan generation may cross class lines. But one wonders, for response may be cultivated by what happens to young lives as a consequence of class position.

Assuming that inflation will be curbed without the price of high unemployment, Bureau of Labor experts have predicted that the nation's labor force will rise by one-fifth by 1980 to 100 million workers, and of these, 26 million will be in the 24 to 34 age group. On the job these young workers will find their lives influenced by two powerful forces—their employers and their unions. Of the two, they, in turn, will no doubt have a greater direct impact on the latter.

Some consequences are already visible. Roughly one out of four union members is under 30, and there is evidence that younger workers are largely responsible for the increased frequency with which rank-and-file union members rejected contracts negotiated by union leaders at the end of the 1960s. In interviewing leaders and young members of the auto- and steel-workers' unions, *New York Times* reporter Agis Salpukas found that the new, younger workers were "better educated and want treatment as equals from the bosses on a plant floor . . . ; do not want work they think hurts their health or safety, even though old-timers have done the same work for years; want fast changes and sometimes bypass their own union leaders and start wildcat strikes." Salpukas reports union men concluding, "There is a challenge to management's authority to run its plants"—to hire, lay off, assign, transfer and promote employees, and to determine the starting and quitting time and hours worked.

The reader of this book, I hope, will discover that these things are not so new as the young believe. The young workers, who provided much of the excitement in organizing the CIO in the 1930s, too, often found the old-timers reluctant about seizing the plants in a sit-down strike. Today's impatience, after all, rests upon yesterday's achievements. This is implicit in one incident cited by Salpukas. A Steel Worker staff representative, Manuel Fernandez, recalled a three-day wildcat strike in a brick-manufacturing plant which followed the disciplining of a worker by a foreman for carelessness in operating a lift truck. "The older generation would have filed a grievance," Fernandez said. "The young people have no faith in that. They want it settled right away. There's a big explosion coming in the industrial unions and the young people are going to come out on top."

In history's perspective this statement is not so revolutionary as it sounds. AFL-CIO president George Meany was, I believe, closer to the mark when he said, "All the labor leaders of the past were young men dissatisfied with working conditions when they started to build unions. And from what I've seen of today's young worker, I think the future of labor is going to be in good hands." Indirectly, however, Meany did indicate one difference with the past of great importance. The young dissatisfied workers of the past expended their energies in building new institutions. Now a new generation is growing up—coming to power—within an already established institution. And the young do have different priorities. To oversimplify, young workers tend to prefer immediate wage gains over such deferred benefits as improved pensions. But even this is a complicated matter. Early retirement may open up more desirable jobs for young workers and create an interest in pension demands among the young in industry. The young, too, are more apt to be dissatisfied with present leadership, a feeling they share with black workers now coming to the fore within many unions. The black upsurge within the unions has many of the characteristics of generational change and indeed may be viewed fruitfully in that light. And, too, young workers frequently play a leading role in the organizing of new unions among public employees, farm workers and in the service industries. The picture is complex, and today's young will no more escape history than did their elders.

On job issues, so far as I can judge, the impatience of young workers with "things as they are" falls within the traditional in-plant, anti-boss militancy of generations of American workers. Much more crucial, in my opinion, is the political question: Are young workers going to be more political than previous generations? And, if so, what kind of politics?

At first glance the prognosis is not favorable. George C. Wallace, the latter-day Know-Nothing, drew more support in the 1968 Presidential race for his candidacy from voters under thirty than from any other age group. Young, that is, relatively young workers were prominent in the "hard-hat" construction workers' demonstrations in the spring of 1970, against long-hairs, peaceniks and other off-beat types. When one looks beneath the surface agitation, however, there are some encouraging signs. For example, the Kraft survey previously mentioned disclosed only one issue on which union members differed widely from an AFL-CIO position—open occupancy in housing, which received only 43 percent in support. But on this issue *young* workers were closer to the official AFL-CIO position in support of open occupancy than were older rank-and-file unionists. Forty-eight percent of those workers under 30 endorsed it.

Alexander Barkin, director of the AFL-CIO Committee on Political Education, put the findings of the Kraft poll into perspective: "More recent prominent issues—like air and water pollution control and consumer legislation—achieve a slightly higher degree of support among younger than among older members. Conversely, issues that dwelled in Congress for years—issues with roots in the 1930s, '40s, and '50s—garner higher support among older than among younger members. Medicare, for exam-

ple, gets 75 percent from members in their 40s and 78 percent
from members 50 and over, while it gets 70 percent support from
members under 30, many of whom apparently view it as a problem that won't crop up for them until far down the road."

One ought not to discount the impact of the work place as an
education. As Michael Harrington remarks in his book *Socialism: Past, Present and Future,* "Workers . . . are concentrated
in very large numbers, subjected to a common discipline in the
work process, and forced—in the defense of their most immediate
interests—to build collective institutions. They therefore have a
cohesion, a social weight, in excess of their members." Even
though, as the Kraft poll discovered, nearly 75 percent of union
members under 40 were suburbanites—as against 50 percent of
*all* union members—they do not escape the discipline of the
industrial processes. Nor will they escape the broader pressures
building up within the trade-union movement—the organization
of the public sector and the upsurgence of black workers within
the unions. Both of these forces tend to be political, the one because it is, after all, their bread and butter, and the other because
so many answers to the problems of the black community are to
be found in politics. Young workers, no matter where they are,
cannot escape these influences. My own observations indicate
that the young men and women who win local union elections
or work on union staffs tend to be more political, more progressive
than their peers—in the plants and in the colleges. The reasons
for this are obvious. These are the union youth who have attended
union educational institutes, read the labor press, participated in
bargaining and other union affairs, and have had to take hard
looks at the gut issues that affect the rank and file.

In sum, I think, the indications are that young workers will
reinforce the recurring involvement of the American worker and
his unions in politics. And, on the whole, I think labor history
shows that this involvement may be described as progressive.
What is unique to worker experience, I suggest, is the necessity
that forces him toward political action and toward involvement in

the issues of the day. Unions, long concerned about health and safety in the plant, are now writing "environmental provisions" defining anew what are acceptable working conditions. The United Farm Workers Organizing Committee, for example, has negotiated a ban on "hard pesticides," including DDT, Aldrin, Dieldrin, Endrin, Tepp and Parathion, in the farm factories of California. The United Auto Workers joined with six conservation groups in urging Congress to set air pollution control standards so tough that they would banish the internal-combustion engine from autos by 1975. The Oil, Chemical and Atomic Workers Union has taken its antipollution drive to the bargaining table, demanding that the oil companies deposit 0.1 cent per barrel of oil refined into a joint fund for research into pollution caused by the oil and gas industry.

Ten years ago, the years of gestation for this book, automation was a hot issue just as inflation seemingly dominates the dawn of the 1970s. Yesterday's issues, of course, have a way of becoming occasions for tomorrow's retrospection. No doubt we will muddle through inflation as we did automation even though both are likely to persist, varying in magnitude as economic activity waxes or wanes, as problems for our society. Significantly, both automation and inflation as well as a host of other critical issues, including the latest fashionable one of environmental pollution, raise fundamental questions about the nature of our society. All point to the need for planning. Indeed, they force planning upon us for one does not introduce cybernetic machines costing hundreds of thousands of dollars nor impose wage/price controls lightly. So, too, in ecological matters, the simple edict, "Clean up," embodies so many ramifications that everything we do must be carefully thought out. The question then becomes how can we resolve democratically and responsibly issues that affect us all.

Some answers, I believe, may be found in labor history. In this country, as in other industrially advanced nations, we have relied on collective bargaining to set wages directly and prices indirectly as well as more or less to regulate the introduction of technological change. Now it appears some ecological matters, too, may be resolved through workers' demands for adequate health safeguards. Blinkered by our myths of free enterprise, we tend to view collective bargaining as a voluntary act. But it is not so unrestrained as one might think. The law, general trends in the economy and public opinion all place restraints in varying degree upon the negotiators, setting the limits as to what is permissible as well as what is attainable. In this light collective bargaining is an instrument of public policy, a technique of social and economic planning. Its importance to our policy is underscored by an act of Congress: unions are the only voluntary institutions within American society that are required by law to be democratic.

Obviously collective bargaining cannot solve all our problems. It cannot rebuild our cities, clean up our streams or purify our air. Nonetheless, organized labor remains the major force pushing consistently for legislative programs that will do something about such matters. Moreover, organized labor is the only force persistently lobbying for full employment. No major piece of economic, social or civil-rights legislation now enacted into law could have passed Congress without the active support of the labor movement.

No democratic institution, however, can afford to rest on past laurels. Recent developments in the public sector, among black and young workers ensure, one hopes, that the labor movement will not. The cycle of inflation and unemployment cries out for resolution. The hungry of the world are as yet unfed; the poor are ill-housed. A world economy of plenty lies within the grasp of man, and the vast multinational corporations reach out to encompass the globe. Of all the institutions of modern society, trade unions are most central to nearly all its vital concerns. Rooted in the work place and in the day-to-day experience of working people, unions reach out through political action to embrace all the issues of war and peace, of poverty and plenty, and of economic, political and social democracy. Churches have their moral authority, corporations, economic power, and the universities, intellectuality, and each, in its own fashion, reaches outward but none ties the individual to the social fabric so closely as do the unions. Speaking in 1871 on "The Foundation of the Labor Movement," Wendell Phillips described the motto of the workingman of the United States as: "Short hours, better education, co-operation in the end, and in the meantime a political movement that will concentrate the thought of the country upon this thing." One hundred years later the labor movement is still working at that particular job. Or so I believe its history suggests.

# NOTHING EXPECTED
# BUT BY LABOR

WE BEGIN WITH WORK. THIS IS THE REALITY THAT CONFRONTED nearly all the migrants to American shores, from the first settlers at Jamestown to the latest Puerto Rican hopefully disembarking from a night-flight jet at New York's Kennedy International Airport.

The gentlemen adventurers whose arrival at Jamestown so exasperated Captain John Smith were lured here by the thoughts of gold dancing feverishly on their brains. All they needed, they thought, was a touch of "Spanish Luck" and their fortunes would be made. "Why, man," declared a 1605 play on the glories to be found in America, "all their dripping pans are pure golde, and all the chaines with which they chaine up their streets are massive gold; all the prisoners they take are fettered in golde; and for rubies and diamonds, they goes forth in holy dayes and gather 'hem by the sea-shore, to hang on their children's coates and stick in their children's caps, as commonly as our children wear saffron-gilt brooches and groates with holes in 'hem." Once the fortune-hunters landed on the inhospitable shores of Virginia, however, it was the harsh dictum of Captain Smith that those who would eat must work that kept them alive. "Nothing," said Smith, "is to be expected thence, but by labor."

Ultimately, of course, the dream of gold gave way to something more prosaic but infinitely more substantial and lasting. It was, as Charles Beard noted, "the man fired by the passion for owning a plot of ground who led the vanguard of settlers all along the frontier from New Hampshire to Georgia; to him cheap land meant freedom, to his family a rude but sufficient comfort." Behind the settlers were the supporting troops, the Colonial merchants and traders of the seaboard cities. The frontier husbandman exchanged potash from his burned-over clearings for an ax and other tools, for kitchen utensils, for a bit of lawn or some linens for his wife, for powder and shot, shoe buckles, and a twist of tobacco. Towns grew as white pine marked for His Majesty's Navy, barrels of salted fish, and furs crowded the wharves. Houses had to be built, articles manufactured for trade and local consumption. Craftsmen were needed; there was a continual shortage of skilled labor. "When you send again," Captain Smith pleaded, "I entreat you rather send but thirty carpenters, husbandmen, gardners, fishermen, blacksmiths, masons, and diggers up of trees' roots, well provided, than a thousand such as we have." To induce a shoemaker to migrate in 1629, Massachusetts Bay Colony "gave him fifty acres of land and £10 a year for his services." Windsor, Connecticut, wooed a currier with a house, land and "something for a shop." But so great was the town's fear that they would lose the leather craftsman they stipulated that the property was to belong to him and his heirs only on condition that "he lives and dies with us and affords us the use of his trade."

As is often the case in frontier society, wages were high. Governor John Winthrop of Massachusetts Bay Colony complained in 1633 that the "scarcity of workers caused them to raise their wages to an excessive rate." Almost three decades later, a discouraged New Englander wrote that "help is scarce and hard to get, difficult to please, uncertain, etc." Gabriel Thomas, a Pennsylvanian historian, wrote in 1698, "Poor people can here get three times the wages for their Labour they can in England." Colonial workmen commanded anywhere from 30 to 100 percent higher real wages than did contemporary English workers. Wages exceeded the English scale by up to 100 percent for skilled workers and up to 50 percent for unskilled workmen. Massachusetts carpenters in 1701 secured 58.4 to 61 cents a day; in 1712, 83.3 cents. After a drop by 1743 to 40 cents a day in specie, carpenters' wages leveled out to about 67 cents a day from 1751 to 1767. Common labor in Massachusetts commanded a daily wage of 33 cents in 1752; 25 cents in 1758–61; 17.8 cents in 1762; 22 cents in 1777; and 79 cents in 1779.

Irked by the "excessive rates" charged by workmen, the Colonial governments sought to regulate wages. In 1630, the Massachusetts General Court ordered that "carpenters, joyners, bricklayers, sawers, and thatchers shall not take above 2 s. a day, nor any man shall give more, under paine" of a stiff fine. If workers "have meate and drinke" the pay was proportionately less. But the attempts to regulate the wages of masons, mowers, sawers, "taylors," "tylers," or wheelwrights soon failed. Employers overbid, and laws penalizing overpayment of wage rates were soon repealed, although legislation exacting fines from workmen who accepted more than the fixed rates continued in force for some time after. In the Colonial mind there was little doubt that there was a connection between high wages and high prices. Colonial legislatures frequently tried to regulate both, or wages by price controls. The most comprehensive attempt, the famous "assize of bread," which regulated the price of bread by proportions of ingredients, weight and price of wheat, lasted the longest. After the adoption of the Constitution, master bakers in New York refused to bake because the local assize was too stringent.

Clearly, it was exceedingly difficult for the colonial authorities to regulate wages and prices in the bustling, expanding urban centers along the Eastern seaboard. Boston, the largest town in North America, was described in 1744 by the traveling Scotsman

Dr. Alexander Hamilton as "a considerable place for shipping and carrys on a great trade. . . . The people of this province chiefly follow farming and merchandise. Their staples are shipping, lumber, and fish." The good doctor, who toured the colonies shortly before the outbreak of the American Revolution, also recorded the growth of more basic manufacturing in his *Itinerarium*—a visit, for example, to an iron works outside of Philadelphia, "where they were casting cannon, where I thought they made but bungling work of it, spoiling ten where they made one." But America's iron masters, possibly under the stimulation of demand created as a result of the French and Indian Wars, were soon doing much better. In 1700, the Colonies produced one-seventieth of the world's iron supply; by 1775, one-seventh. Indeed, when the Revolution dawned, the Colonies had more blast furnaces and forges than England and Wales combined. On the Brandywine in Delaware, Oliver Evans perfected machinery for cleaning, grinding, cooling, bolting, and barreling grains without manual operation. Using his system, six men closing barrels could convert annually 100,000 bushels of grain into flour. By the eve of the American Revolution the outlines of the future development of manufacturing were clearly discernible. New York City alone possessed a small linen factory with 14 looms, a paper mill, a beaver hatter manufacture, a glass house, two breweries, a spermaceti candle works, and a number of shipyards. In Colonial mill and furnace works, a semiskilled manufacturing work force took root and grew as industry expanded. Weaving and shoe manufacturing developed a "putting out system," or farming out work to the homes of craftsmen, which characterized the infant stage of these two important manufactures. Indeed, as the Royal Governor of New York warned London, a people who could clothe themselves handsomely without the help of England would soon think of governing themselves.

The burgeoning Colonial industry further intensified what was almost a chronic shortage of labor, especially skilled labor. Many of the free workingmen attracted to the colonies by offers of special advantage or high wages soon saved enough money to buy land, plentiful and cheap, and set up in farming on their own. For a time, the colonies were favored by an active colonization policy back home. Many Englishmen believed that the home isle was overpopulated and that the unemployed, poor and vagrant classes should be shipped off to the New World as fast as possible. The authorities, at first, were inclined to overlook the zealous recruiting activities of the colonial companies. "Spirits" or "crimps" virtually kidnapped colonists. But others in England were concerned lest the mother country lose too many of its own skilled workmen and fail to maintain a large enough labor supply to keep down wages and manufacturing costs. In time, these views began to prevail in official circles. Following the Stuart Restoration, as England became a great commercial and industrial power, the authorities began to discourage the emigration of free workmen, preferring instead to export convicts. In 1765, Parliament actually went so far as to forbid the emigration of skilled craftsmen as a means of preventing the spread of closely guarded manufacturing secrets and of maintaining an adequate supply of highly trained labor at home.

To meet the growing demand for labor, the Colonies turned to bound white labor and Negro slaves. It is estimated that up to 80 percent of the immigrants to America before the Revolution were indentured servants or Negro slaves. "The ships," wrote Hugh Jones in 1724 (*Present State of Virginia*), "bring over frequently white servants, which are of three kinds. 1. Such as come upon certain Wages by Agreement for a certain Time. 2. Such as come bound by Indenture, commonly call'd Kids, who are usually to serve four or five Years; and 3. those Convicts or Felons that are transported, whose Room they had much rather have than their Company; for abundance of them do great Mischiefs, commit Robbery and Murder, and spoil Servants, that were before very good: But they frequently there meet with the End that they deserved at Home, though indeed some of them prove indifferent good."

The bound white servant included many who voluntarily bound themselves for a term of years to pay for passage. But a goodly number were also hustled aboard ships, carried here against their will and sold into bondage. Indentured servants usually served for specific terms, generally from three to seven years. The redemptioners or "freewillers"—those who signed an indenture with a recruiting agent to pay the cost of passage, which averaged about £10—served a term of two or three years. These, according to some estimates, accounted for 60 to 77 percent of total immigration until 1776. The Hogarthian "rogues, vagabonds, and sturdy beggars" and the Moll Flanders transported to the Colonies generally served seven and fourteen years in bondage.

Bonded servitude preceded Negro slavery in the colonies. The first slaves in the New World were subdued Indians. History records that the first American slaver, the ship *Desire* out of Boston under Captain William Pierce in 1638, carried a number of Pequod Indians, captured during the border war, to the West Indies, where they were sold into slavery. In 1644, the *Desire* fetched slaves from Africa, who were traded in the Barbados for wine, salt, sugar and tobacco, thus setting up the "tragic triangle" followed by the Yankee slavers. The first Negroes brought to Virginia, in 1619, apparently were treated like bonded servants. Twenty arrived on "a Dutch man-of-warre," along with a "cargo" of ninety white women, brought over to ensure the future of the colony. One of the twenty Negroes, history records, became a free man after two years, taking on the Christian name of Anthony Johnson. His son, Anthony, was the first Negro child baptized in America. Johnson soon acquired a plantation and a number of slaves of his own. Slavery, at first, was unpopular and grew slowly. In 1681 there were 6,000 white servants to 2,000 slaves in Virginia.

But the need to keep the hogsheads filled with tobacco required regular tilling by disciplined workers. Transported convicts were too unruly, although the Negro slaves were frequently no more tractable. But it is easier to break the spirit of a man who is completely uprooted from his homeland and culture and set down amidst total strangers than that of those imprisoned or transported among their own people. In the end the difference was one of color; it was easier to capture a runaway black man than an escaped white man. Until 1808, when the slave trade was prohibited, between 300,000 and 400,000 black slaves were imported into the territory now known as the United States. Another 250,000, it is estimated, were smuggled in after that date and down to 1860. Thanks to the slavers the Negro workmen of today can claim a longer lineage in America than most of their white fellow workers, if that is any comfort.

Conditions were harsh for those who were sold into bondage on American soil, white or black. There is even some dispute as to whose immediate lot was actually worse. In his *Letters from America*, William Eddis, describing conditions observed by him about 1770, wrote: "Negroes being a property for life, the death of slaves, in the prime of youth or strength, is a material loss to the proprietor; they are therefore, almost in every instance, under more comfortable circumstances than the miserable European, over whom the rigid planter exercises an inflexible severity. They are strained to the utmost to perform their allotted labour. . . . There are doubtless many exceptions to this observation, yet, generally speaking, they groan beneath a worse than Egyptian bondage." On the other hand, John Hammond, nearly a century earlier, in 1656, declared that "The labour servants are put to, is not so hard nor of such continuance as Husbandmen, nor Handicraftmen are kept in England. I said little or nothing is done in winter time, none ever work before sun rising nor after sun set, in the summer they rest, sleep—or exercise themselves five houres in the heat of the day, Saturdayes afternoon is always their own, the old Holidayes are always observed and the Sabbath spent in good exercises."

Conditions, no doubt, did differ among colonies and among masters. Significantly, however, those in bondage, white or black, continued to rebel or run away; the whites out of hope, the blacks out of desperation. White indentured servants rebelled in 1661–62 in Virginia's York and Gloucester counties. In 1712, Negro slaves in New York, bound by a blood oath, rebelled, killing nine whites. Twenty-one slaves were executed. Of their leaders, Clause was put on the rack; Robin hanged in chains to die slowly; and Kuako burned alive. In Stono, South Carolina, in 1739, twenty Negroes armed themselves and began a freedom march to Florida. They struck down all they met, excepting an innkeeper who was "a good Man and kind to his slaves," before they were halted. A year later, another rebellion, and the enraged citizens of Charlestown hanged fifty Negroes—ten a day. A bounty was set on the scalps of any Negroes trying to escape to Florida. Clearly, the blacks had the worst of it, although Governor Berkeley of Virginia, by drowning in blood Nathaniel Bacon's uprising in 1670, caused Charles II to cry out, "The old fool has taken more lives in that naked country, than I for the murder of my father."

Redemptioners and convicts often did better than gentlemen on the rugged frontier. W. J. Cash reminds us that Adam Thoroughgood, who became the greatest planter in Norfolk, entered the colony as an indentured servant. Enough others did likewise to keep up the hopes of the white bondsmen, but no such luck blessed the fortunes of the black men who were forced into slavery. Indentured servitude was too costly, or so the largest employer of labor, the plantation owner, believed. An indentured servant cost on the average of £2 to £4 a year in capital investment. A slave could be purchased for £18 to £30. For this, the owner received a lifetime of service plus windfall profits from the sale of slave progeny.

Eventually, the indentures and the system of redemption and the dumping of convicts on Colonial soil all died out. Slavery, however, lasted until the Civil War wracked the nation with a pain that still lingers. Indeed, the cleavage between black and white workmen was set in Colonial times and has lasted with detrimental results to this very day.

Although colonial society was an open one—for whites—by comparison to European society, the rudiments of a working class did exist in the larger urban centers. The Founding Fathers were well aware of this. After the Revolution, James Madison in the Tenth Federalist paper wrote, "The most common and durable source of factions has been the various and unequal distribution of property. Those who hold and those who are without property have ever formed distinct interests in society." British working-men, as early as 1689, began to act in concert to secure better working conditions. But similiar action in America, in a sense, waited on the American Revolution. In part, this was due to the sheer newness of American industry; in part, due to the openness of American society. The American journeyman could—and frequently did—expect to set up on his own within a short time of learning his trade. Laborers could hope to strike out for the frontier and make a go of it by farming. There was still a good deal of cheap and available land about, some of it even close to the cities of the Eastern seaboard.

But it is also true that some of the energy that might have gone into workingmen's agitation or organization was funneled into the brewing tempest that ended in a complete break between England and her Colonies. The ideals of 1776 appealed to artisan, laborer, master craftsman, merchant-capitalist and tradesman alike. Organized in the revolutionary Sons of Liberty, the artisans and laborers provided the muscle for riots in Boston, New York, Philadelphia and Charlestown. The offices of stamp agents and the houses of royal officers were pillaged and razed. In Boston, the Sons of Liberty broke into the residence of an astounded lieutenant governor, sacked the premises and pitched the governor's property out into the street. The class nature of the activity of the Sons of Liberty is overlaid by our prevailing mythology. It was also disguised by its association with the general upheaval that took place prior to the American Revolution and by its leadership, which was frequently middle or upper class. However, that the mechanics and laborers did go further than the merchants and lawyers intended is attested to by the warning of Gouverneur Morris: "The heads of the mobility grow dangerous to the gentry, and how to keep them down is the question." This early association of the colonial workingman with the promise of the American Revolution was later to be an inspiration to the founders of the American labor movement.

But the first American unions drew their lessons from the Colonial organization of master workmen and craftsmen. These in turn, it seems, were inspired by the example of the English guilds, although the guild system as such was not transplanted successfully to Colonial soil. As early as 1644, the Massachusetts General Court placed shipbuilding under the supervision of a chartered company, patterned after contemporaneous English guilds, and four years later granted similar rights to the shoemakers and coopers. The officers of the guild were empowered to examine mechanics and might procure from the courts an order to supress any they did not approve "to be a sufficient workman." However, these charters were not renewed, and the guild system as such failed to take root. But organization among the crafts continued and by the American Revolution, master silversmiths, coppers, wigmakers, and others were organized by crafts. Intercraft organizations for economic and philanthropic ends also existed.

The first "strike" in America is said to have taken place when bakers in New York City in 1741 combined "not to bake bread but on certain terms." The records, however, are uncertain, and David J. Saposs, in the monumental *History of Labor in the United States* edited by John R. Commons, argues as others have since that "the strike in question was rather a revolt of master merchants against regulation of prices by public authorities than a strike of journeymen to maintain wages against employers." Earlier, in 1677, the licensed cartmen of New York engaged in a similiar action when they "combined to refuse full compliance when ordered to remove the dirt from the streets for threepence a load." Both the cartmen and the bakers rebelled against a price that was insufficient to cover both their operating expenses and their wages. When the cartmen refused to haul and the bakers to bake, they, according to Saposs, "acted in the dual capacity of merchants and laborers" and clouded their claim as the first workmen to strike in America. A purer claim may be made on behalf of Charlestown's Negro sweeps, who, in 1761, "had the insolence" to refuse to work "unless their exorbitant demands are complied with." Otherwise, the first genuine labor strike did not occur in America until 1786, when the Philadelphia printers "turned out" for a minimum wage of six dollars a week.

The Colonial skilled craftsman frequently combined within his person the functions of merchant, master and journeyman. Typically, his work was "bespoke" work; that is, the craftsman made his product in his own shop to the order of his customers. Before long, however, as the growth of cities expanded his market, the master workman began to employ journeymen, workers with a handicraft or trade. He also began to stock "shop work" for a more generalized retail trade. Ultimately, the three guildlike functions began to sort themselves out. The merchant-master functions melded and the journeyman function spun off. One result was the formation of employer and worker organizations. The masters, apparently, first felt the import of changing times. At any event, the associations of masters usually preceded the organization of journeymen's associations, or trade unions. The master-merchants organized to eliminate "unfair" competition and cutthroat prices. The Carpenters Company of Philadelphia was organized in 1724 to establish a "book of prices"; the master cordwainers of the same city banded together in 1789 "to consult together for the general good of the trade and determine upon the most eligible means to prevent irregularities in the same." The masters also organized to improve production as did the Associated Housewrights of Boston, who, in the 1780s, promoted "inventions and improvements in their art." The first continuous organization of wage earners in America was that of the Philadelphia journeymen shoemakers, organized in 1792.

So, the Colonial period ended with the organization of employ-

# **II**

## *THE SEEDTIME OF UNIONISM*

THE COLONIAL CRAFTSMAN, OR ARTISAN, AT THE TIME OF THE
American Revolution enjoyed a considerable amount of freedom and status. The artisan and the free farmer, each with his
plot of ground, were the two pillars on which a free society would
rest. This was the Jeffersonian belief. But the opening up of new
markets in the South and West created a new set of economic
conditions. These conditions undermined the independent existence of the artisans in the growing cities. The master workman
faced the choice of becoming a merchant-capitalist himself or a
journeyman. Trade was no longer a local affair. Hard-pressed by
growing competition, the merchant-capitalist pressed his journeymen the harder, cutting his labor costs whenever he could. The
ancient skills were broken down; labor was divided so that a
cordwainer, for example, no longer made the whole shoe. The
journeyman cordwainer became a workingman limited to a
single operation. The journeymen, in reaction to this threat to
their long-standing independence, good living conditions and
status, formed the first trade unions. But their grievances as workingmen were more general than the immediate difficulties they

experienced as journeymen within their own crafts, and as a result, the American labor movement was born. The transition from the early job-conscious journeymen's associations to the broader socially conscious workingmen's political movements was a matter of three decades. The first unions were organized in the 1790s; the labor movement was born in 1827. Within those three decades, the economy had moved from mercantile capitalism to incipient industrialism.

The labor movement, at first, was in rebellion against a rising industrialism. As such, it made common cause with the middle-class, transcendentalist reformers, largely based in New England, against the new conditions. This was the period of utopianism, communal experiments, agitation for land reform and free public education. But by the time of the Civil War, the middle-class reformers, who had sought in various ways to escape confrontation with the new industrialism, finally succeeded by becoming absorbed into the antislavery movement. Workingmen, unable to escape so easily—though some did by way of the Gold Rush and the Homestead Act of 1861, which opened new land—developed an indigenous leadership, some of it with a socialistic cast, and began to organize their own institutions for confronting inevitable industrialism.

When the first census was taken, in 1790, the population of the newly formed United States was just over 3,900,000, of whom some 750,000 were slaves. Life still was largely rural; only three percent of the population lived in the six towns of more than 8,000—Philadelphia, New York, Boston, Charlestown, Baltimore, and Salem. Communication was still poor; John Fitch's steamboats barely made it up and down the Delaware. President John Adams spent three days in making the journey from Philadelphia to the new capital in 1800. Short on capital, short on skilled labor and short on machinery, manufacturing consisted largely of the village sawmill or gristmill on the edge of a convenient stream.

Yet, a change was clearly discernible by the turn of the century. In 1791, Alexander Hamilton, in vigorous pursuit of his policy of promoting American manufacturing, was able to report some 70 paper mills, a cotton-yarn mill operating with American-made spinning frames, a woolen mill, glass works, brick kilns, and a growing number of forges and thriving blast furnaces. The outbreak of war between Great Britain and Napoleonic France in 1793 accelerated American interest in coastal and river commerce. Straining teams of four to six broad-chested horses hauled as much as two tons of merchandise in white-topped Conestoga wagons westward over the Alleghenies to the new farm communities and returned laden with wheat, corn and rye.

This was, in Richard Hofstadter's phrase, the "seedtime of American industrialism." Jefferson's Embargo Act of 1807, which confined American ships to port, and later, the War of 1812, cut off American capital from overseas trade and turned investment to domestic manufacturing. A Federal highway—built at a cost of $7 million—pushed its way west through the Cumberland Gap, reaching Wheeling, West Virginia, in 1817. A mania for canal building spurred a network of navigable waterways in New York, Pennsylvania, Ohio, Indiana, and other states. Work on the Erie Canal commenced on July 4, 1817; on July 4, 1825, 363 miles of canal from Albany to Buffalo were opened for traffic.

The development of transportation opened new markets for American retail merchants. From ordering and stocking goods for resale to customers in their own retail shops, the merchants of the Federal period began to supply retailers in the South and West. The shoe industry provides the classic example of this transition. "My little capital being laid out in stock," John Bedford, a Philadelphia shoe merchant, testified at the Philadelphia cordwainers' trial for conspiracy in 1806, "and no way of vending it at home, an idea struck me of going southward, and endavor there to force a sale. I went to Charlestown at the risque of my life, for the vessel in which I went had like to have been lost at sea. I put my articles at an extremely low price, by which I had but little profit, in order to induce people to deal with me. I got two customers at Charlestown; from there I went to Norfolk, Petersburgh, Richmond and Alexandria; and in all of those places I obtained customers."

Others did likewise. And the margin of profit was small enough and the risk great enough for the early merchant capitalist to press his journeymen very hard indeed. As a result the skilled mechanics were the first to organize into unions, not factory or mill hands. By organizing with his fellow, the journeyman sought to protect his standard of life against the encroachments of the merchant capitalist and the competition of the semiskilled. The first strikes took place over the prices of the journeymen's work; only later did strikes occur over wages, a somewhat different concept that embodies an entirely different social relationship. The standards of the skilled shoemaker were being undermined by the new methods of manufacture developing in the shoe towns of New England, which ultimately doomed the new unions springing up in Philadelphia, New York, Baltimore, and Pittsburgh. In Lynn, a cheaper grade of shoe was made through the division of labor; each worker made a part of a shoe. Since the whole family frequently engaged in the work, actual earnings increased while labor costs remained relatively low. In addition, as an early historian of Lynn noted, "every well-to-do shoemaker had his garden, and a pig-sty somewhere on the premises." The Lynn shoemaker, in fact, was somewhat better off than the hard-pressed, more highly skilled cordwainers.

Wages of the unskilled, actually, were rising at the time as the wages of skilled remained constant or declined slightly, even though the cost of living rose sharply. In 1784, common laborers were paid less than $4 a week but by 1810, their wages had increased to $7 or $8 a week. This explains, in part, why cotton mill hands did not organize or strike in the early 1800s—there were some 100,000 in 1815—although their English counterparts were already forming unions. (In England, wages in the mills were actually depressed, the opposite of the initial American experience.) As for Lynn there was no thought of unionization until the 1840s, when conditions worsened for the shoe worker and the day of the cordwainer was past.

However, there are other reasons for the lack of spontaneous strikes, or organization, in the mills at this time. Many of the first factory hands were women or children. Samuel Slater opened his first mill in Pawtucket in 1790 with seven boys and two girls, ages 7 to 11. In Lowell of the early 1800s, where young women (over 10 years of age) operated the loom and spindle, work in the mill was a pleasant and profitable change from farmwork; initially there was nothing to induce these girls to organize unions or strike. As for the children, they lacked experience. Whatever the reason—wages, age or sex—the mill hands were laggards at unionization. The first American unions were journeymen's associations, formed as a protest against the new conditions brought on by expanding markets.

Philadelphia, the "cradle of liberty," was also the cradle of American unionism. In 1790, Philadelphia numbered some 42,000 souls. It was also a city of many crafts, whose practitioners were strong enough to resist for a time the encroachments of the new mercantile-capitalist age. The first continuous organization of wage earners, that of the Philadelphia shoemakers, organized in 1792, lasted but a year. Two years later, the shoemakers organized a more lasting union, the Federal Society of Journeymen Cordwainers. It lasted until 1806, when members of the society were tried for conspiracy. The Federal Society conducted the first organized walkout—a strike of nine or ten weeks in 1799.

Printers organized in New York, and then, Philadelphia, in 1794 and 1799 respectively. Later, the printers in Albany, Boston and Washington organized as did the shoemakers in Baltimore and Pittsburgh. Actually, spontaneous strikes preceded the formation of unions in many trades. The first strike for a ten-hour day, for example, occurred in May, 1791, when the Philadelphia house carpenters spontaneously downed tools. They had no organization; the strike was unplanned and lost. It and other strikes of the time, such as those of the Baltimore tailors and sailors and the 1817 shipbuilders' strike in Medford, Massachusetts, were ephemeral in character and left no lasting organizations. They simply serve to underline the unrest of the journeymen of the day.

David J. Saposs characterized this early period of trades unionism as "dormant." While there was some activity, it was almost entirely local in character and did not involve any large numbers of workingmen. Nevertheless, many of the practices now associated with trade unions—especially the craft unions—were developed at the time. Tenuous contact did exist between organizations in different cities, for example. History records that the Philadelphia Typographical Society loaned the Franklin Typographical Society of New York City, $83.50 for the relief of members "distressed" as a result of an epidemic, possibly the first example of union fraternity on record. This was a seed from which future international unions grew. The first wage scale was drawn up by the New York printers in 1800. The printers also exchanged "price lists," in an early attempt to establish a national wage policy. The first paid "walking delegate" was employed by the Philadelphia shoemakers in 1799. It was his job to visit the various shops "to see that the journeymen are honest to the cause." The first "sympathetic" strike also occurred at this time. When the Philadelphia bootmakers struck in 1799 for higher prices, the shoemakers were also ordered to "turn out." And, the first "general strike" occurred in 1809, when the New York cordwainers struck the firm of Corwain and Aimes and discovered that the work was farmed out to other employers. The union then declared a strike against all masters. Strike benefits, too, were first paid in this formative period. But these were usually in the form of loans, which members were expected to pay back, although the unions or benefit societies sometimes "forgave" the loan. In 1805, the New York shoemakers set up the first permanent strike fund. The early unions also provided sickness and death benefits out of surplus funds—when they had them at hand.

The early unions, especially the cordwainers, also managed to establish what we would now call a "closed shop." They refused to work alongside non-members; in one case, the Philadelphia cordwainers even refused to eat at the same boardinghouse where non-union men boarded. By use of the boycott, the cordwainers managed to compel employers to hire only union men.

Collective bargaining as we now know it, however, did not exist. Individual bargaining remained the prevailing mode. The journeymen shoemakers, for example, went about setting a price for their work in just about the same fashion as their employers, the master shoemakers, set a price on their goods. The journeymen simply met and set a scale of wages and pledged "not to work for any employer who did not give the wages, nor beside any journeyman who did not get the wages." But this not entirely satisfactory method soon gave way to a rudimentary form of collective bargaining. Journeymen's associations and masters' organizations that lasted any length of time began appointing committees to meet jointly to discuss demands.

This incipient bargaining process, however, was brought to a halt by a series of court cases that developed when the harassed master cordwainers invoked the common-law prohibition against criminal conspiracy against the growing strength of the journeymen's associations. The masters sought to lower prices in order to compete with rivals in other cities for the expanding markets in the newly settled territories in the South and West. The journeymen vigorously contested the price cuts. Each of the six conspiracy cases—Philadelphia (1806), New York City (1809), two in Baltimore (1809) and Pittsburgh (1814 and 1815)—followed a hard-fought strike.

The Philadelphia case is the most important to our history, and, as it happens, it is the one we know most about. Historians owe much to the conscientious court reporter, Thomas Lloyd, who sensed history in the making—"the most interesting law case, which has occurred in this state since the revolution"—and sent a transcript of his notes to the governor and state legislature. The Philadelphia case was rooted in a labor dispute over wages that occurred in 1805, the year before the actual court case. The master cordwainers had, after Christmas in 1804, reduced the price of labor to $2.50 per pair of boots. The workers resented the cut but took no action until the busy season in 1805, when they demanded that the prices of their work be set at prevailing prices in New York and Baltimore—an increase of 25 cents to 75 cents a pair, depending on the nature of the boots. The demand was rejected and the journeymen "turned out." George Pullis and seven of his co-workers were arrested, though not immediately prosecuted. The strike ended soon after the arrests, the workers' morale apparently destroyed, and the journeymen returned to work.

The case of the eight cordwainers was caught up in the embittered political struggle going on at the time between the Federalists and the Jeffersonians. The Federalists represented the commercial interests and controlled the courts. (In the New York and Pittsburgh cases, the masters apparently financed, at least in part, the prosecution.) The Jeffersonians, alarmed at the growth of industrialism, took up the cause of the cordwainers. In Philadelphia, incidentally, the workmen possessed the right to vote; other states had a more restricted franchise at the time.

The eight cordwainers were indicted in January, 1806, and charged with the crime of "a combination and conspiracy to raise their wages." The case was prosecuted by Jared Ingersoll, "the foremost protagonist of the English common law" and a leading Federalist. Caesar A. Rodney, a prominent Jeffersonian, represented the eight cordwainers. The jury of nine merchants and three masters sustained the chief charge, as laid down by recorder Moses Levy, a leading Federalist judge, to the effect that: "A combination of workmen to raise their wages may be considered in a two fold point of view: one is to benefit themselves . . . the other is to injure those who do not join their society. The rule of law condemns both."

In vain, Caesar A. Rodney pleaded "that the spirit of the revolution and the principle of the common law are opposite . . . if applied it would operate an attack on the rights of man." The jury obviously agreed with the recorder, who, pointedly, noted that what the defendants were doing was "artificial regulation . . . , an unnatural, artificial means of raising the price of work beyond its standard, and taking an undue advantage of the public." The defendants were found guilty, fined $8 each and costs, and jailed until the fines were paid.

Out of the Philadelphia cordwainer case evolved a legal doctrine holding that workers acting in concert to raise wages were engaged in a criminal conspiracy under the common law. As Charles O. Gregory notes in *Labor and the Law*, this doctrine "served as a formal vehicle—a legal abracadabra, if you please —in the name of which English and American judges . . . made labor unionists conform to the principles of classical economics." The doctrine of criminal conspiracy, as set down in the Philadelphia cordwainers case, acted as a check on early unionism until it was set aside in 1842 in a Massachusetts case (*Commonwealth* v. *Hunt*) that, as it happened, involved another generation of bootmakers.

The doctrine that a combination of workmen to raise their wages was a criminal conspiracy was applied in some nineteen cases during the early decades of the nineteenth century. The prosecution—or threat of prosecution—of workers' organizations on this charge no doubt hindered the early development of trade unions. But in some instances the public outcry against prosecution was sufficient to cause juries to find for the defendants. In 1842, Massachusetts' Chief Justice Lemuel Shaw set aside the doctrine of criminal conspiracy in *Commonwealth* v. *Hunt*. He dismissed an indictment of conspiracy against the Boston Journeymen Bootmakers Society for a strike to force the dismissal of a non-member on the grounds that the indictment did not set forth any agreement to engage in a criminal act. The decision by a highly respected judge did away with the use of the doctrine of criminal conspiracy as a means for the control of unions, although it cropped up from time to time after the Civil War as a means of breaking strikes. The lasting impact of the cordwainers cases lies in the precedent set—not in matters of legal doctrine but in legal redress. Employers came to rely on the courts to restrain unions and, in effect, the courts came to set the community's policy towards unions, until the New Deal reversed the practice and Congress set down a national policy towards unionism in the Norris-LaGuardia Act and the Wagner Labor Act.

The conspiracy cases may have also helped to turn workingmen's thoughts to politics. Irate workingmen held mock trials of judges and hung them in effigy in more than one city. The spread of the franchise gave workingmen hope that perhaps their votes might reverse the run of unfavorable court decisions. They hoped through the vote to elect their own judges. Massachusetts granted the franchise to workingmen in 1820, New York in 1822; and Pennsylvania in 1790 had already extended the right to vote to all who paid any kind of state or county tax.

The recession that followed the end of the War of 1812, when cheap goods from Europe again flooded American markets, all but destroyed the first unions. The industrial crisis, which reached its depth in 1820, caused a great many businesses to shut down, threw a great many workers out of employment. The only survivors among the unions of this drastic depression were a few that functioned as benevolent societies.

But the opening up of the navigable rivers in the West, which made the steamboat practicable, stimulated an economic revival in the mid-1820s. This, in turn, sparked a renewal of trade-union activity. Renewed prosperity stirred workers to make demands for improvements in wages and working conditions. Unorganized strikes occurred in many trades, and more stable organizations began to take root among the craftsmen—hatters, tailors, house and ship carpenters, house painters, stone cutters, weavers, nailers, and cabinet makers. The factory workers organized at this time. They were the first to use the word "union" to designate their organizations, as contrasted to the journeymen's "associations." Women became active. In 1824, the women workers struck alongside the men in the mills of Pawtucket, Rhode Island. In the next year, the first all-female strike occurred when the tailoresses of New York struck for higher wages.

But the agitation for higher wages soon paled beside that for the ten-hour day. Workingmen in the growing industrial centers were stirred in 1825 by reports of a strike for a ten-hour day by some 600 Boston journeymen carpenters. The strike was lost but it launched what amounted to a nationwide movement for the shortened day. The workingmen's struggle soon spilled over into the political arena as "farmers, mechanics and workingmen" rallied to the cause.

The next rebellion against the then current practice of working "sun up to sun down" broke out in Philadelphia when the journeymen carpenters struck in June, 1827, for the ten-hour day. The painters, glaziers, and brick layers joined in the agitation, though it is not clear whether or not they struck over the issue. This action did give birth to the first effective city central labor organization, the Mechanics' Union of Trade Associations. Out of this grew the first labor party in the world, the Working Men's Party.

# III

## *FURROW TURNERS AND HUGE PAWS*

"A MORAL EXCITEMENT, NEW IN ITS NATURE AND RAPID IN ITS progress," wrote Francis Wright, America's first suffragette, in 1830, "pervades the world. . . . The Priest trembles for his craft, the rich man for his board, the politician for influence. . . . From the people—ay! from the people, arise the hum and stir of awakening intelligence, enquiry and preparation." The rise of workingmen's parties during the years 1828, 1829, and 1830 in Philadelphia, Boston and New York—and ultimately of statewide movements in each of these key industrial states—provided a heady, yeasty brew for early radicals and workingmen alike.

The new "moral excitement" that moved the attractive chestnut-haired suffragette soon claimed the "farmers, mechanics, and workingmen"—and even a few factory operatives in New England. The New England "furrow turners" and "huge paws," as they were dubbed in the contemporary press, formed what amounted to the first industrial union in the United States, the New England Association of Farmers, Mechanics and Other Workmen. One of the characteristics of industrial unionism is a greater interest in political action than one finds in craft unions.

The CIO of our day is a case in point. The New England work-men—and subsequently workmen in other states—rallied behind platforms espousing the abolition of imprisonment for debt, uni-versal free education, a mechanics lien law (making wages the employer's first obligation in bankruptcy), the abolition of child labor, credit, currency and land reforms. Behind these diverse issues was a deeply felt resentment of privilege and a desire for equality.

The first workingmen's parties and movements were largely made up of native Americans. Between 1790 and 1830 only 400,000 immigrants entered the country, whose population had grown to nearly 13 million. The "Spirit of '76" was very much alive in the United States of the 1830s. And, as they exercised their newly acquired franchise, workingmen and their allies de-manded what they deemed to be the essence of that spirit. "The objects we have in view," declared a Philadelphia working-men's association, "are hallowed by the sympathy of patriotism —it is the finish of the glorious work of the Revolution." In short, the workingmen's chief grievance turned on what Samuel Whitcomb, Jr., in an address to the Working Men's So-ciety of Dedham, Massachusetts, declared to be a "continued prevalence of irrational, anti-republican and unchristian opinion in relation to the worth and respectability of *manual labor*." Workingmen agreed with the *New England Working Man's Ga-zette* when it saw "all attempts made to degrade the working classes as so many blows aimed at the existence of our free po-litical and civil institutions."

Labor historian Selig Perlman once wrote that labor turns "to politics as a measure of depair." Yet, this does not seem to be the case in the 1830s. Labor's first turn towards politics strikes one as anything but a measure of despair; it was, if anything, a measure of expectation. It paralleled the general rise of popular hopes in the country at large that found its expression in Jacksonian de-mocracy. But it would be a mistake to assume an identity of interests between the workingmen's parties and the Jacksonians.

Eastern workers were divided in allegiance; New York labor voted for Jackson but Philadelphia labor did not. Among the Jacksonians, as Richard Hofstadter reminds us, "the democratic upsurge was closely linked to the ambitions of the small capitalist." The initial effect of the Jacksonian Revolt was the liberation of the "rural capitalist and village entrepreneurs" from the credit bonds imposed by the Hamiltonian Bank of the United States. Broader issues, however, linked the small entrepreneur with the workingman in opposition to the bank. Under the guidance of Philadelphia's aristocratic Nicholas Biddle, the bank was considered by both a center of privilege. Workingmen, too, unwisely blamed all banks for a system of payment that consistently cheated them of their due. Employers frequently paid their employees in notes on suspect or distant banks at par. But these notes could not be spent except at substantial discounts. Workmen, thereby, were defrauded by as much as a third or more of their pay in some instances. The continued existence and growth of a national bank and currency system was the only insurance against such practices. But the workingmen failed to see this because they were beguiled by the illusion that abolition of the Bank of the United States would mean easy credit and, therefore, easy entry into entrepreneurship. This failure serves as a classic example of the conflict of class interests that occurs so frequently in the history of American labor within the workingman himself.

Over the long run, Jacksonian economic policy (protective tariffs, the bank veto and paper money), as Professor Arthur Schlesinger, Jr., ruefully concedes in *The Age of Jackson*, "on the whole promoted the very ends it was intended to defeat." It cleared the way for the subsequent growth of giant corporations and for the lobbying of special privilege. More importantly, the Jackson revolution also overturned Jeffersonian federalism—with its emphasis on decentralism and encouragement of "the art of associating together" within a federal framework. In this context, the workingmen's political movements of the 1830s were Jeffersonian rather than Jacksonian, for structurally, these parties were worker's councils, an economic or industrial equivalent of the town meeting. This form of organization has recurred many times in the history of labor, in widely separated places—the Paris Commune of 1871, the American Knights of Labor in the 1890s, the Russian soviets of 1905 and 1917 (before the Bolshevik subversion of the idea), the CIO in the auto and rubber cities of the 1930s, and in Hungary during the revolution of 1957. All these were expressions of rebellion by working people against the centralizing tendencies of their respective times.

The workingmen's parties of the 1830s were short-lived, although the movement spawned some 50 newspapers in fifteen states and organizations of varying strengths in most of the states from Maine to Georgia and west to Missouri. By 1834, the workingmen's parties had all but disappeared, either because of internal dissension, as in New York, or because workers succumbed to the blandishments and superior political tactics of the old-line politicians. However, workingmen continued to exert considerable influence on the old parties. Workers in the Eastern cities, increasingly, tended to vote on ethnic lines—the Americans and British immigrants supporting the Whigs, and the Irish and Germans the Democratic Party. Both parties, as a result, found it worthwhile to woo the workingman. In 1835, there was a brief revival of independent political action on the part of workingmen in New York. Former supporters of the city's workingmen's party called a meeting to choose their own, rather than Tammany's, candidates for the state elections. An attempt was made to sabotage the meeting by shutting off the gaslights. But the workingmen were prepared and continued their meeting by lighting candles with the new friction matches, known as "locofocos." The locofoco faction was strong enough to elect the nation's first trade-union Congressman in 1834, Ely Moore, the president of New York General Trades Union. Tammany, even then a wise old tiger, soon made peace with the locofocos and thus ended another flurry of independent political action by labor.

The 1830s saw a further breakdown in the crafts, a development inherent in the rise of merchant capitalism. Wholesale orders grew, and employers increased the division of labor, prompting the *Mechanics Free Press* to complain that "what made one trade formerly, now makes a half dozen." The journeymen's associations were generally found wanting and unable to cope with the new trend. The individual trade associations were too small to confront successfully the employers. The organizational structure of the workingmen's parties, possibly, suggested a way out to the workingmen of the day, who, as the parties died out began to organize city federations, or councils, of the respective craft organizations. The city central labor council soon became the dominant form of organization in the mid-1830s. Groups in various cities corresponded with one another. From this exchange of ideas grew the first national trade-union federation, the National Trades' Union, formed in 1834. But the National Trades' Union was unable to do much more than hold an annual convention in each of the next three years. It expired in 1837, a victim, along with most of the labor movement, of the panic and the ensuing depression.

The city labor councils, however, had won a major victory. In the spring of 1835, the building trades of Philadelphia struck again for the ten-hour day. This time they managed to win, establishing—for the skilled trades at any rate—a standard workday that lasted until the 1890s. In 1840, President Martin Van Buren, a New Yorker who owed much to the support of workingmen in that state, issued on March 31, an executive order establishing the ten-hour day on all government works. The one notable exception to the pattern established by the Philadelphia building tradesmen was New England. In a few New England cities, the carpenters, masons and plasterers secured the ten-hour day, but for the rest, the day's toil stretched from sun up to sun down. The sturdy Yankee artisans were defeated in their campaigns for the ten-hour day by the mill owners, who feared that their factory operatives would also demand shorter hours. In the Lowell mills, for example, operatives averaged 11 hours, 24 minutes a day in

December and January, and 13 hours and 31 minutes a day in April. Over the year, Lowell factory operatives averaged 12 hours, 13 minutes a day, or 73½ hours a week. Later, in the 1840s, the mill owners reduced the workday by a half-hour in response to the growing public pressure for shorter hours. But their move was, in many instances, deceptive: many mills, adopting the practice of the Middlesex mills, fixed their clocks so that the operatives would think they left work at seven o'clock when actually it was closer to eight o'clock.

The defeat of the New England artisans on the ten-hour day issue reflected the growing power of the factory in the political and economic life of our nation. It is difficult today to conceive of an alternative to the factory system, and we forget that originally many considered the factory system both alien to and destructive of American ideals and standards. "The factory system contains in itself the elements of slavery," declared *The Voice of Industry* in 1846. This was a widely shared belief among independent artisans, Jeffersonian farmers and New England transcendentalists. Henry David Thoreau, mulling over his thoughts on the lonely shores of Walden Pond in 1845, wasn't the only one to ask, "Where is this division of labor to end?" The Puritan conscience is a stern taskmaster and it, too, was bothered by the red-bricked factories springing up along the waterways of New England. They were worried lest the direct importation of the English *laissez-faire* system of hiring whole families, especially of children, lead to immorality among factory operatives. In Rhode Island, this did lead to widespread exploitation of child labor.

Francis Cabot Lowell, however, held a different vision, a marriage of morality and manufacturing. When he established his first mill in Waltham, boardinghouses were built for the farm girls who came to work in the mill. There was careful supervision over their morals as well as living condition. The Waltham system also flourished in the new mill town erected at Pawtucket Falls on the Merrimack River and named after the Boston manufacturing visionary. It also spread to other mill towns throughout New England.

Lowell—"That wonderful city of spindles and looms,/And thousands of factory folk."—was indeed a marvel. To it, flocked the girls from nearby farms for a year or two of work. Work in the mills during those early years of Lowell paternalism was not arduous by comparison to farm toil. Girls still had energy enough after a long day to study and read; even within the mills, it was reported, girls had enough time on their hands to snatch a page or two of reading in books brought to work for just those precious moments. Lowell, declared a French visitor, "Resembles a Spanish town with its convents, but in Lowell you meet no rags or Madonnas, and the Nuns of Lowell, instead of working sacred hearts, spin and weave cotton." There is a striking parallel between the paternalism of Lowell and "utopian" experiment of Robert Owen at New Lanark, Scotland, a decade or so earlier. There was the same moral concern, emphasis on education and the righteousness of work. Both Francis Cabot Lowell and Owen believed that a moral and rational factory life was possible; both hoped by stressing moral turpitude to convert the opponents, especially the middle-class opponents of the factory system, to the new way of the future.

While the mills remained close by the farms, unemployment was almost no more than a vacation back home. But a change was sweeping New England that would soon transform the whole country from predominantly a rural nation to a manufacturing one. The mills were crowding the farms out; escape to the farm ceased to be feasible, unemployment became something to be feared. The factories themselves changed. "Once they were light, well ventilated, and moderately heated," wrote Harriet H. Robinson, once a Lowell girl and author of *Loom and Spindle*. "Each factory building stood detached, with pleasant sunlit windows, cheerful views, and fresh air from all points of the compass. But these buildings are now made into a solid mass by connecting 'annexes,' and often form a hollow square, so that at least one-half the operatives can have no outlook except upon brick walls, and no fresh air but that which circulates within this confined space."

A similar process occurred in the shoe industry, which entered the factory age during the 1840s. By the time Thoreau fled to Walden, the cotton mills began to pass out of the hands of the original paternalists into absentee ownership. By 1840, Nathan Appleton, sometime congressman and advocate of protective tariffs and of sound banking, with his Boston associates created in eastern Massachusetts a miniature replica of the corporatism of the twentieth century. They controlled banking, railroad, insurance and power companies as well as textile mills scattered over the state.

Under the new owners, the famous Lowell paternalism became a respectable cover for a rigid near tyranny. Workers who protested, sought to organize, or engaged in the agitation for the ten-hour day were fired, blacklisted, and hounded from the industry. It became more difficult for the mill owners to recruit innocent farm girls. "Slavers," long, low, black wagons, cruised the farms in upper New England, enticing the girls to the mill towns with promises of work so easy they could "dress in silks and spend their day reading." But the reality was quite something else. A Holyoke manufacturer, for example, found his hands "languorous" in the early morning because they had breakfasted. He then began to work them without breakfast and "got 3,000 more yards of cloth a week made." Turnover in the mills remained high, and the New England girls, who had the alternatives of other careers or marriage, chose them over the mill. Their place was taken by immigrants, mostly Irish, supplemented by lesser streams from England, Germany, France, and Canada. This pattern was to repeat itself many times in the course of the history of American manufacturing.

"Modern society seems to me to be rushing to some new and untried conditions," declared a fretful John C. Calhoun in 1837. The Panic of that year washed out a good many businesses and created large-scale unemployment in the cities. (The depression left one-third of the working population of New York City unemployed, for example.) The effects of the severe crisis of 1837 did not entirely disappear until the gold rush of the 1850s. "Thirty years ago," the land reformer George Henry Evans wrote in 1844, "the number of paupers in the whole United States was estimated at 29,166, or one in three hundred. The pauperism of New York City now amounts to 51,600, or one in every seven of the population." Hard times made life that much more difficult for the immigrant workmen who were arriving daily in larger numbers. Employers found it difficult not to use this to advantage. When, for example, the Irish laborers in New York City organized a benevolent society and went on strike in 1846 to raise wages from 65 cents a day to 87½ cents a day, the contractors broke the strike by hiring a cargo of freshly landed Germans. The Irish tried to defend their jobs by driving the Germans away, but the military were called out and the Irish workmen overcome. Earlier, in 1842, a strike of Pittsburgh puddlers and boilermakers was broken in a similar fashion. Riots broke out and some of the puddlers seized one of the mills, despite some pistol-waving by the mayor, in a forerunner of the sitdowns of 1937. But the mills were soon reopened with imported help.

As a result of the uncertainties and turbulence of the times, the middle-class reformer moved to the fore as a spokesman for reform and for labor in the 1840s. It was an "era of lost causes" and the last fling at stopping industrialism by the artisans of the old order—the shoemakers and their like. The various reform groups of the 1840s frequently embraced workingmen, artisans and their masters, and the small mercantile capitalist. They saw the new capitalist as alien to the "producing classes." Although the reformers frequently sounded like revolutionists, Norman Ware warns us against taking the language of the agitators at face value. "Essentially," he notes, "the protests of the forties were conservative, defensive in temper and purpose." As a striker of the time declared, "the employers were the revolution-

ists and levelers who want to uproot the old order." The protests
were also escapist.

Of the three dominant strains of reform in the 1840s, only the
cooperators came close to grappling with the real situation confronting the workingmen. The cooperators sought with limited
success to establish producer and consumer cooperatives in several industrial centers. The most famous of these was that of the
iron moulders of Cincinnati in 1848. The moulders, who had lost
a strike the previous year (a common stimulus for this kind of
endeavor), organized a Journeymen's Moulders' Union Foundry
by raising some $2,100 among themselves. They kept their profits
in the business, and by 1850, they had added $5,692 to their
original capital. But they were unable to weather the depression
of the following year. Ultimately, however, the failure of the in-
dustrial-cooperative movement in the United States must be attributed to the lack of a stable and homogenous working population. The cooperative movement enjoyed a much greater success
in Europe, where these two factors prevailed.

The Associationists, a much more middle-class movement, attracted attention from disenchanted workingmen in New England
and elsewhere. The Associationists were influenced by the doc-
trines of Charles Fourier, a Frenchman who sought to make industry attractive and efficient by preaching the need for an industrial community. Although Fourier is often considered somewhat
of a socialist, he is rather a forerunner of Elton Mayo and that
school of sociology which believes that more production can be
got out of happy workers than out of the dissatisfied. Fourier
realized, as few did at the time, that industrialism was uproot-
ing old social ties, creating insecurity and anarchy. Fourierism
was a "back fire against red revolution," an attempt to create
new social ties within the new industrial order. But the middle-
class Americans who took to Fourier were in flight from the
new order. They picked up Fourier's idea of community, turned
it into a way of escaping the factory life they saw rising about
them. Brook Farm, for example, was essentially a pastoral retreat

from industrialism. Here American Fourierism took root for awhile and died.

The American Fourierists, or Associationists, chiefly in the persons of Albert Brisbane and his editorial chief, Horace Greeley, did preach to the workingman. (Greeley was the first president of the International Typographers Union, founded in 1850.) They sought to convince the workingmen of the value of phalanxes and the new community life. They also crusaded against child labor and in favor of the ten-hour day. They served to awaken middle-class consciences to some of the worse evils of industrialism. But they preached, too, that the worker and his employer, insofar as the latter was a producer, shared a common interest. Greeley, and other Associationists, tended to frown on strikes and put their faith in the employer's efforts to elevate the workingman, rather than in the workers' own collective strength. This, as one would expect, led to a certain disenchantment between the Associationists and workingmen's organizations. The middle-class reformer was caught up more and more in antislavery agitations, from which workingmen, by and large, stood aloof until the dawn of the Civil War.

While Associationism and cooperation as movements had largely died out by the end of 1840, agrarianism continued to attract followers from all walks of life. Largely due to the persistence of George Henry Evans, who first became active in the workingmen's parties of the 1830s, land reform began to grow in the public imagination as the solution to all the evils of the day. Evans was born in England in 1806 and he emigrated to America at the age of fourteen with his father and brother. An avid reader of Thomas Paine, he seems to have picked up the kernel of his land-reform proposal from Paine's *Agrarian Justice*. Evans may also have been influenced by Thomas Skidmore, a New York machinist active in the workingmen's party at the same time as Evans, who advocated an equal division of all property. Evans, as editor of the *Workingman's Advocate*, picked the idea up and propagated it in the columns of his paper. After the failure of the workingmen's party, Evans withdrew to a farm in New Jersey. He came out of seclusion in 1844 and launched, with some followers, the National Reform Association. By this time, however, equal division of property had been dropped for the equal division of land, especially the free land to the West. With a single-minded doggedness, Evans cornered politicians into supporting his proposal. Evans did not live to see his agitation bear fruit. In 1849, worn out and penniless, he returned to his farm, where he died seven years later. His National Reform Association also died. Evans' life-long campaign ultimately paid off in the Homestead Act of 1862, which granted 160 acres to any citizen, free of charge, on proof of occupation and cultivation. It was, however, a far cry from the equal division of property to the Homestead Act of 1862. Thirty-five years later, Henry George revived the doctrine of natural rights in property to work out the idea of a single tax on land. He, too, would rally workingmen to his cause as Evans did in his time.

Nonetheless, the three strains of 1840s' reform—Associationist, cooperativist, and agrarianist—failed because they did not meet workingmen's needs. Each was tried—for workers, too, wanted to escape their lot—but found wanting. To survive, workingmen and their organizations had to accept industrialism. An anonymous workingman of the 1850s put his finger on it: "Suppose we had the means, we know nothing about the cultivation of the land—we have all our lives worked in a factory and we know no other employment." In the 1850s, the workers in the special crafts began to develop a technique and an approach of their own; they cast off all notions of community of interest between journeymen and their bosses. The printers' union, the first permanent national organization of labor, is a case in point. At the first convention of the Typographical Union, the delegates came to the conclusion that "It is useless for us to disguise from ourselves the fact that, under the present arrangement of things, there exists a perpetual antagonism between Labor and Capital.

. . . one side striving to sell their labor for as much, and the other striving to buy it for as little as they can."

In the 1850s the first real attempts were made to establish permanent and exclusive organizations of skilled workmen. Rules of apprenticeship, closed shop, minimum wage, initiation fees, dues, strike benefits, union hiring halls were all utilized in the attempt by the skilled craftsmen to set themselves apart from the unskilled immigrants. Attempts at setting up national organizations were made by hat finishers, cigar makers, upholsterers, building tradesmen, lithographers, painters, silver platers, cotton mule spinners, stone cutters, iron moulders and others.

The discovery of gold created a shortage of skilled workers, which helped organization by the craftsmen and boosted their wages. Economist Thomas G. Carey estimated that the gold rush drained off, in addition to vagabonds and the like, some 50,000 workers. But while this helped the craftsmen organize—a shortage of skilled workers always enables those holding the precious skills to set the terms of their employment—in the long run it also cramped the development of permanent, lasting national unions. The drain of the westward movement—gold and free land—was just too much. Workers, who might have sustained unionism, went West. The new unions of the early 1850s did not, with a few exceptions, survive the depression of 1857–62.

There remain only a few words to be said about labor's attitude towards slavery and the antislavery agitation prior to the Civil War. The invention of the cotton gin by that ingenious Yankee Eli Whitney made cotton king and slavery immensely profitable to the Southern plantation economy. The workingmen of the North took a fairly dim view of the activities of the early abolitionists because the abolitionists had—with the notable exception of Wendell Philips—ignored the plight of the "wage slaves." Ely Moore, labor's first congressman and the first president of the National Trades Union, in 1839, told the House of Representatives that emancipation would bring the Negro slave into the labor market in competition with the Northern white worker.

And, in that event, said Moore, "the moral and political character, the pride, power and independence of the latter are gone
forever." John Finch, a New York printer who was active in the
formation of the first general trade union, declared in 1833, "It
is a well-known fact that the blacks of the south enjoy more
leisure, time and liberty, and fare quite as well as the operatives
in the northern and eastern manufactories." With this in mind,
it's not surprising to find Northern labor reacting favorably when
Southern spokesmen lashed out against "wage slavery" as a
means of needling the abolitionists and offering a backhanded
defense of slavery itself.

But, in the end, the Southern argument was self-defeating: if
there was no essential difference between "wage slavery" and
slavery, then there was no inherent reason that all workers, white
or black, free or not, should not be slaves; slavery, in Southern
eyes, was the safest and most durable basis for society. Most
Southerners shrank from this logical conclusion of their argument.
But some did not. George Fitzhugh, a Virginian lawyer, won a
national reputation by advancing just this argument. This provided the abolitionists with the ammunition they needed to win
over the free workingmen of the North to their side. Nonetheless,
workingmen remained skeptical until the guns were fired at Fort
Sumter. A national convention of workingmen met in Philadelphia on February 22, 1861. It was called to order by William
H. Sylvis, a leading spirit in the moulder's union, and proceeded
to set forth its "opposition to any measure that will evoke civil
war." But once the thunder of the guns began to rumble in
Charleston, South Carolina, the Northern wage earners rallied to
the union cause. Entire local unions enlisted at the call of President Abraham Lincoln. Sylvis helped to recruit a company of
moulders.

# IV

## *DRAWING CLASS LINES*

THE CIVIL WAR UNLEASHED THE DEMONIC IN AMERICAN LIFE; NO-
where is this more apparent than in the explosive growth of industry. Capital accumulated out of wartime profits searched for
investments; the new trusts in oil, iron, steel, copper, coal and
coke, sugar and railroads rose as giants in the land. The tariff
wall, erected by a Congress ever mindful of the needs of the new
powerful business interests of the North, protected from foreign
trade the opening markets of the West and the reviving South.
Combination was the order of the day as the corporation with its
giant steam-powered turbine replaced the water-powered mill as
the chief manufacturing establishment of the nation.

The accomplishments of the new age were prodigious. "Two
pounds of ironstone mined upon Lake Superior," wrote that
cagey Scotsman Andrew Carnegie, "and transported nine hundred miles to Pittsburgh; one pound and one-half of lime, mined
and transported to Pittsburgh; a small amount of manganese ore
mined in Virginia and brought to Pittsburgh—and these four
pounds of materials manufactured into one pound of steel, for
which the consumer pays one cent." Railroads—Walt Whitman's

"emblems of motion and power: pulse of the continent"—soon linked the nation with bands of gleaming steel.

"There's Millions in it!" The feverish cry of Mark Twain's Colonel Sellers in *The Gilded Age* echoed in Wall Street. Jay Gould, William H. Vanderbilt, Collis P. Huntington, James J. Hill, and Edward H. Harriman in railroads; John D. Rockefeller in oil; Andrew Carnegie in steel; Jay Cooke and J. Pierpont Morgan in finance; William A. Clark in mining; and Philip D. Armour in beef and pork—these were the Gogs and Magogs transforming American industry in the years that followed Grant's triumph at Appomattox.

In 1860, slightly more than a billion dollars was invested in manufacturing and there were only 1.5 million American industrial wage earners. By the end of the century, capital increased to more than 12 billions and the number of wage earners to 5.5 million. While population from 1850 to 1900 trebled (from 23,192,000 to 79,995,000) and the product of agriculture nearly trebled ($1,600,000,000 to $4,717,070,000,000), the value of manufacturers increased elevenfold ($1,019,107,000 to $11,-406,927,000). Within twenty-five years of the assassination of Abraham Lincoln, America had become the leading manufacturing nation in the world. "What England had once accomplished in a hundred years," declared Charles Beard, "the United States had achieved in half the time."

This awesome expansion accelerated the changes that we find in embryonic form in the eastern seaboard cities of pre-Civil War America. The factory system, once confined to the mill towns of New England, now spread over the industrial heartland of America. It hastened the decay of the old ways of doing business and the decline of the crafts. Artisans found their work further divided; small businessmen found it increasingly difficult to survive the violent ups and downs of the business cycle, especially in face of competition from the corporations. Small wonder, then, that class cleavage increased sharply as the century drew to a close.

Andrew Carnegie, at the height of his career as a philanthropist, declared that "the millionaires who are in active control started as poor boys and were trained in the sternest but most efficient of all schools—poverty." C. Wright Mills has shown that opportunity was more prevalent for ascent from the lower classes for men born 1820–49 and who came of age in the post-Civil War period than for the preceding generation (born 1790–1819) and the subsequent (born 1850–79). Of the 1820–49 generation, some 43 percent of the business elite came from the "lower" or "lower middle" classes. The comparable figures for the earlier generation is 37.2 percent; and 29.3 percent for the later.

Significantly, many of the leaders of labor in the late 1850s, 1860s and the 1870s were competent workmen who, in the course of their lives, were in and out of business. William H. Sylvis, the first outstanding figure in the American labor movement, made the move from journeyman to part proprietorship in a Philadelphia foundry in the early 1850s. His father, a wagon maker, too, was in and out of business most of his life. William, the second son of ten children, was born of Irish-French parentage, on November 26, 1828 in Armagh, Pennsylvania. The panic of 1837 destroyed the elder Sylvis' business and he was forced to tramp from place to place in search of work. William went to live with a well-to-do family and worked on the farm in return for his upkeep. When he became 18, William and his father attempted a joint venture in a wagon shop that proved unsuccessful. Sylvis then became an apprentice iron moulder, trying his hand alternately as journeyman and independent entrepreneur, until 1852 when he married and moved to Philadelphia.

When his employer sought to impose a 12-percent wage reduction, Sylvis, in 1857, joined his fellow iron moulders in a strike. He became secretary of his shop committee and an active member of the "Committee on Corners," a strike committee that posted men at the corners of the streets to watch for scabs. Sylvis was among the handful of men who kept their pledge not to return at reduced pay. In January, 1858, he was elected recording secretary of his local union. The rest of his life was devoted to the labor movement.

Sylvis was a remarkable man by any standard. Self-educated, he managed to secure only about three months of formal schooling as a lad. It is said that he learned to write only after being elected secretary of his local union and was obliged to carry on correspondence with other local secretaries. He was an avid reader, especially of politics and economics, though his letters showed a "lamentable deficiency" in spelling and grammar throughout his life. Sylvis was a founder, in 1859, of the National Molders' Union, serving first as secretary-treasurer and then as president. Along with William Harding, president of the International Coachmakers' Union, Sylvis helped to found the National Labor Union. Though he was unable to be present at the first congress of the NLU in 1866 because of illness, Sylvis later served as president of the short-lived federation. In 1867, Sylvis' name was put forward by labor and other periodicals as a possible vice-presidential candidate on an independent ticket with Congressman S. F. Carey of Ohio, a supporter of the eight-hour movement and a monetary reformer. Sylvis was the first American labor leader to seek a relationship with international labor. In 1867, he proposed that the National Labor Union send a delegate to the Lausanne Congress of the First International Workingmen's Association. No funds were available, but the suggestion was the first of its kind from an American labor leader. In 1869, A. C. Cameron, a Chicago labor leader, was sent to the Basel conference of the International as a delegate by the NLU. Sylvis was also the first to suggest a department of labor be added to the federal government. Sylvis died unexpectedly, at the age of 41, on July 26, 1869, from a stomach ailment.

Sylvis, of course, wasn't the only labor leader of the time who had seen "better times." James L. Wright, who helped Uriah Stephens to found the Knights of Labor, rose to become a manager of a large clothing store from a humble birth in County Tyrone, Ireland, on April 6, 1816, and an apprenticeship as a tailor. The depression of 1857, however, returned him to the ranks of the wage earners. He then helped organize the Garment Cutters' Association, the immediate predecessor of Local Assembly No. 1 of the Knights, in 1862, and was president when it was dissolved in 1869.

Charles Litchman, who became the grand secretary of the Knights of Labor, was born in Marblehead, Massachusetts, on April 8, 1849, the son of a shoe manufacturer. Litchman started in life as a salesman for his father's firm. Then he went into business on his own but ran afoul in the panic of 1873. In 1874, employed in a shoe factory, he first took up with the Knights of St. Crispin, a secret organization of shoemakers. He later became Grand Scribe of that organization and, when it folded in 1878, entered the Knights of Labor. Terence V. Powderly, the Grand Master Workman of the Knights during most of the Order's career from 1879 to 1893, himself could never make up his mind as to his role in society. Born of Irish parentage at Carbondale, Pennsylvania, on January 22, 1849, Powderly became a switch tender at sixteen, and a year later he entered a machine shop. He joined the Knights in 1876, entered the Greenback campaign of 1876 and was elected mayor of Scranton in 1878, a position he retained until 1884. He also joined his brother in a tea and coffee business, investing $1,000 in 1882. It failed a year later. Later, he became part owner and manager of a grocery business, which also ultimately failed. Perhaps his failures as a businessman and as a labor leader can be ascribed to these divided loyalties. Nonetheless, Powderly was, in his own way, typical of many who became leaders of the troubled workingmen of that era. In contrast, it must be said that Samuel Gompers, Powderly's great rival and the leader as well as founder of the American Federation of Labor, suffered no such disability. His was a single-minded devotion to the cause of the craftsmen.

As the fortunes of the early labor leaders fluctuated, so did those of the workingmen and the unions. The Civil War, at first, caused a paralysis of business and an increase in unemployment.

But this soon passed, and labor activity once again increased as economic activity picked up. Workmen revived dormant local unions, or organized new ones. The pattern of development followed that of the movement in the 1830s; the local unions banded in city central bodies, or trades' assemblies and attempts were made to organize national unions as well as to federate the trades' assemblies. But the national unions were largely "national" in name only. The Typographical Union survived as a benefits organization. The Machinists and Moulders, both organized in 1859, served as the barest of springboards into reform for their respective leaders, Jonathan Fincher and William H. Sylvis. Although some twenty-three national unions were organized between 1861 and 1871, the casuality rate was high. Few, indeed, lasted, until the formation of the American Federation of Labor in 1886, when national unions truly began to lead the American labor movement. Actually, the times were not ready for the national union. Industry itself, which, after all, serves as the incubator for trade unions, was barely national in scope. National markets were still unfolding. National consciousness, although greatly stimulated by the "war to save the union," needed to patch the wounds of the civil conflict before national leadership would be acceptable, both politically and economically, in business or in labor.

For the period, toward the end of the Civil War and immediately following, the trades assemblies were the source of labor's strength. The first trades' assembly was organized in Rochester, New York, in March, 1863, and the movement soon spread to every industrial center of any consequence. This city-wide organization of workingmen, as was the case in the 1830s, was a mixed body of local trade unions, workingmen's clubs and reform societies. For the worker, such an organization appeared to meet their needs in rallying support for strikes, mounting boycotts, serving as a center for advice and aid. It also served as a training ground for those trying to set up organizations that were national in scope, including many who were to be active in the Knights of Labor.

Industry changed radically and rapidly in the post-Civil War era, and workingmen soon felt the need for something more in the way of organization than city-wide trades' assemblies. Robert Gilchrist, the anti-war labor leader of 1860 and president of the Louisville, Kentucky assembly, tried to call a national convention of trades' assemblies in early 1864, but without success. However, a second call later in the year resulted in the short-lived International Industrial Assembly of North America. The organization never met again but is significant nonetheless because its constitution made provision for a strike fund to be financed by a per capita tax on the membership. The idea was later adopted by the Knights of Labor and the Cigar Makers with greater success. The Cigar Makers' version became the basis of the "new unionism" that gave rise to the American Federation of Labor.

The demise of the International Industrial Assembly left a leadership vacuum. The depression that started in 1866 weakened the brief revival of national unions and possibly prevented their filling in the gap. However, the economic downturn revived worker interest in reform, greenbackism and the eight-hour day. Ira Steward, a self-taught Boston machinist, revived the shorter-hours movement of the first half of the nineteenth century by his demand for an eight-hour day. Steward also added an economic theory of growth to the argument for the shorter day, giving an ideological cast to the workingmen's demand for more leisure and time for "self-improvement." Steward's theory was expressed in the popular couplet:

"Whether you work by piece or work by day,
Decreasing the hours increases the pay."

The notion that cutting the work day, or work week, will increase employment still has currency in the labor movement. It is embodied in the AFL–CIO's current proposal for fluctuating the length of the work week in order to maintain full employment;

the idea being that, when joblessness increases, the work week is to be cut until all who want work are once again employed.

Steward's agitation resulted in the formation of eight-hour leagues throughout the United States. Taking a tactical leaf from Evans, the land reformer, the leagues sought pledges from candidates favoring the issue; those who would not sign were opposed by the league.

The campaign for the eight-hour day also provided the stimulus for the formation, in 1866, of the National Labor Union, another attempt at political reformism by America's workingmen. The strength of the National Labor Union rested upon the local trades' assemblies. It soon became more and more political, ultimately giving birth to the National Labor and Reform Party, in 1872, which died the same year when its nominee for the presidency declined the honor. The National Labor Union, however short its existence, did leave a mark. The first permanent labor lobby was established in Washington, D.C., in 1868 to press for a department of labor. A. C. Cameron, the editor of the Chicago *Workingman's Advocate*, was sent to the Basel conference of the International Workingmen's Association. The eight-hour day for federal employees was adopted by Congress in 1869, largely as a result of National Labor Union agitation. Illinois, Wisconsin, Connecticut, Missouri, and New York passed state laws. But these laws were ineffective, because they permitted contracts requiring ten hours or more a day. The eight-hour day was legal only in the absence of such agreements and employers made certain that their employees signed contracts for the longer day. The depression of 1873 wiped out even this small gain. The issue was not to be revived seriously until 1886. But the federal victory did last; in 1872, President Grant issued a proclamation prohibiting any wage reductions in carrying out the eight-hour day for federal employees.

The race question cropped up at the 1869 conference of the NLU. Prior to the convention, in an address to workingmen, the NLU declared: "Negroes are four million strong and a greater proportion of them labor with their hands than can be counted from among the same number of any other people on earth. Can we afford to reject their proffered cooperation and make them enemies?"

"What is wanted," the address continued, "is for every union to help inculcate the grand ennobling idea that the interests of labor are one; that there should be no distinction of race or nationality; no classification of Jew or Gentile; christian or infidel; that there is one dividing line, that which separates mankind into two great classes, the class that labors and the class that lives by others' labor."

However, as so many labor conventions since have done, the NLU meeting evaded the issue; postponing any action, after debate, and against the better judgment of Sylvis. "We are all one family of slaves together," he argued. "The labor movement is a second Emancipation Proclamation." The convention, however, did seat Isaac Myers, president of the Colored National Labor Union, as a delegate.

Following the failure of political action in 1872, the national unions called a series of national congress in the years 1873 to 1875. But these annual meetings were largely ineffective. John Siney, founder of the Miners' National Association, quit in disgust because the congresses promised no help for the miners. Two new secret societies—the Industrial Brotherhood and the Sovereigns of Industry—also flourished at the time. The latter was a cooperative movement in the tradition of the Associationists and Brook Farm. Not much is known about the former. But the merits of the two were debated at a national congress in 1875 with the Industrial Brotherhood the apparent winner. Thereupon, both seem to have expired, leaving little behind except, in the case of the Brotherhood, a preamble and some platform measures that were subsequently adopted by the Knights of Labor.

The Panic of 1873, precipitated by the failure of the country's leading brokerage house, Jay Cooke & Company. and the collapse of railroad speculation, led to widespread unemployment. What bad times could do to a union is illustrated by the fate of the Knights of St. Crispin, whose development paralleled that of the Knights of Labor and which was to provide the latter with ideas and personnel. The Crispins were organized secretly in Milwaukee on May 7, 1867, a year before the Knights of Labor were launched in Philadelphia. Shoemakers, following the Civil War, were particularly hard-hit by the industrial revolution. The invention of the McKay pegging machine hastened the development of specialization and speeded the growth of the factory system. The new machinery enabled employers to hire "green hands" to replace old-line craftsmen. The Crispins started to protest. By 1870, the membership had reached 50,000, making the Crispins the largest union of the day. Its strikes in 1869–70 were successful, and the manufacturers of Lynn were forced to sign agreements with the Crispins. But it was a Pyrrhic victory. The Crispins were fighting a lost cause. They opposed the introduction of the new machines and prohibited their members from teaching their craft to others. In the end, the machine had its way. The employers of Lynn combined and, in 1872, broke the union. The Panic of 1873 helped to administer the *coup de grâce;* the Crispins lost most of their strikes that year, and the organization expired a year later.

The defeat of the Crispins was paralleled elsewhere. The unions were destroyed by the hard terms exacted by employers, many of whom, in their turn, failed as a result of the industrial crisis of the 1870s. The fall of the Miners' National Association, for example, left the kind of vacuum in leadership and organization that the Knights came to fill so well. In December, 1874, under the leadership of Mark Hanna, the bituminous coal operators of Ohio's Tuscarawas Valley decided to reduce the miners' scale from 90 to 70 cents. Hanna, who was the first industrialist to recognize the common sense of negotiating with representatives of one's employees, convinced the mine owners that they ought to sit down with the mine union. Three representatives from each side were chosen (Hanna was one of the employers) and a well-known Ohio judge, S. J. Andrews, appointed chairman of the wage committee. The decision went against the miners and a rate of 71 cents was set. But one operator, irked by the failure of the other employers to order a general lockout against the miners' demand for a check-weighman, revenged himself by offering to pay his men 80 cents. This was so much fuel to the passion of union militants, who were, in any case, restive over the pay cut handed down in the arbitration. The miners appealed to their officers to be released from the award. This was granted reluctantly and the operators were forced to pay the higher rate. But the incipient process of collective bargaining—involving joint conferences and arbitration—was destroyed for a decade. Within two short years, the 35,000-member miners' association was destroyed by incessant strikes.

Despite the counsel of their leaders, the miners struck frequently, bringing on the arrest of John Siney, president, and Xingo Parks, a youthful union organizer, for violation of the Pennsylvania criminal conspiracy law. Siney was exonerated, Parks sentenced for "inciting to riot." The association fell to pieces. By 1876 both the anthracite and bituminous coal miners were without a union. (A second union, confined to the anthracite fields, was destroyed by a long strike in 1874–75.) The anthracite miners came under the sway of the "Molly Maguires," a terroristic offshoot of the Ancient Order of Hibernians. In Ireland, the Hibernians led the struggles in the '40s against the encroachment of the English landlords. The Irish immigrants adapted the Order to their contest with the mine owners; they ran strikebreakers out of the coal fields. When unionism failed, the young Irish hotheads in the Mollies turned to derailing mine cars and burning breakers. Then they took to the hills to snipe at mine supers and unpopular foremen.

To counter the depredations of the Mollies, the operators called in Allan Pinkerton, a secret service agent who won quite a reputation spying on the Confederacy. Pinkerton sent a young Irishman, James McParlan, into the anthracite coal fields with instructions to ingratiate himself with the leaders of the Mollies. McParlan, possibly the first labor spy in American labor history, did so in the manner of the Vautrins the world over by suggesting ever greater deeds of terror and intimidation. McParlan, under the assumed name of James McKenna, rose to be secretary of his district of the Mollies. The case against the secret order broke in 1875, when arrests were first made. The secret agent took the stand and, largely on his unsupported testimony, fourteen Mollies were imprisoned and ten—the guilty along with the innocent— were hanged. The secret order was crushed, and the rudderless miners began to drift into the Knights of Labor.

The apparent collapse of the economy and the collapse of the unions stimulated interest in socialism and in the financial nostrums of Greenbackism. The latter, with its faith in inflationary fiat by paper money, overshadowed the early socialist movement and, perhaps, accounts for socialism's failure to take root in the discontent of the times. The Greenbackers sought to have the government lend its credit to cooperative associations of workingmen, hoping thereby to drive capitalism out of existence. But the appeal of Greenbackism is found in the expectation of the man without capital—small businessman, farmer, or workingman— that such credit would give him an even break in business with rich, Wall Street financed competitors.

The early socialist movement is of interest, primarily because it provided a training ground for P. J. McGuire, Adolph Strasser and Samuel Gompers, the founding triumvirate of the American Federation of Labor, as well as other labor leaders of the last quarter of the century. The socialists, following the lead of McGuire, were active in the unemployment demonstrations that followed the Panic of 1873. On January 13, 1874, thousands of red-sashed workers marched into Tompkins Square in New York City at the behest of P. J. McGuire and the socialist-organized Committee of Public Safety. Mounted policemen greeted the marchers with a billy-club charge; hundreds were injured. Throughout the day, police flying squads carried the terror throughout the East

Side of New York. The violence served the authorities well; the radical movement on the East Coast came to a temporary halt. Young Sam Gompers, who, with his temperamental and fiery friend McGuire, witnessed the bloody outcome of the demonstration, was convinced of the futility of political radicalism. The Tompkins Square riot marked the start of Gomper's journey to pure-and-simple unionism. His friend came, in the end, to the same posture but at a much later date.

After the riot, an embittered McGuire declared: "These scurvy knaves know not the volcano ready to burst beneath their feet and blow them to atoms." The rhetoric may have been excessive, but the explosion was not long in coming. "Strikes," warned the New York *Railroad Gazette*, January 3, 1874, "are no longer accidents but are as much a disease of the body politic as the measles or indigestion are of our physical organization." Before the "Great Upheaval" of 1877, America was scarcely aware of the existence of a labor movement. Middle-class Americans rested secure in the belief that the country was immune from the revolutionary viruses rampant in the mid-19th century Europe. The Tompkins Square riot and a peaceful demonstration in Chicago a month earlier were put down as local disturbances caused by "foreign" workmen. The powerful were confident that they could handle any outbreak of mob violence. Did not Jay Gould boast, "I can hire one half of the working class to kill the other half"?

Significantly, the first great clash between capital and labor occurred "on" the railroad. "In the year 1871," wrote Henry Adams, "the West was still fresh and the Union Pacific was young." Two years earlier, on May 10, 1869, at Ogden, Utah, the last spike connecting the Union Pacific and the Central Pacific was driven into the roadbed. Thirty-three thousand miles of railroad were built between 1867 and 1873. Railroads were also the first major combines in finance and business to come to the attention of the public; they were also the first to inspire near-universal hatred.

Hard times following the Panic depressed wages although the

railroads continued to pay dividends of eight and ten percent. Grievances piled up as the lines of the jobless men seeking work grew outside rail employment offices. Hours were long—15 to 18 a day. The pay frequently was in arrears on too many railroads. Trackmen on the Erie lived as squatters in shanties on land alongside the tracks, a long-established custom. Suddenly, without warning, they were ordered to pay ground rent of $20 to $25 a year or vacate. Some railroads deprived their employees of the customary passes needed to carry them to and from their work. One engineer on the Lake Shore Line was paid 16 cents in wages to run a train from Collinwood to Cleveland. He then had to pay a fare of 25 cents to report back to his superior in Collinwood. When the president of the Pennsylvania and Reading ordered the locomotive engineers, in 1877, to quit their weak and ineffective union—the Brotherhood of Locomotive Engineers, organized in 1863—the engineers planned a surprise strike but were defeated through the spy tactics of the Pinkertons. If the railroads ignored any way of degrading or insulting their men, it goes unrecorded.

In 1877, the Pennsylvania led the way in cutting railroad pay by ten percent. Robert H. Ammon, a young Pennsy brakeman, organized a secret Trainmen's Union that was to be an industrial union of all railroad employees—engineers, conductors, brakemen, firemen, trackmen, shop men. The union spread within a matter of weeks along the Pennsy network, to the Baltimore and Ohio, the Erie, and the Atlantic and Great Western. A simultaneous strike was planned, but dissension arose and the movement collapsed. This was the immediate background of what became the Great Upheaval of 1877.

On July 11, the Baltimore and Ohio announced its ten-percent wage cut: a first class fireman, under the new scale, would receive but $1.50 a day; this came to an average, at best, of $5 or $6 a week on the basis of the four-day week then worked. Out of this the men were expected not only to support a family but pay living expenses while on the job. The men grumbled. Company president Garrett patiently heard out the complaints of his men but remained firm, confident that those who chose to quit, or the troublemakers, would be easily replaced.

On July 16, the day the new scale went into effect, the trains were manned as usual, although 40 firemen and brakemen on freight trains in Baltimore refused to work and had to be replaced. But as the day wore on, reports of "trouble," "discontent," and "insubordination" poured into the main office. At Martinsburg, West Virginia, firemen abandoned their trains. The mayor arrested the strike leaders but had to release them in the face of threats from an angry, growing crowd. By morning, the strike had assumed "alarming proportions." A B & O vice-president called on the governor of West Virginia for militia; two companies were sent, shots were exchanged between the militia and the strikers. The ranks of the strikers were swelled by townspeople and nearby farmers; the two companies of militia soon went over, officers and all, to the strikers. The latter ruled Martinsburg until federal troops arrived.

The tremors spread along the railroad tracks, setting off civil conflagrations at nearly all the chief rail centers of the country. Riots occurred in Baltimore, Altoona, Scranton (where the miners joined in), Buffalo, Toledo, Louisville, Chicago, St. Louis, and San Francisco. "Since last week," John Hay wrote on July 24, 1877, to his father-in-law, prosperous Cleveland financier Amasa Stone, "the country has been at the mercy of the mob, and on the whole the mob has behaved rather better than the country. . . . the government is utterly helpless and powerless in the face of an unarmed rebellion of foreign workingmen, mostly Irish." Federal troops were called out to quell disorders in Reading—where 11 people were killed and 20 wounded in a single day—and in Baltimore. The one city where no violence or bloodshed occurred was Allegheny City, across the river from strife-torn Pittsburgh, where Robert H. Ammon's trainmen's union still retained some organization and controlled the city throughout the strike. But elsewhere the walkouts of the railroaders set off community-wide riots that revealed the depth of the popular hatred of the rail barons. In Pittsburgh, where public feeling ran high against the Pennsy, almost the entire city turned out to loot and burn the railroad's property after the militia fired on the strikers. Many businessmen openly supported the strikers because they felt that they were discriminated against in freight rates by the railroad.

When the trainmen left their trains and took command of the Pittsburgh junction railroad switches on the morning of July 19, the railroad called on the governor for aid. But the local militia ordered out by Governor John F. Hartranft openly sympathized with the strikers. A detachment of 1,000 troops from Philadelphia was ordered to Pittsburgh, arriving on Saturday, July 21. The Philadelphian troops marched out on Liberty Street to disperse the strikers and were met by a crowd of men, women, and children. Some stones were thrown by boys—much in the manner of the Boston Massacre some hundred years earlier—and the militia opened fire. Twenty persons were killed and 29 seriously wounded. The troops were forced to retreat by the angry, swelling mob and were soon trapped in the Pennsy roundhouse by some 20,000 enraged men and women. The mob looted to provide itself with arms and munitions; three pieces of artillery were captured from the state troopers. A carload of coke was saturated with oil, set afire and run against the roundhouse. The besieged militia shot their way out—killing and wounding still more—and fled to Sharpsburg.

A fire broke out in the freight cars lined up outside Union Depot. It soon spread and, before it ran its course, the fire had destroyed 104 locomotives, 2,152 cars of all sorts, and 79 buildings. The total loss to the railroad, according to Pennsy president, Colonel Thomas A. Scott, exceeded $5,000,000. But as the fire burned itself out, so did the riot. The next day, a hastily gathered volunteer militia found it easy to disperse the remaining handful of looters.

The Great Upheaval of 1877, in turn, burned itself out as did the Pittsburgh fire and riot. The strikers were too disorganized to prevail for long against the superior strength of federal troops and the militia. Yet, the relationship of labor to capital was irretrievably changed. The old master-journeyman relationship was forever buried with the ashes of the Pittsburgh roundhouse. Frightened by the glare of flame-fed riots, civil authorities reinforced the militia. The massive armories of our larger cities are monuments to that fear. The courts revived the old doctrine of conspiracy and applied it with renewed vigor to the unions. "The prospects of labor and capital both seem gloomy," Hay wrote on August 23 to his father-in-law. "The very devil seems to have entered into the lower classes of workingmen, and there are plenty of scoundrels to encourage them to all lengths."

While the strikes were lost, the morale of workingmen, oddly enough, did not suffer correspondingly. Labor parties flourished in the years following the Great Upheaval. One of these was the Greenback Labor Party. The Greenback movement, up until that time, had been largely agriculturally based. Immediately following the outbreaks of 1877, workingmen's parties either sprang to life or were created in the industrial centers of the country. But as the railroads knit the nation together with ribbons of steel, so grievances held in common brought the farmers and workingmen together. Both shared a common hatred of the growing power of the railroad barons. Alliances were struck in Ohio and Pennsylvania that were encouragingly successful at the polls in the fall of 1877. These led to the formation of a Greenback Labor Party in February, 1878. Leaders of the Knights of Labor, fresh from their own first national general assembly, attended the Greenback Labor convention in Toledo, Ohio. Trevellick was temporary chairman and Robert Schilling, Ralph Beaumont, and Uriah Stephens were delegates. In the spring, Powderly, who became Grand Master Workman of the Knights a year later, was elected Mayor of Scranton, Pennsylvania, on the Greenback Labor ticket. The Greenback vote in the fall congressional elections was over one million, and fourteen representatives were elected to Congress. For a moment, it appeared that a successful farmer-labor coalition was in the making. But the appearance was illusory; on

January 1, 1879, the redemption of greenbacks in gold began. The volume of currency increased, heralding the return of prosperity. The ties between the farmer and workingman snapped. The Greenback Labor Party went out of existence with its disparate elements swallowed up by the Democratic Party, while others went into the growing Socialist Labor Party.

Thereafter, the Knights of Labor came into their own as a national organization.

# V

## *THE NOBLE AND HOLY ORDER*

THE YEAR 1869 WAS A BAD ONE FOR THE CLOTHING TRADE IN Philadelphia. The Civil War boom petered out and the Garment Cutters' Association, a benefits society organized in 1863, found it difficult to survive. After considerable discussion, the members of the Association met on December 9, 1869, to divide the remaining funds and to dissolve their organization. But nine of their number were dissatisfied with the decision to disband. So, after the others left, they stayed on in the hall of the American Hose Company on Jayne Street to form a new secret society.

Soon cryptic calls to meetings of Local Assembly No. 1 of the Knights of Labor appeared on sidewalks, fences and walls—five stars and a circle enclosing a triangle. Anonymously signed meeting notices also appeared in the press, hinting at hidden power. Slowly, under the leadership of Master Workman Uriah S. Stephens, the organization began to grow. In the fall of 1870, the first "sojourner," a ship's carpenter, was admitted to the assembly of cutters. He, however, was not a full member, paid no dues and was allowed to remain only until enough of his own craft could be secured to "swarm" and form an assembly of their own. "The sojourner," Terence V. Powderly, who was to lead the Knights for most of their years, wrote in his autobiography, *Thirty Years of Labor*, "was admitted that he might become a missionary among his fellow tradesmen." In the summer of 1872, the ship carpenters and caulkers who had sojourned in Local Assembly No. 1 swarmed to form the second assembly of the Knights of Labor. In this fashion, the Knights grew steadily until it became the dominant labor organization of the 1880s.

The defeat of the Crispins—and of other unions—was not lost on the Knights of Labor. It reinforced their general distaste for strikes. The Knights—as other unions of the time did—placed great emphasis on arbitration, by which they meant the peaceful settlement of disputes and not a referral to a third party for settlement, as we now understand the term. The reluctance to strike was later to prove to be the tragic flaw in the makeup of the Knights of Labor. But in the midst of the grim depression, avoidance of strike action seemed to be the better part of wisdom. So did secrecy, another major tenet of the Order. Employer blacklists were all too effective, and the Knights can't be blamed for believing that secrecy was one way of avoiding dismissal for activity on behalf of the Order. However, secrecy touched yet another nerve. Uriah Stephens was—as were a number of other yearly leaders of the Knights—a Mason, an Odd Fellow, and a member of the Knights of Pythias. All of these are organizations with elaborate—and secret—rituals and "mysteries." Stephens, and the others, no doubt, carried a fondness for this sort of thing over to the Knights of Labor. In doing so, he apparently hit on a formula, if not for success, at least for staying alive and growing during difficult times.

Secrecy, reinforced by an elaborate ritual and high-sounding titles, gave the Knights a sense of power beyond that actually exercised during the early growth of the order. This, of course, acted as a lodestone to workingmen who felt that their pride of craft was being undermined by the new industrialism. The hidden power of the Knights was a counter to the burgeoning power of corporate industry. It also gave the individual Knight a sense of belonging; indeed, it was one of the great strengths of the Order that it offered a new community to replace the disintegrating community of craft and trade.

The Noble and Holy Order of the Knights of Labor became the vessel into which poured the discontents of workingmen chafing under the yoke of the new industrialism.

The appeal of the Knights—"That is the most perfect government in which an injury to one is the concern of all"—fitted the new mood. The Knights welcomed them all—workers in every field, women as well as men, Negroes in the South, immigrant "greenhorns" in the North. Rank-and-file sojourners during the years from 1869 to 1878 spread the gospel among carpenters, gold beaters, mechanics, mill workers, miners, railroaders, and others. The Order's constitution provided that three-fourths of every Assembly must be composed of wage earners. Professional men, small businessmen and farmers, however, were welcomed to join. Indeed, all were welcome, except "Bankers, stock-brokers, professional gamblers, lawyers, and those who in any way derive their living from the manufacture or sale of intoxicating liquors." Sober-sided delegates to the first national assembly denounced "the recent alarming development and aggression of aggregated wealth," called for democratic cooperative effort "making knowledge a standpoint for action, and industrial and moral worth not wealth the true standard of individual and national greatness." Their goals, in truth, were modest: the establishment of bureaus of labor; the setting up of both producers' and distributors' cooperatives; the reserving of public lands for genuine settlers—"not another acre for railroads or speculators"; the substitution of arbitration—what is really meant here is negotiations—for strikes; and anti-child-labor clause; and demand for equal pay for equal work for men and women.

"I do not claim," declared Uriah Stephens, "any power of prophecy, but I can see ahead of me an organization that will cover the globe. It will include men and women of every craft, creed and color; it will cover every race worth saving."

Norman J. Ware, the sympathetic historian of the movement, summed it up this way: "A monopoly against monoplies, said the Knights. After that they did not know, but time would tell. So they advanced toward solidarity, followed every trail that promised to lead them out of the morass of the wage system or make it comfortable to them, threw the nation into hysteria, and departed, making the way clear for business unionism and the bankruptcy of deals."

The rise and fall of the Knights is dramatically reflected in the normally dry-as-dust statistics of membership. In 1879, the year of the second national assembly of the Order, membership stood at 9,287; within a year, it was up by 20,000, dropping back to 19,422 in 1881. Thereafter, membership rose steadily to reach 111,395 in 1885. But in 1885–87 the Knights increased mightily to reach a peak of 729,677 members. At the peak in February, 1886, some 515 assemblies were organized within one month. "Never in all history," declaimed labor journalist John Swinton, "has there been such a spectacle as the march of the Order of the Knights of Labor at the present time." Estimates of the Order's membership ran considerably higher, up to 2.5 million in some instances. The Knights' officers, flushed with success and in the manner of political leaders everywhere, exaggerated their strength, boasting of 10,000 assemblies and a membership of over a million. But the march was of short duration; scarcely a year later, the membership declined to 548,000 and to 259,000 in 1888. By 1890, the Order was down to 100,000 and before the Gay Nineties expired, the Noble Order was all but dead.

To understand the magnificence of the failure of the Order, we must set the structure of the Knights against that of prevailing industry. The Order was that all-encompassing vessel, the one big union. As such it counterposed an alternate form of organization for the new age of industrialism to that posed by the dominant corporatism. "The tariff is the mother of trusts," intoned Henry O. Havemeyer, who should have known since he was the father and president of the Sugar Trust. Combination certainly was the order of the day as the Carnegies, the Goulds, and the Rockefellers became the undisputed masters of the provinces of steel, rails, oil, and nearly everything else. The industrial magnates remade the image of America so successfully that we can scarcely imagine any other-possible, probable, or otherwise.

The Knights, however, flourished at a different time, when combination was, relatively speaking, in its infancy. The Order never was, as the Congress of Industrial Organizations was to be, an adaptation to a mold cast by the industrial corporations. It was, rather, a substitute, an alternate way or style, howsoever tentative, to that set by the plutocracy of wealth and power.

As an all-inclusive organization, the Knights offered—when it had to do so—the autonomy that the craft unions craved and ultimately deified in the American Federation of Labor. It also offered haven for incipient industrial unions, such as the coal miners' and the brewery workers' unions. But it drew these—as well as its district assemblies which were, in turn, delegated bodies based on the older form of workers' organization, the local single craft or trade union—to a central, national federation in much the same way the Constitution drew the states together into a federal union. (The AFL, properly speaking, was a confederation of equally autonomous unions and not a federation.) The Knights, unlike many of the earlier national unions, grew from the grassroots, evolving naturally and when it suited its sojourner-recruited members, a structure that would fit industrialism to the needs and wants of the workingman and his allies—the professional man, the farmer, the small businessman. The Order, subconsciously perhaps, represented a working out of the Jeffersonian strain in American life in the strange waters of the new industrialism that contained so much that is foreign to the democratic spirit. It was the hope and dream of the Knights to find a workable substitute for the corporate capitalism that threatened to engulf the traditional independence of the American workingman. (The craft unionism of the AFL actually bypassed corporate capitalism. Its strength rested in the carpenters and the cigar makers; the Knights, say what you will about their weaknesses, had the brass to confront Jay Gould.)

"The Knights of Labor is not a trade union—it is a union of all trades and callings; it furnishes the great heart through which the life-giving current may flow strong and healthy to every part of labor's mighty frame." So reads Powderly's invitation to the skilled steel workers—the boilers, puddlers, rollers and beaters— in the Amalgamated Association of Iron and Steelworkers to join the unskilled under the banners of the Knights. It was his conviction—shared by the Knights—that a bringing together of the skilled and unskilled would make them both invincible. The failure to carry off this marriage was the ultimate failure and tragedy of the Knights. But the Order did try. Sometimes in spite of itself, for the leadership, by and large, did not live up to the task set by the Order's own ideals and aspirations.

Terence V. Powderly was no John L. Lewis. With his great drooping blond handlebar moustache and steel-rimmed spectacles perched on a Roman nose, the balding, high-domed Powderly was a great talker. He was also a sensitive and vain man." The position I hold," he asserted in 1887, "is too big for any ten men." At that, the slender, blue-eyed ex-machinist held down too many other jobs in addition to the chieftainship of the Knights. In part, this was due to the inadequacy of the remuneration that went with the exalted post of Grand Master Workman. Powderly, in 1886, finally was granted a decent salary. But it came too late. When he was finally discarded by the Order several years later, all that was left for him was a minor position with the government in Washington. This underlying economic insecurity drove the man to devote too much of his time to other projects at a time when the Knights could have used all his energies and talents.

Nonetheless, Powderly was the wrong man to be at the helm when the final storm broke and the organization was nearly swamped by the influx of new members. Powderly was a born agitator but he was not a very aggressive man. He could never, for example, bring himself to regard the strike as an essential weapon in the workingman's armory. The Knights' general distastefulness for strike action was widely shared among union leaders of the day. It was, after all, deeply rooted in experience; labor was too frequently defeated to take up lightly so explosive a weapon. Yet, it wasn't a weapon of their own choosing. Lockouts flourished as frequently as strikes and it was hard in many cases to draw the distinction. The men who flocked to the Knights during the mid-1880s were often caught up by one or the other. Even where the unions preferred negotiation, or arbitration, that choice was rarely a real one; recognition had to be won first and that—almost inevitably in the history of unionism—means strike. Powderly could not see this. And for a man who believed in arbitration, or negotiation, he was a poor negotiator. This was largely because his heart wasn't in it. According to Ware, Powderly "believed in the peaceful settlement of disputes but he believed even more strongly in not having disputes to settle." Powderly wanted to educate the working class into the new cooperative society; he failed to recognize the need for fighting one's way to build a new world.

Toward the end of his stewardship of the Knights, Powderly received a wire from Wisconsin asking him to settle a strike of 1,500 men. "We never had a meeting yet," the disgruntled Master Workman wrote to an aide, "that some such thing did not turn up to hamper and embarrass us." Strikes and lockouts, however, did take place and the Knights perforce were compelled to try to cope. Repeated attempts were made to set up a Resistance-Defense fund but none was entirely successful.

Small wonder then that—given Powderly's squeamishness and the Knights' skittishness toward strike action—the Order should run into difficulty in its first strike on a national scale. Typically, the trouble arose out of an implied promise to deliver aid and comfort when there was no chance of doing so. An implication, incidentally, may have been rooted in the Knight's past as a closed, secret society. But it is an attribute of such societies that they often give the appearance of strength where none exists. This is a kind of deception, I think, that explains a good deal about some of the courses taken by the Knights; why, for example, the Knight rank and file was often too eager to strike while the leadership was too reluctant to say, "Hold on now." In any event, this is just about what happened in the telegraphers' strike, the first major national strike action taken by the Order.

On July 19, 1883, following a period of organizing among telegraphers, John Campbell, their district master workman, called a strike of all commercial telegraphers. Initially, the strike was a success. Two companies—American Rapid and the Bankers and Merchants—agreed to a 15-percent pay hike, abolition of Sunday work without extra pay, and other improvements. But the Gould-backed Western Union decided to break the union. The Knights did what they could, issuing an appeal for funds, which raised some $1,600. The executive board of the order ponied up another $2,000 out of the general fund. But the total was not sufficient. The strike was called off on August 17 and the 4,000 Western Union men straggled back to work as best they could.

That year was a bad one for the Knights, and for labor generally. Workers struck fruitlessly against reductions in wages occasioned by the general industrial recession that winter. The Knights were indirectly involved in a series of lost strikes—the Fall River spinners; the Hocking Valley (Ohio), Indiana, and Pennsylvania coal miners; Troy (N.Y.) moulders; and the Philadelphia carpet weavers. Significantly, none but the carpet weavers was a strike directly led by the Knights. Those that were so led—the glass workers, Philadelphia shoemakers, and the Union Pacific shopmen—were successes.

This may have been due to a more hard-headed turn among the leadership of the Order. Robert Layton, then secretary, realistically argued: "If a strike is right and inevitable, support it; if not, ignore it and save trouble to all concerned. But for the sake of truth let us cease to condemn strikes and refuse to assess for them while we just as strongly yet indirectly indorse them by the issuing of those delusions known as appeals."

The potential possessed by the Order for the workingmen of the day was demonstrated in a strike of Union Pacific shopmen. It was this strike that set off the skyrocketing growth of the Order—from 50,000 to 700,000—in the three short years from 1884 through 1886. On May 4, 1884, the railroad shopmen in Denver downed their tools to protest a wage reduction. Leaderless and without organization, they turned to Joseph R. Buchanan, editor of the *Labor Enquirer* and a leader of the Denver Knights. Within twenty-four hours, the shopmen developed an organization and the entire Union Pacific system rolled to a halt. The company capitulated four days later, and the wage reduction was withdrawn. The railroad, however, reacted in a fashion typical for the times. Caught by an upsurge of organization, employers frequently extended what amounted to union recognition with fingers crossed until a moment presented itself to break the union. This the Union Pacific did later in the summer, when a notice was posted in the Ellis, Kansas shops, announcing a ten-percent cut in wages for fifteen first-class machinists. Twenty men who were active in the Knights and the May strike were also discharged in Denver. Two days later, on August 13, 1884, the Knights responded with a strike call, again downing the railroad. On August 18, the company gave way, agreeing to a restoration of the wage cut, the jobs of the twenty men, and an agreement to discuss and arbitrate other grievances.

The significance of the Knights' victory was not lost on railroad men. In the following year, the Knights were called in to lead a strike against the Gould system, embracing the Wabash, Missouri, Kansas and Texas, and the Missouri Pacific. More than 4,500 men were out. They were backed by the "runners"—the locomotive engineers, brakemen, and conductors. The Union Pacific Knights' assembly kicked in $30,000 and Buchanan was sent out to aid the strikers. Knights of Labor assemblies were organized along the striking roads and the solidarity of the rail men resulted in a quick victory, wages were restored and strikers reemployed in March, 1885.

Once again the rail employers crossed fingers. The Wabash, then in the hands of receivers, on August 18 laid off a majority of the shopmen at Moberly, Missouri, in an effort to bring their union to heel. The Knights pointed out that this was in direct violation of the March agreement and sought in vain to meet with the Wabash receivers. Failing a meeting, the Knights ordered all members on the Gould system to refuse to handle Wabash rolling stock. Gould, the power behind the scenes, was unwilling to risk a strike of the magnitude of the great rail strike of 1877. He therefore requested a meeting with the Order's general executive board. The railway magnate pledged that he "would always endeavor to do what was right" and threw his weight on the Wabash board behind a settlement favorable to the Knights. The "runners" (the operating trainmen), incidentally, failed to back the shopmen in this dispute, thereby giving the victory of the Knights an even greater significance in the eyes of American workingmen.

For the first time in American labor history, a labor organization had met on an equal footing with a giant of industry. The rush to join the Knights was soon on, and the country would never see its like again until the rise of the Congress of Industrial Organizations in the mid-1930s. Within the space of one month—February, 1886—515 assemblies were organized. So many flocked to the standard of the Knights that the executive board was alarmed and declared in March, 1886, a moratorium on organizing for forty days to give the swollen Order time to digest the newcomers.

Organization of the Knights was not confined to the United States. A. G. Denny was sent to Europe in 1885 to organize glass workers. Assemblies were formed in Sunderland, England; Charleroi, Jumet, and Brussels, in Belgium. Additional assemblies were organized in places as far apart as Australia, New Zealand, and Ireland.

Success, however, stretched the Knights beyond its capacities as an organization. There was some recognition of this among the leadership of the Order. When the Southwestern men—Gould employees on the Missouri Pacific and the Missouri, Kansas, and Texas—wanted to strike in sympathy with the Wabash shopmen, the Knights' general executive board wisely refused permission. But in the end the Order's officials were unable to restrain the overconfident Southwestern railmen. They firmly believed the Order to be invulnerable and were eager to strike for the eight-hour day and $1.50 a day "for all laboring men." By 1886, the railroad interests on Wall Street, too, were eager for a showdown with the Knights. Gould was ready, as he had not been a year earlier, to break the union. Minor Southwestern officials effectively needled the shopmen with petty annoyances. On February 18, 1886, a foreman of the car-shop at Marshall, Texas, was discharged. He had, apparently, permission to take a leave of absence to attend a district assembly meeting but was not taken back on his return. Martin Irons, district Master Workman, seized the chance to call a strike that he was convinced was inevitable.

Irons sent a telegram to the Dallas headquarters of the railroad demanding that company officers meet with him in Marshall, or else a strike would be called. Receiving no reply, Irons called out the Knights on the Missouri Pacific on March 6. The strike soon spread over 5,000 miles of track in Missouri, Kansas, Arkansas, Indian Territory and Nebraska and involved over 9,000 shopmen, yardmen and section hands. The strikers seized railroad equipment whenever they could, "killing" locomotives by removing key parts. Violence flared whenever the strikers resorted to force to keep the unsympathetic engineers, firemen, brakemen and conductors off the job.

The leaders of the Order, trapped between the militancy of the rank and file and the adamancy of the railroad officials, met with Gould and other company officials, but to no avail. Congress appointed a committee to investigate. The railroads were asked to agree to arbitration by a citizens committee from St. Louis. The road refused and the committee asked the Order to call off the strike in the public interest. This the Knights' executive board did on May 4, 1886. This capitulation unhappily coincided with the collapse of the eight-hour strikes.

The success of the Order, following the rail strikes of 1884 and 1885, was paralleled by a revival of craft unions, both within and outside of the Order. But a Knights of Labor group within the Cigar Makers fostered an internal quarrel that pushed an irate Adolph Strasser and iron-willed Samuel Gompers into founding another national labor center, the Federation of Organized Trades and Labor Unions. The immediate predecessor of the American Federation of Labor, however, did not do so well in face of the prosperity enjoyed by the Knights. The craft-union group was all but dead when it declared, at the instigation of P. J. McGuire's Brotherhood of Carpenters and Joiners, that the eight-hour work day should begin on May 1, 1886. It was a meaningless gesture, given the actual strength of the Federation and its affiliates. Perhaps bitterness against the Knights prompted the audacious but otherwise empty motion. Gompers and company were well aware that, while the issue might be a popular one with workers, Powderly viewed the eight-hour demand as a panacea.

As it was, the matter was taken out of the hands of both Gompers and Powderly. Workers eagerly took to the proposal, and organizers for the Knights seized upon the issue as a popular rallying cry and means of organizing new assemblies. (Organizers were paid by local assemblies and, therefore, were not easily subjected to the control of the Order's executive board.)

Oscar Ameringer, in his delightful autobiography, *If You Don't Weaken*, gives a picture, perhaps somewhat exaggerated, of the pull the eight-hour-day movement exerted on the workingman of the day. Ameringer, then a youthful German immigrant, worked in a Cincinnati furniture factory. He recalls:

> The work was monotonous, the hours of drudgery ten a day, my wages a dollar a day. Also, spring was coming on. Buds and

blue hills beckoned. And so, when agitators from the Knights of Labor invaded our sweat shop, preaching the divine message of less work for more pay, I became theirs from toe to forelock. The general cause of labor did not enter my head—all I knew was that what these organizers talked about was what I wanted. . . .

The prelude to the revolution was the May Day parade in which I marched, bloody upheaval in heart and dagger beneath my coat tail. Only red flags were carried in that first May Day parade, and the only song we sang was the *Arbeiters Marseillaise*, the battle cry of the rising proletariat. Even the May Day edition of the *Arbeiter Zeitung* was printed on red paper. . . .

Unfortunately for the pending revolution, the forces of law and order in the city made no attempt to interfere. Whether plutocracy had already abdicated or, considering that it takes two to make a fight, had taken the wiser course, I never discovered. And so we just marched and marched and sang and sang, until with burning feet and parched throats we distributed our forces among the saloons along the line of march where we celebrated the first victory of the eight-hour movement with beer, free lunch and pinochle.

Next day the strike started. It was a jolly strike. Victory was dead certain, for did not almost everybody belong to the Knights of Labor? Butchers, bakers, and candlestick makers, doctors, preachers, grocerymen and boarding-house keepers. What could be easier? With everybody quitting work the surrender of plutocracy was a foregone conclusion. In addition, there was the union treasury. The first week "out" married men received six dollars in strike benefits, single men, three. The second week out was not so good. Married men received three dollars and single men nothing. And the third week out all were placed on a basis of American equality, everybody getting nothing. . . .

Unhappily for the Ameringers, an explosion in Chicago's Haymarket Square on May 3 put an end to the eight-hour dream for a time. Chicago, during the early 1880s, became the center of the revolutionary currents then swirling subterraneously in America. The eight-hour movement, in turn, became a focus for the activity of the Chicago radicals—anarchists and socialists. On May Day, 1886, 40,000 workers struck for the shorter day; their number doubled within the next four days. An additional 45,000, mostly packinghouse workers, were granted the shorter day without a strike.

On the third day of May, striking lumber-shovers met near the

McCormick reaper works to hear August Spies, a strike leader and anarchist editor of the *Arbeiter Zeitung*, and to appoint a committee to meet with lumber yard owners. During the course of the meeting, about 200 left to go to the McCormick works to harass strikebreakers, who were then leaving work. Within fifteen minutes, some 200 policemen arrived on the scene wielding clubs to break up the crowd. Others at the Spies meeting hurried to join their fellow workers. They were met by the police, who fired upon the strikers, wounding many and killing four.

Spies, indignant, rushed to his office and issued a call to a mass meeting for the following day at 7:30 P.M. at Haymarket Square. There was some question whether or not the authorities would allow the meeting to proceed at all. Spies' call, though understandable in the heat of passion, was inflammatory: "Workingmen Arm Yourselves and Appear in Full Force!" But Mayor Carter H. Harrison wisely gave permission, and the meeting was held as scheduled, with about 3,000 workingmen present. Spies and Albert Parsons, an anarchist prominent in the Chicago Knights, spoke to an orderly crowd. A rainstorm threatened and by the time the third speaker, Samuel Fielden, rose to speak, the crowd was down to a few hundred. Spies and Parsons left as did Mayor Harrison, who was on hand as an observer. The mayor called the local precinct station at 10:00 to report that all was quiet. Then he went home to bed.

Shortly after the mayor left the scene, Inspector John Bonfeld, who had a reputation for brutality, marched into the Square with a detachment of 180 men. The gathering was ordered to disperse. Fielden cried out. "This is a peaceful meeting." There was a brief pause. Suddenly, a bomb exploded among the police, wounding 66 (seven died later). Hysterical, the police fired round after round into the stunned crowd, killing several and wounding 200.

The identity of the bomb thrower remains unknown to this day, although the suspicion will not die that the police knew more than they let on. The leaders of the Chicago anarchists were arrested. Eight were tried amidst hysteria—August Spies, Michael Schwab, Samuel Fielden, Albert R. Parsons, Adolph Fischer, George Engel, Louis Lingg, and Oscar Neebe. Although there was not a shred of evidence linking these men to the bomb, seven were sentenced to hang; the eighth, Neebe, was sentenced to 15 years' imprisonment. Fielden and Schwab petitioned for clemency; their sentences were commuted to life. Lingg committed suicide by exploding a dynamite tube in his mouth. On November 11, 1887, the others died bravely on the gallows. The three who remained in prison were subsequently pardoned by Governor John P. Altgeld.

The effect of the bomb, as Samuel Gompers noted, "was that it not only killed the policemen, but it killed our eight-hour movement for a few years after, not withstanding we had absolutely no connection with these people." In October, 1886, the Chicago packers took away by lockout the eight-hour day they had granted without a strike in May.

"The bad news from Chicago," recalled Ameringer, "fell like an exceedingly cold blanket on us strikers. To our erstwhile friends and sympathizers the news was the clarion for speedy evaporation. Some of our weaker fellow Knights broke ranks. The army of the social revolution was visibly melting away." The respectable labor organizations at first disassociated themselves from the Chicago anarchists completely. But as the trials wore on, the eight defendants came to be viewed as martyrs by some, and as unjustly accused by many more within the ranks of labor. The newly formed American Federation of Labor, while condemning violence on principle, pleaded for mercy for the sentenced men. The Chicago Knights also demanded that the sentences be set aside, although that Assembly had initially recoiled in horror from the Haymarket affair. But Powderly, who was privately sympathetic to the plight of the condemned, refused to join any public appeal for clemency for fear of associating the Knights with anarchy and violence. "Better," he said, "that seven times seven men hang than to hang the millstone of odium around the standard of this Order in affiliating in any way with this element of destruction."

On this ignominious note, the Noble and Holy Order of the Knights of Labor entered into its decline.

# VI

## *THE CARPENTER*
## *AND THE CIGAR MAKER*

THE AMERICAN FEDERATION OF LABOR WAS BORN ON DECEMBER 8, 1886, in Columbus, Ohio, of an act of desperation and a gesture of defiance on the part of a handful of trade unionists who feared that their struggling unions would be swallowed by the then flourishing Knights of Labor. Most of the delegates arrived a day earlier to bury a predecessor organization that had proven itself ineffectual as a center for those trade unionists who were disaffected with the Knights. The Federation of Organized Trades and Labor Unions, founded in 1881 by a dissident group from the Knights, was consciously modeled after the British Trades Union Congress. It was organized to look after the legislative interests of trade unions, an objective that was deemed sufficient while relations with the Knights remained fairly friendly. By 1884 it was clear, even to its own leaders, that the Federation of Organized Trades and Labor Unions could not hope to survive. As an organization it was pretty much a failure; its annual income never exceeded $700 and the number of delegates to its annual conferences fell from 107 to a bare handful. A depression in 1884 further aggravated matters. The successes of the Knights attracted even the staunch craftsmen the Federation founders had hoped would rally to its standard.

But the craft unionists who still clung to the idea of a national center of their own were reluctant to give up. The crafts were hard pressed. On one hand, technological change threatened their skills; on the other, the rising tide of semiskilled and unskilled workers threatened their jobs. To join hands with these workers within the Knights must have seemed to the craft unionists the last ignominious blow, a final doom. In addition, most of the Federation leaders had jurisdictional or factional bones to pick with the leaders of the Knights. Some, like the carpenters, were outright dual unions, bitter rivals to like organizations within the Order. While merger, or some sort of rapprochement with the Knights seemed inevitable by the end of 1884, the Federation leaders hoped, by keeping their organization alive, to strike a better bargain.

As a desperate, dying gesture, the Federation called for the universal adoption of the eight-hour day by May 1, 1886. The results—the establishment of the American Federation of Labor and the ultimate demise of the Holy Order—must have surprised the man who devised this piece of grand strategy, P. J. McGuire.

The proposal was ingenuous to say the least. By a vote of 23 to two, the delegates representing some 50,000 at the FOT&LU's 1884 convention "Resolved . . . that eight hours shall constitute a legal day's labor from and after May 1, 1886, and that we recommend to labor organizations throughout this jurisdiction [the United States and Canada] that they so direct their laws as to conform to this resolution by the time named." The whole proposition didn't have a prayer unless taken up by the mushrooming Knights. And though its rank and file took to the idea well enough, the leadership was reluctant. While Powderly, the Grand Master Workman of the Order, was temperamentally opposed to any action of this sort, part of his opposition to the idea may have stemmed from the very effrontery of the Federation.

After all, his organization was being asked to undergo the risks while the Federation had little to risk or to offer.

In any event, as noted in the previous chapter, the Knights' rank and file dragged its leaders into the eight-hour movement with disasterous consequences for their organization. The Knights might have survived the Haymarket affair and its aftermath if the organization had not been wracked by an acrimonious debate over its future course. As the Order grew, the lines became more sharply drawn between trade unionists and the "union haters," those who envisioned the Order as an amorphous all-embracing organization of workers, farmers and small businessmen. Indeed, the balance between these two forces seem to have been such that the presence of the Federation of Organized Trades and Labor Unions drew off enough unionists to allow the weight of the anti-union faction to carry the day.

Significantly, the Richmond Assembly of the Knights in 1886—the highpoint of the Order's career, with 658 delegates representing over 700,000 members—was the scene of the final defeat of the faction that favored the unions. "It was at Richmond," notes Joseph R. Buchanan, the Denver leader of the minority faction, "that the seal of approval was placed upon the acts of those members who had been bending every energy . . . to bring an open warfare between the Order and the trades-unions." The elections of an anti-trades-union majority to the Knights' executive board ensured the defeat of any peace overtures between the Knights and the trade unionists in the Federation of Organized Trades and Labor Unions. (Both had appointed committees to explore this possibility, but nothing came of it.) The trades unions scheduled a conference for December in Columbus, Ohio. An open declaration of war upon the trades unions by the Knights guaranteed a successful meeting. Later, the adverse effects of the eight-hour movement and the drift of the Knights away from the cities to become an organization of mechanics, small merchants and farmers assured the success of the American Federation of Labor.

The infant Federation benefited from the mistakes of its rival, much as the Congress of Industrial Organizations was to do a half-century later. At Columbus, Samuel Gompers, the president of the new organization, was able to report with evident satisfaction, that the eight-hour strikes had greatly stimulated the growth of trades unions and would have been more successful but for the "fickle" attitude of the "leading members of the Knights of Labor."

While the Knights dared to dream of becoming the one big union, the trade unionists held to much more modest goals. The Knights were all inclusive, the AFL exclusive. The Order was a true federation of local and district assemblies, although it permitted a fair amount of autonomy to affiliated unions. The AFL became a loose confederation of powerful national unions. In the beginning, the new trade-union group, as Philip Taft has pointed out in *The AF of L in the Time of Gompers*, did carry on substantial organizing activity. It was a center for disseminating information and mobilizing aid for the newly organized. But as the individual affiliates of the Federation grew in power, they prevented more vigorous action on the part of the Federation and its officers simply by refusing to furnish the financial resources. This development coincided with the decided conservative swing taken by the Federation after the turn of the century, a swing that was rooted in the desperate years following the defeat of the Pullman strike by use of the federal injunction. So, by default as it were, autonomy became the keystone to the structure of the American Federation of Labor.

The development of autonomy—the sacred principle that no affiliate of the AFL, or its executive council, could intervene in the affairs of any other affiliate—was reinforced by the ethnicization of the unions. It is not uncommon, even today, to find craft union locals consisting almost entirely of members of one ethnic group. We associate, for example, the Irish with transportation; the Jews with the needle trades; and the Italians with construction. The craft unions came into existence during a period of heavy immigration. Frequently, the immigration of unskilled workmen was encouraged by employers to break down high labor costs. The unskilled immigrants were also seen as a threat to established skills. To protect their jobs, their craft and skills, skilled workmen frequently formed unions based on exclusion of recent immigrants, or of other ethnic groups. Autonomy, in part, was developed to prevent any likelihood of the national labor center's insisting that a trade should be open to all qualified workmen.

"In the building trades," declared Colonel Richard T. Auchmuty, a pioneer of industrial schooling, "we have mechanics from England, Ireland, France, Italy, and Germany, and we have mechanics who are our own countrymen. Each nationality usually follows some particular trade. In New York, for instance, the stone masonry is mostly done by the sons of Italy; Englishmen and Irishmen lay the brick. When the heavy work of putting on the beams, or of framing and placing in position the roof trusses, begins, seldom an English word is spoken; the broad shoulders and brawny muscles of the German provides the motive-power. Irishmen and Americans in about equal number do the carpenters' work. In the plumbing trade, where science is as needful as skill—thanks, perhaps, to the interest the master plumbers have taken in the plumbing school—our own countrymen will soon have control. Where delicate artistic work is required, we find the Frenchman and the German. In all the trades, except the plumbing, we find the best workmen, those who command the steadiest employment, are of foreign birth."

Needless to say, each group protected its own as it organized its trade. The process—and results—were markedly different in industry where employers followed a deliberate policy of pitting one immigrant group against another as a means of forestalling unionization. In a report made by John R. Commons following a visit to a large Chicago packing company in 1904, he notes: "I saw seated around the benches of the company's employment office a sturdy group of Nordics. I asked the employment agent,

'How comes it you are employing only Swedes?' He answered, 'Well you see, it is only for this week. Last week we employed Slovaks. We change about among the different nationalities and languages. It prevents them from getting together. We have the thing systemized. We have a luncheon each week of the employment managers of the large firms of the Chicago district. There we discuss our problems and exchange information. We have a number of men in the field who keep us informed. . . . If agitators are coming or expected and there is considerable unrest among the labor population, we raise the wages all around. . . . It is wonderful to watch the effect. The unrest stops and the agitators leave. Then when things quiet down we reduce the wages to where they were.' " This deliberate policy is one reason that unions failed to secure an early foothold in industrial plants. Among the skilled trades, ethnic lines reinforced craft solidarity. But among the unskilled in the factories, worker solidarity was defeated by the babel of tongues.

The trade unions, of course, also gained strength from the desire of the craft unionists to protect skills threatened by the new age of machinery as well as the fear of being inundated by the semiskilled and unskilled immigrant masses then flooding Eastern cities. Later, particularly in the South, craft unionism, especially in the building trades, became the way for whites to drive out skilled Negro craftsmen, who had established a precarious foothold in postbellum Southern cities. Finally, the tight bonds of craft unionism enabled craftsmen to survive during a decade of murderous class warfare between the new industrialists and the more militant unions, some within the Federation and some without.

"The various trades," states an address by the founders of the American Federation of Labor, "have been affected by the introduction of machinery, the sub-division of labor, the use of women's and children's labor and the lack of an apprentice system, so that the skilled trades were rapidly sinking to the level of pauper labor. To protect the skilled labor of America from being reduced to beggary and to sustain the standard of American workmanship and skill, the trades unions of America have been established."

The impulse that led to the founding of the American Federation of Labor finds its best and fullest expression in the three men who left the stamp of their personalities and philosophy upon the new Federation—Samuel Gompers, Peter J. McGuire, and Adolph Strasser.

Strasser, the least known of the three, was born in Germany in 1844, where he apparently participated in the labor movement before coming to the United States in the early 1870s. In 1874, he became the national secretary of the Social Democratic Party of North America, a predecessor organization to the Workingmen's Party and to the Socialist Labor Party. (P. J. McGuire, then a young man of 22, was also on the executive board of the SDP.) Strasser soon became deeply involved in the political factionalism within the socialist and labor movement of the day, a kind of infighting that was particularly bitter in New York City. Strasser's practical bent—he once informed a Congressional committee, "We are all practical men"—led him to side with the trade-union faction as against the more politically oriented socialists. This factional struggle erupted within the Cigar Makers Union, presided over by Strasser. He had the energetic support of the youthful Samuel Gompers, who headed a large New York City local against the political socialists, who as it happened had the active support of the Knights of Labor. Thus, an intramural struggle within the Cigar Makers became the seedbed for the warfare betwee.. the craft unionists of the AFL and the Knights of Labor.

Strasser and Gompers worked together to revamp the structure of their union to meet changes then occurring within the cigar-making trade. To avoid the union, the employers began to farm out work to men, women and children, who worked at home in the teeming tenements of New York City. Strasser formulated a counter strategy that involved improving the benefit structure of the union in order to strengthen the tie beween the member and his union. The Cigar Makers' president, who was "something of a Prussian," according to Norman Ware, laid down a framework for his union that later became a model for other unions, especially those in the needle trades. Complete authority over the local unions was invested in the hands of international officers; dues were increased to build a reserve in funds; a far-reaching benefit system was adopted as a practical method for tying the member to his union. The pattern was authoritarian and had a wide appeal for the business unionists who came to dominate the American Federation of Labor. Strasser lived to the ripe old age of 95; he died in 1939.

Peter J. McGuire, founder and master carpenter of the Brotherhood of Carpenters and Joiners of North America, was in many ways the complete opposite of Strasser. His was an undisciplined, thoroughly romantic intellect. He supplemented the Prussian stodginess of Strasser and the pompousness of Gompers with an Irish flair for flamboyant oratory. McGuire, Ware says, "undoubtedly supplied what ideas the American Federation of Labor had for its foundation."

The secretary of the fledgling Federation was born in 1852 of Irish immigrant parents on New York's lower East Side. He became an apprentice joiner in 1867. What little formal education the young Irish lad had was supplemented by an avid attendance at the free lectures and courses offered by Cooper Union. There he met Samuel Gompers and the two became lifelong friends, despite a profound difference in temperament. When club-swinging cops broke up the Tompkins Square unemployment demonstration in 1874, McGuire became, if anything, more radical, developing a devotion to socialism that was to remain with him all his life while Sam Gompers became convinced of the futility of political radicalism, a conviction that remained unshaken until his death.

The young McGuire was a natural-born joiner and organizer. He was a leader of the Social Democratic Party of North America, the Workingmen's Party and the Socialist Labor Party. In 1880, he turned away from direct political work to trade-union affairs. McGuire began building a union of his own trade in St. Louis, where he had moved in 1878. Soon his tremendous energies were caught up feverishly in building a national carpenters' union.

McGuire became an opponent of the Knights of Labor in much the same way as Strasser and Gompers; all three happened to fall within the same caucus. A carpenters' local fell out with McGuire, who was *the* national office of the Brotherhood of Carpenters. The dissenters refused to pay dues; they were opposed by a loyal McGuire man. The dissenters, as has happened time and time again in American labor history when workers could choose between two existing organizations, bolted to the Knights. Still, McGuire was not anxious for an open break. When a carpenters' Knights of Labor Assembly in Troy, New York, refused to work with Brotherhood carpenters, McGuire proposed an "exchange of cards." But E. S. Turner, secretary of the Order, did not even extend the courtesy of a reply to McGuire's request. McGuire then initiated a series of trades-union conferences that led directly to the founding of the American Federation of Labor.

As Robert A. Christie, author of the history of the carpenters' union, *Empire in Wood*, points out, the eight-hour-day movement "may be likened to a cocoon into which utopian unionism disappeared, to emerge four years later as job-conscious unionism." This was pretty much McGuire's doing. He proposed the campaign to the Federation of Organized Trades and Labor Unions; he led a renewed effort in 1890 that won the eight-hour day for the nation's carpenters. This gave the Brotherhood the competitive edge in wages and working conditions that finally drove the Knights of Labor carpenter assemblies from the field. And since the Brotherhood of Carpenters was the chief AFL union of the day, this victory became an AFL success.

For McGuire—and, for that matter, for the unionists—the retreat from the idealist in social unionism to "pure and simple"

unionism was not without its price. For McGuire, the labor movement was "a great democratic training school" for the future
management of industry by the worker himself. Pure and simple,
or business unionism had nothing to do with such ideas. In retreat from the great drama of one big union, McGuire and others
like him gave up, or at least put off to some distant future, the
radical notion of remaking the new industrial age over into their
own craft-proud image. Instead, the leaders of the American Federation of Labor developed what Selig Perlman calls "a philosophy of pure wage-consciousness." It signified, says Perlman, "a
labor movement reduced to an opportunistic basis, accepting the
existence of capitalism and having for its object the enlarging of
the bargaining power of the wage earner in the sale of his labor."
At its best, business unionism won higher wages and decidedly
improved working conditions for skilled workmen. But without
the guiding star of idealism, business unionism frequently de-
teriorated into outright racketeering. Frank Feeney, quoted in
Louis Adamic's *Dynamite* is the prototype of this fallen leadership. "Sure, I'm a grafter. When you hear that Frank Feeney
goes after somethin' you make up your mind he's gettin' his
price. I'm for Frank Feeney."

P. J. McGuire, who did not have it in him to be "for" P. J.
McGuire, drifted into alcoholism. McGuire's personal tragedy
aptly paralleled that of business unionism. Liquor magnified his
faults. Never a careful administrator, he became more careless. In
the end, his union, now an outfit of fat and sleek business agents,
expelled McGuire for misappropriation of funds. That McGuire,
ill and tortured by the failure of his achievement to live up to his
aspirations, spent the money to defray the cost of his illness did
not matter. That his salary in the past had been spent to keep the
union alive did not matter. McGuire's successors did not care a
fig for the years of service at little or no salary and at an unknown
cost to his health. They hungered for his power, his influence over
the rank and file. "To speak of McGuire's owing the union
money," writes Christie, "or the union's owing McGuire money

in 1901 was a travesty in every sense but the legal one." In the light of the subsequent development of the union, McGuire's successors couldn't have minded so much the money as they did his clinging to the old illusions.

McGuire died a pauper in Camden, New Jersey, on February 15, 1906. His last words were: "I've got to get to California, the boys in Local 22 need me." Christie comments: "He might better have saved his waning breath. The boys in Local 22 did not need him. They had but recently placed one Patrick H. 'Pin Head' McCarthy, politician and labor boss extraordinary, in power." Christie, of course, may be wrong. Under "Pin Head" the boys in Local 22 needed P. J. McGuire more than ever.

They still had, of course, Sam Gompers. That incredibly ugly, squat, iron-willed old man was the guiding genius of the American Federation of Labor from its inception to his death in 1924. It is difficult to conceive of Samuel Gompers as ever having been young. Legend has it that he spent his youth reading Marx and other socialist classics to his fellows as they rolled cigars. His, clearly, was not a youthful temperament. But then life was not easy for Samuel Gompers. He was born on January 27, 1850 in London of Dutch-Jewish parentage. His parents brought him to the United States in 1863, already a thirteen-year-old apprenticed cigar maker. The young Gompers knew poverty at first hand and didn't much like it.

Despite his early fondness for theorizing, Gompers soon developed a hard-minded realism, which he devoted to the cause of the skilled workingman: "I am a workingman," he once declared, "and in every nerve, in every fibre, in every aspiration, I am on the side which will advance the interests of my fellow workingmen. I represent my side, the side of the toiling wage-earning masses in every act and in every utterance." Yet, Samuel Gompers yearned for respectability for himself and for the craftsmen; he did not like the lumpen proletariat, the unskilled masses. He did not share that compassion for the unfortunate exemplified by his contemporaries Eugene Debs and Emma Goldman. For them, prison was an acid test of one's faith in the working class; for Gompers, prison was to be avoided. He was arrested only once in his life, for talking to a picket in 1879. He apparently found the experience unnerving. "That was one of the most uncomfortable days I ever spent, sitting there in the dirt and filth and vermin surrounded by men of unclean bodies and minds who used vile language. Fortunately for the effect on me, there was only one day of it."

Gompers, clearly, was more at home smoking cigars, having a drink, and swapping stories with "the boys." William D. "Big Bill" Haywood, leader of the Western Federation of Miners and a Wobbly, called Gompers "vain, conceited, petulant, vindictive." He was all of that—and more. Pompous, histrionic on the platform, his figure—short-legged, stocky, capped by a massive head with its big and mobile features, wide mouth, eyes made large by steel-rimmed spectacles, and broad forehead capped by tufts of disorderly hair—dominated the American Federation of Labor for thirty-eight years and, for better and for worse, shaped the character of America's longest-lived labor organization. (In 1895, Gompers was defeated as president by John McBride of the United Mine Workers. McBride had the backing of the socialist wing of the Federation, yet Gompers remained a powerful figure, recapturing the presidency the following year.) At the 1890 Federation convention, Gompers spelled out the basic philosophy that was to guide him throughout the rest of his life: "The trades unions pure and simple are the organizations of the wage workers to secure their present material and practical improvement and to achieve their final emancipation."

# VII

## *THE BITTER BREAD OF SURVIVAL*

THE FOUNDERS OF THE AMERICAN FEDERATION OF LABOR SET A difficult task for themselves. To secure immediate, practical gains for the American wage earner was not easy. Thomas Scott, president of the Pennsylvania Railroad, following the Haymarket affair stated the typical employer reaction to the efforts of their employees to organize: "Give the working men and strikes gun bullet food for a few days, and you will observe how they will take to this sort of bread." It was bitter bread, indeed, that fell to the union organizer, whether affiliated to the AFL or the Knights. Initially, the Order bore the brunt of the anti-union attack. (AFL unions sometimes, it must be said, benefited by scabbing on locked-out or striking members of the Holy Order.) The Federation survived the period simply because employer attention was given over to the smashing of the Knights. Every strike undertaken by the Order after 1886 was lost. Employers organized strong associations to fight the Knights, making liberal use of the lockout, the blacklist, armed guards and detectives. Agreements with the Order were broken as soon as convenient since employers considered them as contracts signed under duress and, therefore, not to be honored. The new Federation of craft unions, however, did not escape unscathed; its membership grew but slowly, from 140,000 in 1886 to about 275,000 in 1893, where it remained for most of the next decade. We can see what happened by comparing the eight-hour-day victory of the Carpenters in 1890 to the defeat suffered on the same issue by the mine workers the following year.

The leaders of the new Federation—and particularly P. J. Mc-Guire—realized that in the demand for an eight-hour day they had an effective organizing tool and rallying cry for the country's craftsmen. The gains won by the strikes of May 1, 1886 were subsequently wiped out in the period of reaction following Haymarket. To recover these losses, McGuire proposed a change in tactics. Instead of a general strike of all trades over the issue, said McGuire, let one trade lead the way, then others might follow one by one. The Carpenters, the largest and the most rapidly growing union within the Federation, was a natural choice to take the lead, as it had in 1886. May 1, 1890, was the date picked for the second test. That year over 23,000 carpenters in 36 cities won the eight-hour day; another 32,000 in 234 cities secured a nine-hour day. As the Carpenters aggressively pushed for the shorter work day, they extended their control over their trade and jobs. The men owned their own tools and worked in local markets. As itinerants, carpenters threatened one another almost as much as did the new machinery, division of labor, and the collapse of apprenticeship standards. The eight-hour day was the measure McGuire seized to give the carpenter and his union some measure of control over his job. Craft-pride combined with job control and a benefit system proved to be the basic strength of the craft unions, enabling them to survive the perilous decades on either side of the century mark. Just as the sense of solidarity, of universal brotherhood, was the revolutionary contribution of the Knights to the labor movement, control—or ownership—of the job was the revolutionary contribution of the American Federation of Labor.

An attempt to meld the two—job control and solidarity—was

made in such unions as the United Mine Workers and the Brewery Workers. Significantly both were offsprings of the Holy Order that found a home within the AFL. Nonetheless, the United Mine Workers was a poor choice to carry on the second year of the Federation's drive for an eight-hour day. The mine union was still weak, barely recovered from the factionalism between the pro-Knights and pro-AFL miners. And, neither the AFL nor the coal miners' union possessed the strength to take on the coal masters, the founding barons of the new order of industrialism. Before May 1, 1891 rolled around the UMW became embroiled in a disastrous strike in the Connellsville (Pa.) coke region, and the eight-hour movement had to be abandoned. Despite this setback, the eight-hour day was standard in 1891 for all building trades in Chicago, St. Louis, Denver, Indianapolis, and San Francisco. A majority of the trades worked an eight-hour day in New York, Brooklyn, and St. Paul. A new pattern was evolving for the workday, one that has lasted to the present.

The defeat of the miners at Connellsville was a curtain raiser for a far greater clash between the unions and the new concentrated power of industry—the Homestead (Pa.) strike of July, 1892. On one side were ranged the workmen of the Homestead works of Carnegie Steel and their union, the 25,000-member Amalgamated Association of Iron and Steel Workers, the most powerful union in the country at the time. On the other side was the chief barony of the new age, the Carnegie Steel Company, a forerunner of United States Steel Corporation, which owned and operated twelve steel and coke works in the vicinity of Pittsburgh, employing 13,000 workers. The company controlled almost the entire steel market of the country. From coal and coke to steel and its products, the control of the corporation and the new trusts extended in society. As Henry Adams noted, "A banker's Olympus became more and more despotic over Aesop's frog-empire. One might no longer croak except to vote for King Log, or—failing storks—for Grover Cleveland; and even then could not be sure where King Banker lurked behind."

The new magnates were not given to worrying over employee relations, except possibly a few "paternalists," such as George Pullman. Mark Hanna, industrialist and politician, was the rare coal operator who saw no profit in fighting his workers. During the 1894 Pullman strike, Hanna outraged the members of the Cleveland Union Club by proclaiming that "a man who won't meet his men half way is a God-damn fool." And Andrew Carnegie's Scot Presbyterian soul was troubled. He went so far as to write: "The right of workingmen to combine and to form trades unions is no less sacred than the right of the manufacturer to enter into associations and conferences with his fellows. . . . My experience has been that trades unions upon the whole are beneficial both to labor and to capital." Carnegie even showed unexpected understanding about the reasons violence frequently broke out during strikes. "To expect that one dependent upon his daily wage for the necessities of life will stand by peaceably and see a new man employed in his stead is to expect much." As sympathetic to labor as this sounds, Carnegie's enlightenment was well grounded in a realistic evaluation of labor's place in the corporate scheme of things. Carnegie Steel Company was well endowed with a good location, close to raw materials and with convenient transportation. Competitors survived because they could save on labor costs. But the Amalgamated Associations' demand for uniform wages for the same class of labor throughout the industry, if achieved, would deprive Carnegie Steel's competitors of that advantage.

This is pretty much what happened. While significant competition existed, the union was fostered. Prior to 1889, relations between the company and the union were friendly. But in that year, the appointment of Henry Clay Frick, the "Coke King" of Connellsville, as operating head signaled a change in company policy. Frick came to Carnegie Steel with an anti-union reputation. With most of its competitors driven from the field, the giant steel company no longer needed the union and was not about to share any of its power with a rival within its plants. A short strike ensued in

1889, which the union won. An agreement was signed, providing for a fluctuating wage scale that would rise and fall with the per-ton price of steel above a minimum price of $25 a ton. But relations between the union and the company were strained. During the negotiations Frick had demanded the dissolution of the union—a harbinger of trouble to come, or so the union men believed. At the time, they tended to absolve the absent Carnegie, who was in Europe on an extended stay, from blame for the shift in company policy. But there is no question but that the canny Scot approved of the course taken by Frick. Just before the contract expired on June 30, 1892, Carnegie dictated a memorandum putting the men on notice that the firm henceforth was to be non-union. The notice was never posted; the action was vetoed by Frick as too openly provocative.

Henry Clay Frick, rather than Carnegie, was the representative man of his day. Born in 1849, he was raised on his father's farm in Westmoreland County, Pennsylvania, where four generations earlier a maternal ancestor had come from the Palatinate. His grandfather, a pious Mennonite, was the original distiller of Old Overholt rye whiskey. As a young lad, Frick worked on his father's farm, leaving at 13 to go to work in his uncle's store. His talent for businesslike efficiency developed early, and he soon moved on to become a proficient bookkeeper in his grandfather's distillery. After his grandfather's death, young Frick moved into the coke business. Borrowing money from his mother's estate, his father and neighboring farmers, he consolidated his holdings and earned his first million by his thirtieth year. A righteous self-willed man, Frick neatly complimented the disciplined power of the gigantic steel mills of the Carnegie Corporation. Under his management, Carnegie Steel Company, Ltd., capitalized at $25,000,000 in 1893, grew to the point where it was to command a price of $300,000,000 from J. Pierpont Morgan seven years later. The United States Steel Corporation, built around the properties Morgan bought from Carnegie, was capitalized at $1,402,846,000 in 1900.

Frick, as a Congressional investigation later found, was clearly eager for a showdown with the union. Homestead, the scene of the struggle, is located on the left bank of the Monongahela River, seven miles east of Pittsburgh, where its 12,000 souls lived clustered around the riverside works of Carnegie Steel. Here the company turned out, with a workforce of 3,800, boiler plates, beams, structural steel of all kinds, and armor plate. The monthly payroll totalled $200,000; wages ranged from 14 cents an hour for common labor to $280 a month for skilled workmen. But most of the latter were getting $200 or less a month.

Negotiations began in February, 1892, and dragged on for three months. Finally, the company unilaterally announced a new scale pegged to a $23 a ton, which represented a wage cut of 18% to 26%. The workmen at Homestead hung Frick and a mill superintendent in effigy on company property, by then so fortified that local citizens dubbed the works "Fort Frick." A hose was turned on the men sent to cut the figures down. Frick thereupon used the incident to shut down the Homestead works, two days before the agreement expired on June 30.

As the events at Homestead soon showed, craft unionism confronted by corporate power soon takes on the cast of industrial unionism. The Amalgamated was an AFL craft union, and there were only 800 skilled union men at Homestead. Confronted with an adamant Frick, the skilled men called a mass meeting of all the men, at which the 3,000 mechanics and common laborers decided to stand with the union men. An advisory committee—the kind of workers' council that is central to industrial unionism—was formed, not only to direct the strike but to run the town itself. Hugh O'Donnell, a young workman of exceptionable ability, headed the committee, which included, among others, W. T. Roberts, Hugh Ross and John McLuckie, a burgess of Homestead who provided a link of legitimacy between the advisory committee and the regularly constituted government of the town. The steel works and all approaches to the town were kept under a strict watch. No one could enter without the consent of the committee; on five minutes' notice, a thousand men could be mobilized anywhere within the area. Saloons were policed to keep a check on drunkenness and noisy, provocative gatherings. When a force of twelve deputies arrived on July 4, they were escorted to the river and shipped back to Pittsburgh. The workers feared that they had come to make way for "blacksheep," as scabs were then dubbed.

Meanwhile, Frick pushed through arrangements—initiated before the lockout—with the Pinkerton agency for 300 armed men. On the night of July 5, this force was towed up the river on barges to the Homestead works. At dawn the townspeople turned out to greet the Pinkertons. As the barges neared the shore, the crowd surged through a company fence. The Pinkertons were warned off, but a plank was shoved out and the guards began to disembark. An unknown person fired a shot, providing an excuse for the Pinkertons to fire a volley into the crowd, drawing first blood. The women and children fled out of range of the guns; their menfolk crouched behind the steel, pig iron, and scrap stacked in the mill yard and returned fire. The Pinkertons took shelter in the barges. The steamboat that had towed the barges fled downstream, leaving the invaders without means of escape.

When the Pinkertons finally ran up the white flag, about five o'clock in the evening, three detectives and seven workers lay dead and scores were wounded on both sides. The Pinkertons were shipped back to Pittsburgh after some roughing up by the women of the town, whom the committee unsuccessfully tried to restrain. Homestead settled down to wait; the wounded were cared for, the dead buried. All the damage done to the mill was repaired, the fence rebuilt; and the regular company watchmen were replaced by a guard of workingmen.

On July 12, Governor Robert E. Pattison of Pennsylvania responded to company pressure and sent state militia to take over the peaceful town. Other steel workers in the Pittsburgh area went out on strike in sympathy with the locked-out Homestead men. The company pressed legal action against the Homestead leaders.

Six indictments were secured, three for murder, two for riot, and one for conspiracy. As Samuel Yellen notes in *American Labor Struggles*, "The leadership of the men was buried beneath bail bonds." In the fall, twenty-seven of the Homestead leaders were indicted for treason against the State of Pennsylvania. Although the men of Homestead were vindicated in the courts, their cause was lost. The union treasury was depleted. On November 17, the remnants of the Homestead lodges of the Amalgamated voted to lift the ban against working for Carnegie Steel. The power of the union in the steel industry was smashed.

What this means in human terms was uncovered in a survey of working and living conditons made by Margaret F. Byington some fifteen years later. She found a wage of $9.90 a week standard for a twelve-hour day, with a 24-hour stretch every two weeks when day and night shifts were exchanged. That the union's absence made a difference comes out in Miss Byington's comparison of wages of unionized common laborers in nearby bituminous mines—$2.36 for an eight-hour day—with those of common laborers in the steel mills—$1.65 for a ten-hour day, or $1.98 for a twelve-hour day.

The Homestead strike also resulted in one of those freakish confrontations of fanatic protagonists which somehow illumine an age. Shortly after noon on Saturday, July 23, 1892, Alexander Berkman, a sensitive, idealistic young anarchist, entered Frick's office and shot the industrialist. Both men, so representative of the extremes of their time, acted with commendable bravery. Berkman persisted against odds in his effort to kill the man who had oppressed the workmen of Homestead; Frick, still conscious through the pain caused by two bullet wounds and two knife wounds, asked that Berkman not be killed.

The Homestead affair had repercussions in the presidential election of 1892. Hitherto, some workmen had sided with employers in seeking protective tariffs under the impression that protectionism would protect their industry, their jobs and their union. Homestead dispelled this notion and Grover Cleveland's antiprotectionist campaign carried the day.

The year 1892 saw several great clashes on the order of Homestead—at Coeur d'Alene in the Idaho silver district, of railroad-yard switchmen in Buffalo, of miners in Tracy City and Coal Creek, Tennessee. These events stirred a new interest in industrial unionism. The Panic of 1893 added a greater impetus. The brewers' national union and the United Mine Workers—both with roots in the Knights of Labor—pushed industrial organization within their respective industries. Unions in the ferrous-metal mines banded together in 1893 to form the Western Federation of Miners; railway workers followed Eugene Victor Debs into the industrial American Railway Union. Debs, then 39 years of age, quit his lucrative position as secretary-treasurer of the Brotherhood of Locomotive Firemen and as editor of the Brotherhood magazine to devote his energies to the new industrial union. The growth of the American Railway Union was phenomenal; entire lodges of the Railway Carmen and the Switchmen transferred to the new union; firemen, conductors, even engineers signed up. But the great influx came from the unrepresented mass—section hands, engine wipers, the maintenance men of the nation's railroads. Within a year, the ARU grew to a membership of 150,000, over half the total strength of all the American Federation of Labor.

Debs and the other leaders of the new union were capable and experienced men. They were aware of the dangers inherent in pitting a hat-waving, thigh-slapping greenhorn organization against the adroit, seasoned men who controlled the railroads. The ARU's first victory—a successful strike on James J. Hill's Great Northern in 1894—made Debs, if anything, more cautious.

George M. Pullman, in 1880, built a model town adjoining the southern edge of Chicago for his employees. Here the company— Marshall Field and the Vanderbilts were major stockholders— conducted a profitable business of manufacturing and repairing

"palace" cars, which operated under contract over 125,000 miles
of railroad, about three-fourths of the country's total railroad
mileage. The Pullman Company paid an annual dividend of eight
percent in addition to increasing its capital stock from $1,000,-
000 in 1867 to $36,000,000 in 1893, with some $25,000,000 in
undistributed profits. During the Panic of 1893, wages were cut
by one-fourth, while dividends were raised by $360,000 all told.
The reduced wages of 1893 ranged from four cents to 16 cents an
hour, which were not munificent by any standard and less so
since the employees had to pay an $18 monthly rent for five room
"pens," "with conveniences." The employees were, of course, free
to live in nearby towns where rents were cheaper, but they soon
discovered that those who lived in Pullman were the first hired
and the last laid off. (Incidentally, just as Stalin's slave camps had
model areas to show impressionable visitors, Pullman had its
flower borders and "green velvety stretches of lawn.") Chicago
supplied Pullman with water at four cents a thousand gallons,
while the company charged its employee ten cents a thousand.
Gas cost Pullman 33 cents a thousand feet, but the tenants paid
$2.25 a thousand. When wages were slashed in 1893, the cost of
living in Pullman remained unchanged. A post-strike investigation
by the U. S. Government revealed that the Pullman workers were
in arrears $70,000 to the company for rent alone. Rev. W. H.
Carwardine, pastor of the Pullman Methodist-Episcopal Church
for two years preceding the strike, reported, "after deducting rent
the men invariably had only from one to six dollars or so on
which to live for two weeks." One man, according to the pastor of
the Pullman flock, "has a pay check in his possession of two cents
after paying rent. . . . He had it framed."

During the hard winter of 1894, the workingmen of Pullman
decided that something had to be done. They began by joining
the American Railway Union; in the spring, they formed a grievance committee and presented their demands to the company for
a restoration of wages to the pre-1893 level. Pullman himself
decided to meet with his workmen on May 9 to explain that he

was keeping the shops open as a philanthropic gesture. Business was poor, he explained, and regrettably wage cuts were essential to enable the company to enter lower bids to secure orders during depressed times.

The men were far from satisfied with the explanation but contented themselves by accepting in good faith Pullman's promise that none of the members of the grievance committee would be fired or discriminated against and that the company would investigate shop conditions. On May 10, three members of the grievance committee were laid off. By noon the next day, three thousand Pullman employees laid down their tools and walked off the job, demanding the reinstatement of the three men, reductions in rent, and a return to the previous year's wage scale. The events of Homestead were reenacted; the Pullman workers formed a workers' council to govern their affairs during the strike, even mounting guard around company property to protect it. The ARU assessed its members three cents a day to support the strikers.

By the time the ARU's first convention opened in Chicago on June 12, there was widespread talk among the delegates of a sympathetic strike and boycott. The victory over Hill and the Great Northern bolstered confidence beyond reasonable expectation of success. Workers in the railroad industry and elsewhere were also resentful as the depressed conditions of the 1890s bore down. Coxey's Army of unemployed marched on Washington, only to disperse anticlimactically when three of its leaders were arrested for trespassing on White House grounds. Clearly, however, as unemployment mounted into the four millions, such expediences would not suffice for long. And out of frustration the railroad workers in the ARU were eager to slash out against their masters. But Debs and the other leaders of the ARU believed the organization too young and too feeble to risk a conflict of that magnitude. Debs refused to permit strikes at other Pullman works and convinced the delegates to the convention to appoint a committee to meet with the company instead of calling for an immediate boycott of Pullman cars. But company officials refused to meet with the ARU delegation. Debs offered to submit the Pullman dispute to arbitration; again Pullman refused. The ARU leaders tirelessly explored every possible avenue for a peaceable resolution of the affair. But the company remained adamant and the ARU leaders found that they could not restrain the delegates forever. The swelling tide of strike sentiment among the delegates was irresistible. An appeal for help from the Pullman delegates caused the rising emotions within the convention to boil over. Thin, trembling with emotion and exhaustion, a wan Pullman seamstress, Jennie Curtis, further aroused the delegates with her account of how the company forced her to repay sixty dollars in back rent her father owed the company at his death, though he'd been with the firm thirteen years. Finally, the delegates had their way. On June 21, they voted unanimously to give the company four days to yield to mediation; if not, ARU members would refuse to handle Pullman cars.

Events marched swiftly and the pacific Debs soon found himself directing what Selig Perlman has called "the only attempt ever made in America of a revolutionary strike on the Continental European model." The so-called Debs Rebellion spread out over the rails. By June 28, 125,000 railroad workers had joined the boycott and twenty railroads were tied up. The ARU found itself pitted against the General Managers' Association, an employer group representing twenty-five railroads rolling in and out of Chicago. The Association, experienced in the ways of strikebreaking, set out to smash the ARU. Pullman cars were deliberately hitched to trains that had never before pulled them, especially to mail trains, in hopes of provoking workers into halting the mail contravening their union's instructions to keep the mail rolling. There was little violence, however, until the arrival of federal troops on July 4. President Cleveland, at the instigation of his attorney-general, Richard P. Olney, a former railroad corporation lawyer, ordered them to Chicago over the protests of Illinois Governor John P. Altgeld. The presence of federal troops stirred up violence, as Debs and Governor Altgeld had feared. On July 5, a crowd that sought to block the movement of a train from the Union Stock Yards was driven away by bayonet and cavalry charges. Chicago was an armed camp. Agent provocateurs of the railroads intermingled with the strikers, stirring up violence. On July 7, when a crowd gathered to protest the movement of a wrecking train by troops, the soldiers opened fire and killed some thirty persons. Rail cars were fired by incendiaries, and a pall of smoke hung over Chicago accenting the gloom that settled over the strike.

Federal troops alone could not break the strike. The railroad brotherhoods were making the best of the opportunity to break up their rival. Gompers held the Federation to a rigid neutrality, which, as his autobiography revealed later, could only further his wish to "maintain the integrity of the Railroad Brotherhoods." When Gompers left Indianapolis for a Chicago meeting of the AFL executive council that had been called to consider what course to take, he was quoted as saying, "I'm going to the funeral of the ARU." When a desperate Debs begged the executive council to declare a sympathetic general strike, Gompers wisely declined to do so, for nothing would have been gained by the added destruction of other unions as well as the ARU. But Gompers had already contributed his mite to the defeat of the rail union by his do-nothing policy. The AFL might have been of great help had it done no more than sought to keep the courts and the federal government out of the dispute and countered the malicious propaganda of the Managers' Association widely disseminated in the public press. But even this it did not do.

The strike was finally broken by the use of the injunction, ironically issued under the Sherman Anti-Trust Act, which had been enacted in 1890 to curb the power of the likes of Pullman and the railroad corporations. The injunction, issued on July 3, ordered the ARU, its leaders and members to restrain from urging railroad employees to stay off the job. On July 7, Debs and other strike leaders were arrested for "conspiracy" and released on $10,000 bond each. On July 17, they were arrested for contempt of court. The four officers of the union opted for jail in order to force a trial. With the leadership in jail, the pressures building up against the strikers began to take effect. Slowly, the strike was strangled. On August 2, the ARU called off the boycott. (The railroads, however, maintained for years a blacklist of all ARU activists.) The strikers at Pullman held out until fall, when imminent starvation compelled surrender. Debs went to jail and on to socialism. Subsequently, he became the standard bearer of the Socialist Party for many presidential elections.

The year of 1894 surpassed even the Great Uprising of 1886 in the number of labor disputes, involving 750,000 workers before the year had ended. But the year was one of lost causes. The Pullman debacle was a loss for the entire labor movement. Employers learned the value of a new weapon, the injunction, which, as one commentator of the day remarked, soon ruled as king. In the vivid words of Alfred Kazin, "The image of a closed frontier, of a corporation economy, of a city proletariat oppressed and rebellious, darkened the mind." The Gay Nineties were not so gay for America's workingmen.

But the last decade of the century was not without achievement for the unions. The stove molders in 1891 worked out the first successful national trade agreement with the Stove Founders' National Defense Association. This agreement was to set a pattern for the collective bargaining agreements that developed during the last decade of the century and the first decade of the next. The AFL managed to hold on to its membership, which rose from 264,000 to 349,000 in the last year of the century. Samuel Gompers that year in a report to the AFL convention declared: "It is noteworthy, that while in every previous industrial crisis the trade unions were literally mowed down and swept out of existence, the unions now in existence have manifested not only the power of resistance, but of stability and permanency." The American Federation of Labor had survived.

# VIII

## *DYNAMITE AND REFORM*

PRESIDENT THEODORE ROOSEVELT, EYES SNAPPING EXCITEDLY behind eyeglasses, awaited a very important guest. Already it was the thirteenth of October and the poor in the cities of the Northeast were clamoring for fuel, and the governor of Massachusetts and the mayor of New York City had warned of the possibility of fuel riots. The anthracite strike was in its 143rd day, running into a cost of $100 million for the railroads, the operators and the miners. John Mitchell, the gentlemanly president of the United Mine Workers and leader of the 140,000 anthracite strikers, had agreed to send the men back to the pits, leaving the dispute to arbitration by the President or a Presidential commission. But the operators were obdurate; the spirit that moved them was that of George Baer, president of the mine-owning Philadelphia and Reading Railroad, who had just written to a troubled stockholder, "The rights and interests of the laboring man will be protected and cared for—not by the labor agitators, but by the Christian gentlemen to whom God has given control of the property rights of the country." The President fumed, impotent before the power of the coal barons. As he wrote to Mark Hanna, "From

every consideration of public policy and of good morals they should make some slight concessions." But they wouldn't budge. And, continued the President to Hanna, "the attitude of the operators will beyond doubt double the burden on us while standing between them and socialistic action." So, it was with considerable relief that the President greeted his visitor that fall day. J. P. Morgan, head of the New York banking house, was, as always, to the point: "The operators will arbitrate."

"Great is Mr. Morgan's power," wrote Washington correspondent A. Maurice Law, "greater in some respects than that of President or Kings." Roosevelt, who at another time waved his fist beneath the elder Morgan's astonished nose, was properly grateful. "If it had not been for your going into the matter," he said, "I do not see how the strike could have been settled at this time."

Anthracite, unlike soft coal, does not fall to pieces when burned, but burns from the inside out. The anthracite strike of 1902 generated a good deal of heat. Yet for the first time, as Selig Perlman has noted in his *History of Trade Unionism in the United States,* "a labor organization tied up for months a strategic industry and caused wide suffering and discomfort to the public without being condemned as a revolutionary menace to the existing social order calling for suppression." Indeed, the government in the person of President Roosevelt took an opposite course from that of President Grover Cleveland when he sent federal troops to Chicago to quell the Pullman strike eight years earlier. The President intervened as a mediator, effecting a settlement by means of a Presidential commission empowered to hold hearings and to issue an award.

In passing, it is also of note that the collective bargaining agreement was subjected to—and passed—a severe test during the course of the strike. Mitchell was hard pressed by many within the union to call out the bituminous miners in sympathy with the anthracite strikers. This course was entirely in accord with the traditions of the labor movement as well as those of the

mine workers' union. Instead, Mitchell chose to live up to a contract signed earlier with the bituminous operators, upholding the principle that, once a bargain is struck, both sides adhere to it during the lifetime of the agreement. Mitchell's course of action was not entirely altruistic; he assessed the soft coal miners a dollar a week for support of the hard coal strike, a levy that yielded over $2 million. As a result the strikers were able to hold out for five months. Nonetheless, an important principle had been upheld, a collective bargain adhered to. When both parties realized that the other would observe its agreement for a stated period of time, collective bargaining as a process took a long step forward.

The anthracite coal hearings before the President's commission, presided over by Judge George Grey of Wilmington, Delaware, lasted just about as long as the strike. The United Mine Workers' case was presented by Clarence Darrow. At one point in the hearing, the noted advocate remarked that the operators' "social advantages are better; they speak English better; they can hire expert accountants; they have got the advantage of us in almost every particular." Judge Grey, according to Darrow's biographer Irving Stone, then glanced over the battery of twenty-one corporation counsels, murmured, "Except the lawyers." Darrow, incidently, asked that the books of the operators be opened for examination by the commission, a revolutionary demand for the times and one that has been echoed in our day by Walter P. Reuther.

After examining 558 witnesses and accumulating some ten thousand pages of evidence, the commission issued its award on March 21, 1903. It was no clear-cut victory for the union—such as it won by a strike in the election year of 1900—but the public certainly considered the award a triumph for Mitchell and the miners. The award called for an increase of 10 percent in the rates paid contract miners, with a scale tied to rising coal prices; an eight-hour day for engineers, firemen and pumpmen and a nine-hour day for "company men"; and the miners secured the

right to elect their own check weighmen and their check docking bosses. During the three-year life of the award, all disputes were to be submitted to a six man board of conciliation—three representing the operators, three the miners. Failing agreement by the board, an umpire was to be appointed by the courts. However, the commission failed to grant the union recognition, an omission that led Mother (Mary E.) Jones, a mine-union organizer and famous militant, to comment, "Labor walked into the House of Victory through the back door." Its tenure in the house was also uncertain. While the commission's award barred strikes and lock-outs for three years, it allowed employers to discharge workmen without reference to the board of conciliation. There was, in other words, no guarantee that a man could not be fired for union activity. The miners were not to win protection against this sort of retaliation for another thirteen years.

When operator George F. Baer finished his able presentation of the operator's case before the commission, Mitchell crossed the room and shook the coal operator's hand. "To this day," McAllister Coleman wrote in his history of the union and the industry, *Men and Coal,* "veteran diggers speak of that gesture with perplexment." Possibly, speculates Coleman, Mitchell wearied with warfare, wanted peace with honor. "At all events," Coleman concludes, "from that time on, the course of the president of the UMWA, ran more and more to concilation."

As the new century wore on, this became the dominant mood of labor officialdom.

Samuel Gompers, for example, joined the National Civic Federation, an august body of industrialists and civic leaders founded by Senator Mark Hanna and others in 1900. Hanna served as president until his death in 1904; he was succeeded by August Belmont. Gompers was vice-president of the organization. Using the Civic Federation as a forum for airing labor's views, Gompers believed, would help the unions win acceptance from the more respectable elements of the community.

Socialists, radicals and other union militants, of course, vehemently criticized Gompers for banqueting with plutocrats while workers starved. The industrialists, for their part, viewed the Civic Federation as a means of easing serious social tension. Respectable labor was to join with respectable capital to fend off the rising tide of socialism. However, there was opposition within industry ranks to this conciliatory approach. John Kirby, then head of the National Association of Manufacturers, took his co-equals to task for joining with the likes of Gompers in an effort to achieve industrial peace. There is, said Kirby, "a great danger to the best interests of our common community" in the civic Federation's sympathetic support of Gompers and trade unionism.

The support, of course, was limited; there was no molly-coddling of the Wobblies and suchlike. However, until World War I generated the antiradical hysteria of the Palmer raids, the energies of the Civic Federation were usefully expended on divising methods for maintaining industrial peace and promoting collective bargaining. John Mitchell in 1908 doffed his miner's soft black hat for the derby of the Civic Federation. He became the full-time head of the trade-agreement department of the employer-union groups. According to its secretary, Ralph Easley, the Civic Federation helped to settle more than 100 strikes, and wholly or partially failed in only 18 other cases, during the first years of the group's existence. For this, Mitchell and Easley deserve much credit. No doubt the growing acceptance by industry of collective bargaining and the observation of trade agreements was due to the efforts of the Civic Federation. It was, in its way and time, a forerunner of President John F. Kennedy's labor-management advisory council, a place where labor and management could—and did—exchange views.

Yet, the Civic Federation was unable to head off the anthracite strike of 1902. Nor was it any more successful in inducing J. P. Morgan "to start right" with a positive labor policy in his newest endeavor, the United States Steel Corporation. And, when it came right down to it, the National Civic Federation was no more interested than the American Federation of Labor in encouraging industrial unionism. A craft union, as we saw in the Homestead strike, after all represented only a minority of the new work force in the industrial concentrations springing up throughout the land and, therefore, posed no real threat to the magnates at dinner with Sam Gompers. In the end, the Civic Federation came to devote most of its energies to combating "radicalism" and much less to promoting amicable relations with labor. After Gompers' death, the organization declined, eventually dying out in the early 1930s.

The profound differences that existed within the labor movement—between the AFL and the Industrial Workers of the World—also existed within the AFL itself. The Socialist Party of Eugene Debs grew rapidly during the early years of the twentieth century and its strength and influence within the Federation grew proportionately, for not all the socialists in the labor movement followed Debs into the IWW. Max Hayes, socialist leader of the Typographical Union, warily refused to join with Debs in founding the IWW. He believed that the formation of the IWW meant "another running fight between Socialists on the one side and all other partisans on the other. . . . If there is any fighting to be done I intend *to agitate on the inside* of the organizations now in existence." This pretty much came to be the position of the Socialist Party union activists—and of Debs, who, as we have seen, dropped out of the IWW in 1908—with the anarchists and trade-union syndicalists clustering around the IWW.

Gompers, of course, fought the socialists, who, in the early 1900s, seemed to be on the threshold of becoming a major political force. In 1908, Eugene Debs rode the "Red Special," a rented locomotive and sleeping car, for sixty-five days, speaking five to twenty times a day, to reach over 500,000 people. In the spring of 1910, the party experienced its first victory at the polls. Milwaukee and Schenectady elected socialist mayors; socialists were in the state legislatures of New York, Massachusetts, Pennsylvania, Minnesota, and Rhode Island. Victor Berger was sent to Congress by the voters of Wisconsin. By fall of 1911, over 500 socialists held office. The growing electoral strength of the socialists was also reflected within the trade-union movement.

To fend off the socialists, Gompers enlisted the support of the more conservative elements within the Federation, largely to be found within the building tradesmen and among the Catholics. The conservative wing of the Federation was not immune to the nationalism that seized Americans during the Spanish-American War and the period following. In the eyes of these new Americans, socialism appeared as a foreign importation—a view fostered within the labor movement by Gompers, who, because of his youthful flirtation with the ideas of Karl Marx, claimed to have first-hand knowledge of this. However, as Professor Marc Karson points out in his study of Roman Catholic Church influence within the AFL, *Labor Unions and Politics,* "the weakness of socialism in the American Federation of Labor at the close of World War I was, in part, a testimonial to the success of the Catholic Church's opposition to this doctrine." Karson concludes: "Aided by the predominantly Catholic officers of the international unions and by the large Catholic rank and file in the AFL responsive to their Church's view on socialism, Catholicism helped to account for the moderate political philosophy and policies of the AFL, for socialism's weakness in the AFL, and, therefore, for the absence of a labor party in the United States."

Gompers, in fact, may have not had much choice in face of the pressures on him from the socialist left and from the Catholic wing of the Federation. To throw his lot in with the socialists might have, as Gompers well knew, fostered a Catholic split away from the House of Labor. Gompers was as opposed to the development of a religious labor organization along the lines of the Christian labor organizations to be found in Europe as he was to left-wing unionism. He believed in one national center for trade unions in the United States. Failing an ideology, such as the one possessed by the Knights of Labor, which, incidently, managed to encompass both Catholics and the radicals, Gompers had little choice but to tack with the more conservative winds blowing through AFL convention halls. It was also a policy that paid off: at the turn of the century, the Federation membership barely topped 550,000; by 1914, it reached the two-million mark.

Outside the increasingly stodgy atmosphere of Federation conventions, the AFL ark was buffeted by other winds. The opening years of the century were turbulent—and fateful—years indeed. The complacency of the Gilded Age gave way rapidly before the advancing waves of reform. The discontent of the laboring masses was felt at another level by the middle-class reformer who set about with remarkable vigor to set things aright.

The great disparity between unrestrained wealth and dismal poverty was all too apparent. Greed, corruption in high places, and the social evils festering in the slums of the nation's chief cities were mercilessly exposed in Lincoln Steffin's *Shame of the Cities,* published in 1904. A year earlier Ida M. Tarbell unveiled the mysteries of Standard Oil in her monumental history. Upton Sinclair's *The Jungle* exposed the fetid and sordid hog butcher of the world, Chicago. The muckrakers altogether gave the great trusts and the growing power of the corporations a racking that still lingers in our culture. A growing body of informed opinion agreed with William Allen White when he declared, "The problems facing Theodore Roosevelt are problems concerning the distribution of wealth." This was not far, in genteel terms, from the views of the socialists agitating in the forgotten corners of industrial America. The Social Gospel of Dr. Washington Gladden and Walter Rauschenbusch filtered through the Protestant denominations to broad segments of the middle class. "If the banner of the Kingdom of God is to enter through the gates of the future," declared theologian Rauschenbusch, "it will have to be carried by the tramping hosts of labor."

As the discontent of the working masses percolated upwards, it became distilled in the middle-class reformism of the Rough Rider's Square Deal: "We are neither for the rich man as such nor for the poor man as such; we are for the upright man, rich or poor." An admirable sentiment that did justice to a significant departure taking place in American government. As Charles Beard observed in *The Rise of American Civilization,* "[Theodore] Roosevelt was the first President of the United States who openly proposed to use the powers of political government for the purpose of affecting the distribution of wealth in the interest of the golden mean." In a letter to reformer Jacob Riis, Roosevelt himself made the same point: "So far as it can be done by legislation to favor the growth of intelligence and the diffusion of wealth in such a manner as will measureably avoid the extreme of swollen fortune and grinding poverty. This represents the idea toward which I am striving."

The accomplishments of the new reformers were many and lasting. Populist agitation combined with labor strife and Protestant conscience to prod the middle class into action. A wave of political reform washed over the entrenched political machines of the day. The "Wisconsin idea" of reform through legislative and administrative advances, as in the income tax and railroad regulation, spread, with Senator Robert M. LaFollette as its most articulate spokesman. The 16th amendment to the Constitution, the so-called income tax amendment, was adopted in 1913, as was the 17th, which provides for the direct election of U. S. Senators. Sixteen states—mostly Western—had adopted by 1912 the initiative and referendum as measures ensuring greater democracy. In 1906, Congress enacted the Hepburn Act, which strengthened the regulatory power of the Interstate Commerce Commission. The Pure Food and Drug Act (which forbade the manufacture, sale or transportation of adulterated foods or drugs in interstate commerce) and the Meat Inspection Act (aimed at the conditions in the meat packing industry exposed by Upton Sinclair) were both passed the same year. Conservation of the country's national resources made significant headway when President Roosevelt set aside over 148 million acres for national forest lands. By 1912, a considerable body of state social legislation relating to wages and hours, the employment of children and women, and safety and health conditions had been enacted as state legislatures responded to pressures generated by radicals, reformers and the labor movement. Maryland, in 1902, adopted the first workmen's compensation law; Oregon, in 1903, adopted a ten-hour law for women in industry; Illinois, in 1911, adopted the first law providing public assistance to mothers with dependent children. Massachusetts, in 1912, established a commission to fix wage rates for women and children, establishing the first minimum-wage law. President Roosevelt's antitrust policy was carried on with increasing vigor by President William H. Taft's attorney-general, George Wickersham.

Yet, the reformers failed to provide adequate legal protection for the chief self-help endeavor of working people, their unions. The Clayton Anti-Trust Act, reform's best effort in this direction, declared that "the labor of a human being is not a commodity or article of commerce." Labor organizations, therefore, were excluded from the provisions of the antitrust laws. The act, adopted in 1914, forbade the use of injunctions in labor disputes unless a court decided that one was necessary to prevent irreparable injury to property. The act was an attempt to set aside court decisions applying the Sherman Anti-Trust Act to labor, and especially the use of the boycott by unions. Nonetheless, "labor's Magna Carta," as the act was hailed by the AFL executive council, fell far short of securing labor's right to bargain collectively and the worker's right to freely choose an organization of his own making to represent him. The courts quickly seized upon the act's legal vagaries to restore the dismal status quo for struggling unions.

This state was not one of grace. Despite Gomper's efforts to win acceptance from the community at large through his speeches at the grand banquet of the National Civic Federation and elsewhere, the AFL faced constant harassment in the courts and at the hands of the employers. In 1903, confronted by a noticeable rise in trade-union strength, "the employing interests" banded together to launch the Citizens' Industrial Association, an anti-union clearinghouse with headquarters in Indianapolis, Indiana.

The Association did not last very long but, in the opinion of labor historian Philip Taft, it "undoubtedly inflicted grave wounds" on the unions. The National Association of Manufacturers also played a leading role in molding employer and public opinion against what it termed "trades union tyranny." Perhaps of more importance were the employers' trade associations, such as the National Metal Trades' Association, which specialized in promoting the open shop, providing strikebreakers, and planting industrial spies.

As an organization of autonomous unions, the AFL was ill-armed to counter such attacks. The more powerful affiliates preferred to do their own organizing and declined to put up the wherewithal for AFL organizational efforts. This barred a combined, united assault on anti-union strongholds. So the Federation fell back on the union label and the boycott. Union members—and the public—were encouraged to buy union-made products. While individual unions were responsible for establishing the use of the union label within their jurisdiction, they frequently called upon the Federation to give users of the label wider publicity. Unionization, in this way, became a positive business asset and incentive, for it meant more business, or so it was argued, for unionized firms. To put the bite on reluctant employers, the unions turned to the boycott. However, the use of this more militant weapon was undertaken with the greatest of reluctance by the AFL. It was not to Gomper's taste, but the pressures on the Federation to take the lead in boycott action intensified as the employers' attack on the unions increased.

In the end, however, the courts forced the Federation to drop this weapon from its arsenal. In the Danbury Hatters' case (*Lawlor* v. *Loewe*), the Supreme Court of the United States opened the way for the widespread application of the Sherman Anti-Trust law to the unions. In March, 1902, the United Hatters of North America called a strike and proclaimed a boycott against Dietrich Loewe and Company and its products. The boycott apparently succeeded, for the company, in September, 1903, sued the 240 members of the Hatters in Danbury for treble damages of $240,000 under the Sherman Anti-Trust law. Workers' homes were attached, pending the outcome of the suit. After fourteen years of legal wrangling, the Supreme Court upheld the right of the company to sue the individual members of the union for actions undertaken by their officers and confirmed the final amount of the judgment against them, $252,130.90. The AFL spent $98,756.02 in fighting the case. The labor movement could ill-afford to allow the burden of the judgment to fall upon the homes and slender bank accounts of the Danbury hatters, so the AFL convention of 1915 called for the donation of one hour's pay from union members to meet the damages. The case cost the far from affluent labor movement more than $420,000.

The actual cost was greater. Workers became wary of joining unions for fear of being sued. The AFL was forced to discontinue its "We Don't Patronize" listing in the *Federationists*. (In part, this came about as a result of a parallel case involving the Buck's Stove and Range Company. Gompers was indicted because of an editorial he wrote protesting the injunction that forced him to take the stove company's name off the "We Don't Patronize" list. For this effrontery to the majesty of the courts, Gompers nearly went to jail. A compromise solution worked out by lawyers saved Gompers from this indignity.) The upshot of both cases was the dropping of the boycott by the Federation as a weapon against recalcitrant employers.

The boycott troubles of the AFL were a factor in the general drift toward radicalism by labor around 1912. Further impetus came from the organization of the needle trades in New York in 1910 and 1911. The success of the socialist-led International Ladies Garment Workers' Union not only boosted AFL morale and membership but strengthened the socialist wing within the Federation. (The men's clothing industry was organized by the Amalgamated Clothing Workers, founded in 1914. The ACW remained outside the AFL because of a jurisdictional quarrel with an AFL affiliate.) The needle-trades unions were to pioneer a new socially-conscious unionism that welded the socialist-industrial union concept of solidarity to the pragmatic craft-union-AFL concern with the collective-bargaining agreement. The garment unions, through negotiations, won an entirely new spectrum of gains in employer-financed, union-controlled pensions, health and welfare benefits, and the like that are now a permanent part of the fabric of welfare unionism. In the early decades of the century, however, the avowedly socialist leaders of the needle trades worked to further political unionism within the framework of the AFL.

Their arguments were reinforced by increased employer opposition to the unions and the growth of violence on the industrial scene. "Violence," Sam Gompers testified before a Congressional committee, "is not a recognized part of labor's plan of campaign. . . . Labor needs to be strong in numbers, in effective organization, in the justice of its cause, and in the reasonableness of its methods. It relies on moral suasion." The sentiments were admirable but were not entirely in accord with the facts. Hard-pressed unionists at times had to fall back on naked force to protect not only their rights, but their very lives. In 1909, for example, the Wobblies fought a pitched battle with the police at McKees Rocks, Pennsylvania, in which about a dozen men were killed on both sides. They finally drove the police from the streets, ending further violence and ultimately winning the strike against the Pressed Steel Car Company.

Alongside this "open" class warfare, however, there existed a more pernicious guerilla war between the unions and employer associations. The sustained guerilla warfare opened the way into organized labor for racketeering and gangster muscle. "The brutal force which money can exert in America in the workshop," J. Ramsay McDonald wrote in 1912, "the corrupt force it can exert on the bench and in the capital of every State, make it the most natural thing imaginable for labor to contemplate a resort to such force as it can command—dynamite, sabotage, bad work, the revolutionary strike." The Wobblies, as we have seen, did not hesitate to proclaim that capitalist oppression made such counter-thrusts on the part of labor inevitable. But it was the conservative AFL building trades that provide the classic example of the development from militant unionism to racketeering. Dynamite, easily available on the building site, at first the last resort of desperate men fighting to hold their jobs and decent working conditions, became a weapon of terror and of the shakedown in the hands of labor racketeers such as Owen "Skinny" Madden and Sam Parks, who bossed the building trades of New York at the beginning of the century. Trade-union leaders who hired guns to counter the hired guns of employers frequently found themselves at the mercy of their supposedly hired hands.

This particular development within the labor movement reached a tragic climax in the famous McNamara case in 1911. The case had its roots in a long-standing industrial quarrel between the Ironworkers and the strongly anti-union National Erectors' Association. The employer organization launched a vigorous open-shop campaign within its industry in 1906. By driving the union to the wall, the employers forced out a more militant leadership—John J. McNamara, president of the Ironworkers, and his brother and "outside" man, James B.

Los Angeles, at the time, was a stronghold of anti-union forces headed by the aggressive publisher of the *Los Angeles Times*, Harrison Gray Otis. In the morning of October 1, 1910, shortly after 1 A.M., as the *Times* employees were "putting the paper to bed," there was "a dry, snappy sound" in Ink Alley at the rear of the building, followed by a deafening explosion. The building was completely destroyed and twenty lives lost. The *Times*, as soon as it could get out an edition (a matter of a day or two), charged that the dirty work was done by an agent of the unions. A tremendous award was offered but there were no further developments until Christmas night, 1910. The California State Federation of Labor conducted an investigation and claimed that the evidence showed that the explosion had been caused by gas. But on Christmas night a bomb wrecked the Llewellyn Iron Works, where a strike was in progress. From there, it was an easy matter for private detective William J. Burns to trace the second explosion, if not the first, to the Ironworkers. Burns arrested James B. McNamara and Ortie McManigal, a member of the union, in Detroit. McManigal confessed. The other McNamara was soon under arrest and transported to California.

The trial soon became another *cause célèbre* within the labor movement. Great sums of money were raised for the defense of "the boys." Clarence Darrow was retained as defense counsel; Sam Gompers visited the McNamaras in prison and even took the unprecedented step of endorsing Job Harriman, the socialist candidate for the mayoralty of Los Angeles. Before the jury was impaneled, the chief investigator for the defense was arrested and charged with bribing a juror. Darrow, worried, began to look for a way out. He faced a possible prison sentence for the alleged jury bribing; the McNamaras faced almost sure death. So the great lawyer became convinced that the only way to save the lives of the two men was to have them plead guilty and take a prison sentence. The prosecution proved to be amenable, and especially so after the Erectors' Association approved the deal. The Association, for its part, accepted the proposition because of pressure put on it by employers in Los Angeles who were worried about the outcome of the mayoralty race. The two defendants entered their plea just five days before the election. Socialist Job Harriman was soundly defeated as a result of the resentment and disillusionment felt by labor in the city. A shocked Sam Gompers declared, "I have been grossly imposed upon." A month later, the leaders of the Ironworkers were indicted for conspiracy to transport dynamite in interstate commerce. At the trial it was shown that between 1909 and 1911, eighty-seven structures erected by non-union labor had been dynamited at the direction of the McNamara brothers and Ortie McManigal. The employers, however, were not without knowledge of this development or perhaps without guilt of connivance in this use of violence. H. S. Hockin, a member of the executive board of the union, privy to the dynamiters' plans, was also on the payroll of the employers. The thirty-eight ironworkers were convicted and Ironworker president Frank Ryan was sentenced to seven years in prison. An attempt to implicate the AFL and Gompers failed. The rule of dynamite, however, did not end with the McNamaras.

# IX

## *THE TROUBADOURS OF DISCONTENT*

"THE AVERAGE WAGE EARNER," MINEWORKERS' PRESIDENT JOHN Mitchell declared in 1903, "has made up his mind that he must remain a wage earner. He has given up the hope of a kingdom come, where he himself will be a capitalist, and asks that the reward for his work be given him as a workingman."

Whenever this reward was denied or its achievement frustrated, workingmen became radical or turned to the radicals for leadership. "The labor men are very ugly," President Theodore Roosevelt wrote to Senator Henry C. Lodge in 1906, "and no one can tell how far such discontent will spread. There has been during the last six or eight years a great growth of socialistic and radical spirit among workingmen and the leaders are obliged to play to this or lose their leadership." It was a realistic assessment of the prevailing mood among great sections of the working class of America during the early decades of this century. It was altogether characteristic of this development that Mother Jones— "Pray for the dead, but fight like hell for the living"—should find it necessary to resign from her post as organizer for the more militant of AFL unions, the Miners, a year after the 1902 anthracite settlement. That year she became a founder of the Industrial Workers of the World, the fullest expression of that radical impulse among American workingmen, the dream of one big union.

The Wobbly came from the West in the person of William Dudley "Big Bill" Haywood and his Western Federation of Miners. As Gompers worked to set off the skilled workmen as the "aristocracy of labor" within the AFL, the Wobblies rode the rails to spread the message of "one big union for all." "We are going down in the gutter," declared Big Bill, "to get at the mass of the workers and bring them up to a decent plane of living." Before they were done, the Wobblies had marched across the wheatlands of the mid-Western plains, chopped into the lumber camps of the Northwest, and aroused downtrodden textile workers in the industrial Northeast. They spun out their dream on "Father" (Thomas J.) Hagerty's "Wheel of Fortune," an organization chart that would establish an industrial democracy along industrial spokes branching out of an administrative hub. Strumming "songs to fan the flames of discontent," Wobbly troubadours stirred rebellion across the land.

"Big Bill" was a representative man, a product of the changing West, where the Western Federation of Miners carried on an open, violent class war with the mine owners and operators in the 1890s and early 1900s. For a time, as armed miners seized control of mines in Telluride and Cripple Creek districts in Colorado in 1901 and 1903, it was a real question as to who controlled the state—the miners or the militia. The tone of the WFM, as Louis Adamic points out in *Dynamite*, "came from adventurous American frontiersmen who suddenly found themselves in the degrading position of workingmen—thousands of feet under the earth." Their energies and enterprise, frustrated by the close of the West and of business entrepreneurship, found new expression; the Wobblies, in truth, were "pioneers," but on the new industrial frontier. Exploited, working under intolerable conditions, they did not hesitate to take to firearms to protect their rights through their union. In 1897, Ed Boyce, the president of the WFM, urged the Idaho and Colorado locals of the union to form rifle corps, "so that in two years we can hear the inspiring music of the martial tread of 25,000 armed men in the ranks of labor."

Haywood, a Bunyanesque figure with a voice to match, was a natural leader for these frontiersmen-turned-miners. He was a son of the Rockies, a ranch hand turned miner. The men admired him for his great physical courage and capacity for booze. Blind in one eye, Big Bill also shared their defects. A great agitator, Haywood wasn't much as an organizer. Unquestionably, he was a master of the direct statement. On January 2, 1905, he strode to the podium in a small hall in Chicago, picked up a loose piece of board, rapped for order, and shouted: "Fellow workers! This is the Continental Congress of the Working Class. . . . The aims and objects of this organization shall be to put the working class in possession of the economic power, the means of life, in control of the machinery of production and distribution, without regard to capitalist masters." Thus was the IWW born.

Troubadours, however, make notably poor organizers. The infant IWW was torn with socialist factions hauling one way and anarchists, trade unionists and others, pulling other ways. Indeed, the IWW seemed destined to go the way of its deceased predecessor, the American Labor Union, within a year of its founding. But the arrest of Big Bill Haywood for the murder of an ex-governor of Idaho temporarily brought the warring factions together.

On December 30, 1905, Frank Steunenberg opened the gate of his home in Caldwell, Idaho. A piece of string was tied to the gate; at the other end was a crude bomb that tore the sheep rancher to bits. A member of the Western Federation of Miners, Harry Orchard, was arrested on suspicion. He confessed, charging that Haywood, Charles Moyer, president of the WFM, and George A. Pettibone, a Denver businessman and a WFM familiar, had hired him to murder assorted mining bosses. Their motive in the Steunenberg case, according to Orchard, was revenge upon the ex-governor, who had called out the militia during the Coeur d'Alene strike of 1899. The Idaho law officials, overlooking the legal niceties of extradition, arrested the three men and spirited them out of Colorado for trial in Idaho.

The selection of Clarence Darrow for the defense and of William E. Borah for the prosecution heightened the natural drama of the case. The trial opened on May 9, 1907. The state, however, could not prove its case against Haywood, and the big, burly miner was acquitted along with his two companions. Labor viewed the case as an attempted frame-up. The emotions generated illustrated the bitterness surrounding the near-open class war then taking place between the mining interests and the unions. The trial also served to unify temporarily the various factions within the labor movement; even the various craft unions within the AFL rallied to aid Haywood and his companions. For the Wobblies, the trial provided the necessary breather in factionalism that enabled the organization to survive the first year of its existence. But once the trial was over the rivalries commenced again. The Western Federation of Miners withdrew, leaving the IWW to Big Bill and the soapbox agitators who were to dominate and set the style for the "One Big Union" for over a decade. The anarcho-syndicalists were in charge; in the spring of 1908, the Wobblies dropped the last reference to political action from the preamble to the order's constitution. As a result, Eugene Debs quietly dropped out of the IWW.

The direct-action philosophy of the Wobblies, however, carried a great appeal for the migratory laborers of the West—the harvest hands who moved across the Great Plains following the giant combines threshing wheat—for carefree lumberjacks and longshoremen and seafarers. For a time, around 1912, it seemed likely that the IWW would repeat the sudden growth experienced by the Knights of Labor during the great upheaval of 1886. Itinerant Wobbly soapboxers shouted their revolutionary message on streetcorners across the country. Incidently they provided an inestimable service to American democracy in the free-speech fights that occurred in San Diego, Spokane, Fresno, Sioux City, and elsewhere between 1909 and 1915. The martyrdom of Joe Hill and Frank Little enriched the folklore of the labor movement. But the IWW never developed into a major rival of the AFL; its membership never topped 250,000. However, the far-ranging organizers of the IWW did awaken the labor movement to the plight of the migrant worker of the West and of the immigrant factory worker in the East. It demonstrated that unskilled workers, speaking many tongues, could be welded together to form a fighting organization. Widely different temperaments and ethnic antagonisms could be overcome as the IWW showed in the Lawrence strike of 1912 and the Paterson silk strike of 1914. To the oppressed immigrant, the IWW brought a message of hope that is America.

Lawrence, Massachusetts, in 1912 was at its height as a textile center. Of its 85,000 population, some 25,000 were mill hands. Most of them were immigrants, largely Italian, but also Russian, Syrian, German, Polish, Belgian, Armenian, English, Irish, Portuguese, Austrian, Jewish, French-Canadian and Lithuanian. When the mills ran full time, the average weekly wage was $8.76, with a third of the work force earning less than $7, and 17.5 percent earning $12 or more. In slack time, a frequent occurrence in the textile industry, wages fell to $2.30 and $2.70 a week. Wage earners had a hard time to support their families; women and children were pressed into service. Massachusetts law prohibited the employment of children under 14, but half the children of Lawrence between 14 and 18 worked in the mills. Children were undernourished; the infant death rate was high, 172 deaths out of every 1,000 live births. Only six other cities in the United States had a higher rate and four of these were textile centers.

When the Massachusetts state legislature cut working hours for women and children under 18 from 56 to 54 hours a week as of January 1, 1912, the mill owners extended the shorter work week to all hands. A committee of Lawrence workers sought in vain to meet with their employer, the American Woolen Company, the chief principality of the Woolen Trust, to discuss the effect of the reduction in hours would have on earnings. The cut wasn't much—about 3½ percent of weekly earnings. But it was serious to workers worried about "short pay." On Thursday afternoon at the Everett cotton mill, pay envelopes were distributed carrying the wage cut instituted without warning. The weavers, mostly Polish women, stopped the looms, left the mills saying to company officials who attempted to explain the pay cut, "Not enough money."

The next morning sullen workmen streamed to work from their crowded, dark, wooden three- and four-story tenements. The distribution of pay envelopes at other mills showed that the pay reductions were general. Someone, tradition has it, shouted, "Goddamn it to hell! Let's strike!" In any event, around 9 o'clock in the morning workers began shutting down the looms at the Washington mill. They congregated outside the mill and marched to another where they called out the workers. As the strikers milled in the streets, the City Hall bells tolled a riot alarm, the first in seventeen years. That afternoon a telegram was sent to IWW executive board member Joseph Ettor to come to assist the conducting of the strike. By evening, 10,000 mill workers were out.

Ettor, a magnetic personality in his mid-twenties, arrived in time to help shape the organization of the strike. He was Brooklyn-slum-born and raised in Chicago. His Italian father, a militant proletarian, was severely wounded by the Haymarket bomb. Young Ettor took to the Wobblies as naturally as Yale men take to Wall Street brokerage houses. Despite his youth he brought with him to Lawrence wide-ranging experience as an organizer; his first work having been to organize the debris workers after the San Francisco earthquake in 1906. He was an invaluable asset for the inexperienced, unskilled mill hands of Lawrence.

Before the walkout began, there was little labor oganization in Lawrence. The AFL craft unions had a membership of about 2,500; the IWW had some 1,000 out of the great mass of the unskilled. These, however, turned to the Wobblies for leadership when aroused to the point of rebellion. The AFL United Textile Workers, which represented the handful of craftsmen in the industry, had turned a deaf ear to appeals for help from the unskilled. In Lawrence, the UTW refused to join the walkout and John Golden, president of the AFL union, did his best to break the strike. As in Homestead some twenty years earlier, the workers' response to crisis took the industrial form of organization. A strike committee of 50 met each morning to hear reports, investigate complaints and formulate plans. Because of language differences, the strikers were organized by ethnic groups, each electing representatives to the central strike committee. The major problem facing the committee, aside from the nigh impossible task of keeping order, was that of providing relief for the 50,000 strikers and dependents. An appeal for funds brought in a $1,000 a day for the duration of the ten-week walkout from other labor oganizations, socialist groups, and private individuals all over the country. The committee's efficient handling of relief was instrumental in preventing strikers from wavering in the face of extreme provocation from the employers, the city authorities, and the militia.

Panicky city fathers had called for the militia almost immediately after the start of the strike. Martial law was soon imposed upon the hapless city. As the strike spread to Fall River and Haverhill, the governor ordered out additional troops. Thirty-six strikers were arrested and, without opportunity to defend themselves, sentenced to a year in prison. Dynamite was planted by company spies in a cemetery, a tailor shop and a shoe shop next to the print shop where Ettor received his mail. A peaceful demonstration on January 29, organized by the strike committee to dispel rumors that the strike was collapsing, ended in clashes with the police and the milita. That evening, Anna LaPizzo, a young striker, was killed. Strikers on the scene insisted that the shot was fired by a police officer. Ettor and Arturo Giovannitti were arrested and charged with "inciting and procuring the commission of the crime in pursuit of an unlawful conspiracy."

Giovannitti, who had joined Ettor in the leadership of the strike, was an Abruzzi-born poet whose talents, after turns as minister, clerk, theological student, mission preacher, and tramp, finally brought him to the editorship of an Italian radical newspaper in New York. A powerful, incisive speaker, he was in charge of the relief work during the strike until his arrest.

Arrests became more frequent as the authorities bore down on the strikers. Haywood, and other officers of the IWW—William Yates, James P. Thompson, William E. Trautmann, Elizabeth Gurley Flynn—rushed to Lawrence to replace the jailed IWW leaders. The employers tried to lure the strikers back to work by setting the mill machinery into motion. But as the *New York Times* reported, "Not a single operative was at work and not a single machine carried a spool of thread."

To ease the burden of the strike on the families of the Lawrence mill hands, the strike committee borrowed a technique from Belgium, France, and Italy and arranged to send the children of the strikers to sympathetic families elsewhere. The plan was successful and some 400 children were placed in temporary foster homes before the authorities decided to intervene. They declared that no more children would be allowed to leave the city. When the strikers attempted to send 40 more children to Philadelphia on February 24, they were greeted by the police at the rail station. Women and children were clubbed and thrown into a waiting truck.

The violence of the police attack, however, had unexpected results. It "settled" the strike. As protests rolled in from all over the country, company officials began to think twice about meeting with the union. On March 12, the strike ended in a victory for the IWW. The Lawrence mill hands won wage increases from five to 25 percent and these were extended throughout New England to some 200,000 or more textile workers. That fall Ettor and Giovannitti were acquitted.

The Lawrence strike was the Wobblies' greatest triumph. As

Jim Thompson declared, "Every hour that the strike lasted the One Big Union idea was spreading like wildfire. The strikers of Lawrence were actually teaching the country how to fight." But the One Big Union failed to leave a lasting organization behind.

After the strike victory, the IWW had a membership of 14,000 in Lawrence. In October, 1913, there were only 700. There are several reasons for this—unemployment and the disillusionment of the workers. The employers instituted a speedup immediately after the wage increases went into effect; they also succeeded in establishing a spy system within the mills. Nevertheless the IWW must bear proportionate responsibility for the loss for failing to provide a lasting leadership. In 1915, Selig Perlman found that only one of eight local IWW leaders who were active in the strike still remained in Lawrence.

Nonetheless, the direct-actionist Wobblies in the years before World War I began to move from freewheeling agitation to more solid organizational achievements. "As a union advances from an ephemeral association to a stable organization," Selig Perlman wrote in *A Theory of the Labor Movement*, "more and more emphasis is shifted from wages to working rules." This is exactly what happened to the Wobblies before they went under the wave of super-patriotism brought on by World War I.

The trade-union strain within the IWW, of course, had always existed within the organization, although it receded into the background during the free-speech fights of 1909–15. In 1907, for example, the IWW established thoroughgoing job control in Goldfield, Nevada, over both mine jobs—miners as well as carpenters—and town jobs—cooks, waiters, hotel personnel, etc. Vincent St. John, for many years secretary-treasurer of the IWW, proudly recalled: "Under the IWW sway in Goldfield the minimum wage for all kinds of labor was $4.50 per day and the eight-hour day was universal. . . . No committees were ever sent to any employers. The unions adopted wage scales and regulated hours. The secretary posted the same on a bulletin board outside of the union hall, and it was the LAW. The employers were forced to come and see the union committee."

A decade later, the Wobblies applied the lessons learned at Goldfield and elsewhere to the organization of harvest hands in the grain belt, lumber workers of the West coast, the road construction hand, and the shoreside and seagoing maritime workers. The IWW enjoyed considerable success, entering the period of its greatest growth. As Philip Taft notes in his study of the IWW in the Grain Belt published in *Labor History* (Winter 1960, Vol. I, No. 1) "Were it not for the intervention of World War I [this development] might have transformed the IWW into a powerful economic organization of unskilled and semiskilled workers."

But World War I did intervene. IWW publications were suppressed and IWW halls shut down. In June, 1917, the federal government indicted the whole top leadership of the IWW under the wartime espionage laws. Over 150 were jailed. The IWW, in the end, was destroyed by continual harassment by the federal authorities during the war and the prosecutions under various state criminal syndicalist statutes following the war. Big Bill Haywood jumped bail after his conviction, seeking haven in the Soviet Union, where he died in 1928, lonely and bewildered by the outcome of a revolution he never quite fully understood.

# X

## *THE SEEDLINGS*
## *OF CORPORATE WELFARISM*

ALTHOUGH THE FIRST TWO DECADES OF THE CENTURY WERE
marked by labor strife, today's widespread acceptance of unions
among employers is rooted in that bitter period. By the time the
United States entered World War I, unions were recognized in
many important industries. But of greater importance was the
shift in attitude toward employee relations on the part of such
giants as U. S. Steel and the Rockefeller complex. Both changed
their attitudes as a result of strikes that ended in defeat of the
unions. But the new attitudes made possible the corporate family
of today that embraces both the unions and management.

The change in attitude that took place was much more rudimentary in form in steel than within the Rockefeller oil-mining
interests. Oddly enough, this meant, in the long run, unionization
of steel and the flourishing of company unions within the oil
industry. But the basic management attitude is the same in both.

John A. Garraty, in a fascinating study, "U. S. Steel versus
Labor: The Early Years," published in *Labor History* (Winter,
1960), relates labor policy debates within the company to a
struggle for control of the corporation between the steelmen, rep-

resented by Charles M. Schwab, and the financiers, represented by Judge Elbert H. Gary. The steelmen favored autonomy of the individual companies within the corporate setup; the financiers wanted more centralized control. Neither was particularly friendly toward labor, especially organized labor. "If a workman sticks up his head," argued an ironmaster, "hit it." The steelmen wanted freedom to slug it out with the unions since they were confident of their own strength. But the financiers, much more conscious of the new trust's vulnerability in the public eye, were a good deal more cautious.

Actually, the union, such as it was, hardly concerned steelmen or financiers. After the Homestead strike, the Amalgamated Association of Iron, Steel and Tin Workers entered into a permanent decline. Organized on craft lines, the union failed, despite the lessons of Homestead, to adapt to the shifts within steel leading to mass production. The growing numbers of unskilled and semiskilled workers were ignored by the AFL craft union. The nature of the work force had also changed; in 1900, 35 percent of all steel workers were immigrants; by 1908, the figure had increased to 57.5 percent. Slovaks, Croats, Magyars and Poles were among the newest immigrants; few of them had any experience with urban industrial life. A difficult human mixture for an industrial union to organize, it was virtually impossible for the exclusive craft union.

Nonetheless, the Amalgamated held a precarious toehold in the steel industry as the century began. The organization of the United States Steel Corporation raised the possibility of expanding this tiny beachhead through an industry-wide strike. When the union struck the American Tin Plate Company, a U. S. Steel subsidiary, in 1901, the company was willing to compromise. It accepted the wage demand and offered to permit the unionization of several mills. The union then made a serious error of judgment. It interpreted the concessions as a sign of weakness and extended the strike to all subsidiaries of the steel company. Forced to fight back, the corporation reopened its mills with strikebreakers—many were the new immigrants coming into the industry—and whipped the union. The contract specified "non-union mills shall be represented as such, no attempts made to organize, no charters granted."

The Panic of 1907 and the declining fortunes of the industry in 1908 and early 1909 no doubt helped shape the decisions of U. S. Steel to rid itself of the remnants of the union that still clung on after the 1901 debacle. In 1907, Judge Elbert H. Gary gave the first of his famous "Dinners" for the nation's steel producers. Gary pleaded "like a Methodist minister at a camp meeting" with his competitors not to lower prices. "What we want," he declared, "is stability—the avoidance of violent fluctuations." Thus did the Indiana judge usher in the new age of corporate responsibility.

But the new age as yet had not extended to the unions. When the Amalgamated struck American Sheet and Tin Plate Company in 1909 after the U. S. Steel subsidiary announced that it would not renew its contracts with the union, the Steel Corporation serenely sailed on, ignoring the union. The strike finally folded on August 10, 1911. "After 1909," notes Garraty, "U. S. Steel, and the rest of the industry, were to remain on an open-shop basis for more than a quarter of a century."

Indirectly, however, the strikes fostered a new corporate welfarism. George W. Perkins, chairman of the Finance Committee of U. S. Steel, took an interest in improving employee relations. Perkins, a Morgan partner, was one of the great trust organizers. He organized International Harvester for Morgan as well as other corporate groupings. Competition, he held, had become "too disturbing to be tolerated. Cooperation must be the order of the day." Perkins also believed that corporations had obligations to labor. The corporation, he declared, must "people-ize" modern industry. Profit sharing, social insurance, and pensions were to be the cement of the new order. In true cooperation, declared Perkins, there would be "socialism of the highest, best and most ideal sort." Perkins was well in advance of his time; Mussolini would put forth much the same set of ideas a quarter of a century later in his plans for a corporate fascism.

After the 1901 strike, Perkins put forward a stock-ownership plan based on selling company stock on the installment plan to everyone "from the President to the man with pick and shovel." As owners of stock, argued Perkins, U. S. Steel employees would take a greater interest in their jobs and in the corporation that employed them.

Few steelworkers, however, could afford to buy the stock, sold at $82.50 a share. About ten percent of the 122,000 workers who made less than $800 a year contracted to buy a single share. Nonetheless, the skilled worker, say, who bought a share for $82.50 in 1903 received over the next five years $125.05 in dividends and bonuses. In addition to the regular dividend, he also received for each share $5 a year extra if employed continuously by the corporation and if he had "shown a proper interest in its welfare and progress." The five-dollar bonus, however, was not distributed each year, but held for five when the corporation "by its own final determination" handed out the accumulated money to the "deserving."

"The elimination of the unions from U. S. Steel plants," concludes Garraty, "made way for the paternalistic philosophy of men like Gary and Perkins." Model towns were developed with cheap and, for the times and the skilled men, adequate housing, a departure from the sharp practices of the Pullman Company a decade earlier. Schools, playgrounds and recreational facilities for steelworkers were also provided. In 1911, the Corporation set up a Bureau of Safety, Sanitation, and Welfare— stimulated in part by the new workers' compensation laws—to promote improved practices in these fields throughout the corporation. Along with accident prevention, the corporation developed a program for compensation. By the end of 1911, Sunday work was almost entirely eliminated and the seven-day week a thing of the past. A pension plan was developed whereby any worker with twenty years' service could retire at sixty at a pension equal to one percent of his monthly pay for each year of service. The way to avoid labor troubles, the bankers then in charge of U. S. Steel believed, was to look after the workers' welfare. This they did, especially for the skilled elite, though the benefits were tinged with a false and demeaning charity. The result was the birth of the corporate family, though the unions were not included until after 1937.

In the case of U. S. Steel, corporatism came to welfarism by chance and drift, nudged along perhaps by the strikes of the Amalgamated. But the Rockefeller interests came to adopt the same posture as a result of a cataclysmic event, the bloody Ludlow, Colorado, massacre of 1914.

The Rockefeller complex had grown beyond the possible personal surveillance of any mortal man. Though John D. Rockefeller controlled the Colorado Fuel and Iron Company, the largest coal mining company in Colorado, through his ownership of 40 percent of its stock and bonds, he had "not the slightest idea" of the wages, rents, or living conditions of the miners who were technically in his employ. "Such details as wages, working conditions, and the political, social, and moral welfare of the 15,000 or 20,000 inhabitants of his coal camps," declared a report of the U. S. Commission on Industrial Relations, "apparently held no interest for Mr. Rockefeller, for as late as April, 1914, he professed ignorance of these details. Yet he followed, step by step, the struggle of his executive officials to retain arbitrary power and to prevent the installation of machinery for collective bargaining, by which abuses might automatically be corrected, and he supported and encouraged this struggle in every letter he wrote to his agents." Rockefeller was standing pat on the principle of the open shop. Each miner, in his view, was to strike his bargain with the company. Anything less would be to turn control of the company over to outsiders—"disreputable agitators, socialists, and anarchists." The result of such a policy for the miners was, of course, a far-reaching social and economic tyranny.

In September, 1913, some 9,000 miners with their families and personal belongings left their "shabby, ugly, and small" company houses in the company camps to establish tent colonies at the edges of the Southern Colorado coal fields. Their fifteen-month strike was not so much an economic strike for better wages and working conditions as it was a rebellion against company domination of every aspect of their lives. Chief among their demands, for example, was recognition of the union, the United Mine Workers; the right of the miners to trade at any store they pleased and to choose their own boarding places and doctors; and the enforcement of the Colorado mining laws. Among the economic demands were a ten-percent wage increase to correspond to rates in Wyoming; an eight-hour day; the election of checkweighmen; and payment for so-called "dead work"—brushing, timbering, removing falls and so on.

The companies imported armed thugs from Texas, New Mexico and West Virginia, who were readily deputized by complaisant law enforcement officials. Violence hovered in the air. Rifle pits were dug in the hills adjacent to mining properties and equipped with machine guns, rifles, and searchlights. An armored automobile—nicknamed the "Death Special" by strikers—was constructed in the Colorado Fuel & Iron Company Pueblo shops. To protect themselves, the miners armed.

Sporadic gunfire, resulting in a few deaths on both sides, brought in the militia and the imposition of martial law. For a time, an uneasy peace settled down over the Colorado coal area. The militia were ultimately withdrawn with the exception of Company A and Troop B of the Colorado National Guard, which were largely composed of professional gunmen and adventurers who were economically dependent on the coal operators. These were left to guard the largest tent colony, outside of Ludlow, Colorado. Rumors that the colony was to be wiped out rippled amidst the flapping tents. Understandably, the miners seized their rifles and took up positions in nearby arroyos when the militia mounted a machine gun on a hill overlooking the camp and set off two bombs. (Later, the guardsmen maintained that the bombs were merely set off as signals.) No one knows who fired the first shot, but there is no question about the outcome. The militia poured machine-gun and rifle fire into the tent colony. The battle raged for twelve hours; one boy and three men were killed, one a militiaman.

Then, on orders from their officers, the militia poured coal oil on the tents of Ludlow and set them afire. Women and children, who had huddled in pits dug as protective cellars beneath the tents, fled in terror. The militia looted at will; took three prisoners and killed them while they were unarmed and under guard. In one pit, eleven children and two women of the colony were found suffocated or burned to death.

As the news of Ludlow spread, armed workers marched from the surrounding districts. For ten days, open rebellion reigned, which ended upon the arrival of Federal troops. Rockefeller became a target of the mass indignation that followed the news of Ludlow across the nation. He hired Ivy L. Lee, publicity agent for the Pennsylvania Railroad, to help undo the bad publicity. He also hired W. L. Mackenzie King, formerly Minister of Labor for Canada, to discover some means of fostering friendly cooperation between capital and labor. But even the intervention in the interest of compromise on the part of President Woodrow Wilson failed to save the embattled Colorado miners. The suppression of the strike proceeded to the bitter end.

But after the unquestioned defeat of the strike, the Colorado Fuel and Iron Company unveiled a plan for improved employee relations. The so-called Colorado Industrial Representative Plan, or the Rockefeller Plan, was a fruit of Mackenzie King's labors. It called for the election of Joint Committees on Industrial Cooperation and Conciliation composed of representatives of the company and of the employees. The individual worker was to have the right to appeal grievances from local officials and to send representatives to the Joint Committee. Cooperation was to supplant the antagonism between capital and labor fostered by the union. According to John D. Rockefeller, Jr., in an article ghosted by Ivy Lee, the plan "brings men and managers together, facilitates the study of their common problems, and it should promote an understanding of their mutual interests."

In the fall of 1915, the plan was launched with a bright blaze of publicity. At the suggestion of Ivy Lee, Rockefeller toured the mines. He danced with nearly every woman at a mining town social function. It was all very democratic; William Hood, a colored miner, asked: "An' I wants to know, suh, when I'se goin' tuh git in on de pension list?" Rockefeller, "Well, I'm not on the pension list myself, yet, William." "Yes, but you-all ain't doin' no laborious labor." The trip and the plan was an instant success. In October, 1915, 2,404 of 2,846 voting employees (4,411 were eligible) cast ballots in its favor.

The Rockefeller Plan served as the model for the many variations of the company union that have flourished in the years since its inception in 1915. Indisputably, it has been responsible for nearly fifty years without a major strike within Standard Oil of New Jersey, the parent company of the Rockefeller complex.

Today's corporate welfarism is rooted in the Rockefeller Industrial Representative Plan and the welfare experiments of U. S. Steel during the first quarter of our century.

# XI

## NO LONGER ALIEN

AMERICA AT WAR WITH GERMANY WAS FAR FROM UNITED. THE rumblings of discontent were not solely confined to pacifists and radicals. Sam Gompers, who had exorcised pacificism from the American Federation of Labor, was having difficulty holding the unions in line. With the outbreak of war, Gompers pledged the full support of organized labor. But he failed to ask for, nor did he secure, a labor policy in return for what was, in effect, a no-strike pledge. Even hulking William Hutcheson, the Scotch-Irish president of the Carpenters, who favored the war effort but wanted the closed shop on government work, rumbled that the government was aiding anti-union employers.

Despite the AFL's support of the Wilsonian war effort "to make the world safe for democracy," labor was a lukewarm supporter of the preparedness parades of 1916. Tom Mooney and Warren K. Billings, in 1917, sat in the death house at San Quentin, charged with throwing a bomb during a preparedness day parade in San Francisco the year before that resulted in the death of eleven and the wounding of forty spectators. In Petrograd at the peak of what John Reed called "Ten Days That Shook the World," Russians surrounded the American embassy chanting "Mooni," virtually holding American Ambassador David R. Francis responsible for the lives of two union organizers. (Mooney and Billings were both pardoned some twenty years later, a somewhat belated recognition of the unfairness of their trials.)

Fully conscious of these swirling currents, President Woodrow Wilson, on November 11, took the night train to Buffalo for his first trip out of Washington and his first public address since America had entered the war. The next morning, accompanied by his wife and a grim cordon of soldiers, Wilson entered the American Federation of Labor convention hall. With a "thrill of pride," Gompers introduced the first President of the United States ever to address a labor convention.

The Presidential presence amounted to official recognition of organized labor. Though he came to plead the continuance of the no-strike policy—"Nobody has a right to stop the processes of labor until all the methods of conciliation and settlement have been exhausted"—Wilson went on to lay the cornerstone for what has since become public policy in labor relations. "We must," said the President, "do what we have declared our purpose to do, see that the conditions of labor are not rendered more onerous by the war, but also that we shall see to it that the instrumentalities by which the conditions of labor are improved are not blocked or checked." Although he may not have realized it as he hurried back to Washington, President Wilson had significantly changed the relationship between the federal government and organized labor. Never again would the national bodies of labor be in serious opposition to the government. Labor's implicit faith in the national government had finally borne fruit; in short, organized labor was now a part of the establishment.

World War I, in fact, helped to make the American Federation of Labor a permanent and lasting organization by giving it the strength to survive the 1920s. First, there was the sheer growth in membership, which was fostered by the government's wartime labor policy as well as the wartime flourishing of the economy. In the two years from 1917 to 1919, unions expanded with balloon-like rapidity. The meat cutters and butcher workmen, for example, grew from a tiny organization of fewer than 10,000 into a respectable 85,000-member organization. The railway clerks bounded from a bare 7,000 to over 71,000; the electrical workers grew from 42,000 to 131,000. These were a few of the big jumps that brought the membership of the AFL up from slightly over 2 million in 1916, before America entered the war, to twice that number in 1920.

Concomitant with the growth of union membership were economic gains. By late 1916, war prosperity edged up the cost of living and stimulated a movement for higher wages. The virtual end to immigration created a labor shortage that also helped to press wages upward. The movement for the eight-hour day spilled over from the munitions industry to others. A threat of a rail stoppage by the four operating Brotherhoods—engineers, firemen, conductors, and trainmen—followed by the intervention of President Wilson resulted in the enactment of the Adamson Act in 1916, which established the basic eight-hour day for rail operatives.

But membership growth and economic gains were outweighed by the *de facto* recognition afforded the unions by the government. President Wilson's address to the AFL Buffalo convention actually capped a change that began with his election in 1912. "Hereafter," writes Perlman, "for at least seven years, the Federation was an 'insider' in the national government." While Perlman may have put the case too strongly—Max Lerner notes in *America as a Civilization* four decades later that "the prevailing attitude in the major parties is that, like a mastiff [labor] must be kept tolerably content, but under no circumstance admitted into the house"—labor, after Wilson, was no longer alien in Washington. During the Presidential campaign of 1912, Gompers' discreet leanings toward Wilson were deemed sufficient to warrant the assurance that labor "would not be disappointed with the

labor program he would outline in his inaugural address."
William B. Wilson, a Democratic congressman from Pennsylvania and former secretary-treasurer of the United Mine
Workers was appointed Secretary of Labor, an appointment that
had been made "at the instigation of Samuel Gompers," according to the *New York Times*. Wilson established the Federal Mediation and Conciliation Service, a significant development in the
new dispensation.

With America's entry into the war the goodwill of labor became crucial to national policy and economic planning. Gompers
and other Federation leaders established the American Alliance
for Labor and Democracy to present the views of patriotic labor
and to counter those of the radicals and pacifists in the labor
movement. (At the end of the war, the effort of Alliance secretary
Robert Maisel to turn the organization into an antiradical intelligence service forced its discontinuance.) Maintaining the economy on a wartime footing required labor cooperation and several
steps were taken to obtain it. Among these, though not directly a
labor measure, was the cost-plus terms of government contracts,
which stimulated employer willingness to bid wages up and
dampened any willingness to risk strikes. Labor, for the first time,
was represented on a host of public and regulatory agencies, from
the Advisory Council of National Defense to fuel, food, emergency construction and war industries boards. But the prolifera-
tion of agencies proved to be too cumbersome for the wartime
administration of labor relations. So, in April, 1918, the War
Labor Board was established. It was charged with the mediation
and conciliation of disputes in war-connected industries. The
labor policy framed by the War Labor Board later became the
basis for much of the New Deal legislation in labor relations and
the basis for public policy toward labor under all subsequent
Administrations. The board and other government agencies im-
plicitly recognized the right of workers to bargain collectively
through representatives of their own choosing. To give guts to
this policy, the board held that workers were not to be discharged

or subject to any discrimination because of union membership. Furthermore, union rates were to be paid where they had been customary in the past and a "living wage" was to be applicable to all workers; in fixing wages, reads a World War I directive, "minimum rates of pay will be established which will insure the subsistence of the worker and his family in health and reasonable comfort." The eight-hour day was to be recognized where the law required it and to be settled in other cases "with due regard to government necessities and the welfare, health and proper comfort of the workers." Finally, strikes and lockouts were to be abandoned as means of achieving union or employer goals. Enforcement, since the board foreswore compulsory arbitration, depended upon government and public suasion, which was effective enough during the war. In almost every instance, the decision of the War Labor Board—a tripartite board consisting of labor, management and public members—was accepted without either strikes or lockouts.

Yet, the recognition so readily afforded the unions by the government was not extended by industry. By and large, the board's policy turned on the simple extension of the *status quo*, with the exception of the railroads. Here government operation resulted in the direct extension of trade unionism, since the government as employer in this instance gave full official recognition to collective bargaining. In the coal industry, which also fell under government administration, the union was already well established; the government merely solidified an existing arrangement. Steel, though a basic industry, remained non-union and a stronghold of the open shop. The government's favorable labor policy was of no help to the unions in this vital industry. Nonetheless, by the end of the war, the AFL had reached the permanency and strength to give weight to President Wilson's remark, made some years earlier at the dedication of the AFL Building in Washington, that no future President would be able to ignore the organized labor movement.

There was another side of the Wilsonian coin, however: In the future, no union could afford to ignore the federal government.

As the nation returned to normalcy with Warren Gamaliel Harding, the value of even the limited protection afforded to organized labor by the Wilson Administration became painfully clear. With the liquidation of the various "pro-labor" wartime agencies and the restraints of wartime patriotism severed, the number of strikes and lockouts increased slowly from 1.2 million workers involved in 1918 to 4.1 million in 1919. The postwar strike wave lasted four years, involved nearly 8.5 million workers, and ended in total defeat for organized labor. Justice Louis D. Brandeis once remarked, "Europe was devastated by war, we by the aftermath." Nowhere was this more true than of the labor movement.

Certainly, this ran contrary to the expectations engendered by the "war to end war." "Democracy is infectious," a *New Republic* editorial proclaimed in 1917. "It is now as certain as anything human can be that the war. . . will dissolve into democratic revolution the world over." Nor was America to be exempt. For did not President Wilson cable from Paris, in May, 1919, to a special session of Congress, a call to "a new organization of industry," a "genuine democratization of industry," and a "cooperation and partnership based upon a real community of interest and participation in control"? A special mention was made of the rights of workers to share "in some organic way in every decision" that affected their welfare. True, these vague formulations fitted the corporate welfarism of George W. Perkins and the company unions spawned by the Rockefeller Industrial Representation Plan as well as the craft unionism of the AFL. But it was also a promise of a new era for labor, or so unionists believed.

Nothing is won without struggle and the unions really wanted nothing more than that their struggle should be given an even break. The beginnings were auspicious enough to suit the AFL. The slump that followed the end of the war lasted only three months. The expansion of the auto industry sparked growth throughout basic sectors of the economy—steel, machine tools, petroleum, rubber, roads, and public construction. The output per manhour in industry was to rise about 40 percent during the 1920s. The initial burst of prosperity helped to bring union membership to a peak in 1920 and the first few strikes of the postwar period ended in victory for the unions. Sixty thousand clothing workers won the 44-hour week. Building, printing, and metal trades workers soon scored a similar success. A textile strike in Lawrence, Massachusetts, won the 48-hour week and a 15-percent wage hike.

But there were ominous notes. In February, 1919, a shipyard strike of 32,000 in Seattle, Washington sparked a general strike. A labor guard patrolled the city streets, and a workers' council representing the 110 unions involved dominated all phases of city life. But the movement was soon brutally smashed.

In August, a group of deputy "peace officers" rushed a mine workers' picket line at West Natrona, Pennsylvania, outside an Allegheny Coal and Coke Company mine. One striker was mortally wounded. Fannie Sellins, a 49-year-old grandmother, mother of a son killed in France, and a United Mine Workers' organizer moved out of danger some children who were playing nearby. She then ran back to plead with the officers, who were still clubbing an unconscious picket, to let up. One officer hit her on the head; she fell, tried to escape. Someone shouted, "Kill that goddamn whore!" Three shots were fired; then a final shot in the head and Fannie Sellins lay still. An eyewitness reported that another deputy "picked up her hat placed it on his head, danced a step, and said to the crowd, 'I'm Fannie Sellins now.'" Despite a plethora of witnesses, no one was ever punished for the murder. The mood of that fall in Seattle was captured by John Dos Passos in his novel *1919:* "The wobblies whose leaders were in jail, in Seattle whose leaders had been lynched, who'd been shot down like dogs, in Seattle the wobblies lined four blocks as Wilson passed, stood silent with their arms folded staring at the great liberal as he was hurried past in his car, huddled in his overcoat, haggard with fatigue, one side of his face twitching. The men in overalls, the workingstiffs let him pass in silence after all the other blocks of handclapping and patriotic cheers."

It was the great steel strike that began on September 22, 1919, that marked the end of labor's wartime fortunes, underscored the weakness of the protection afforded labor by the Wilson Administration, and encouraged an employer offensive that set back the labor movement for a generation.

Steel was the one major industry where the wartime blessings of the federal government had done labor little or no good. U. S. Steel's opposition to unions remained adamant. "Our corporation and subsidiaries," declared Judge Elbert H. Gary, chairman of U. S. Steel, in refusing to meet with an AFL committee shortly before the strike began, "although they do not combat labor unions as such, decline to discuss business with them." The country's largest corporation, he added stands "for the 'open shop,' which permits one to engage in any line of employment whether one does or does not belong to a labor union." To enforce the open shop, union men were fired, blacklisted throughout the industry. Gary denied that this was the case. But President Buffington of the Illinois Steel Company was more frank: "We don't discharge a man for belonging to a union, but of course we discharge men for agitating in the mills."

Agitation in the steel mills began before the war ended. Hours were long; 60 percent of the industry's employees worked a 12-hour day, while in nearby unionized mines, the eight-hour day and 44 hour week were standard. Wages for the semi- and unskilled were low although the industry boasted of high wages and a fully developed welfare program. This aspect of steel labor policy was designed to bind the highly skilled, English-speaking minority to the companies. Others—the overwhelming majority—were not so fortunate. The situation of a Polish steel worker, with eight children, who applied to the Pittsburgh Red Cross for relief, is a case in point. The minimum budget set up by the Home Service Division of the Red Cross for this family was $180.75 a month. With three members of the family employed earning a total of $143 a month in normal times, they could not make ends meet. A Commission of Inquiry set up by the Interchurch World Movement found steel wages to be inadequate to sustain a minimum of comfort—set at annual earnings of $2,024 in 1919—for 72 percent of the steel workforce. As for the unskilled, who alone made up 38 percent of the industry, their annual earnings fell below the budget for minimum subsistence—$1,456 a year in 1919. The average annual earnings of skilled labor in steel, significantly, was above the minimum for comfort. The corporate welfare program was similarly suspect. Stock subscriptions turned on "loyal service"; pensions could be severed at will for "misconduct"; and employees turned out of company houses if they dared strike or question management's right to manage in any way.

Encouraged by the War Labor Board's forthright defense of collective bargaining, moved by signs of discontent among the nation's steel workers, and stimulated by organizing successes elsewhere, chiefly among the packinghouse workers in Chicago, the American Federation of Labor began to prepare a steel organization campaign in 1918. Union strategists also believed that the industry would be unable and unwilling to suspend production—to sustain a lockout to defeat unionism—because immediate profits were too tempting. (U. S. Steel profits in 1917 alone amounted to over $253,608,200.) The initial impetus to organize steel came from the Chicago Federation of Labor, then a militant center of union activity flushed with the recent packinghouse successes. The chief tactician was William Z. Foster, then a general organizer for the Brotherhood of Railway Carmen. Foster, a first-class organizer, was born in Taunton, Massachusetts, in 1881. He started work as a sculptor's apprentice at the age of ten and, before becoming a labor skate, served at one time or another as a type founder, factory worker, steam engineer, steam fitter, railroad brakeman, fireman, logger, salesman, streetcar motorman, longshoreman, and farmer. He joined the IWW before the war and became a leading proponent of syndicalism. Later he joined the Communist Party, ending his life as that rather tragic figure, an American radical caught in the coils of a totalitarian ideology. But in 1918 he was back within the folds of union orthodoxy and ready to storm the strongest anti-union citadel in the country.

Foster believed he had an answer to the craft rivalry that had proven to be a stumbling block to the organization of steel. The Chicago Federation sent him to the St. Paul convention of the AFL to request an immediate AFL "conference of delegates of all international unions whose interests are involved in the steel industries, and of all State Federations and City Central bodies in the steel districts, for the purpose of uniting all these organizations into one mighty drive to organize the steel plants of America." The essence of the plan, Foster wrote later, "was quick, energetic action." The idea, he added, "was to make a hurricane drive simultaneously in all the steel centers that would catch the workers' imagination and sweep them into the unions en masse despite all opposition, and thus to put Mr. Gary and his associates into such a predicament that they would have to grant the just demands of their men." Unfortunately for the timing of the steel drive, the AFL wasn't so easily moved. Foster's proposal was accepted but the conference itself was put off for 30 days. On August 1, 1918, a National Committee for Organizing Iron and Steel Workers was formed, composed of the representatives of 24 participating unions. John Fitzpatrick, president of the Chicago Federation of Labor, was elected chairman and Foster, secretary-treasurer. Though funds were few and slow to come in, the drive got underway in September. Aware of the difficulty of tackling Pittsburgh, home of the industry, the Committee decided to encircle the steel center with organized districts. Union organizers appeared in Youngstown, Cleveland, Buffalo, Sharon, Johnstown, and Wheeling. Earlier successes in Gary, South Chicago, Hammond, and Joliet prompted the industry to extend the basic eight-hour day and other minor concessions. In early 1919, the drive moved on Pittsburgh.

At the next convention of the AFL, Fitzpatrick was able to

report the unionization of 100,000 steel workers. Encouraged by this, the convention instructed President Gompers to request a meeting with steel company officials. The companies remained officially silent, while making their answer plain enough in the mills by the discharge of union militants. The pressure for a strike grew. A month-long poll of the 100,000 organized workers showed a 98-percent vote for a strike. Again and again, representatives of the organized steel workers sought meetings with company officials. Rebuffed, they requested that Gompers ask President Wilson to try to arrange a conference. Gompers appealed to the President, but in vain. Reluctantly, the steel organizing committee set a strike date. Suddenly, there appeared a request from President Wilson that the strike be postponed until after a meeting of an Industrial Conference that had been called for October 9 in Washington. Gompers joined the President in his request for a deferment of action.

Nonplussed, the steel workers' committee delayed in making a decision. Meanwhile, the pressure for a strike grew apace. Discharges for union activity increased sharply, and the organizing committee feared that postponement would cause the effort of a year to be dissipated in scattered and futile strikes. On September 18, the committee wrote: "Mr. President, delay is no longer possible. We have tried to find a way out but cannot. . . . This strike is not at the call of the leaders, but that of the men involved." On September 22, 1919, some 275,000 steel workers quit work. The strike was on. Before the month was out, some 300,000 to 350,000 were out on strike. Foster estimated that the strike was then 90-percent effective.

What President Wilson had in mind when he requested postponement until the October Industrial Conference is not known. At the conference of representatives of capital, labor, and the public, Gompers made a bid for arbitration of the steel strike. This modest proposal was defeated through the efforts of Judge Gary, who was present as a public member of all things.

Soon, with all the excitability and brutality of Cossacks, company police and state troopers were riding down steel-worker picket lines. Since so many of the nation's 400,000 steel workers were recent immigrants, speaking many tongues, industry propagandists diligently spread the idea that the strike was un-American. During the strike, an old pamphlet by Foster proposing syndicalism was revived and circulated. Foster protested that he had long since changed his ideas and offered to resign from the strike committee. But this was rejected by the committee. Because of the "U. S." in the title of the chief steel corporation, the immigrant strikers were encouraged by company propagandists to believe the company was an arm of the federal government and, therefore, the strike was in reality a rebellion against the government.

The jails were jammed with strikers. Terror ruled the steel towns. From Pittsburgh to Clairton, twenty-five miles along the banks of the Monongahela, 125,000 men were under arms. The deputy police at Braddock, Pennsylvania attacked a funeral procession from ambush, clubbing the mourners into flight. Mounted policemen rode down children on their way home from school; the parishioners of a Catholic priest sympathetic to the strike were mercilessly clubbed one Sunday after leaving services. Industrial spies whispered stories of Italian defections into Serbian ears and of Serbian back-to-work movements into Italian ears. In mid-October giant posters appeared on steel town streets proclaiming the failure of the strike and with a giant Uncle Sam, finger pointing at the looker from over the smoke of a steel mill, shouting, "Go Back to Work," "*Idite Natrag Na Posado,*" "*Chodte Nazad do Boboty,*" etc. in seven different languages. Negro strikebreakers were imported, in an effort to fan the flames of racism and break striker morale.

Slowly, the companies broke the backbone of the strike. Terrified workers began to drift back to the mills. The successful suppression of all civil rights in the steel towns prevented the union from reaching the strikers with the truth about the state of the strike. Finally, ancient jealousies began to disrupt the strike leadership. The AFL contributed little in the way of cash, the 24 unions involved still less. Outside unions were more generous: the International Ladies' Garment Workers' Union contributed $60,-000 and the non-affiliated Amalgamated Clothing Workers $100,000 to the strike fund. But various participating unions began to quarrel over the disposition of the members. Too much time and energy were dissipated by strike leaders in efforts to conciliate differences and maintain harmony. In the end, disharmony prevailed; the Amalgamated Association of Iron, Steel and Tin Workers all but defected altogether, ordering its members back to work shortly after the strike began in many plants, on the grounds it had contracts to observe. Later, it was discovered that the companies had managed to reach some of the officers of the 24 strike-participating unions and, therefore, were privy to union strategy and able to foment discord.

An attempt was made to mediate the strike by leading churchmen. But, in the end the strike collapsed. On January 8, 1920, it was called off. The workers had sustained 20 deaths, wage losses between $86,000,000 and $112,000,000, in a three-and-one-half-month battle over nine states and involving more than 300,000 workers. The companies had won.

"The United States Steel Corporation," the Interchurch Commission of Inquiry summed up, "was too big to be beaten by 300,000 workmen. It had too large a cash surplus, too many allies among other businesses, too much support from government officers, local and national, too strong influence with social institutions such as the press and the pulpit, it spread over too much of the earth—still retaining absolutely centralized control—to be defeated by widely scattered workers of many minds, many fears, varying states of pocketbook and under a comparatively improvised leadership. The 'independent' steel companies gave the Corporation solid speechless support; not a spokesman was heard but Mr. Gary."

# XII

## *THE AMERICAN PLAN*

WITH THE GOVERNMENT NOW FOLLOWING A HANDS-OFF LABOR relations policy, belligerent employers eagerly went after the unions. The successful smashing of the steel strike of 1919 marked the beginning of four years of intensive union busting that ended in 1924 with a visibly shaken labor movement. Taking advantage of the hysteria left over from World War I, employers linked their drive for the open shop to Americanism. The open shop, they said, would give "equal opportunity for all and special privileges for none." National Association of Manufacturers' president John Edgerton in 1923 solemnly declared: "I can't conceive of any principle that is more purely American, that comes nearer representing the very essence of all those traditions and institutions that are dearest to us than the open-shop principle."

These traditions found ironic expression in the mutilated body of ex-soldier Wesley Everest turning beneath a bridge in the glare of auto headlights near Centralia, Washington. Everest was a lumberjack who had the temerity to believe that he and his fellow Wobblies had a right to defend their hall from armed invaders.

He was mutilated by a respectable businessman and hanged by the best elements in town interested in keeping the lumber camps open shop.

The murder of Everest was not an isolated event, though it was on the extreme of a spectrum of terror that ran from the cowing of individual workmen with the so-called yellow-dog contract to the gunrunning of strikebreakers past indignant picket lines. On December 10, 1917, the United States Supreme Court, in the *Hitchman Coal Company* v. *Mitchell* case, held that an individual contract not to join a union was valid, that inducement to join a union was a breach of contract, and that the right to strike was not a right to instigate a strike. While the government held an upper hand as industry's chief customer, the Hitchman decision was, so to speak, held in abeyance. But once industry was freed of governmental restraint, the decision that legalized the yellow-dog contract became the chief weapon in the anti-union arsenal of the 1920s. Before getting a job, the prospective employee had to sign an agreement that he would not, while employed, join a union or attempt to organize his fellows. Sanctified by law, the yellow-dog contract enabled employers to seek injunctions barring violations of contract. Thus, all strikes where yellow-dog contracts existed became illegal; if they continued, they became strikes against the government itself. Open shops, in reality, became closed non-union shops, where a union member who acknowledged his affiliation was either discharged or denied employment.

Workingmen, however, clung to their unions. But no more willing to commit economic suicide than anyone, they frequently signed yellow-dog contracts with crossed fingers. The spread of the yellow-dog contract, first prominent in the New England textile industry in the 1870s, to coal, hosiery, street-railway, and shoe industries in the 1920s did not lessen industrial strife. Despite court enforcement of the yellow-dog contract, employers obviously needed another string to their anti-union bow. As union activity of necessity became more secret, industrial espionage became widespread in American industry during the twenties. Private detective agencies serving a heady industrial cocktail—one part spy, four parts strikebreaker—flourished like speakeasies across the land, "the biggest lot of blackmailing thieves that ever went unwhipped of justice," according to detective William J. Burns. One AFL official estimated that there were 200,000 spies at work in 1928. The annual income of the three leading agencies during the decade was estimated at $65,000,000. Pearl Bergoff, chief of a leading strikebreaking agency, charged the Erie Railroad $2,000,000 to smash the 1920 switchman's strike. The introduction of armed hoods as "finks" (strikebreakers) or as "nobles" (armed guards) by industry facilitated the entry of the Arnold Rothsteins and Al Capones into the lucrative business of industrial racketeering.

The missionary work on behalf of the open shop—and incidentally on behalf of the industrial spies—was carried on by proliferating employer associations. By late 1920, New York had over 50 organizations dedicated to propagandizing the open shop; Illinois, 46; Michigan, 23; and Connecticut, 18; with other states following suit. In January, 1921, 22 state organizations met in Chicago to draw the assorted local bodies together under the so-called American Plan.

The Plan by any standard, perhaps excepting the unions', was a smashing success. To take one example: The tactics of the American Plan were taken up by the National Metal Trades Association, boosting the income of the employers' group, from dues and initiation fees, from $127,696 in 1918 to $541,236 in 1921 as employers eagerly sought the blacklisting, spy, and strikebreaking services offered by the Association. NMTA's effectiveness can be measured against the precipitous decline in the membership of the International Association of Machinists, chief union in the industry, from 330,800 in 1920 to 77,900 in 1924.

The Machinists' loss was only one example of the general rout suffered by labor during what was a disastrous decade for workingmen. The wartime gains of the Meat Cutters in the packinghouses of Chicago were wiped out in 1921. Belligerent employers crushed the Seamen's strike of the same year. In 1920, the United Mine Workers was the largest union in the country, with a membership of 500,000 and with over 60 percent of the miners organized. The coal depression and internal feuds over the decade eroded the union away to less than half that size. Gangsters and communists racked the garment unions, especially in New York, crippling their growth. By 1929, the anticommunist, though still radical, leadership of the International Ladies' Garment Workers' Union had saved but a shadow of their former selves from ruin at the hands of the communists. The ILGWU was penniless and had barely 32,000 members.

Union membership in the entire nation, according to Leo Wolman, peaked at 5,047,800 in 1920. By 1923, it was down to 3,622,000. Thereafter, it drifted steadily downward to 2.9 million in 1933. In 1920, union membership constituted 19.4 percent of nonagricultural employees; in 1930, the percentage dropped to a scant 10.2. The expanding auto industry, the backbone of 1920s' prosperity, fended off unionization with little difficulty. An abortive effort at organizing the auto workers in 1926 ended in the usual quarrel over jurisdiction, saving the employers the trouble of having to meet the unions head on. Only a bare trace of craft organization could be found in the electrical equipment, rubber, cement, textiles, chemical, and food industries. There were no effective unions in the oil or nonferrous mining industries. The Mine, Mill and Smelter Workers, heir to Big Bill Haywood's Western Federation of Miners, had all but disintegrated. Unions were nearly unheard of in banking, insurance, the retail and wholesale trades, and utilities, not to mention the professions and domestic and personal services.

The American Federation of Labor's response to this setback was anything but encouraging. Its only fling at militancy during the decade was the halfhearted support and endorsement given to the 1924 Progressive Presidential campaign of Senator Robert M. LaFollette. Faced with a choice between Coolidge and John W. Davis, J. P. Morgan's counsel, the unions turned to the nominee of the newly formed Progressive Party. Backed by reformers, socialists and the unions, the Wisconsin champion of the public welfare rolled up an impressive vote for a third party. He carried Wisconsin, beat out Davis in ten other states, and racked up a total of 4.8 million votes. But that wasn't enough for the AFL, or the railway brotherhoods, who were old in leadership and somewhat hidebound as a result. The unions soon after the election withdrew their support of the new political venture.

The exception to the general decline of organized labor is found in the craft unions, especially in the building trades, which actually grew from 789,500 in 1923 to 919,000 in 1929; and the printing trades, which showed a smaller increase of 150,900 to 162,500. In the building trades the unions held their own by superior muscle, maintaining control over the supply of labor in local product markets. They were not adverse to the use of dynamite, and racketeering frequently flourished alongside the business-as-usual unionism of the building trades.

The railroad Brotherhoods were another exception. Their decline in membership was a modest one, from 596,600 in 1923 to 564,600 in 1929. The Brotherhoods were already firmly established in the industry when the federal government seized the railroads during World War I. The government directly fostered collective bargaining and established a system of national adjustment boards for the hearing of grievances and the settlement of disputes. When the railroads were transferred back to private hands in 1920, Congress made provision for continuing the system, with final appeal of a dispute lodged with a Railway Labor Board. However, the rail strikes of 1921 and 1922 undermined the authority of the Board, and the unions began to push for its abolition. Nonetheless, the need for some mechanism for resolving disputes remained clear to both the unions and rail management. A series of conferences were held between railway executives and union officials that ultimately resulted in the Railway Labor Act of 1926.

This Act, with amendments, served the industry reasonably

well until recently. Collective bargaining was institutionalized. Employees were guaranteed the right to pick representatives of their own choosing, a right later upheld in the courts in the Texas & New Orleans case. Later a National Railway Adjustment Board was created to hear and settle grievances under existing agreements. A mediation system was established, voluntary arbitration provided for, and an emergency disputes procedure set up. A National Mediation Board was set up to handle disputes concerning representation, bargaining units, and contract terms. If mediation failed, the Railway Labor Act called for arbitration. And as a last resort the President may appoint an emergency board of three members to hear the dispute and make recommendations. There can be no strikes or lockouts for 60 days after the President appoints the Board. However, Board recommendations are not binding and the unions are free to strike after the 60-day period ends. The rail unions, unlike the rest, were thus recognized as a legitimate part of the industry, junior partners if not co-equals with rail management.

The AFL did not fare so well as the railroad Brotherhoods, although it retained enough influence as a Washington lobby to be of help to the Brotherhoods in passing the Railway Labor Act. Sam Gompers died on December 13, 1924, and the leadership of the Federation fell into the more complaisant hands of William Green. The choice was an historical accident, but apt. When Gompers died, Matthew Woll, a confirmed craft unionist who was considered "crown prince" of the Federation, made his bid for the AFL's top spot. But he was opposed by the leaders of two powerful AFL affiliates, the Carpenters and the Miners. Green was the compromise candidate, acceptable to a group of labor curmudgeons who wanted to lead, rather than be led as they were by Gompers.

Green was born on March 3, 1872, of an English coal miner and his Welsh bride, in Coshocton, Ohio. Reared on Hardscrabble Hill, he soon absorbed his father's union philosophy and at sixteen, lacking the money to follow his religious bent into the Baptist ministry, he entered the mines. He liked to recall that he once taught the largest Baptist Bible class in Coshocton. Something of a joiner, he was a proud Elk, Odd Fellow, and Mason. Articulate, though pompous—Westbrook Pegler once unkindly called him the "All-American mushmouth"—he gradually rose through the hierarchy of the United Mine Workers from local secretary to president of the strategic Ohio district of the union, and, later, statistician for the International. He served in the Ohio Senate for two terms (in 1911–15) as a Democrat, sponsoring the basic workmen's compensation act of Ohio. In 1913, he was elected secretary-treasurer of the UMW and a short time later became a vice-president of the AFL.

Green was to give voice to the AFL's drift toward respectability and to its desire for cooperation with industry during the latter half of the 1920s. Although the many years spent in the mine left their marks on his complexion—blue spots deep beneath the skin—he had the air of a small-town businessman. He wore a heavy gold watch chain across an ample midsection and conservative, well-tailored clothes. Kind eyes crinkled behind a pair of steel-rimmed glasses on a somewhat cherubic face. A decent and humane man with a warm sympathy for the oppressed, Green could not command the respect of his tough-minded peers. As Benjamin Stolberg caustically noted: "He can continue to lead the American Federation of Labor as long as he follows the hard men on its Executive Council—Tobin, Duffy, Rickert, Woll . . . they all tested his strength. They found him weak. They are for him." Green shunned conflict and was hard put to live up even to his own modest leadership aspirations, "to find a basis of accommodation, harmonize conflicting opinions, to settle differences which arise, not among enemies, if you please, but among the family, of organized labor." William Green, as historian Arthur Schlesinger aptly put it, "brought the Harding virtues to the leadership of American labor."

Increasingly, trade unions were to be justified on the grounds that they would "increase production, eliminate waste, and maintain continuity of service." Perhaps drawing on its wartime experience, when the unions sold themselves to the government on exactly those terms, the AFL began to woo big business in like fashion. The new respectable posture called for cooperation with capital. The unions, too, wanted to preserve the *status quo:* workers were not to organize, wrest their own way from recalcitrant employers. Unions were to be recognized by enlightened employers, who were to stand with the unions as upholders of existing order and staunch opponents of Bolshevism. "More and more," declared Green in 1925, "organized labor is coming to believe that its best interests are promoted through concord rather than by conflict." Unions, he added, "will increasingly concern themselves to see that management policies are efficient. Unless management is efficient, labor standards cannot keep advancing."

The minor growth of labor banking in the 1920s illustrates the strange *cul-de-sacs* union thinking lodged in during the decade. The first labor bank opened in Washington on May 15, 1920. It was launched by the officers of the International Association of Machinists. But the big push in labor banking came from the Brotherhood of Locomotive Engineers, which opened its Co-operative National Bank later the same year in Cleveland, Ohio. The Brotherhood retained 51 percent of the original capital stock and sold the rest to members of the union. Dividends of ten percent were announced. The bank received wide publicity and within a few months deposits hit the $1,000,000 mark. Four years later, deposits were more than $26,000,000.

Warren Stone, the grand chief of the Brotherhood, was a labor bank enthusiast. His ideas and energy and the success of the Cleveland bank generated much of the excitement about labor banking during the 1920s. Enthusiasts saw the labor bank as a means of mobilizing the financial resources of working people in order to extend union power. Employers of union help were to receive financial aid from the banks. Labor bank funds were to be used to finance and control certain basic industries. Stone was so enthusiastic that he declared that the strike was a thing of the past. And many believed him.

Interest in labor banks mushroomed. The New York State Federation of Labor, the Brotherhood of Railway Clerks, the International Printing Pressmen's and Assistants' Union, the Order of Railroad Telegraphers, the American Flint Glass Workers' Union, the International Ladies' Garment Workers' Union, and the Amalgamated Clothing Workers experimented with sponsoring and owning banks. The Brotherhood of Locomotive Engineers alone sponsored eleven banks during the late 1920s. By the time the labor bank movement reached its peak in 1926, there were 36 labor banks with combined resources of more than $126,000,000.

The decline of labor banking, however, was just as precipitous as its rise. The stock market crash of 1929 unhinged the labor banks just as badly as it did the regular banks. Only four labor banks reopened their doors after the crash. Two have since folded, leaving the Amalgamated Clothing Workers' banks of New York and Chicago as the sole survivors of the labor bank era.

The American Federation of Labor's ventures into labor education were less subject to economic fluctuations than the unions' dream of banking glory but no less doomed. In the early 1920s, a group of labor intellectuals and educators (among them historian Charles Beard and his wife, Mary) organized the Workers' Education Bureau. At first the Federation welcomed the Bureau and its efforts warmly. In 1923 an agreement was worked out that gave the AFL control over the Bureau's executive committee. An intensive program of teaching and publishing was launched. Universities, notably the University of California, were encouraged to give special classes for trade unionists. Economics, history, parliamentary procedure and other subjects were tailored to fit the needs of workingmen. But soon protests could be heard in the wings against the independence of the Bureau's staff and activities. Crusty Andrew Furuseth of the Seamen complained that the books published by the Bureau took a viewpoint opposite to that held by the Federation. Soon the educators and the labor bureaucrats were at odds. Ultimately, the differences were resolved when the Bureau was swallowed up by the AFL as a regular department. Safely digested, official worker education became intellectually tame stuff and soon faded into the background.

The fate of Brookwood College, labor's only venture in full-time education, was much more honorable. But then there was never much cordiality exchanged between labor officialdom and the radical workers' two-year college. Located at Katonah, New York, in Westchester County, Brookwood was founded in 1921 by A. J. Muste, an ex-Dutch Reform minister who went to preach to the Lawrence textile strikers in 1919 and, much to his own astonishment, found himself leading a successful strike. Shrewd and visionary, Muste had a pretty good idea of what a workers' college should be. While his students were to remove themselves to "a peaceful, pastoral setting, away from the feverish and exhausting struggle in the factories, mills and mines," they were not to absent themselves from the concerns and doings of the labor movement. When several students and instructors in 1926 joined John Brophy's effort to "Save the Union" from John L. Lewis, trouble for Brookwood from the AFL officers was inevitable. The Federation ordered an investigation by Matthew Woll, not the most sympathetic of men toward workers' education, and subsequently, in 1928, requested that national and international unions withhold financial support. Nonetheless, Brookwood managed to survive until 1937, when a lack of funds finally forced it to close its doors. Over the years, Brookwood trained an impressive number of people who played a leading role in the founding of the Congress of Industrial Organizations and have since filled many positions of leadership in the unions. Among them were two Reuther brothers, Victor and Roy, Julius Hochman, a vice-president of the International Ladies' Garment Workers' Union, Rose Pesotta, an ILGWU organizer active in the Akron sit-downs, and Clinton S. Golden, who with other Brookwood graduates was active in the founding of the Steelworkers.

Meanwhile, along with pretty near everybody else, the AFL stood pat with Herbert Hoover, awaiting "the day when poverty will be banished from this nation." Though prices rose rapidly enough during the late 1920s, wages remained fairly stable, reflecting the weakness of the unions. Between 1923 and 1929, output per man-hour in manufacturing rose by 32 percent, while hourly wages rose by a little over eight percent. A National Industrial Conference Board survey shows weekly earnings advancing from $26.54 in 1923 to $28.24 in 1929; average hourly earnings moved from 54 cents to 58.1 cents over the same period. At the same time, regional differences were markedly disparate; the common labor rate in basic steel, for example, ranged from 27.09 cents in the South to 45.6 cents in the Great Lakes district in 1929.

And, like some uneasy whispering from the underground, the discontents of the unemployed were heard in the charities. "My experience," Samuel Insull, the utility magnate, once noted, "is that the greatest aid to efficiency of labor is a long line of men waiting at the gate." There were many men doing just that. The absence of government statistics makes it impossible to report the actual number, but informed guesses make it clear that the prosperity of the twenties was accompanied by heavy unemployment. Technological change displaced a growing number of workers. Some economists estimate that unemployment as a percentage of the labor force never fell below ten percent from 1925 to 1929. More conservative estimates place the percentage floor at better than six percent.

Clearly, something was wrong. But few discerned the economic difficulties until the stock market tumbled in October, 1929. Yet, a report that summer in the mill towns of the Southern Appalachian Piedmont—Henderson, Elizabethton, Gastonia, Marion, Danville—foreshadowed for those who cared to listen, the mid-thirties' uprising of the industrial worker. The wave of strikes that flashed down the Piedmont like a spring freshet were spontaneous protests against low wages, long hours, and the stretch-out, or speedup. At first, the "lintheads," as Southern mill hands were called by their contemptuous employers, were not concerned with the right to organize, or to bargain collectively. But soon after a walkout started, the lintheads called for help. Two unions—the AFL United Textile Workers and the communist-led independent National Textile Workers' Union—hurriedly answered the call. The efforts of both unions were countered by employer-sponsored violence.

Admittedly, textile employers were hard-pressed. They had come South to avoid high wages. The cost of manufacture, according to the Mitchells, in a typical Southern mill was 16.8 percent less than in a typical Massachusetts mill, a difference of $6.73 a spindle, of which $4.53 was due to a saving in labor costs. In 1927, average weekly earnings were $19.16 in the four leading New England states and $12.83 in the four leading Southern states. The Southern mill hands, fresh from the surrounding farms and with a much lower standard of living, found even these low wages attractive at first. But soon after the move South, the industry was seriously depressed. Japan captured vital markets overseas, while at home changes in fashion along with the introduction of rayon cut into the demand for cotton cloth. Hard-pressed by overproduction and ruinous competition, the cotton mill operators turned to the stretch-out to effect labor savings. Under the stretch-out, workers were given additional machines to care for without a commensurate increase in pay. Weavers were stretched from 24 to 48 looms and up to 96 looms.

As W. J. Cash notes in his *Mind of the South*, the stretch-out "violated the whole tradition of the South." Wrenched out of their easygoing ways, Southerners were put under sharp-eyed Yankees with their ever-present stop watches. It was too much.

The 1929 strike wave began at Happy Valley, near Elizabethton, Tennessee, where 3,000 American Glanztoff Corporation employees walked off the job and demanded a wage increase in line with a nearby plant owned by the same firm. Called upon for assistance, the United Textile Workers sent a Brookwood-trained organizer, Alfred Hoffman, to do the job. An injunction brought out the other plant in sympathy and soon after, the strike ended in what was apparently a victory. But soon union members complained of discrimination. AFL troubleshooter Edward F. McGrady reported that the company had discharged more than 300 for union activity despite promises to the contrary. McGrady and Hoffman were kidnapped by a group of armed men, taken across the state line with warnings not to return. However, they ignored the warning and returned to file charges. Five prominent businessmen were arrested but were never brought to trial. A short time later the two plants walked out again in protest against the discharge of union members serving on a grievance committee. State troops were brought in; violence erupted; some 1,250 strikers were arrested for violating an injunction against picketing.

Ultimately, the United States Labor Department intervened and managed to mediate a settlement. But the management once again launched an attack on the union. UTW members were fired, a company union was promoted along with a paternalist welfare program. The union was whipped.

Happy Valley, however, was but a curtain raiser for the events at Gastonia and Marion, North Carolina. Gastonia is of particular interest because of the role played by the communists. On January 1, 1929, a stocky, tow-headed Yankee, Fred E. Beal, arrived in Gastonia, the combed-yarn center of the South. Disillusioned over the Sacco-Vanzetti case, he had turned to the Communist Party. The communist-led National Textile Workers' Union was only too happy to send him to Gastonia; Beal was an old textile hand himself and had a way with the mill workers. He soon had the nucleus of a union at the Loray Mill, the largest in the area, with 3,500 workers. Management, through a spy, soon uncovered the secret union and discharged five of its members. The next day both shifts hit the bricks and shut down the mill.

Once Loray management had rejected the trade-union demands of its employees, the communists were free to move in on the strike. Exploiting the grievances of the strikers and their hunger, the communists through their front organization, the Workers' International Relief, raised a good deal of money. But later, when the money was needed in the South for relief, it was found that the WIR was notably deficient in providing groceries, although voluble enough about fund-raising in the North. The strike began to break under the strain; pickets were unable to prevent strike-breakers from entering the mills and union headquarters was demolished by a band of masked men under the conveniently sleepy eyes of state troopers. The holdouts retreated to a tent city, where songstress Ella May Wiggins helped to keep up morale. Beal walked uneasy among the tents, surrounded by silent, armed mountain men.

On an early night in June, after a demonstration at shifttime had been dispersed by deputy sheriffs, Chief of Police O. F. Aderholt arrived at the tent colony with four officers and without warrant. A scuffle started with a union armed guard, shots rang out in the night air, and the five officers were wounded, Aderholt fatally. Beal and six other union leaders were arrested on a murder charge.

During the course of the trial of the seven NTWU leaders, Ella May Wiggins rode a truck to a union meeting. Vigilantes pumped a round of shots into the truck and the twenty-nine-year-old mother of five fell into the arms of wizened Charlie Shope, crying, "Lord amercy, they done and shot and killed me." The five Loray employees charged with the crime were acquitted despite the presence of witnesses. But Beal and his fellows were not so fortunate. Four, including Beal, received sentences of seventeen to twenty years; the rest, five to seven years. While out on bail, pending appeal, the seven fled to the Soviet Union.

Beal remained in the Soviet Union until 1933, when he could take Stalin's totalitarianism no longer. Back in the United States he went into hiding only to have his former comrades reveal his whereabouts to the police. He had made the mistake of telling the truth about the Soviet Union in a brief autobiography published in 1937. Jailed a year later he was pardoned in 1942 after intercession on his behalf by Norman Thomas, William Green and other labor leaders. He died in 1954 of a heart attack, a lonely forgotten man.

The events of Gastonia were repeated with variations in Marion, North Carolina, later in the summer of 1929. This time, however, the AFL United Textile Workers bore the brunt of the employer attack. Six strikers were killed, and 25 wounded before the strike ended in defeat for the workers and their union.

Chill winds blew across the Piedmont that winter. William Green went south, carrying the message of moderation to the mill owners without avail. The UTW, under the valiant leadership of Francis Joseph Gorman, attempted another sally south, tackling the Dan River mills in Danville, Virginia, only to go down before the Virginia National Guard. The defeat was compléte.

But men would remember and a new mood would descend on America. The winds of revolt that stirred the Piedmont in 1929 would soon sweep across the land. In 1933, the usually benign William Green told a Congressional Committee that if Congress did not enact a 30-hour law, labor would compel employers to grant it "by universal strike." The Senator from South Carolina, Hugo Black, leaned across the table: "Which would be class war, practically?"

"Whatever it would be," said Green, "it would be that. . . . That is the only language that a lot of employers ever understand—the language of force."

A new mood, indeed.

# XIII

## "THE RUBBISH" AT LABOR'S DOOR

FOR MOST AMERICANS, THE DEPRESSION BEGAN WITH THE CRASH of the stock market in 1929. The break came around noon on October, 24; by 2:30 the ticker tape was nearly two hours late. The blue-chip stocks—steel, telephone, copper—fell two, three, five and ten points between sales. Other stocks became unmarketable. That afternoon the heads of six leading banks met at Morgan's, each pledging $40,000,000 to cushion the market. Thomas W. Lamont, Morgan partner and spokesman for the "bankers' pool," informed newsmen, "It seems there has been some disturbed selling in the market." Five days later, it was all over. Panic-stricken, scrambling, yelling traders dumped 16.4 million shares on October 29 alone. The average prices of 50 leading stocks, as compiled by the *New York Times*, fell nearly 40 points. General Motors lost nearly two billion dollars in paper value. By the time Wall Street was able to take a weary breather a few weeks later, the stocks listed on the New York exchange had fallen over 40 percent in value— a paper loss of 26 billion dollars. No one yet has reckoned the psychological loss.

During the 1920s—"It was borrowed time anyhow," wrote F.

Scott Fitzgerald in 1931—the giddy ascendency of the stock market hid disconcerting economic and social weaknesses from the bemused eyes of a nation. "By 1927 a widespread neurosis began to be evident," Fitzgerald noted, in classmates committed to insane asylums and the suicide of contemporaries. There were other signs: the persistence of unemployment despite the boom and the weakness of the labor movement, although unions normally prosper as the economy prospers. The aging American Federation of Labor was unable to break the open shop and yellow-dog contracts prevailing in the expanding mass-production industries, with disastrous consequences for the labor movement and, possibly, for the American economy.

The stock market crash brought the rest of the economy down with a sharp tumble. Unemployment began to mount at the rate of 4,000 a week. In the White House, President Herbert Hoover manfully shut his eyes and blocked his ears and sought to reassure a shattered nation. "What this country needs," he told Raymond Clapper in February, 1931, "is a good, big laugh." While Hoover waited for what the country needed, national income, which had topped 87 billion dollars in 1929 tumbled to 41.7 billion dollars in 1932. Gross private domestic investment at 15.8 billion dollars in 1929 was down to 1.3 billion dollars in 1933. The Federal Reserve Board index of manufacturing production slid from 110 in 1929 to 57 in 1932. Wage payments collapsed from 50 billion dollars to 30 billion dollars. Unemployment rose—four million in 1930; 11 million in 1932, hitting a peak of nearly 13 million in 1933. In the Senate, John Nance "Cactus Jack" Garner seesawed between a desperate effort to balance the budget by a national sales tax and a 2.5-billion-dollar pump-priming public works measure. William Green informed a 1930 Congressional Committee that in Detroit "the men are sitting in the Parks all day long and all night long, hundreds and thousands of them, muttering to themselves, out of work, seeking work."

As hot winds blew over Washington's Anacostia Flats in the

summer of 1932, marchers of the Bonus Expeditionary Force sang:

> "Mellon pulled the whistle,
> Hoover rang the bell,
> Wall Street gave the signal
> —And the country went to Hell!

Even the nation's chief humorist began to talk of revolution. "Ours may be the first nation to go to the poorhouse in an automobile," cracked the crag-faced, rope-twirling, ex-cowpoke Will Rogers. But, he added, "you let this country go hungry and they are going to eat, no matter what happens to budgets, Income Taxes or Wall Street values. Washington mustn't forget who rules when it comes to a showdown."

Then came the legendary first hundred days of the administration of Franklin D. Roosevelt. "It's more than a New Deal," declared Harold Ickes. "It's a new world. People feel free again. They can breathe naturally. It's like quitting a morgue for the open woods." But even before the hundred days began on March 4, 1933, people had begun to act. Angry farmers spilled milk, leaving it to curdle on the cement highways; armed with rifles they held bids down to a dollar as frustrated sheriffs auctioned off foreclosed farms. The unemployed demonstrated, organized and marched, demanding relief. In Detroit, where 30–50 percent of the wage earners were out of work, the communists organized a "hunger march" on Ford's River Rouge plant in Dearborn. Gunfire from Ford's secret servicemen, headed by the notorious Harry Bennett, killed four men. Socialists and radicals of all persuasions organized unemployment councils. The unemployed began to pool resources. In Seattle, shoemakers, carpenters, tailors, laborers practiced their trades in return for surplus wood, fish, apples, and potatoes. Many of the self-help and barter groups in 30 states developed their own script money.

Three times as many workers struck in 1933 as in 1932, 812,000 as against 243,000. More, many more were to strike in 1934. Increasingly, the sole issue became union recognition.

Workingmen once again struggled against their fate, seeking a new way to achieve their needs and wants.

Even before the advent of the New Deal, the Norris-LaGuardia Act of 1932 freed the unions of injunctive restraints leveled by federal courts against boycotts, picketing, and strike action. Yellow-dog contracts were no longer enforceable in the federal courts. But the big lift for organization came from Sections 7a and 7b of the National Industrial Recovery Act enacted on June 16, 1933. The Recovery Act sought to foster industrial self-government under a National Recovery Administration and its famous Blue Eagle Codes. Section 7a guaranteed the right of collective bargaining and Section 7b imposed on the President the responsibility of encouraging "mutual agreements" between employers and employees on the "maximum hours of labor, minimum rates of pay, and other conditions of employment." Such agreements were to become parts of the NRA codes.

That summer, sound trucks bearing banners emblazoned, "The President wants *you* to unionize," invaded the coalfields of Kentucky, West Virginia, Pennsylvania, and Illinois as well as the garment centers of New York, Philadelphia, Cleveland, and Chicago. Within two months, the United Mine Workers added 300,000 members to its ranks; the International Ladies' Garment Workers' Union, 100,000; and the Amalgamated Clothing Workers, 50,000. The AFL executive council in 1934 reported with wonder: "Workers held mass meetings and sent word they wanted to be organized."

At the Philco Radio plant in Philadelphia, an ebullient twenty-one-year-old James B. Carey organized a Walking, Hunting, and Fishing Club. Before long the club transformed a company union into an independent organization. The new union asked for a contract; Carey and his fellows insisted that the NRA made collective bargaining national policy. The company dissented but agreed that word to that effect from NRA administrator, General Hugh S. Johnson would be satisfactory. The youthful unionists immediately piled into two old automobiles and rattled off to

Washington. On the way, they bought a newspaper and tore out a picture of the General. Once in Washington, door by door, they systematically searched the Commerce Building until they found a square-jawed face that fit the picture they carried. After outlining their case, Carey demanded, "Haven't we got law on our side?" Johnson agreed. "Well, then," said Carey, "sign your name; management won't take our word for it." The NRA administrator signed. The unionists returned to Philco and, buoyed by their triumph, swept management into a closed-shop agreement, a 36-hour week, and pay increases that ranged from 69 to 150 percent over the old rates.

For a time, it seemed as though America trembled on the verge of a new civil war. Most managements were not as complaisant, or wise, as Philco's. Employers reacted to the demand for union recognition by their employees with increasing violence. Barbed-wire fences and sandbag fortifications began to ring the plants of some of America's industrial giants. Citizens' Law and Order Associations sprang up, liberally financed by employers and well-armed. Through the streets of company towns swaggered hoods and thugs, sworn in as special deputies to uphold the law. From January 1934 to July 1936 General Motors spent $994,855.68 on an industrial spy system. From testimony before a subcommittee of the Senate Committee on Education and Labor, the so-called LaFollette Civil Liberties Committee, it was estimated that American industry spent at least $80,000,000 on labor spies and anti-union agents in 1936 alone. At the height of the strife-torn summer of 1934, special deputies shot two pickets in the back in Kohler, Wisconsin, a company town. Josephus Daniels, from North Carolina, wrote President Roosevelt, "Mill men put arms in the hands of the men in the mills and the Governor called out the State Guard, at the request of the owners. . . . In nearly every instance the troops might as well have been under the direction of the mill owners." So it went across the nation.

Workers scored a few victories at great cost. In Toledo, Ohio, tin-hatted National Guardsmen were mobilized one spring day to protect at bayonet point strikebreakers at the Electric Auto-Lite Company plant. Showered by beer bottles and bricks flung by indignant strikers, the guardsmen opened fire. Two people were killed and hundreds tear-gassed and wounded. The threat of a general strike, however, soon brought the company around. Federal mediation helped to work out a settlement pretty much on union terms.

A general strike, that is, a city-wide strike of all or mostly all workers achieved a similiar result for striking longshoremen in San Francisco. A strike of truck drivers, which all but choked off Minneapolis, also ended in a partial victory. Significantly, each one of these revolutionary strikes ended with federal intervention. The day had passed when workers' councils could hope, as did the Wobblies in Goldfield or the steel workers for a brief time at Homestead, to seize and govern a city. The San Francisco strike, which began on the docks and haphazardly spilled·over to paralyze a city, merely succeeded in provoking federal intervention. It folded within four days and the longshoremen accepted arbitration. The National Longshoremen's Board, set up under the auspices of the Blue Eagle, awarded the union recognition, raised longshore pay and shortened dockside hours. A hiring hall was established under the joint control of the employers and the union. A side effect of the strike was the establishment of Australian-born Harry Bridges and a communist leadership over the West Coast dockers. The dockers stuck to Bridges—as they have ever since—even though he had opposed accepting arbitration. Joseph P. ("The Waxer") Ryan, president of the International Longshoremen's Association, disavowed the strike altogether. Ryan, like most AFL leaders, was not having anything to do with "radicalism."

The Minneapolis truck strike is significant, not only because of the intransigent militancy of the strike leadership but also because out of it came the present power of the Teamsters' Union. Minneapolis, a communication and marketing center for Minnesota, Wisconsin, and the Dakotas, lies along the Mississippi River where it tumbles through a narrow gorge and over St. Anthony Falls. In 1934, it was a citadel of the open shop. A powerful Citizen's Alliance flourished. But with the arrival of the NRA and Section 7*a*, the city truck drivers began to organize under the leadership of Ray Dunne and his brothers, Miles and Grant. Ray had been a Wobbly, then a communist. He started out as a drayman for a lumber company, became too independent for the increasingly Stalin-dominated party, and was expelled in 1928 as a Trotskyite. A natural leader, Ray Dunne had the confidence of the Minneapolis drivers. His talent for union generalmanship evidenced itself as he and his aides deployed their forces in the truckers' conflict with the employers. The employers refused to meet with the union despite the Regional Labor Board's appeal that they do so. (This was one of the weaknesses of the NRA and the early National Labor Relations Board set up in 1934. It could recommend but could not enforce collective bargaining in the courts despite Section 7*a*.) The union, which had its own newspaper, sound trucks and its own hospital, struck on May 12, 1934. When the city's "better" elements volunteered to be sworn in as "special officers" and were armed with badges and guns, the truckers collected iron pipes and baseball bats.

On May 22, 1934, twenty thousand people gathered in Minneapolis' central marketplace. The armed deputies were determined to get the trucks rolling again, the strikers just as firm in their resolve not to let a wheel turn. After a period of uneasy waiting, there was a scuffle and the melee began. When the dust had settled, two special deputies, one the scion of a best family, lay dead amidst strikers cradling broken heads. Governor Floyd Olsen, though sympathetic to the striking truckers, had no choice. He mobilized the National Guard and forced an uneasy truce on the union and the employers. The communists accused Ray Dunne and his lieutenant, Farrell Dobbs, of selling out to the Alliance. But the strike leaders continued to negotiate in good faith until the employers, still hoping to smash the union, broke off talks. Trucks again stopped rolling.

The police sent out an armed convoy to escort a strikebreaker through the city streets. The unarmed strikers, countered, blocking the road with another truck. The police, armed with shotguns, without warning fired into the second truck and a gathering crowd. Sixty-seven were wounded, most shot through the back, and two were killed.

Class war threatened to throttle the city. Working with haste, federal mediators proposed a settlement. Governor Olsen declared that, unless the plan were accepted by both sides, he would declare martial law. The union agreed but the employers refused. The National Guard moved in on the embattled city. But this time the Guard was not used as a strikebreaking instrument on behalf of the employers. When the union balked at moving certain crucial trucking, the Governor ordered a raid of strike headquarters. But he followed through with a similar raid, two days later, on the Citizen's Alliance. Negotiations were resumed; slowly the employers, at first singly, then in groups, began to give way and signed up with the union on the basis of the federal mediators' plan. After four months of conflict, violence and death, the strikers secured, according to Dunne, "substantially what we have fought and bled for since the beginning." The workingmen and women of Minneapolis celebrated for 12 hours when the trucks again rolled.

Bolstered by their victory, the Dunne brothers and Dobbs began to extend the jurisdiction of their local. They did so over the opposition of Dan Tobin, then paladin of a relatively small Teamsters' union with scarcely 100,000 members. But Dobbs, head of the tiny Trotskyite Socialist Workers' Party, was, as Jimmy Hoffa once noted, "a far-seeing man. He used to talk by the hour about what was going to happen to this country, and we'd listen." One of the things Dobbs talked about was the growing importance of over-the-road long-distance trucking. To organize the over-the-road drivers, Dobbs and the Dunnes devised the simple stratagem of requiring that all drivers coming into Minneapolis terminals be union members. The Minneapolis Teamsters then organized a District Drivers' Council to coordinate the activities of teamsters locals throughout the region. They won the first uniform contract for over-the-road drivers in 1938.

By the outbreak of World War II, the Minneapolis leadership held a strategic position in the Midwest and within the trucking union. They also opposed America's entrance into the war. This gave Tobin what he needed and President Roosevelt was obliging to a long-time supporter. The Trotskyite leaders of the Minneapolis Teamsters' local were imprisoned, the first victims of the wartime Smith Act, to the huzzahs of the communists.

Tobin, as it happened, not only opposed the Dunnes politically, but he was also against organizing "the rubbish," as he called the unskilled on the periphery of the trucking industry. But others within the Teamsters were not so fastidious, including a Seattle business unionist, pudgy Dave Beck, and a Detroit tough, James Riddle Hoffa. They observed the growth of the Minneapolis local with interest and adopted the useful tactics devised by the Dunne brothers and Dobbs. Beck, and subsequently Hoffa, made use of the district councils to extend their power within the union and over the industry. The Teamsters grew from 135,000 members in 1937 to 530,000 in 1941. As Walter Galenson points out in *The CIO Challenge to the AFL*, "The period of the nineteen thirties was characterized fully as much by the rise of the Teamsters as it was by the establishment of the CIO." For this, and their subsequent growth, the powerful trucking union owes much to the Dunne brothers and Farrell Dobbs.

If 1934 was the year of great gains for garment workers, coal miners, factory workers in Toledo, truck drivers in Minneapolis, and West Coast longshoremen, it was also a year of defeat for countless thousands in the auto, steel, textiles, rubber and metal mining industries. Some of the blame lies at the doorstep of the moribund AFL. While majestic John L. Lewis, the effervescent youthful David Dubinsky, and suave Sidney Hillman seized the slender opportunity proffered by the NRA, the Dan Tobins, Maurice Hutchesons, and Bill Greens rumbled on about "keeping

faith" with the ghost of Sam Gompers. "To us was given a charter," Tobin railed against industrial unionism at the 1935 Atlantic City AFL convention, "and Gompers, McGuire, Duncan,
Foster and the others said: 'Upon the rocks of trades autonomy,
craft trades, you shall build the church of the labor movement,
and the gates of hell nor trade industrial unionism shall not prevail against it.'"

Most of the strikes of the turbulent years preceding the founding of the Committee for Industrial Organization within the AFL
in 1935, were led by rank-and-file leaders. A surprising number of
these strikes were condemned by AFL officialdom. About the
others, there was a scarcely concealed distaste. When Norman
Thomas interceded on behalf of a group of Italian workers seeking a union, Bill Collins, AFL Director of Organization, told the
lanky socialist leader, "My wife can always tell from the smell of
my clothes what breed of foreigners I've been hanging out with."
The workers of the mass-production industries were knocking at
the door of the House of Labor, getting little or no response
except a fearful withdrawal from the strife-torn scene. Bill Green,
said Ben Stolberg maliciously, felt about the unorganized the way
"an old and impotent man feels about a young and desirable
woman. He wants her, yet he is afraid."

But the AFL wasn't the only force at fault. The NRA promised
more than it could, or would, deliver. Federal intervention, as we
have seen in the West Coast longshore strike and the Minneapolis
strike, was the decisive factor in the end but there were exceptions. The use of federal power was more often halfhearted and
ineffectual. "At the beginning of his administration Roosevelt
was an acquaintance, not a friend, of organized labor," writes
historian Richard Hofstadter in *American Political Tradition*.
"Although he was eager to do something about the poorest-paid
workers through the NRA codes, his attitude toward unions themselves was not over cordial." While John L. Lewis in the coalfields valiantly invoked Section 7a as pro-labor, employers were
as successful, if not more so, in interpreting the law in the courts

as favoring the establishment of company unions. By the spring of 1934, one-fourth of all industrial workers—say 10 million— were employed in plants with company unions. Almost two-thirds of these were organized under NRA auspices. Company unions flourished in the steel, rubber, petroleum, and chemical industries, among others. Hugh S. Johnson, the square-jawed, truculent NRA chief, approved NRA industry codes that had no place for organized labor despite the provisions of 7a that called for the fostering of collective bargaining. According to Brookings Institute economists, Johnson's interpretations of the Recovery Act "had the practical effect of placing the NRA on the side of anti-union employers in their struggle against the trade unions. . . . The NRA threw its weight against labor in the balance of bargaining power." Franklin D. Roosevelt's concept of a "partnership in planning" between business and government had no place for organized labor, even as a very junior partner. By the time the Supreme Court of the United States had killed the NRA in 1935—*Schecter* v. *U.S.*, the so-called sick chicken case—disillusioned workers were calling the NRA the "National Run Around." "Labor's public enemy No. 1," cried Heywood Broun, "is Franklin D. Roosevelt." Rebellious workers had little chance against the massed power of the giant corporations, the adverse weight of the government, and the inertia of the American Federation of Labor. During the last days of the NRA, a new National Labor Relations Board was set up under the chairmanship of Lloyd K. Garrison, Dean of the Wisconsin Law School. Garrison and his associates did the best they could but were powerless to act in the face of almost universal employer opposition. Employers simply ignored the Board. To give the N. L. Board some teeth, Senator Robert F. Wagner, Democrat of New York, sought to introduce a bill that would enable the Board to order representation elections, define and prohibit unfair labor practices (such as employer-dominated company unions, discriminatory discharge of union members, or the refusal to bargain in good faith), and power to enforce decisions. But the Administration

remained cool. Donald Richberg, a Presidential advisor on labor questions, was actively hostile to the unions. By June, 1935, Roosevelt, already worried about the 1936 Presidential elections, changed his mind. Huey Long was mustering too much support from the disaffected. The Supreme Court tore up Roosevelt's plan for labor and industry, leaving the President with little to lean on in the campaign ahead. Always flexible, the Country Gentleman in the White House turned left. Suddenly, Wagner found the Administration behind his bill as well as behind a strong holding-company act and a bill imposing a stringent tax on wealth. Larger expenditures and a better wage scale were promulgated for a new relief program under the Works Progress Administration. These measures, along with a Social Security measure, became the foundation of a second New Deal, the New Deal of liberal and labor legend.

All that remained was for labor to act. That summer at Atlantic City, John Llewellyn Lewis threw, in James Wechsler's phrase, "one of the most deliberate punches in modern history" at lumbering Bill Hutcheson and, indirectly, at the American Federation of Labor. The delegates voted for the craft-union *status quo* 18,204 to 10,933, giving the decision, so to speak, to the Carpenters' chief. The day after the convention had adjourned, Lewis met with Philip Murray, Thomas Kennedy, John Brophy of the Mine Workers, Charles P. Howard of the Typographical Workers, David Dubinsky of the International Ladies' Garment Workers' Union, Max Zaritsky of the Hat, Cap and Millinery Workers, and Thomas MacMahon of the Textile Workers. On November 9, they formed the Committee for Industrial Organization, with the addition of Thomas Brown of the Mine, Mill and Smelter Workers and Harvey Fremming of the Oil Field, Gas Well and Refinery Workers. On November 23, 1935, Lewis wrote a terse note: "Effective this date, I resign as vice-president of the American Federation of Labor." At the AFL convention in 1936 at Tampa, Florida, Matthew Woll prepared a lengthy report condemning the "ingratitude" of the CIO unions. The executive council recommended suspension of the offending unions. In March, 1937, William Green instructed city and state central bodies of the Federation to expel all delegates from the suspended ten CIO unions. The following year the Committee for Industrial Organization became the Congress of Industrial Organizations. The split within the House of Labor was now complete.

Whether or not the split was inevitable is perhaps moot. Though the AFL and the CIO fought and raided each other for nearly twenty years, there were many within both organizations who worked conscientiously for unity. Dubinsky and his ILGWU in the end refused to join the other CIO unions as a second national labor center, preferring to go it alone until readmitted to the AFL in 1940. AFL historian Philip Taft argues convincingly that, had the AFL truly stuck to its basic organizational principles, the separation need never have taken place. The conflict over the organization of workers in the mass-production industries during the 1930s revolved around "principles of craft autonomy," which guaranteed affiliated unions jurisdiction over all workmen doing the work in a specific craft or occupation and guaranteed no interference in internal affairs. Jurisdictional quarrels were traditionally resolved by time, persuasion, and conciliation. The early Committee for Industrial Organization might easily have become, so Taft argues, a department of the AFL, as the Building Trades were then and the Industrial Union Department is now within the AFL-CIO, if the Federation had settled the issues that divided the CIO unions and the craft unions on a practical basis and if it had shown its usual lack of haste in resolving controversies that concerned autonomous unions. Ironically, the present AFL-CIO powers to intervene in the internal affairs of constituent unions flow indirectly from this hasty suspension prompted by the very unions that today would like to retain the old autonomy.

The haste was perhaps unavoidable. The split—though it turned on questions of jurisdiction and autonomy within the AFL—developed out of a conflict between generations. The lead-

ers of the AFL were men of advanced age in 1936; the leaders of
the new CIO unions, if not the original founders of the Committee, were young men in their twenties and thirties. Only John L.
Lewis, as Professor Walter Galenson has pointed out, "had the
genius to bridge the gap between the generations and to put his
experience as an AFL organizer and AFL international union
president at the disposal of the forces which were thrusting the
semiskilled industrial worker to a place in the sun alongside the
craftsmen."

Paradoxically, the split had a liberating effect on the AFL. The
Federation entered the mid-thirties crusty, fusty, craft-ridden,
and just plain suspicious of the appeals for organization from
auto, rubber, and steel centers. After the split it responded with a
vigor that nearly surpassed its rival, the new CIO. During the last
four months of 1936, the AFL payroll for organizers was
$82,000; the corresponding figure for the last four months of
1937 was $466,000. In 1937, the AFL had a membership of 2.8
million; the CIO, 1.5 million. By 1941, the AFL had a membership of 4.5 million to the CIO's 2.8 million. Galenson concludes
in his study of AFL and CIO rivalry, *The CIO Challenge to the
AFL*, that "the expansion of trade unionism from 1936 to 1941
had one overriding characteristic: it extended the power of labor
into new and strategic sectors of the economy." That extension
was largely due to the energies and character of one man, John L.
Lewis.

John Llewellyn Lewis was a miner, and a miner's son. He was
born on February 12, 1880, of Welsh parentage in Lucas, Iowa, a
small community. His father, Thomas Lewis, was active in the
Knights of Labor; two years after the birth of his eldest son, Tom
Lewis was blacklisted for his part in a successful strike. Until the
blacklist was lifted in 1897, the growing Lewis family—six sons
and two daughters—moved repeatedly throughout the Midwest as
the senior Lewis shifted from job to job. John L. entered the
mines as a husky lad of fifteen. Back in Lucas at 17, young John
L. sponsored traveling shows ranging from Shakespeare to per-

forming dogs. He also read avidly and widely, with his future wife, Myrta Bell, the daughter of the Yankee doctor in town, guiding him to the Bible, Dickens, Homer, and Shakespeare. At twenty-one, the restless youth went west, to mine copper in Montana, silver in Utah, coal in Colorado, and gold in Arizona. In Hannah, Wyoming, he helped carry out the torn bodies of 236 coal miners killed in the Union Pacific Mine disaster of 1905. This experience, along with the silicosis that shadowed the later years of his father, inspired Lewis' life-long passion for mine-safety legislation.

"The miner," as Saul Alinsky notes in his biography *John L. Lewis,* "knows that he digs death as well as coal, and the death tonnage is appalling." From 1910 to 1945, 68,842 miners were killed and 2,275,000 injured.

In 1906, John L. returned to Lucas, where he married Myrta Bell a year later. An ambitious man, Lewis decided that, to make his start in life, he needed a broader base than Lucas. In 1909, the Lewises moved to Panama, Illinois, the heart of the Montgomery coalfields. "Lewis from Illinois," writes Alinsky, "would mean more to the miners than Lewis from Lucas, Iowa." Lewis' judgment was accurate as well as acute. Within a year, with the help of his five brothers, John L. captured the Panama local of the United Mine Workers. He was the local's one-man grievance committee and, a year later, state legislative agent for the union. After a mine explosion that killed 160 miners, Lewis single-handedly bullied the state legislature into passing safety legislation and a workmen's compensation law. This brought him to the attention of old Samuel Gompers, who in 1911 appointed the husky miner a field representative and legislative agent for the AFL. The burly Welshman and the stubby Dutch-English Jew made a curious pair. Lewis learned much from the crafty AFL tactician; in return he stood guard whenever Gompers went on a binge. Though Gompers groomed Lewis carefully, the miner was not destined to replace the cigar maker as the leader of the AFL. Once while he was still in the mines, Lewis allegedly was attacked by a vicious, man-killing mule, Spanish Pete. He reportedly felled the mule with a right-hand blow and finished him off with an iron bar. Realizing that the act might cost him his job, the young Lewis covered the wounds with clay and reported to the foreman that the mule had died of heart failure. With the same mixture of brute strength and quick thinking, Lewis built a strong personal machine within the mine union. While on the AFL payroll, he travelled widely through the minefields, was lavish with his expense account, and became friends with key mine leaders throughout the country. As a result, in 1916 he was offered the post of chief statistician for the union. Subsequently, he was named a vice-president by UMW president, Frank Hayes, an ineffectual alcoholic. Lewis ran the union, becoming president in 1920 of the largest single union within the AFL with a membership of 500,000.

Confronted with the catastrophic conditions of coal mining during the 1920s, Lewis fought a rearguard action—"We will take no backward steps"—chiefly aimed at preserving his power within the union. As acting president of the union, he had called off the 1919 strike under pressure from President Wilson and an all-embracing injunction. "I will not fight my government," intoned Lewis, "the greatest government on earth." The statement was to haunt him in later years (during the World War II coal strike) and was taken at the time by UMW militants as an ill omen. Ruthlessly, Lewis suppressed his opposition. John Brophy, the gentle English-born socialist, who tried to cope with the coal crisis by pushing for nationalization and stimulating cooperative stores in mining communities, was driven from the union. So was Powers Hapgood, a Harvard man with a mission and beloved by the miners. Hapgood, the son of a socially minded Indianapolis businessman, puzzled Lewis. According to McAllister Coleman, Lewis once sent for Hapgood and asked him what he was doing in the fields. "Organizing," said Hapgood. "Not writing a book?" queried Lewis. At the end of the decade, these men and other opponents of Lewis as well as hundreds of thousands of miners were no longer in the UMW. Small wonder, then, that during the summer of 1933 the coal operators were stunned by the vigor of the Lewis-sponsored organizing drives that recouped the fortunes of the ailing UMW.

As Lewis looked on scornfully, Michael F. ("Grandmother") Tighe, leader of the AFL steel union, kept his union to a manageable membership of 5,000 that year. It wasn't easy to do; some 100,000 steel workers applied for membership in 1933 and 1934. In auto, inept AFL leadership succeeded in reducing union membership from about 100,000 in 1934 to 10,000 by the winter of 1935. "The American Federation of Labor," concluded Lewis, "is standing still, with its face to the past." Convinced that industrial unionism was the answer to the problem of getting organized labor off dead center, Lewis laid his plans. The Mine Workers' exposed position in the so-called captive mines—mines owned by steel companies—gave Lewis an added interest in organizing steel. As Lewis told Alinsky, "Every year as we sat down to negotiate with the coal operators, they could . . . justify their unreasonable position [against a wage increase] by citing the lower wages of the unorganized steel workers." The rising clamor of the unorganized at the closed door of the AFL and the passage of the Wagner Labor Act convinced Lewis that the time was ripe. During the Atlantic City AFL convention, bushy-browed Lewis walked across a hotel lobby to tap slender Powers Hapgood on the shoulder. "Let's go upstairs, Powers," he said to the organizer he had drummed out of the miners. Upstairs in the hotel suite, Lewis said, "We're about to go into a campaign . . . that will be everything you dreamed about and everything you've talked about. We're going out to fight for those things, and we're going to get them. You see, Powers, I've never really opposed those things. I just never felt that the time was ripe and that trying to do those things back in the days when we had our violent arguments would have been suicide for organized labor and would have resulted in complete failure. But now the time is ripe; and now the time to do those things is here. Let us do them." "Lewis stopped talking," Hapgood later recalled, "and I just can't tell you how I felt. It was just as if everything I dreamed of had finally come to pass." Lewis also brought his old foe John Brophy into the CIO as executive director. Adolph Germer, slugged by Lewis' men in 1932, was assigned to Akron, where he directed the first major CIO strike, the 1936 Goodyear Tire and Rubber strike. On June 13, 1936, Lewis set up the Steel Workers' Organizing Committee with another miner, Philip Murray, as director.

# XIV

## *THE REVIVAL OF AN OLD DREAM*

THE CENTURY-OLD DREAM OF INDUSTRIAL UNIONISM NOW CEN-
tered on the Congress for Industrial Organization. But the aspirations of the mass-production workers that now thronged to the
CIO were much more modest than those that agitated the members of the workingmen's parties of the 1830s, the Knights of
Labor, or the Wobblies. Each of these on their own terms and in
their own times sought to remake society over into their own
image of what ought to be. The CIO was a successful adaptation
of revolutionary industrial unionism to the corporate world of
this century. It reinforced corporate welfarism; it did not seek a
new world. "Labor does ask for and demand," thundered John L.
Lewis, cold gray eyes snapping under beetling eyebrows, "a voice
in the determination of those policies that affect the human element in industry. . . . It wants a place at the council table when
decisions are made that affect the amount of food that the family
of a worker may eat, the extent of education of his children, the
kind and amount of clothing they shall wear, the few pleasures
they may enjoy." Socialists and ex-socialists like Hillman and
Dubinsky, or like the youthful Reuther brothers in Detroit,

Trotskyites, communists of varying hue, and ex-Wobblies broadened Lewis' business-*cum*-industry unionism to include a concern with political action and social welfare. But they no more succeeded in radicalizing the CIO than did American business in opposing the new wave of unionism that swept over the industrial centers of New Deal America.

For, in truth, the giant corporations established after much travail by the Rockefellers, Fords, Morgans and lesser captains of industry defeated all those who had a vision of another America, from Henry Adams to the Wobblies. The corporation clearly was here to stay. Under the NRA, for a brief period, big business and big government were avowed "partners in planning." Since then, they have been unofficial though sometimes strained kissing cousins. The private governments of the corporate world are in many ways the larger partner, though not always the dominant one, in this uneasy relationship. It was, in part, to offset possible domination by industry that government fostered collective bargaining. The countervailing power of the unions, in John Kenneth Galbraith's revealing phrase, was cultivated by the government to equalize the balance between it and big business.

Here, too, the CIO departed from its predecessors. Lewis not only welcomed government intervention, but fostered it. He was the architect of Section 7*a* of the NRA, or so he claimed; he certainly made the most of it. Lewis also quickly seized upon the advantages offered under the Wagner Act and by the revitalized National Labor Relations Board. One reason for the hesitancy of the AFL old guard to organize those clamoring for unions, it must be said, was a fear of the very same governmental interference that Lewis sought so eagerly. Voluntarism was the doctrine that held that labor might better rely on its own strength and had nothing to gain from the state. Only by relying on their own organizational strength, the AFL leaders believed, could workers resist the pressure of employers, avoid being tripped up by a change of administrations, and survive economic adversity. The coming of the CIO, however, changed all that. The CIO not only brought industrial unionism to the mass-production industries, but it also brought the government into labor relations to stay.

But this was by no means a sure thing as CIO sound trucks began to roll through the streets of Akron, Detroit, and Pittsburgh as well as countless shoe and textile towns. After the passage of the Wagner Labor Act in 1935, key business spokesmen denounced it as "invalid." Earl F. Reed, counsel to Weirton Steel Company and chairman of a committee of lawyers called together by the American Liberty League, an organization of businessmen and conservatives, declared, "I feel perfectly free to advise a client not to be bound by a law that I consider unconstitutional." Two years later, the Supreme Court upheld the act, in *NLRB* v. *Jones and Laughlin Steel Corp.*, but labor's troubles with employers were not exactly over. Although the government played a crucial role in the survival of the CIO as an organization, America's leading corporations in rubber, steel, and auto recognized it only after a near-revolutionary wave of sit-down strikes rolled through the mills and plants.

The sit-down strike ran like a fever through the strike-racked body of American industry in 1936 and 1937. "You'd be sitting in the office any March day of 1937," Myra Wolfgang, an AFL Hotel & Restaurant Employees' business agent recalled, "and the phone would ring and the voice at the other end would say, 'My name is Mary Jones; I'm a soda clerk at Liggett's; we've thrown the manager out and we've got the keys. What do we do now?' And you'd hurry over to the company to negotiate and over there they'd say, 'I think it's the height of irresponsibility to call a strike before you've ever asked for a contract,' and all you could answer was, 'You're so right.' " It was the forerunner of a revolution that never fully developed. From September, 1936, to May, 1937, sit-downs directly involved 484,711 workers. "It was like we was soldiers," a General Motors sit-downer told Lewis' biographer Saul Alinsky, "holding the fort. It was like war. The guys with me became my buddies. I remember as a kid in school readin' about Davy Crockett and the last stand at the Alamo. You know, mister, that's just how I felt. Yes sir, Chevvy No. 4 was my Alamo." For a brief time, the CIO teetered on the brink of the revolutionary industrial unionism of the Wobblies.

In the end, however, the CIO drew back from the brink. The great bulk of the sit-downers had no wish to overthrow either their employers or the country. They did realize, however, that they had hold of a good thing, a practical tactical advantage over the forces with which they had to cope to win union recognition. In their book, *The UAW and Walter Reuther*, Irving Howe and B. J. Widick tell an amusing anecdote that underscores this. A veteran sit-downer recounted to a friend of the authors in great detail how the men prepared for a sit-down—prepared barricades, policed the plant and even thought of using the fire hose to repel attackers. "But," asked the listener, "suppose the city turned off the water." "They couldn't have done that," replied the shocked unionist. "That would have been against the law." Needless to say, American industry took a far different view of the sit-downs—one paradoxically that was actually closer to that of naive radicals who saw revolution in every factory—than that taken by the strikers themselves.

A cold winter blizzard hit Akron, the rubber capital of the world, along with the first CIO strike on February 17, 1936. For four weeks, rubber workers camped out in 68 shanties and tents strung along an 11-mile perimeter surrounding Goodyear Tire & Rubber Company's huge plant. "The two agitators in this strike are Goodyear hours and wages," noted a strike leader. Wage cuts in November, 1935, and January, 1936, sparked sporadic sit-downs. When the company discharged 137 workers without notice, Goodyear workers began to sit down at their machines. That night, workers in threadbare overcoats and belted mackinaws marched through roaring winds. By the second day, 10,000 were out on strike and the world's largest rubber factory was at a standstill.

At Akron, the rubber workers developed tactics that subsequently became characteristic of most CIO strikes. When police threatened to open the plant, the union massed thousands before the plant gate. The police wisely did not attack. No violence occurred. When a Law and Order League was formed and word went out that it would attack the picket line, the union leased the facilities of the local radio station, which then became a kind of city-wide sound truck. Strikers were instructed to keep tuned in all night. From eleven o'clock at night, McAllister Coleman, a veteran socialist, union publicist, and newsman, directed a program of entertainment and newscasts until eight o'clock in the morning. Union and civic leaders later credited this imaginative use of radio with forestalling the vigilantes and preventing a serious conflict. The strike wound up on March 22 with the recognition of the union as a spokesman for its members. In July, 1937, *Business Week* declared editorially: "Akron is from nine months to a year ahead of the national procession in labor recovery. It was in Akron that the Committee for Industrial Organization made its first stand in a big industry. . . . Today all the big rubber companies in Akron are dealing across the table with unions."

Akron was a morale-building curtain raiser for CIO struggles in steel and auto. When sit-downs began breaking out in the auto industry, John L. Lewis tried to head them off. He had hoped to organize steel first. But once he saw that curbing the impetuousness of the auto worker was useless, Lewis committed all of CIO's strength to back the struggling United Auto Workers. The auto union was founded in August, 1935, following the AFL Detroit debacle of the year before. After a year under officers appointed by the Federation, the new union cast off the Federation-appointed leadership for a new group of its own officers. Homer Martin, an ex-Baptist minister from St. Louis with a gift for agitation, was elected president. Wyndham Mortimer, an ex-coal miner, associated with the Communist Party faction within the union, was elected vice-president. George Addes, a shrewd, hard-headed Toledo Auto-Lite strike leader was elected secretary-treasurer. John L. Lewis contributed $100,000 for organizing, a munificent sum to the hitchhiking delegates who slept six to a room in South Bend, Indiana, site of the 1936 auto workers' convention. Richard T. Frankensteen, a raucous, fleshy ex-football tackle, brought the independent Chrysler workers' union into the UAW fold after a brief struggle with the company. Walter P. Reuther, a fiery, redheaded socialist, enlarged his growing West Side (Detroit) local by a five-day sit-down at the Kelsey-Hayes wheel plant. Despite these acquisitions, the chief target of the UAW-CIO drive remained the giant of the industry, General Motors Corporation.

GM, controlled by the Du Ponts and J. P. Morgan, had recovered handsomely from the depression. In 1934, its net profit was $167,000,000; in 1936, $227,940,000. In 1935, the individual worker received an average (yearly) wage of $1,150; the same year, GM president Alfred P. Sloan knocked down $374,505 and vice-president William S. Knudsen, $325,868. Whatever rancor the auto worker may have felt at the discrepancy was sharpened by the speed-up. "Sit-down" was their reply to the Corporation's rejection of their demands for union recognition.

The auto workers' war with General Motors began on November 18, 1936, in the Fisher body plant at Atlanta, Georgia, spread to Kansas City, then Cleveland. It soon centered on Flint, Michigan, heartland of the GM empire. By January 1, 1937, 112,800 of GM's 150,000 production workers were idle.

In Flint, where over 50,000 of a population of 165,000 toiled in GM's Chevrolet, Buick, and Fisher body plants, UAW members routed the Flint police in what is known affectionately in union annals as the "Battle of the Running Bulls." It was the only attempt made to forcibly remove the strikers from the plant. Governor Frank Murphy sent some 1,500 national guardsmen to Flint and restrained city officials who wished to issue wholesale injunctions. Murphy prevailed upon the UAW to vacate the plants in return for a GM agreement to negotiate. On January 15, 1937, GM sit-down strikers left plants in Detroit and Anderson,

Indiana. The Flint workers were due to vacate the Fisher body plant two days later.

A newsman, however, uncovered an exchange of telegrams between GM and the so-called Flint Alliance. The Alliance, organized by a Flint businessman, had attempted to engineer a back-to-work movement among the Flint auto workers. It also requested a collective-bargaining meeting with the company. GM agreed, according to the telegrams. Angered auto workers refused to leave the Flint plants. GM officials agreed to meet with Secretary of Labor Frances Perkins but refused to meet with John L. Lewis. Scowling, Lewis informed the press that labor expected the President to help the strikers in every reasonable way. Roosevelt, in turn, chided Lewis for his plea and rebuked the company for refusing to meet with the CIO leader.

Meanwhile, in Flint the situation became critical for the striking auto workers. They were beginning to feel the strain and their morale crumbled as Washington remained inactive. Something dramatic was needed. On the night of January 27, Roy Reuther, the first organizer and Reuther brother on the UAW payroll; Bob Travis, UAW organizer and Flint strike leader; Powers Hapgood, sent in to help by the CIO; and Kermit Johnson, "Chevvy" union leader, sat down to discuss ways and means. Reuther, who had a freshly laundered shirt in his desk, drew out the cardboard and sketched a plan. Chevvy Number Four, the motor-assembly division still in operation, was the key. Chevvy Number Nine, a ball-bearing plant, lay nearby; Chevvy Numbers Six and Eight, also close by, were points of union strength. What Roy Reuther proposed—and the others accepted—was simple: diversionary moves against Chevvy Number Nine and the other plants while a union task force captured Chevvy Number Four. Secrecy was essential since company spies were plentiful. When the strike leaders proposed the seizure of Chevvy Number Nine, the strikers set up a derisive howl, but in the end they were convinced.

On January 29, GM's plant guards were all mustered at Chevvy Number Nine; alerted, the Flint police hastened to the threatened factory. The UAW women's auxiliary, under fiery Genora Johnson, staged a demonstration in front of Plant Nine. Victor Reuther was in the street with his sound truck; Walter was on hand with reinforcements from Kelsey-Hayes. For more than 30 minutes, a fierce battle raged outside Plant Nine. Tear gas brought tears to strikers' eyes. Windows were smashed; cops, plant guards and strikers exchanged vigorous blows.

Then there was a sudden silence at Chevvy Four; the objective was taken and the union once again had the upper hand. The seizure of Chevvy Four meant the end of the strike. Governor Murphy, furious, threatened to oust the strikers by force; President Roosevelt summoned John L. Lewis and urged him to get the strikers out of the plant. Lewis, adamant, declined, asking instead when GM would start negotiating. Leaving Washington for Detroit, he declared, "Let there be no moaning at the bar as I put out to sea." Murphy had second thoughts and concentrated on pressuring Knudsen to negotiate with Lewis. At their first meeting, he insisted that Lewis tell the men to vacate the plants. Lewis replied, "I do not doubt your ability to call out your soldiers and shoot the members of our union out of those plants, but let me say when you issue that order I shall leave this conference and I shall enter one of those plants with my people." President Roosevelt once again requested GM to meet with the union. Lewis held fast, insisting that GM give the auto union exclusive recognition. The company finally capitulated on February 11 and agreed, at Governor Murphy's suggestion, to recognize and deal with the UAW for the 17 plants closed by strikes. The union had won a significant victory. In a few weeks, UAW membership doubled, rising from 100,000 to 200,000.

Later, in the summer of 1937, the UAW moved on Ford's River Rouge plant. There Walter Reuther, Dick Frankensteen, and other UAW leaflet-passers clashed with Harry Bennett and his crew of Ford servicemen. Frankensteen later testified that fully 50 of Ford's men assaulted Reuther and him. Reuther described the battle at the overpass near River Rouge before an

NLRB hearing. "Seven times they raised me off the concrete and threw me down on it. They pinned my arms and shot short jabs to my face. I was punched and dragged by my feet to the stairway. I grabbed the railing and they wrenched me loose. I was thrown down the first flight of iron steps. Then they kicked me down the other flight of steps until I found myself on the ground where I was beaten and kicked." But the company misjudged Reuther and the auto workers. The beating did not do a bit of good. The UAW came back again and again. After years of battling the union, Ford, in 1941, did a complete about face. Harry Bennett in negotiating with Philip Murray agreed to a union shop, dues checkoff, grievance machinery, seniority, time-and-a-half pay for overtime, premium pay for night workers, and two hours' pay for workers called in but not given work. Ford workers followed GM, Chrysler, and other auto company employees into the union.

CIO's campaign in the steel industry proceeded somewhat differently than that in auto. In both industries there was a clamor for organization from the workers and adamant opposition from the employers. But, in the end, steel was organized from the top down. John L. Lewis was invited to Detroit to lead negotiations by the auto workers. But the Steel Workers Organizing Committee was, from the beginning, a Lewis–Mine Workers' project. As a SWOC convention delegate told R. R. R. Brooks (quoted in *As Steel Goes*), "The Steel Workers Organizing Committee is a democracy. It is a democracy of steel workers, for steel workers, but not by steel workers." Professor Philip Taft points out: "Funds for organizing the steel workers were supplied by other unions whose leaders could claim the right to appoint officers and administrators. Moreover, no objection of any consequence was made to 'outside' tutelage for the outsiders had supplied the finances and the organizing talent that made the union a living reality." Philip Murray, a long-time Lewis lieutenant and a vice-president of the Mine Workers, directed the affairs of SWOC as chairman with the assistance of his former secretary, David J. McDonald, who served as SWOC secretary-treasurer. Other unions had representatives on SWOC but control remained in the hands of the Mine Workers. Twelve international representatives of the Mine union served on the steel staff under the direction of another miner, Van A. Bittner. Between 1936 and May 1, 1942, the UMW loaned SWOC $601,000; the CIO advanced $997,648. But this does not take into account the services of organizers and officials carried on the UMW payroll. Philip Murray himself remained on the UMW payroll as a vice-president until he became president of the CIO. All told SWOC spent, it has been estimated, some $2,500,000 up until the end of the Little Steel strike in 1937, the great bulk of which came from the United Mine Workers.

The United Steel Workers Union held its first constitutional convention in 1942, after six years of existence as SWOC. The difference between the two CIO giants—steel and auto—is perhaps best illustrated by the following, possibly apocryphal, anecdote. During the steel union's first convention in 1942, R. J. Thomas, the president of the contentious, democratic, fractious, and proud auto union, sat on the platform next to Murray during a heavy-going discussion that preceded adoption of the steel union's constitution. At one point during the debate, Murray leaned over to Thomas and said, "R. J., that fellow down there causing the ruckus is one of your boys." R. J. Thomas, always willing to oblige a friend, replied, "Why didn't you say so, Phil? I'll go down and speak to him." This the UAW leader did. Thomas called the UAW man off the convention floor and asked him what he was doing at a steel convention. The delegate explained that his auto local had helped to organize a couple of small steel locals in Detroit and, in return, they had sent him to the steel convention as a delegate. Thomas allowed as to how that was nice of the gang. Then, he added, "you know Phil Murray is a friend of ours; why give him so much trouble? Lay off, why don't you?" "But, R. J.," spluttered the auto worker, "I'm only trying to get them to adopt *our* constitution."

Shortly after its formulation in 1936, SWOC set out to woo the many company unions that then existed in the steel industry. SWOC experienced a moderate amount of success, especially in the plants of United States Steel, where the company unions were still young and inexperienced. By winter, the union had signed up a majority of the employees of Carnegie-Illinois and other U. S. Steel plants. The steel workers girded themselves for a battle with the industry giant. But the unionization of U. S. Steel was a John L. Lewis triumph, pure and simple. On March 2, 1937, after two or three months of secret meetings between Lewis and Myron C. Taylor, chairman of U. S. Steel's board of directors, the corporation and SWOC signed an agreement that granted SWOC recognition. Many lives had been lost since Homestead in successful attempts to reach that goal. Now the chief bastion of the open shop had fallen without so much as a solitary picket. The United Auto Workers–General Motors agreement was reached a week earlier as a result of a long and bitter sit-down strike. Lewis and Taylor avoided that kind of high-cost settlement. Lewis' triumph was truly historic and laid the cornerstone not only for collective bargaining as we now know it, but also for present-day corporate welfarism. The paternalistic philosophy of Gary and Perkins was to be shored up by the massive bargaining power of the steel union, now a recognized junior member of the corporate family.

Lewis' stunning success at signing up U. S. Steel stimulated countless CIO drives in the electrical, rubber, men's clothing, textile, meat, petroleum, and maritime industries. It also started up a flock of rumors explaining U. S. Steel's about-face. According to one story, Taylor happened to be dining with his wife at the same Washington restaurant as Lewis in December, 1936. Mrs. Taylor noticed the CIO chief and asked her husband, "Myron, I want to meet that man. Bring him over here." Taylor did so and a friendship began that, so the society gossips alleged, ripened into the SWOC–U. S. Steel agreement in March, 1937. Taylor, however, was much more reconciled to the New Deal than his colleagues in the industry. He also benefited from the advice of Tom Moses, president of U. S. Steel subsidiary H. S. Frick

Coal Company, who had negotiated with Lewis and enjoyed a friendly relationship with the CIO leader.

Though personalities may have helped smooth the way for an agreement between Lewis and Taylor, U. S. Steel's decision to bargain collectively with SWOC was based on a businesslike, hard-headed assessment of current economic and political conditions. The GM strike made it clear that the cost of open combat with the CIO came high both in terms of money and public opinion. President Roosevelt, still in his brief leftish phase, was an uncertain quantity. The La Follette Committee was threatening to look into the labor espionage practices of the corporation. But outweighing even these hefty considerations was the presence in the United States of Lord Runciman, president of the British Board of Trade, who was arranging the purchase of steel for Great Britain's rearmament program. Lord Runciman insisted on a guarantee of uninterrupted production before letting contracts. This, in the end, decided Thomas W. Lamont (of the Morgan interests) in favor of collective bargaining in steel. Once Lamont, key to the powerful finance committee of U. S. Steel, was in the line, the rest was a foregone conclusion.

For a time, it appeared that the balance of the steel industry might follow suit. By early May, 1937, Philip Murray was able to announce that SWOC had 325,000 members and contracts with 90 companies, including all the subsidiaries of U. S. Steel and key independents such as Wheeling Steel, Timken Roller Bearing, Caterpillar Tractor, and McKeesport Tin-Plate. On April 12, the U. S. Supreme Court upheld the constitutionality of the Wagner Act, reinstating a number of Jones & Laughlin employees fired for union activity. As a result, the Aliquippa—"Siberia of America"—Steel Company signed with the union after a 36-hour strike in mid-May. The company agreed to grant the union exclusive recognition—a greater concession than U. S. Steel's "members only" clause—if a majority of the workers voted for the proposal in an NLRB election. This they did, 2 to 1, on May 20.

But a worsening of economic conditions (in May, 1937) stiffened the opposition of the Little Steel companies to the encroachments of SWOC. Republic, Bethlehem, Inland, and Youngstown Sheet & Tube Corporation rallied around Tom M. Girdler, president of Republic Steel, to do battle with the steel union. Girdler, a rugged corporate individualist, hated unions. In the Little Steel effort to destroy SWOC, he ruthlessly applied the tactics devised by James H. Rand, Jr., to combat the International Associations of Machinists during the 1936 Remington Rand strikes, the so-called Mohawk Valley Formula. The Formula was widely publicized by the National Association of Manufacturers and has served as text for anti-union tactics ever since. The ingredients of the formula are relatively simple: the plan of attack calls for an employer-conducted strike ballot; the labeling of union leaders as "outside agitators," "communists," and "radicals"; economic pressure on the community by threats to move plants; the organization of a back-to-work movement to cover up the employment of strikebreakers; a show of police and "Citizens' Committee" force; and a grandstand opening of struck plants.

Under Girdler's leadership, the Little Steel companies rejected all overtures from SWOC for collective-bargaining negotiations. By late May and early June, 70,000 were out on strike in an attempt to shut down Little Steel. The bitterness of the strike is highlighted by the Memorial Day Massacre. On May 30, 1937, white clouds scudded across the blue sky above Sam's Place, where the strikers from Republic's South Chicago plant had gathered to hear speakers. The plant lay to the south across a railway track and a field.

It was decided to cross the field and picket the plant to affirm the right to picket, a right upheld in a statement to the meeting by the mayor. Casually, the strikers with their families strolled by twos and threes and small groups toward the plant gates. This holiday spirit was met by gunfire. After intensive investigation, the La Follette Senate Committee concluded, "The first shots came from the police . . . unprovoked." The strolling crowd was in shambles; some strikers retaliated with stones or whatever else

came quickly to hand from the field. But most fled. Ten marchers were shot, seven in the back, three in the side, none in front.
Thirty others, including one woman and three minors, were
wounded; 28 others were so badly beaten they required hospitalization, and some 30 more received injuries requiring medical
treatment. The police reported 35 of theirs injured, none was shot
and only three required hospitalization. "The police," noted the
La Follette Committee, "dragged seriously wounded, unconscious
men along the ground with no more care than would be employed
on a common drunkard."

In Massillon, Ohio, a Republic Steel official demanded of Chief
of Police Stanley Switter: "Why don't you take action like they
did in Chicago?" Switter, who apparently could not do so, was
persuaded to leave town and in his absence "special police,"
sworn in and armed at the instigation of Republic Steel, precipitated a riot in which two strikers were killed, seven wounded,
and 160 others arrested. In Cleveland, Ohio, a strikebreaker's car
crushed a picket to death against an iron fence; a mob wrecked
strike headquarters. In Canton, Ohio, nervous troopers drove
derisive children from playgrounds with drawn bayonets. In
Johnstown, Pennsylvania, Mayor Daniel J. Shields received
$31,456 from Bethelehem Steel during the strike. He headed up a
return-to-work movement and all but turned the city over to vigilantes. In Youngstown, two strikers were killed and 42 injured
during riots there.

With SWOC and Little Steel at each other's throats, the CIO
looked to President Roosevelt for help. Hadn't they contributed
much to the landslide victory of 1936? But on June 30, 1937, an
irritable President snapped out a quote from Shakespeare: "A
plague on both your houses." A frowning Lewis attempted a
parry: "Which house, Hearst or Du Pont?" But it was not
enough; the damage had been done. The Little Steel strike ended
in mid-July as a victory for Tom Girdler. The blow was softened
somewhat for SWOC by an agreement with Inland Steel pat-

terned after the U. S. Steel agreement and secured through the mediation efforts of Governor Townsend of Indiana.

The Little Steel strike precipitated a break between President Roosevelt and John L. Lewis that led to the latter's endorsement of Wendell Willkie in 1940. On September 3, 1937, over a coast-to-coast hookup, Lewis rumbled, a sorely wounded lion: "Labor, like Israel, has many sorrows. Its women weep for their fallen and they lament for the future of the children of the race. It ill behooves one who has supped at labor's table and who has been sheltered in labor's house to curse with equal fervor and fine impartiality both labor and its adversaries when they become locked in deadly embrace."

The defeat hurt and rankled. The CIO lost, for a time, the momentum of 1936 and early 1937. In 1940, Philip Murray complained to the CIO executive board, "So, with all our wind and with all our puffing and blowing we had increased our dues paying membership by about 500,000 in five years, or perhaps 600,000 members." CIO membership peaked in 1938 to slightly over four million; by 1940, it was down to 3.6 million.

The fever induced by the heady wine of plant seizure had run its course. On February 27, 1939, the Supreme Court declared the sit-downs illegal in the Fanstock Steel case. The court in its majority opinion stated: "The strike . . . was an illegal seizure of buildings in order to prevent their use by the employer in a lawful manner." As war clouds darkened over Europe, the steel union shifted its efforts to combat Little Steel from the picket line to the NLRB and the courts. The effects of the Little Steel strike, however, lasted as late as 1945, when Republic paid $350,000 to settle suits brought against the company on behalf of strikers who had been killed or injured. As a result of NLRB proceedings, Republic eventually reinstated 7,000 strikers with back-pay awards amounting to two million dollars. In 1941, SWOC remounted its organizational drive against Little Steel. One by one the companies agreed to abide by results of NLRB elections. In September, 1941, the four Little Steel Companies sat down to bargain. But negotiations were long and drawn out; the talks dragged on until after war was declared in December, and the dispute was referred to the War Labor Board. SWOC's victory became the famous "Little Steel Formula," an award that was the basis of wartime wage increases for all workers. The steel workers won a 5½ cent-an-hour increase based on the decline in their real hourly wages since January 1, 1941. The WLB panel also awarded the union a maintenance of membership clause and a check-off.

# XV

## *WARTIME INDUSTRIAL STATESMANSHIP*

SPITFIRES AND STUKAS CONTESTED FOR BRITISH SKIES THAT SUM-
mer. In America, the jobless were being absorbed into Franklin
D. Roosevelt's "arsenal for democracy"; "Doctor Win-the-War"
was called in to supplant "Doctor New Deal." It was, however, a
slow gathering of strength. On the eve of Pearl Harbor there were
still some seven million jobless in an economy that could not
shake off depression until fully launched into war. In Britain,
World War II brought labor into full partnership in the effort to
defeat the Axis powers and, ultimately, into power on its own in
1945. But the war deflected the radical potential of American
labor, left it still divided though enriched in numbers and enlarged coffers.

Oddly enough, when John L. Lewis kept his campaign pledge
to step down as CIO chieftain—"Sustain me now or repudiate
me," Lewis declared over a nationwide radio hookup in a 1940
bid to defeat Roosevelt—both wings of the American labor movement were in the hands of Lewis protégés. Neither ex-miner William Green, presiding over the AFL, nor Philip Murray, over-
seeing the CIO, would ever be free of the Lewis presence.

Perhaps something of this was in Lewis' mind when he stepped down from the CIO presidency on November 18, 1940. In the public eye, he was a repudiated isolationist, sulking with his America-First and communist allies. Amalgamated Clothing Workers' president Sidney Hillman, who had mustered CIO support, over Lewis' opposition, for Roosevelt during the third-term campaign, was awarded in December, 1940, an appointment as an associate director of the Office of Production Management under William S. Knudsen. Sardonic, Lewis thundered that American labor was in danger of becoming a "tame cat" in the White House. But Tabby could still arch her back and spit. The year before Pearl Harbor was an uneasy one; strikes threatened defense production at, among other plants, Allis-Chalmers—shut down for 76 days in the spring—and at the Inglewood, California, plant of North American Aviation, Inc., seized by the President on June 9. Coal miners struck on April 1 and Ford's gigantic River Rouge plant shut down the following day. A steel strike seemed likely. The communists exploited legitimate workers' grievances skillfully. The number of strikes swelled to a peak higher than in any previous year, except 1917 and 1927. During 1941, more than 4,200 strikes involving over 2.3 million workers caused a loss of 23,000,000 man-days. "Hell is breaking loose all over the place," declared a harried Defense Advisory Commission aide. For a time, it appeared that John L. Lewis once again would engage in a great power struggle.

Nonetheless, the current began to run the other way. In Detroit, Walter P. Reuther first gained national prominence with the suggestion that the idle facilities of the automobile industry be used to produce an estimated 500 planes a day. The AFL demanded full representation for labor on all governmental defense agencies; Philip Murray proposed the creation of industry councils for each major defense industry, consisting of an equal number of labor and management representatives with a government official as chairman, to coordinate production, train workers and promote industrial peace. Hillman was photographed at the

President's side as he telephoned orders for government troops to break up the Inglewood strike. More importantly, Hillman also negotiated an exclusive agreement with the AFL building and construction trades on behalf of government agencies concerned with defense construction. The agreement froze out the CIO's struggling union of construction workers, headed by John L. Lewis' brother Denny, from any share in defense construction. This further weakened Lewis' hold on the CIO. The communists, when Hitler attacked Russia on June 23, 1941, deserted Lewis for Hillman. The "Samson of Labor," as the communists once called Lewis, was in for a shearing.

Lewis, however, as his former first lieutenant Phil Murray well knew, had tremendous recuperative powers. Relying solely upon his miners, Lewis prepared to challenge the growing encroachment of government into labor-management relations. His target was the National Defense Mediation Board, appointed by Roosevelt on March 19, 1941. The issue was the union shop for mine workers in the mines owned by the major steel companies. Lewis feared a wartime erosion of labor's rights unless these "captive" mines were secured by the union shop, where all employees must become and remain members for the duration of a collective-bargaining agreement. This was opposed by the steel companies for fear that it would set a precedent for the steel mills, where SWOC still represented members only. After a shutdown of two days in late October, the dispute was referred to the Mediation Board. On November 10, the Board voted to reject the UMW demand by a vote of 9 to 2. Murray and Thomas Kennedy, the two who voted nay, resigned from the Mediation Board, thus ending its usefulness. In no mood to repeat his surrender to Wilson in 1919, Lewis called out his miners on November 15. Sympathetic strikes swept the surrounding mines in the anthracite belt. Eleven pickets were shot at the Frick coke plant at Edenborn, Pennsylvania. Lewis was denounced for blocking the defense effort, though the truth was with Lewis when he pointed out: "Defense output is not impaired and will not be impaired for an indefinite period." However, the nation could not very well tolerate a coal strike at this critical juncture. Congress had just authorized the arming of merchant vessels; Japanese envoys had opened discussions in Washington. On November 22, Lewis accepted a White House proposal that the captive-mines dispute be arbitrated by a board consisting of Benjamin F. Fairless, president of U. S. Steel; John R. Steelman, director of the U. S. Conciliation Service; and Lewis. The miners went back to work and Lewis, confident that Steelman would see the issue his way, met with his fellow arbitrators. The decision was 2 to 1 for the union shop in the captive mines, but its significance was lost in the day's headlines. The Japanese had attacked Pearl Harbor. It was December 7, 1941.

The significance of the decision, however, was not lost on the leaders of the AFL or the CIO. Lewis, no doubt about it, had pulled a coup of the first magnitude. He was back in form, and at a conference of labor and management summoned by the President to work out machinery for the settlement of wartime industrial disputes, Lewis emerged as the tacit spokesman for the AFL and the CIO. The conferees agreed that there should be no strikes or lockouts for the duration of the war. But they quickly deadlocked on the issue of union security. The industry representatives pleaded for the *status quo*; the unionists insisted that the proposed wartime mediation board be empowered to grant a union or closed shop in plants where the open shop prevailed at the outbreak of war. When Charles R. Hook pleaded for the preservation of the open shop, Lewis replied: "I have heard this open shop talk before. The open shop is a harlot with a wig and artificial limbs, and her bones rattle. But how much production will she give us, Mr. Hook?"

For a moment, it appeared that Lewis might wrest an agreement out of the conference, a victory that would have made him the undisputed spokesman for American labor for the duration of the war, at least. But President Roosevelt cut the conference short on December 23, forestalling any Lewis success. The President accepted the proposed ban on wartime strikes and lockouts. He also declared that he would create a war labor board that must "cover of necessity all disputes that may arise between labor and management." The first skirmish went to labor; the union security issue would be fought out on a case-by-case basis within the War Labor Board. William H. Davis, a former patent attorney and chairman of the National Defense Mediation Board, was named chairman of the new agency created by executive order on January 12, 1942.

Though the President neatly sidetracked Lewis, the mine workers' paladin still possessed another string to his bow. Lewis actually was in a good strategic spot. Two former Lewis aides—Green and Murray—headed the two wings of the American labor movement. The American people were united in their effort to win the war, and the time seemed propitious for unifying the labor movement as well. Lewis could not help but see that a united labor movement would be an invaluable counter to the weight of industry in the nation's councils of war. And such a development certainly would place Lewis himself once again at center stage.

So on January 17, 1942, Lewis, as chairman of the CIO negotiating committee, sent a letter to Green and Murray suggesting the resumption of peace conferences between the AFL and the CIO. Arrogantly, Lewis did not even bother to inform Murray beforehand of the move though he had caucused with the two most powerful men in the AFL—Big Bill Hutcheson of the Carpenters and Dan Tobin of the Teamsters. According to A. H. Raskin of the *New York Times*, an agreement had been reached even on a slate of officers. Green was to retire; AFL secretary-treasurer George Meany was slated to be president of the unified movement. Lewis would represent the CIO as first or second vice-president on an expanded executive council. Murray was to be named secretary-treasurer at $18,000 a year. Green immediately accepted the Lewis invitation. Phil Murray, who first read the letter in the papers, retorted, "No one has the right to trade me for a job." Angrily, he declared that any unity conferences would have to be initiated through his office. Always adept at improvisation, President Roosevelt saved the day for Murray and the anti-Lewis bloc within the CIO by forming a "labor cabinet" of three AFL and three CIO leaders. The so-called Labor Victory Board met from time to time at the White House and served to fend off the Lewis comeback. It also ended for over a decade any merger possibilities between the two national labor organizations.

Although Lewis continued to loom, beetle-browed and glowering, over the labor scene until his retirement in 1959, the failure of the merger coup marked the end of his career as the dominant figure in the American labor movement. Roosevelt outfoxed him, though he might not have succeeded so easily if it had not been for Lewis' overweening pride and blunt arrogance. In classic fashion, Lewis, in the end, was his own best destroyer. Hubris laid him low. Frustrated. a baleful Lewis hounded Phil Murray out of the United Mine Workers but he could not dislodge his former lieutenant from the captaincy of the CIO. In time, Lewis would take his miners out of the CIO, leaving behind a debt that could never be repaid. Then he would reenter the AFL only to leave the Federation after the war to go it alone again.

As for Philip Murray, so gentle a man and so long in Lewis' shadow, he emerged to govern a CIO that had far greater power than in Lewis' day with a hand as resolute as that of his old mentor. Murray, a Catholic with a mystical belief in labor-management-government industry councils, was born in Lanark-shire, Scotland, the son of an Irish immigrant coal miner. His father, William Murray, was active in the Scottish trade-union movement. Young Phil soon entered the mines as his father's helper. On Christmas Day, 1902, the 16-year-old Philip and his father arrived in America as an advance party for the rest of the Murray clan. The young Murray shoveled enough coal to fill three mine cars a day at a dollar a car in Westmoreland County, Pennsylvania. During mine layoffs, Murray played an indifferent outside left at soccer. He was a much better team manager. At night, he studied mathematics and economics, racing through a

60-dollar International Correspondence School course in six months.

Murray first came to the attention of his mates when he upped and smacked a weigh boss suspected of cheating him and others on coal weight at the tipple. A strike ensued. The lanky 18-year-old led a deputation to talk to the general manager of the Keystone Coal and Coke Company. The next day, the Murrays were dispossessed and forced to live in a tent. When hunger ended the strike, four weeks later, Philip Murray was personally escorted to the border of Westmoreland County and told not to return. Out of such stuff is popularity made among militant coal miners. Murray rose rapidly in District 5 of the UMW, a district that covers the rich Pittsburgh bituminous coal seam. By 1912, Murray was an International Board member and four years later he was president of his district. John L. Lewis made Murray a vice-president in 1920. Murray, along with Thomas Kennedy, UMW secretary, made up Lewis' team of negotiators. The canny Scotsman carried in his briefcase a wealth of statistics on coal and allied matters, which he would read in a rolling burr to operators silenced by Lewis' blustering thunder. Murray, until his death on November 9, 1952, was always a first-rate negotiator.

When Murray was first assigned to the Steel Workers Organizing Committee by Lewis, he knew little of steel making except what he knew of the coal-coke end of the process. But with his capacity for absorbing data, Murray soon came to grips with the intricacies of sheet-bar and structural shapes, rail mills and tin-plating processes. It was Murray's patience that carried SWOC from the defeats of 1937 to successful bargaining with the Little Steel companies in the early 1940s.

Murray's temperament was admirably suited to the wartime transition of the CIO from an almost revolutionary industrial unionism—the CIO of the sit-ins—to the syndicalist, adaptive CIO of the postwar era. Murray was a moderate. As John Chamberlain noted in *Life* magazine in 1946, "The Murray mind is not a speculative mind and the Murray psychology is not made for revolution." Murray was influenced by the labor-management-public cooperativism of the Papal encyclicals *Rerum Novarum* (1891) and *Quadragesimo Anno* (1931). He was interested in the post–World War II German experiments in codetermination, in which German trade unionists served as company directors along with representatives of management. Industrial democracy, Murray argued in his book *Organized Labor and Production* written with Morris Cooke, depended on collective bargaining with labor organizations, on one side, "able to regard the interests of the industry as a whole"; and on the other side, organizations of employers "prepared to assume the responsibilities of economic statesmanship." "As younger and better trained men rise into positions of industrial leadership," wrote Murray and Cooke, "there is multiplying evidence of the infiltration of social-mindedness into the stubborn tissue of business self-interest. We see great labor unions taking seriously the idea of responsibility for continued production." Murray's outlook also fit into the spread of the "New Unionism" of the needle trades with its emphasis on employer-financed, union-controlled health and welfare programs. As McAllister Coleman pointed out, Murray "was talking more in the quiet voice of Sidney Hillman than in the sonorous tones of Lewis." Murray's viewpoint, as it happened, dovetailed neatly with wartime-fostered developments in collective bargaining.

Chief among these was a changing attitude toward collective bargaining on the part of management. Sharp opposition to unions had been blunted by court decisions upholding the constitutionality of the Wagner Labor Act. Hard-pressed by the necessities of waging a global war, the government redoubled its efforts to establish labor peace on the home front. The Wagner Act put the government into labor relations as a peacemaker as a matter of public policy; the war made enforcement of the policy imperative. "While the struggle between labor and management certainly did not cease during the war," declares economist Joel Seidman in *American Labor from Defense to Reconversion*, "inevitably it was sharply transformed." Cost-plus contracts, with their guarantee of profits no matter the costs—and, in the civilian sector, price adjustments—took the sting out of wage disputes. The government, rather than collective bargaining, became the chief instrument of wage determination with the War Labor Board's applying the Little Steel formula for wartime wage adjustments (raises were based on a 15-percent rise in living costs from January 1, 1941, to May 1, 1942) and the Stabilization Act of 1942, which authorized the President to stabilize wages and salaries on September, 1942, levels. These developments made it easier for management to accept collective bargaining.

Acceptance of trade unionism by management, especially the management of America's giant auto, rubber, steel, and defense industry corporations was furthered by an ingenious compromise worked out by the War Labor Board on the question of union security. How could the unions preserve their strength when they had given up their chief weapon, the right to strike? During World War I, the existing union and open shops had been frozen for the duration. By agreeing to give up the right to strike at that time the unions did gain government recognition of their right to organize and bargain collectively. These rights were now guaranteed by the Wagner Labor Act. Something more was needed than simple maintenance of the *status quo*, unionists argued, if they were expected to meet their responsibilities in maintaining wartime production. "Union security," says Seidman, "remained a source of conflict, partly because it helped to hold the unions together while the strike weapon was given up and partly because it would influence the postwar strength, and therefore the postwar bargaining position, of the parties." The employer-backed anti-union drives of the post-World War I era and their disastrous consequences for the unions were still fresh in union memories.

The dispute over union security deadlocked, as we have seen, President Roosevelt's hastily summoned labor-management conference following Pearl Harbor. The matter was left to the discretion of the War Labor Board. In a union-security case involving

Inland Steel, one of the Little Steel companies, the Board declared that it possessed the authority under the President's executive order to consider disputes over union status. While it continued to decide the issue on the basis of individual cases, it soon evolved a basic policy in a series of key cases involving the Federal Shipbuilding & Drydock Co., a U.S. Steel subsidiary; the Phelps Dodge Corporation; the Caterpillar Tractor Co.; and others. This policy provided the employee with an escape period of 15 days, during which he could withdraw from the collective-bargaining unit for the duration of the labor agreement. Frank P. Graham, in the Caterpillar Tractor case, stated the WLB majority view: "By and large, the maintenance of a stable union membership makes for the maintenance of responsible union leadership and responsible union discipline, makes for keeping faithfully the terms of the contract, and provides a stable basis for union-management cooperation for more efficient production."

Maintenance of membership was a compromise between the union view favoring the extension of the union shop and management's tenacious opposition to the union shop. It represented an advance for the unions, especially those in the mass-production industries, where, at the outbreak of war, the unions held bargaining rights for members only. Management's continued opposition rested on fears of what maintenance of membership would do to the balance of bargaining power after the war rather than on any real dissatisfaction with wartime performance. Any notions to the contrary were quickly disabused when the government seized Montgomery Ward in 1944 to enforce a WLB decision backing Retail Clerks' International Association's representation rights in the mail-order firm. An era of employer opposition to union recognition came to an end when four U. S. Army soldiers carried Sewell Avery, head of Montgomery Ward, out of his office on April 27, 1944. This dramatic confirmation of the government's wartime labor policy marked the turn within management toward acceptance of collective bargaining.

As a result of the WLB's maintenance of membership compromise, which backed in a reasonable way the unions' demand for recognition, there was no real challenge to union recognition in the post–World War II period comparable to that which developed after World War I. Few historians would dispute the assertion of War Labor Board Chairman Davis that the maintenance of membership compromise was "the greatest piece of industrial statesmanship that I know of." The foundation of collective bargaining as a permanent institution in the United States was firmly laid.

Maintenance of membership, as a device, helped to dovetail the "New Unionism" into the new corporatism. What unionists envisaged as "industrial democracy," sophisticated management came to view as a practical means for the handling of personnel problems within a company structure that had become too unwieldy for the old-fashioned face-to-face relationship to work with equity or satisfaction. Collective bargaining, in this light, became a system for drawing up the rules for employment; and the unions became agencies for enforcing these rules. The usefulness of the unions in this new role was driven home by the wartime experience of management confronted with an influx of new— and, in many instances, unruly—workers. Labor's success may be judged by the record. In 1942 only five one-hundredths of one percent of war work was delayed because of strikes. "That record," declared President Roosevelt, "has never been equaled in this country. It is as good or better than the record of any of our allies in wartime." In 1943, when man-days lost peaked to 13.5 million as a result of work stoppages, WLB chairman Davis placed the time lost in perspective by pointing out that there had been one year of work gained for every hour lost. "It is the best this nation or any other nation has ever done in wartime or peacetime," said Davis.

Wartime stoppages were, nonetheless, so many thorns in the public hide. "Our union," declared R. J. Thomas, president of the United Auto Workers, "cannot survive if the nation and our soldiers believe that we are obstructing the war effort." Many unions took disciplinary action against strike leaders. But others found it difficult to resist when their members demanded action to resolve unsettled grievances, a condition aggravated by a backlog of 17,000 undecided cases before the War Labor Board. "Workers, war-weary and fearful about their postwar future," a Wall Street leader began in the summer of 1944, "seem to be grabbing almost any excuse for a strike these days." And, complained *Labor*, official publication of the rail unions, "American workers have been made victims of any number of raw deals. When they have protested, some bureaucrat snapped, 'Don't you know we are fighting a war?' " To many workers, it seemed that "fighting a war" had become an excuse for inaction, for the postponement of the correction of some wrong. Price increases put a strain on the Little Steel formula, which was finally challenged in 1943 by strikes in the nation's coalfields and on the railroads. President Roosevelt, on April 8, 1943, issued a "hold-the-line" order against further wage and price increases. But the order, as it turned out, no more than stressed the duties of the War Labor Board and the Office of Price Administration. It did nothing to ease labor unrest.

Once again John L. Lewis lumbered into the center of labor discontent. The soft-coal miners, who had already received their full allotment under the Little Steel formula, demanded an increase of two dollars a day, vacation benefits and portal-to-portal pay. Strikes rippled through the coalfields in March and April, 1943. On May 1, the President seized all the nation's coal mines, appointing Secretary of the Interior Harold L. Ickes as coal administrator.

All that critical wartime summer the coalfields rivaled the battlefields for public attention. The miners stayed out of the pits sporadically in April, concertedly for a time in June, and again sporadically in late October. Each time, however, their actions backed up Lewis in the course of his "negotiations" with the government. President Roosevelt threatened to draft the striking miners in June. Union leaders were caught in the unhappy dilemma of favoring the demands of the miners while fearing the course taken by the mine union chief. Their fears were amply confirmed mid-summer, when an angry Congress passed over the President's veto of the Smith-Connally Act. This act empowered the President to seize struck facilities; punished by fine or imprisonment a strike at a plant in the Government's possession; required a 30-day cooling-off period following a strike notice; and prescribed that a strike vote be taken on the thirtieth day by the National Labor Relations Board. Lewis came under widespread attack in the labor movement for giving cause for the passage of a "vicious anti-labor bill."

In October, President Roosevelt again seized the mines. But this time he authorized Ickes to negotiate directly with the mine union. On November 3, Lewis ordered the miners back to work, having negotiated a complicated settlement with Ickes. Technically, the $1.50-a-day wage increase managed to stay within the Little Steel formula as it came from portal-to-portal pay and increasing hours by reducing the lunch period. But the formula had its weaknesses, as the rail crisis a month later demonstrated. An emergency board, under the provisions of the Railway Labor Act, had awarded the railroaders a pay raise of eight cents an hour only to have it vetoed by Economic Stabilization Director Vinson. A strike vote was taken, with 98 percent voting in favor. December 30 was set as the strike deadline. Roosevelt ordered the Army to seize the railroads. In January, a settlement was worked out that gave the railroad workers hourly increases ranging from four to ten cents, plus an additional one to five cents an hour in place of overtime after 40 hours. The Little Steel formula had been stretched if not breached.

Following the coal and rail settlements, the union petitioned the President to adjust the formula to the current cost of living. By February and March, 1945, as the war in Europe drew to a close, the unions urged the President to reestablish free collective bargaining within 60 days of the war's end. The UAW declared that procedures before the WLB were "time-wasting, meaningless rigmarole." The AFL urged an immediate 11-percent pay increase to match increases in the cost of living. In February, 1945, the United Textile Workers, CIO, became the first union officially to void its no-strike policy. On August 18, 1945, four days after the surrender of Japan, President Truman authorized voluntary wage rises that did not affect prices to become effective without WLB approval.

The trade unions came out of the war greatly strengthened. Union membership swelled from about 10.5 million when the Japanese bombed Pearl Harbor to about 14.75 million when the war ended in August, 1945. The new industrial unions of the CIO were firmly established in auto, rubber, steel, and other mass-production industries. The craft unions of the AFL were even more firmly entrenched and were organizing on an industrial basis as well. Union officials, as members of wartime advisory boards, gained a prestige they had not had before the war.

This strength was also reflected in the gains secured, as the unions vigorously prosecuted their cases for wage gains before the War Labor Board. The Board in many cases corrected wage inequities, set equal pay for equal work for women workers, allowed a pattern of fringe benefits to emerge, and made increases to prevent substandard living. These gains are reflected in the increase of real earnings. Average real weekly earnings in manufacturing, $24 in terms of the 1935–39 price levels in 1939, rose to $28.12 in 1941 and reached a wartime peak of $36.72 in 1944. Real hourly earnings rose from 64 cents in 1939 to 69 cents in 1941 and reached a wartime peak of 81 cents in 1944. The Wage and Hour Administrator reported in 1942 that 7.5 million workers received 40 cents an hour or less. The WLB automatically approved increases, first up to 40 cents and later to 50 cents an hour, so by the end of the war no workers got less than 50 cents an hour. These gains should be set against rises in corporate profit after taxes, from $6.4 billion in 1940 to $10.8 billion four years later.

The war also brought about a change in the pattern of Negro

employment. When war broke out, Negroes were largely employed in agricultural, unskilled, or service jobs. A large proportion was unemployed. Although a shortage of workers soon developed, Negroes were frequently excluded from new job opportunities in the expanding war industries. Craft unions that controlled job opportunities also discriminated against Negro craftsmen. A. Philip Randolph, the venerated leader of the Brotherhood of Pullman Car Porters, organized his March on Washington movement as a protest against the exclusion of Negro workers from defense industries. The threatened march brought a quick response from Washington. On June 25, 1941, President Roosevelt issued an executive order establishing a Committee on Fair Employment Practices to investigate complaints of discrimination. This also ordered that all training programs for defense production be administered without discrimination and that all defense contracts require a no-discrimination clause. In May, 1943, the FEPC was given increased authority and a greater budget. However, it never possessed the power needed to give full justice to the Negro worker.

In three years, the FEPC handled 8,000 complaints of discrimination in war industry and government employment and held 30 public hearings. Unfortunately, federal FEPC ended with the war. However, its wartime successes sparked a few states to do likewise, and in 1945 New York, New Jersey, and Indiana adopted state FEPC legislation. Some permanent progress had been scored but not enough.

# XVI

## *THE FRIENDLY WARRIORS*

WORLD WAR II ENDED, FOR MANY, ON AN UNCERTAIN NOTE. BE-
neath the surface cordialities of the Yalta and Potsdam conferences lurked the icy realities of an approaching Cold War. Over
Hiroshima and Nagasaki mushroomed a new fear to cloud men's
minds. Closer to home, fear of unemployment and reduced earnings troubled American workers as they welcomed the dawn of
peace.

Even before the war had ended, cutbacks in war production
resulted in joblessness for some workers and in increasing appre-
hension among others. "They've closed up Willow Run," declared the CIO *Economic Outlook* in the spring of 1945. "They
gave the workers Army-Navy E's and told them to go home because the Government and Mr. Ford didn't want the plant any-
more. Nobody wants Willow Run, the $95-million factory that
produced almost 9,000 Liberator bombers. Nobody wants the
51,950 pieces of machinery. . . . And nobody wants the more than
20,000 human beings who go with the plant." The worried auto
worker unionists were not the only ones concerned over the problems of reconversion. John W. Snyder, director of the Office of

War Mobilization and Reconversion, predicted in August, 1945, that there would be five million unemployed within three months and eight million by the following spring. Others put the figure even higher.

To such dour prospects were added labor's fears of an anti-union drive on the pattern of the open-shop drives of the 1920s. A flood of anti-union legislative measures filled Congressional hoppers. None was passed, but similar measures were enacted in a good number of state legislatures, especially in states where industrialization was limited and unionism weak. After the death of Franklin D. Roosevelt, the new President, Harry S Truman, pleaded for a continuance of the no-strike pledge, at least until his labor-management conference could fashion machinery for the peaceful transition from the war to the new economy ahead. But the President's hopes for a successful labor-management confer-ence were soon shattered. Labor quickly chucked the no-strike pledge. In the last four and a half months of 1945, man-days lost due to strikes shot up to 28,400,000, more than double the war-time peak of 1943, when the coal strikes wracked the nation. This was but a prelude to the great strike wave of 1946.

That year set the nation on the collective-bargaining road to a new corporate welfarism. Over four and a half million workers marched on the picket lines in 1946, a half million more than the previous peak, in fateful 1919. One hundred and thirteen million man-days of labor were lost, three times as many as in 1945 and the largest in our history. Nationwide strikes halted production in coal, auto, electric, and steel industries; maritime and railroad transportation ground to a halt. Yet, for all the ferment and wrathful exchanges at the collective-bargaining table, strikers on the picket line frequently assumed a holiday air. There was a great letting off of steam. But unlike 1919, there was no stoking of revolutionary fires. *Fortune*, in November, summed the year up: "The strikes and strike threats of 1945–46 generated violent emotions, but it was an impressive fact that for the first time a great wave of strikes stirred up almost no physical violence. The strikers of 1945–46 were not desperate men. On the public platform their leaders sounded off with booming phrases directed at the enemy Capital; but privately they, like the strikers, were calm, cool, even friendly warriors."

The difference in temper between 1919 and 1946 was no less striking than the changes wrought in the economy. The impact of unemployment, which rose over a million in 1945 and jumped to 2.3 million in 1946, was cushioned by unemployment insurance, which had not existed in the post–World War I decade. Ex-GI's were aided by the "52–20 Club," a full year of unemployment insurance at $20 a week. Others went off to college careers financed by the GI Bill instead of entering a weakened labor market. Wartime savings, too, helped to tide over many people. As for the unions, their organizational strength—both in membership and treasury—was far greater than that commanded by the unions after World War I.

Management, in 1946, also contributed to the peaceful temper of the great strike wave by not contesting the right of trade unions to exist. It was an exceptional strike where recognition of a union was at stake. Management's decision not to undertake a drive to oust the unions was in part, the unintentional fruit of government planning through taxation. Corporations that lost money during reconversion could get returns on excess-profits taxes paid during the war. This carry-back provision provided an excellent cushion against the postwar strike wave for managements that, in any case, had little zest for an all-out, open war against the unions. As *Fortune* pointed out: "A variety of factors makes strikes fairly cheap, in the short-range view, for some corporations. The excess-profits tax was in force until December 31, 1945; in the first eight months of the year the big war contractors had already made about as much money as they could hope to clear for the whole year; in some cases it was actually more profitable in terms of the 1945 balance sheet to shut down toward the end of the year rather than pay higher wages in advance of price relief." But, though strikes were profitable, sophisticated corporate management was quick to see that strikebreaking and union busting were not. Industry wanted price controls lifted. The President, on August 16, 1945, announced a new policy permitting wage increases on condition that they did not result in price increases. The unions, notably the United Auto Workers, were quick to demand higher wages. The corporations resisted, but in the end gave way, hoping to argue increased labor costs to batter down remaining price controls. Even after controls were removed in November, 1946, negotiated wage increases proved to be useful justification for raising prices still further. As Daniel Bell has demonstrated, postwar strikes and resultant wage boosts, became a fulcrum for raising prices and lowering the break-even point—the lowest level of production that will sustain no loss—for industry. Prices were then "administered" with this in mind. Public assent, or acquiescence, however, was still essential before prices could be raised. The unions served as useful scapegoats in this process, a fact that contributed to management acceptance of collective bargaining as a valuable adjunct to corporate policy. But this usefulness of the unions to management was no certain thing as the curtain rose on strife-torn 1946.

Though the temper of unionists was not, unlike 1919, revolutionary, they did possess a new kind of social consciousness, closely tied to collective bargaining. This was rooted in the developments of the late 1930s and of the war years. Though both the CIO and the AFL continued to be politically active, the new social unionism turned from government and politics as an area for the possible achievement of social reform to hard-bargaining around the table with management over an expanding program of fringe benefits. Postwar bargaining also came to be dominated by a few men who developed "pattern" settlements that washed over the economy in successive two- and three-year waves. To the orotund oratory of John L. Lewis and the mild-mannered presence of Philip Murray, a new insistent voice was added, in the person of an ex-tool and die maker Walter P. Reuther.

Reuther then headed a powerful caucus within the auto union.

As spokesman for the union's General Motors bloc, he became the leader of the UAW's first major postwar strike when he convinced the union executive board to adopt his "one-at-a-time" strategy for tackling the auto companies. Reuther's—and the UAW's—insistence on a wage increase without any increase in the price of cars also brought the fiery auto unionist to the forefront as labor's chief spokesman in the first round of collective bargaining following the end of the war. Reuther's most radical demand—that GM open its books to prove or disprove the union's contention that the auto company could grant a 30-percent wage increase without any increase in auto prices—set the stage for a crucial three-and-a-half-month strike that began on November 21, 1945, when some 200,000 GM workers in 96 plants across the country downed tools.

Walter P. Reuther, the voice of the new social unionism, was born on Labor Day, 1907, in Wheeling, West Virginia. His grandfather fled Bismarckian Germany for the freedom of America. His father, Valentine Reuther, inherited a binding sense of moral duty, which he passed on to his sons along with a lesser measure of his devotion to Debsian socialism. Valentine Reuther started his working life as a brewery worker, ran for Congress on the socialist ticket, and served the labor movement as secretary of his AFL brewery workers' local, and as organizer for his union and for the AFL in the Ohio Valley. On Sunday afternoons, Valentine Reuther set up impromptu debates among his boys: Ted, the oldest, the only one to stay out of the labor movement; Victor, Roy, and Walter, all later active in the UAW. They argued the "social questions" of the day: pacifism, socialism, capital punishment, women in industry, and so on. Their father also taught them that each must have a trade.

Walter quit school in his third year at Wheeling High to take a job as an apprentice toolmaker to help support his family. He soon gagged at the idea of working Sundays, organized a protest, and was fired for his troubles. He went to Detroit, where he broke in as a tool and die maker at Briggs, working the 13-hour night shift for 85 cents an hour. He went on to Ford where he received $1.10 an hour as a full-fledged tool and die man. In 1932, the fiery redhead campaigned for Norman Thomas. A year later, he was fired by Ford for union activity. Then, he and his brother Victor decided to take a hand-to-mouth world tour, using their small store of savings as a start. It was the American grand tour with a difference: they avoided fashionable London, touring instead England's auto plants, textile mills, and coal pits. They arrived in Berlin the day before the Reichstag fire. In Germany, they lived with anti-Nazi students, and succeeded in helping a few over the border into Switzerland. They went on to work 16 months in an auto plant in Gorki, Russia, a city built for the Soviet Government by the Ford company. For a time, apparently, they shared the then-prevalent uncritical attitude toward the Stalin regime. When the truth about Stalin's terror became more widely known, the Reuthers' enthusiasm was quickly dispelled. The brothers very early became outspoken opponents of totalitarian communism, both here and abroad. The two brothers went on for short stays in India, where they caught a glimpse of the Gandhian movement for independence, and in Japan, where they saw something of Japanese militarism. As Irving Howe and B. J. Widick note in their book, *The UAW and Walter Reuther*, "No one could have asked for a more direct education in modern realities."

On their return to the United States, Walter and Victor joined Roy, the first Reuther on the United Auto Workers' payroll, in the drive to organize the auto workers. In 1937, as a volunteer organizer, Walter began amalgamating the scattered and tiny West Side UAW locals into one big local union. The Local grew from 8,000 to 30,000 within a year. The Reuthers played a leading role in the sitdowns. Walter was among those severely beaten by Ford Servicemen in the famous "battle of the overpass" in 1937. In 1940, he came to national attention by proposing that the auto industry utilize idle auto manufacturing capacity for production of much-needed airplanes. His leadership of the

GM strike through the winter of 1945–46 catapulted him into the presidency of the auto union a few months later. The following year he consolidated his strength further by the ouster of his communist-backed opposition from most, if not all, positions of leadership within the union. In 1952, after the death of Philip Murray, Reuther became president of the CIO.

More than any other single union leader in the postwar era, Reuther stirred up management animosity and opposition. Reuther's moderate personal life is a puzzle to management, as it is to many workers. He is not a convivial man, though he can exercise considerable charm on occasion. Reuther does not drink nor smoke, belying the typical image of a union leader as a back-slapping, cigar-chomping politico. Reuther's puritanism sets him off from other labor leaders almost as much as his fondness for the statistics of social reform. George Romney, now Governor of Michigan and former head of American Motors, once said, "Walter Reuther is the most dangerous man in Detroit because no one is more skilful in bringing about revolution without seeming to disturb the existing forms of society." But, in action, Reuther is anything but revolutionary; he is the most pragmatic of social unionists. Reuther also gives the impression of a man operating under considerable tension. Howe and Widick locate the source of this tension within Walter Reuther in "a fatal split in American character between the 'idealist' and the 'realist.'" During the 1945–46 GM strike these two aspects of Reuther's character were fused as he drove his union forward into one of the key labor-management engagements of the century.

The insistence that industry open its books in order to demonstrate its ability or inability to meet wage demands, and the linking of prices, profits and wages signaled a potential expansion of industrial democracy, which had previously meant simple grievance machinery and negotiations over wages and working conditions. The Reuther-UAW demand injected organized labor directly into corporate decision making, if not into the still broader area of economic planning. If the UAW case that wages could come out of profits without price increases had been upheld—and there is reason to believe that the union had a case—then the wage gain for auto workers would have been a gain in real wages. A halt in climbing prices would have given other workers a chance to catch up to the rising cost of living. In his demands upon GM, Reuther managed to meld two disparate trade-union traditions—narrow syndicalism (concern with one's own wages and other job matters) with social unionism (broader concern with the economic standing of all workers). The UAW indicated its willingness to sacrifice the former for the latter when Reuther announced that the union would forego any wage increase if it could be shown from an examination of General Motors' books that a wage increase could not be granted.

Before a Presidential fact-finding board the company did not plead inability to pay. It challenged the board's competence to pass on future profits and rejected the union's effort to make its price policy a collective-bargaining issue. "The dispute," as Joel Seidman has noted, "was vastly more stubborn than a mere collective-bargaining disagreement, or even an issue over a 'principle' such as union security; it was an ideological battle in which the leaders of one side saw themselves as crusaders for social progress and the other as defenders of an established and highly desired way of life."

As America hovered uncertainly between wartime national economic controls and a return to unrestrained corporatism, it seemed, for a moment, that the unions might force a new order of things. Behind the UAW's fight with General Motors loomed the radical impulse to remake American society in labor's image of the workmen's parties, the Knights of Labor, and the Wobblies. It appeared that the Truman Administration agreed with the auto union leaders. The President asserted at a press conference that the ability to pay was always relevant when wage increases were under consideration. After GM stormed out of the hearings before Presidential fact-finders, declaring that the company would not cooperate so long as ability to pay remained an issue, the board recommended on January 10, 1946, an hourly increase of 19½ cents, asserting that it was well within the Corporation's ability to pay. GM rejected the recommendations. The union was now out on strike, its contentions backed by the governmental recommendations.

But collective-bargaining pressures in other industries—where the unions did not stand so firmly on principle as the UAW— forced the government's hand. On January 15, 200,000 members of the CIO's United Electrical Workers struck, followed by an equal number of packinghouse workers on the next day. Five days later, 750,000 steel workers shut down the basic steel industry. Philip Murray, unlike Reuther, made it clear that his concern was with wages, not prices. Industry increased its pressure on Washington to relax the price line. When finally U. S. Steel was assured of a five-dollar-a-ton-increase, Benjamin Fairless quickly settled with Philip Murray. The steel strike ended after 30 days with the 18½-cent wage increase suggested by the President. The price increase, according to the *Chicago-Sun*, netted the steel companies $435,000,000 additional income at a cost of only $185,000,000 in wage boosts.

The rug was none too gently yanked from under Walter Reuther and the UAW. After 113 days, which exausted most of the wartime savings of the auto workers, the GM strike ended on March 13 with a 18½-cent wage boost, the figure set by steel. The electrical, packinghouse, rail and other strikes were all settled on the same "pattern" increase. When wartime price controls were lifted later in the year, on June 30, the postwar wage and price spiral was firmly set, neatly accommodating industry's new system of administered prices. In 1950, partly as a result of the Korean War, the highly organized workers of auto, steel, and other industries partially recouped their losses under spiraling prices when automatic cost-of-living wage adjustments and annual improvement factors (i.e., increases based on increases in production) were incorporated into collective-bargaining agreements. But the unorganized, or poorly organized, workers have yet to catch up to the price spiral set off by management's victory in 1946.

The steel and auto agreements of 1946 set a pattern of wage increases followed by price increases that persisted until the 1960s, when bargaining again changed character. The wage-price spiral, however, was not the sole characteristic of post-World War II bargaining. Walter Reuther may have lost the battle to reshape bargaining closer to the processes of a real industrial democracy; organized labor, however, did manage to cast a new mold for bargaining, a mold that gave a new life to corporate welfarism. Its architect was, of all people, John L. Lewis.

Most labor leaders, with the notable exception of Reuther, were content to follow the wage-increase pattern set by Murray and Fairless. Another exception was John L. Lewis. In 1946, the mine operators were perfectly willing to adhere to the pattern. But a rumbling Lewis was not to be so restrained. He demanded, in addition to the wage hike, a royalty on each ton of coal mined to finance health and welfare services in the mining camps. He also insisted on more adequate safety provisions and the right of the miners to close any mine they considered unsafe. If Lewis was unwilling to push industrial democracy to the limit of union participation in price determination and other aspects of corporate economic planning, he was not at all adverse to push the miners' right for a say in industrial matters that concerned health and safety (Lewis was one of the few labor leaders to oppose the continuation of price control in 1946).

The coal mines shut down on April 1, 1946, as a result of the mine owners' rejection of the union's demands. The miners returned to work during a two-week truce in May. The Government seized the mines just before the truce expired. Lewis and Secretary of the Interior Julius A. Krug sat down to bargain on the terms of the Government's operation of the mines. On May 29, the federal mine administrator and Lewis reached a settlement that ultimately became the foundation for coal peace when the mines were returned to private hands. The Krug-Lewis agreement provided for the establishment of two benefit funds, a welfare and retirement fund jointly administered by management and the union, and a medical and hospital fund controlled by the union. The funds were financed by a five-cent royalty on each ton of coal mined. A federal mine-safety code was to be adopted, the miners to get an 18½-cent wage increase as well as improved vacation benefits. Later in the fall, Lewis again threatened to pull out the miners, contending a violation of his agreement with Krug. Federal Judge T. Alan Goldsborough issued a temporary restraining order but the coal miners shut down the mines, in violation of the injunction, on November 20, 1946. Lewis and the mine union were found to be in contempt of court. Lewis was fined $10,000 and the union $3,500,000, the largest financial penalty ever imposed on a union in the history of the United States. The union lost an appeal to the Supreme Court, which, however, reduced the penalty to $700,000 on condition that the union purge itself of contempt within a reasonable time. The union did so by withdrawing its strike threat.

The Court decision was universally condemned by the trade unions. The AFL executive council declared, "If such orders could sustain contempt charges every labor union would be exposed to financial ruin by the arbitrary caprice of any anti-labor judge in this country." The Goldsborough decision still stands as an ominous precedent. However, its impact on bargaining is imperceptible.

When the mines were returned to the mine owners at the end of June, 1947, after the expiration of the Smith-Connally Act, Lewis secured a new contract raising daily wages from $11.85 for nine hours to $13.05 for eight. The royalty benefit was increased from five cents to ten cents a ton. This, over the years, has increased to 40 cents a ton. By the end of fiscal year June 30, 1960, the funds paid out almost 144 million dollars in benefits; about 79 million dollars in pensions; 61 million dollars for hospital and medical care; 3.7 million dollars in funeral costs and widow and survivor benefits. The working miner had come a long way since the day when his children had to scrabble for coal at the pithead.

The royalty on coal to finance welfare benefits was not, strictly speaking, an innovation. During the 1930s, the needle-trades unions had established a similar welfare-benefit system, employer-financed and union-controlled. But their welfare funds were financed by a tax on payroll; the miners' by a tax on coal mined. This gave the union, as an institution, incentive to back wholeheartedly the mechanization of the mines. As J. B. S. Hardman noted in summarizing Lewis' career in *Labor History* (Winter, 1961), "Thanks to Lewis, the traditionally 'sick' coal industry is doing well. For decades Lewis had urged the captains of the coal industry to behave like 'capitalists,' to consolidate, modernize and mechanize. The leader of the coal miners taught free enterprise the art of enterprising." But though the health of the industry has improved, this is not the case for all coal miners. Mechanization has driven the small "truck" mine, along with a good many miners, out of the industry. Today, some 160,000 men mine coal, a number far short of the "half million" Lewis once had declared would be the optimum. "It's better," he declared, "to have half a million men working in the industry at good wages, high standards of living, than it is to have a million men working in the industry in poverty and degradation."

The decision to favor mechanization in mining was Lewis's last contribution. For a time he sought to make the UMW's catchall District 50 a rival to the two major labor federations. It organized some 200,000 workers in a variety of industries. Lewis became president emeritus of the UMW in 1960 and died at age 89 on June 11, 1969.

Mining today offers a glimpse of one possible future for America in the age of automation. A small number of highly paid workers and prosperous corporate giants will exist alongside terrible pockets of poverty and unemployment. At least, this is the present picture of Appalachia, where a segment of a once great industry is dying.

Meanwhile, as the Lewis drama unfolded in the courts, labor entered its second round of wage increases. The second round ended peacefully, patterned after 15-cent-an-hour wage and fringe benefits package settlements in steel and auto. In 1948, a third round settled on an 11-cent to 13-cent wage increase pattern. That year, the UAW secured the first cost-of-living "escalator" clause in its agreement with GM relating wages to changes in consumer prices as measured by the U. S. Department of Labor's Bureau of Labor Statistics. An "improvement factor" also provided for annual wage increases in recognition of the rising productivity of the economy. The following year, a steel strike was settled on the recommendations of a Presidential fact-finding board that employers contribute six cents an hour toward pensions and four cents an hour toward social insurance for each worker. The UAW's five-year contract, signed with General Motors in 1950, was the model for the earlier part of the postwar decade. It established noncontributory pensions of $100 a month at age 65, along with death, sickness, and accident benefits. It also provided for automatic cost-of-living wage adjustments, guaranteed annual increases, and a union shop.

After a period of wage and price controls, imposed as a result of the Korean War, the unions shaped new demands. Rail negotiations in 1954 brought the number of workers covered by some type of health-welfare pension plan under collective bargaining to approximately 12 million. While the terms of such plans could be liberalized through bargaining, there were few frontiers left to explore in this area of corporate welfarism. However, a group of CIO unions—in the auto, steel, rubber, and electrical industries—did develop a new proposal aimed at reducing the perils of unemployment: the Guaranteed Annual Wage. In 1955, the Ford Motor Co. and the UAW negotiated a three-year agreement incorporating a modification of the guaranteed annual wage, the so-called supplementary unemployment benefits (SUB) compensation plan financed by a company contribution of five cents an hour. Under the SUB system, laid-off workers receive supplementary unemployment benefits of up to 75 percent of their weekly earnings for 26 weeks. By the end of 1955, similar plans were negotiated for more than a million workers.

These gains in collective bargaining accompanied a period of consolidation on the part of American trade unions. In the early 1930s, the ratio of union members to persons at work in nonagricultural establishments was about 1 to 8; by 1945, it was about 1 to 3, and there it has roughly remained.

# XVII

## CROOKS, COMMUNISTS, AND LEGISLATIVE REFORMS

IMMEDIATELY FOLLOWING THE END OF WORLD WAR II, DRIVES to organize in the South and among white collar workers by both the AFL and the CIO failed, victims of jurisdictional rivalries between the two federations and among unions. The great dreams of postwar expansion also came to grief because legislative changes in states where unions had little or no strength all but made it impossible to organize the unorganized. External pressures, such as those represented in the passage of the Taft-Hartley Act in 1947 and a host of state so-called right-to-work laws, coalesced with internal pressures, such as the conflicts over communists and corruption as well as inter-union raiding, to inhibit, if not prevent, any urge to expansion on the part of organized labor.

Much of the distaste caused by labor's wartime strikes still lingered when the great strike wave of 1946 rolled across the country. Much was made of this in the press, and considerable steam was generated for "reform" of the labor law. Feeling against unions at times ran so high that President Truman at one point during the 1946 rail strike, after the government had seized the railroads, secured the passage of a bill in Congress to draft labor during an emergency dispute, by a vote of 306 to 13. Fortunately, cooler heads prevailed, and after the immediate emergency had passed—the rail strike settled—the bill was allowed to die quietly. But the episode did illustrate something about the prevailing temper. Both the AFL and the CIO underestimated the widespread public feeling that the Wagner Act, passed in 1937, was not entirely suitable for the postwar era. Undemocratic procedures within unions, racketeering, denial of equal rights to Negroes, and other abuses, it seemed to many, cried out for some legislative action. But labor stood pat, opposing any reform of the labor law as pure and simple anti-unionism. By doing so, the unions forfeited the game to the more aggressive champions of "reform," who secured the passage of the Taft-Hartley Law over the veto of President Truman in June, 1947. The new law, perhaps, was more punitive than what the moderate majority would have preferred. At any rate, Senator Robert Taft, Senatorial sponsor of the new law, later became the willing backer of amendments, never adopted, designed to ease the law's impact on legitimate unionization.

The AFL attacked the new measure as a "slave-labor bill"; Philip Murray emotionally declared that the measure "was conceived in sin." President Truman, in his veto message, argued that the bill would "reverse the basic direction of our national labor policy." As it turned out, all three were in some measure wrong. Nonetheless, Taft-Hartley was far from being a piece of model legislation.

The ineptness of its emergency-disputes provisions, for example, is still with us. The law provides for the Presidential appointment of a board of inquiry and an 80-day injunction, during which the *status quo* is continued, and for a vote on the employer's "final offer" at the end of the injunction period. Cyrus Ching, former Director of the Federal Conciliation and Mediation Service, in 1948 pinpointed the basic weakness of this approach: "Provision for an 80-day period of continued operations, under injunctive order of a court, tends to delay rather than facilitate settlement of a dispute. Parties unable to resolve the issues facing them before a deadline date, when subject to an injunction order, tend to lose a sense of urgency, and to relax their efforts. In most instances efforts of the service to encourage the parties to bargain during the injunction period. with a view to early settlement, fall on deaf ears." In addition, very few, if any, national emergency strikes have been settled by a "yes" vote on the employer's "last offer." In most cases, this vote has been a waste of time. Nothing has happened to change this view. Jack Barbash, writing for the League for Industrial Democracy, analyzed ten so-called emergency disputes and concluded: "What this analysis adds up to is this: first, settlements were rarely made during the period of the injunction; second, in the cases in which settlements came during the injunction, it is a real question whether the settlement came because of, or in spite of, the injunction; third, in the majority of cases, the injunction made settlement more difficult."

The impact, as it turned out, of Taft-Hartley on the major unions was minimal. As Barbash, who served for a time as staff director for the U. S. Senate Subcommittee on Labor and Labor Management, points out: "The Taft-Hartley law has not appreciably weakened the stronger unions. The law seems to have had the effect, however, of impairing the ability of unions to organize new groups of workers. This has been notably true for the workers in Southern textile and wood-working industries and generally for the so-called white collar workers." There is some dispute about whether the impact of Taft-Hartley alone crippled labor's drives to organize white collar workers. Yet there is no question but that the operation of the law, and the appreciably altered National Labor Relations Board after 1947 (and especially during the Eisenhower Administration) has hurt weak unions. For example, the law provides that an employer's expression of any views does not constitute an unfair labor practice unless it contains a threat of reprisal or promise of benefit; this "free speech" provision allowed in practice a wide latitude to employers combating unionism. This provision *may* not mean so much in an industrial state such as New York, but in the South, generally it has meant the end of many an organizing campaign.

Unlike most Federal legislation, Taft-Hartley in the so-called States Rights clause gave the states the right to pass legislation that could override provisions of the national labor law. As a result, some 21 states passed so-called right-to-work laws following the passage of the Taft-Hartley Act. The common feature of this legislation is the strong anti-union bias. The union-shop and maintenance-of-membership clauses in union contracts, as well as the closed shop (forbidden by Taft-Hartley) are outlawed. While the Taft-Hartley Act permits union discipline of and discharge of any employee who fails to pay his dues, even this minimum discipline is illegal under right-to-work legislation. (As of 1963, 19 states still have this legislation on the books.)

In addition to the prohibitions imposed by the states' right-to-work legislation, labor's organizational gains in the South were eroded away by excessive delay in the processing of unfair-labor charges before the NLRB. The Textile Workers Union, CIO, for example, filed unfair-labor charges against Anchor Rome Mills in Rome, Georgia, sometime in 1952. Seven months later the General Counsel for the NLRB issued a complaint. Eight months later the trial examiner, a hearing officer under NLRB procedure, issued his intermediate report finding illegal coercion on the part of the employer. After another eight months—almost two years later—the NLRB upheld the trial examiner's findings. Meanwhile, the union disintegrated in the face of the employer's illegal act.

Taft-Hartley may be taken as representative of the external pressures the unions labored under in the years immediately following the end of World War II. But if some part of the potential for labor expansion was closed off by such outside pressures, the unions were also partially immobilized by great internal conflicts such as that over the expulsion of the communists from the CIO and of racketeers from the AFL. These activities consumed a great deal of energy. And, until they were resolved, organized labor was in no position to press at the polls for favorable changes in the political climate.

Communists played a small but significant role in the building of the CIO. They controlled a number of important unions: the United Electrical Workers and the Transport Workers Union are examples, one large, one small, of their strength within certain CIO unions. In 1940 the communists' continuing subservience to a political line laid down in Moscow nearly split the CIO. The communists' anti-war phase, which "happened" to coincide with the Stalin-Hitler pact, caused them to rally around John L. Lewis in a fight against Sidney Hillman, already an interventionist and a close supporter of President Roosevelt's. The nomination of Philip Murray forestalled any split at the time Lewis resigned. The split that seemed inevitable was postponed by Hitler's invasion of Russia and World War II unity. Hillman and the communists subsequently worked closely together in the American Labor Party of New York, though Hillman never tolerated communists within his own union. This marriage of convenience, typical of similar arrangements within a number of CIO unions, scarcely survived the end of the war. The Reuthers burst out of the wartime no-strike cocoon with an aggressive militancy that upset the communist toehold within the UAW in 1946. The communists actually favored continuing the wartime no-strike pledge until Stalin reminded his American followers that the line had changed again.

James B. Carey's crusade against the communists in his union, the United Electrical Workers, which was dormant during the war, broke out anew. The 1946 UE–General Electric agreement was widely condemned by anticommunists as a sweetheart agreement between the company, which wanted malleable union leaders in office, and the communists, who saw a quick settlement as a guarantee of their continued power. Within the CIO inexorable pressures began to mount for the expulsion of the communists from positions of trade-union leadership. Joseph Curran, of the

National Maritime Union, and Michael J. Quill, of the Transport Workers Union, in 1947 turned on the communists in the leadership of their unions and ousted the party-liners. In March, 1948, Philip Murray replaced fellow-traveler Lee Pressman with Arthur J. Goldberg as CIO attorney.

In Cleveland in 1949 the CIO finally moved against the communists. Philip Murray, in his opening address, declared: "There is enough room within the CIO movement to differ about many subjects, many ideas, question of reform within the CIO, economics, social and trade-union policy—yes, plenty of room, plenty of room, but there is no room within CIO for communism." The Convention expelled the United Electrical Workers as communist-dominated and chartered the International Union of Electrical, Radio and Machine Workers, headed by CIO secretary-treasurer James B. Carey. The Farm Equipment Workers union was also expelled, its jurisdiction being given to the United Auto Workers. Charges were brought against ten other unions. Nine were later expelled as communist-dominated—the West Coast Longshoremen, Marine Cooks, Food and Tobacco, Communications Association, Fishermen, Public Workers, Mine, Mill, Office Workers, and the Fur and Leather Workers. Since then most of these unions have disappeared, with their memberships' being absorbed into one or another AFL-CIO union. Offsetting this momentary loss in membership was the affiliation with the CIO of the 250,000-member Communication Workers of America, the first major white-collar union.

The action against the communists within the American labor movement was paralleled by the labor movements of other countries. Shortly after World War II, the CIO affiliated with the World Federation of Trade Unions, as did many other noncommunist unions in other nations. But it was soon apparent that the WFTU was in communist hands. Non-communist support of the Marshall Plan and communist opposition to it made the continued affiliation of non-communists with the WFTU impossible. In 1949, the CIO withdrew from WFTU. In December of that year, the democratic unions regrouped their forces to found the International Confederation of Free Trade Unions. (The AFL, which all along had fought the WFTU as communist, also joined with the CIO and the British and French free trade unions in the founding of the new world-labor body.) The ICFTU today represents 141 unions in 109 countries and territories, with a membership of over 56 million workers.

International cooperation between the AFL and the CIO preceded—and paved the way for—cooperation at home. In November, 1952, Philip Murray and William Green died within a few days of each other. George Meany, former secretary-treasurer of the AFL, became president of the Federation. Walter P. Reuther succeeded Philip Murray after a hard-fought battle at the 1952 CIO convention. The drive for the amalgamation of the two labor groups began almost as soon as the two representatives of the older order passed from the scene. The same AFL executive council meeting that elevated Meany, unanimously reactivated a committee authorized to seek unity with the CIO. Less than two weeks later, the CIO convention that elected Walter P. Reuther president, authorized its officers to explore the possibilities of unification. Some six months later, in June, 1953, the foundation for unity was laid with the negotiation of a no-raiding agreement between 65 AFL and the 29 CIO affiliates.

Meanwhile, the American Federation of Labor began the long, arduous task of cleansing the House of Labor of corruption. At the Federation's 1953 convention, the AFL took the unprecedented step of expelling an affiliate, the International Longshoremen's Association, on charges of corruption and racket-domination. It charted a new organization, the International Brotherhood of Longshoremen, to contest the 60-year-old racket-ridden ILA on the docks of the East and Gulf Coasts. Three times the AFL-backed Brotherhood attempted to oust the ILA. The Federation spent close to a million dollars in the drive. It failed, in part because once challenged, the ILA began to act like a union. Under pressure from the Waterfront Commission, the dock union was purged of its worst elements. The ILA began to negotiate contracts acceptable to its membership. In 1960, the ILA was admitted to the merged AFL-CIO. But even this modest house-cleaning would never have taken place if it had not been for the challenge of the AFL drive.

The ILA ouster was a forerunner of the expulsion of the Teamsters Union and two other unions in 1956 as a result of exposures of corruption by the Senate Select Committee on Improper Activities in the Labor and Management Field, headed by Senator John L. McClellan and set up by the Senate in 1957. The ouster of the racket-ridden ILA also helped to pave the way for organic unity between the AFL and the CIO, just as the ouster of the communists from the CIO opened the way for the possibility of merger. The no-raiding agreement became effective in 1954. And on February 9, 1955, a Joint Unity Committee of the AFL and the CIO met to approve the "Agreement for the Merger," which set forth the terms of the merger. During 1955, Arthur Goldberg worked on the various drafts of a proposed constitution. In December, 1955 the AFL and the CIO held their final conventions. On December 5, 1955, the American Federation of Labor and Congress of Industrial Organizations was founded, bringing together in one House of Labor some 16 million workers, over 85 percent of all union members. George Meany was elected president; William F. Schnitzler, secretary-treasurer. Walter P. Reuther became head of the newly created Industrial Union Department and a vice-president of the AFL-CIO.

# XVIII

## *THE LEGACY OF GEORGE MEANY*

THE AFL-CIO IS NOW WELL INTO ITS FIRST DECADE. IF, AS THE psychologists tell us, the "infant years" are the most formative, then we should already be able to determine much of the future character of the organization by examining the changes that have thus far taken place within the Federation.

The labor movement entered the 1950s in the full flush of power. Despite the passage of the Taft-Hartley Act in 1947—immediately denounced by unionists as "a slave-labor law"—the unions scored some of their most impressive gains as the century reached its halfway mark. They negotiated pensions, annual productivity factors, cost-of-living increases, health and welfare benefits, and the guaranteed annual wage. Yet, the expulsion of the communists from the CIO and the struggle against racketeering within the AFL weakened both organizations internally. The election of Dwight David Eisenhower in 1952 brought a more critical attitude toward unions to the White House. Decisions of the National Labor Relations Board began to run against the unions as did the tide of public opinion.

The merger of the American Federation of Labor and the Congress of Industrial Organizations was labor's response to this changed climate. It was also, hopefully, an attempt to cap labor's impressive record of postwar gains with still more daring efforts and greater achievements by the unified House of Labor. Actually, however, as John L. Lewis was quick to point out, the new federation was tied together by "a rope of sand." Many unions were against the merger, while others (especially in the AFL) went along reluctantly, insisting on the continuation of the old AFL tradition of autonomy.

There were many fundamental differences in outlook between the AFL and the CIO that had to be reconciled before a constitution for the merged labor organization could be written. While both organizations were loose federations of autonomous unions, the CIO had, in fact, a far greater degree of centralized authority over its member unions than did the AFL. Whereas in 1949 and 1950 the CIO was able to expel all communist-dominated unions, the AFL would have found it difficult at that time to expel a union for any reason whatsoever—except possibly for nonpayment of dues.

Also, the CIO possessed a greater ideological bent. The leaders of the CIO, too, strongly discouraged such practices as the raiding of the membership of one union by another, racketeering and racial discrimination. The leaders of the AFL may have frowned upon these practices, but they were hardly in a position to do anything about it. As an old-time member of the AFL executive council, George M. Harrison, president of the Railway Clerks, once told me, "I remember when, if you were to say something on the convention floor about another affiliate, the head of that union would get up and say, 'Look, you run your union and I'll run mine.' And that was the end of that."

The man who put an end to autonomy was George Meany, a burly, ham-fisted ex-plumber from the Bronx. Meany, who, like General William T. Sherman, Eisenhower, and Churchill, is an amateur watercolorist, seemed to be the perfect embodiment of the AFL "leave 'em alone" bureaucrat, the least likely union leader to upset the ancient traditions of the craft-oriented federation. He was born into a union family in 1894 on the upper West Side of New York City. His father headed a large plumbers' local, and young George, after a year in high school, quit to become a plumber's apprentice. A journeyman plumber at 22, Meany helped to support his widowed mother and seven brothers and sisters. However, he was no ardent Jimmy Higgins, the youthful jack-of-all-trades of unionism portrayed by Upton Sinclair. Nonetheless, at 28 "Mike Meany's boy" became a plumbers' business agent. Thereafter, his rise within the AFL was as steady and sure as the plumbing skills of his old trade. By the middle 1930s, George Meany was the president of the New York State Federation of Labor. It was widely believed that Meany was Joe "The Waxer" Ryan's boy. Ryan, then head of the ILA, was the powerful boss of the New York City Central Labor Trades Council and dominated the state federation. But if Meany had any obligations to Ryan, he never showed it. He tangled with the Longshoremen's chieftain over the candidacy of Fiorello LaGuardia, whom Meany supported against Ryan's wishes.

Meany was a "safe" candidate for the secretary-treasurership of the AFL, an office he held for some 13 years. He became president of the AFL in 1952, aged 56. He is a massive man, with a slight limp from an old heel injury. A great neck supports a large bald head with a snub-nosed Irish face, while a belligerent mouth with cigar emphasizes Meany's blunt nature. He does not waste time with subtleties. Once president of the AFL and faced with the necessity to act against corruption on the docks, Meany characteristically wasted little time. He took the unprecedented step and as a result the Longshoremen along with "Waxer" Ryan were out of the House of Labor.

Racketeering was the issue that finally shattered the rock of autonomy on which the old AFL was founded. The expulsion of the ILA was the beginning of a centralization process that was furthered by the merger of the two labor groups. Meany, as head of a more or less powerless AFL, was more than willing to give into CIO demands that the constitution for the new Federation provide firm commitments on no-raiding, safeguards against racketeering and racial discrimination, and more authority and strength in the central organization. The new Federation, like the AFL, was subdivided into a number of departments. All the old CIO unions, plus some old AFL ones, formed the Industrial Union Department, headed by Walter P. Reuther. The IUD, the Building and Construction Trades and Metal Trades Departments are the three most important blocs within the Federation. But the AFL-CIO constitution, drawn up with the problem of racketeering in mind, clearly centralizes power.

The key constitutional provision is, of course, the one empowering the AFL-CIO executive council "to conduct an investigation, directly or through an appropriate standing or special committee appointed by the president, of any situation in which there is reason to believe that any affiliate is dominated, controlled or substantially influenced in the conduct of its affairs by any corrupt influence." The provision goes on to state that "the executive council shall have the authority to make recommendations or give directions to the affiliate involved and shall have the further authority, upon two-thirds vote, to suspend any affiliate found guilty of a violation of this section."

Both inside and outside the labor movement, Meany's prestige has risen as a result of his forceful actions to drive out corruption. If it had not been for this prestige, many observers believe that the Teamsters would still be affiliated with the AFL-CIO. Unlike Reuther or Murray, whose strength in the CIO came largely from their presidencies of the giant auto and steel unions. Meany's strength is based solely upon the powers and prestige of the office he holds in the Federation.

Meany, in a sense, skillfully used the corruption issue as a tool to reshape the Federation into his concept of what the labor movement ought to be. A power struggle between James Riddle Hoffa, president of the 1.7-million-member Teamsters with his craft union allies on one hand, and Walter Reuther and his IUD on the other, might have shunted Meany aside and wrecked the infant AFL-CIO. What kept the merger from breaking up, ironically, were the McClellan revelations, which enabled George Meany and his supporters to convert what might have been a splintering off into a casting out of devils—a very different kind of operation, as Lenin well knew. Not only did the expulsion avert a split, but it forestalled any attempt by Hoffa to become the John L. Lewis of today. Once the AFL-CIO had been officially stamped "clean" by the McClellan Committee, the unions expelled for corruption could not conceivably form still another federation of labor as Lewis did the CIO in 1937. Hoffa repeatedly tried to rally around the Teamsters the remnants of the various unions expelled by the CIO and the Federation, without success. His dream of a rival federation, based initially on the unity of all transportation unions, was frustrated by his isolation as a corrupt outcast and ultimately by his imprisonment.

The disciplinary actions taken by the AFL-CIO executive council to eliminate corruption virtually destroyed the principle of autonomy for individual unions within the federation. Until the Teamsters were ousted, many unions still hoped to protect their right to run their own affairs without interference from the Federation. But under the harsh light of the McClellan Committee's probing, the AFL-CIO drew up its own Ethical Practices Code, providing standards against which the conduct of any individual union or union official could be measured. Violations of the code meant that the Federation's officers would invoke the constitutional provisions against racketeering. Armed with these powers, Meany and the executive council picked off some of the most powerful proponents of autonomy within the Federation, the mighty Teamsters among them. Indeed, every action taken against corruption within the Federation since the merger, has been aimed at an AFL union that had insisted on the preservation of autonomy.

A logical extension of present AFL-CIO powers would enable the Federation's executive council to suspend or expel officers in affiliated unions. In effect, this is what happens when the Federation places a union on probation, as it did in the case of the United Textile Workers and the Operating Engineers. (Both actions took place after the expulsion of the Teamsters.) A condition for remaining in the Federation was that these unions oust certain of their officials. All that remains to be done is to alter the AFL-CIO constitution so that the Federation can act directly against delinquent union officials.

Yet, for all the growth of centralization within the AFL-CIO, its powers are limited. Expulsion, for example, has not eliminated corruption; once outside the Federation, an offending union, such as the Teamsters, cannot be touched. Meany has been unable, or unwilling, to mount any serious offensive against the Teamsters Union, placing his hopes for reform largely in the hands of the government. These hopes have borne some fruit—a number of key Teamsters officials, including Hoffa, have been convicted on corruption counts of various kinds.

By placing the merger on a firm footing, where it remains despite the 1968 breakaway of the United Auto Workers, George Meany changed the character of the American labor movement. For many years, for example, the building trades dominated the AFL. Had Meany relied on this powerful bloc in coping with the problems of the merger, he would have had to be much more respectful of autonomy and to tread lightly on the corruption issue.

That he did not do so is clear enough. But what is frequently overlooked is that the power of the building-trades unions within the AFL-CIO has faded as a result. Meany laid it on the line in a historic speech to the Building and Construction Trades Department at Atlantic City on December 3, 1957, just prior to the AFL-CIO convention that expelled the Teamsters Union:

"I happen to be a building-trades worker," said Meany. "My union was a closed union, closed in the fact it did not take in new members [in the 1930s]. . . . When we had industrial work crop up that we felt we should do, we made an effort, if we had any weight or pressure, to get that work for our contractors. . . . We didn't want the people that were on the work. We merely wanted the work. So far as the people that were on the work were concerned, for our part they could drop dead."

Meany didn't go so far as to say that the CIO was right when it split off from the AFL in the 1930s because of the Federation's indifference to the problem of organizing industrial workers. But he came close to doing so—far closer than any ex-AFL official is ever likely to do. "I'm not trying to assess the blame. I am not trying to say what should have been done 30 years ago. I told you what my local union did. We wouldn't have any part of an industrial worker. We wouldn't take them in."

Although Meany, technically, was only telling the building trades that they were pushing their jurisdictional claims too far by claiming craft workers already organized by the industrial unions, he was, in reality, signaling their end as an overwhelming power within the AFL-CIO.

What has replaced the great power of the building trades in the house of labor is still uncertain. A clue can be found by examining the course of union growth and expansion. By the mid-1930s, the craft unions were moribund and the industrial unions (CIO affiliates) were growing in membership and vitality. Today the truly craft-oriented unions are small and self-contained—and are likely to remain so. The Horseshoers, with a membership of 280 in 20 local unions, or the International Association of Siderographers, with a membership of 29 and three local unions, are extreme examples. More typical are, say, the Coopers International, with a membership of 2,632; or the Commercial Telegraphers, with 28,265 members. Meanwhile, the giant industrial unions have reached the upper limit of their organizing potential. Both the auto and steel unions, for example, have some 97 percent of their industries organized. But unions that are no longer clearly craft nor industrial—the Teamsters, the Machinists, the Brotherhood of Electrical Workers, among others—have gained members in recent years. So have the unions of government employees, The Fire Fighters, the American Federation of Government Employees, and the Postal Clerks in the early 1960s were added to the list of 44 unions with a membership of 100,000 or more. The fastest growing union with perhaps the greatest potential for growth, is the American Federation of State, County and Municipal Employees. The United Federation of Teachers, too, has shown vigor in organizing.

The losses to organized labor through automation may be offset by gains in industries that are still largely unorganized, such as the chemical and oil industries. This will mean some shifts in the relative strength of the unions affiliated with the AFL-CIO; it is likely that those unions which have made recent gains in membership will continue to wax while others wane. A general rise in employment, however, causes union membership to bulge. Still one can generalize: unions in mining and manufacturing are not growth unions in the sense that unions in public employment are. Unions that are general in character rather than craft or one-industry based, too, are more likely to expand or at least to hold their own against any broad decline in membership whether stemming from automation or a fall in employment. Power generally comes to rest with those unions which are expanding or continue large in number. For an idea about what the AFL-CIO is like, and what it is going to be and what stamp George Meany will leave on the Federation, we must look to the new men on the AFL-CIO executive council. Some, like Jerry Wurf, dynamic head of the State, County and Municipal Employees, are from the growth unions of public employees, and others, like Paul Jennings, sophisticated chief of the International Union of Electrical Workers, represent workers in the new industries of the age of automation and electronics. The new men on the executive council—Matthew Guinan of the Transport Workers Union, Jennings, Wurf, Frederick O'Neal of Actors' Equity, and I. W. Abel of the Steel Workers—are cut from the same bolt of union-made cloth. Politically they are pragmatists, moving away from the old AFL or, for that matter, the old CIO outlook toward an AFL-CIO overview. As they do, the closer they come to that of the late Walter P. Reuther, the altogether pragmatic ideologue.

Significantly, as time goes on, the Federation is more and more likely to plunge into the internal affairs of affiliated unions. Take, for example, the perennial craft-industrial union jurisdictional quarrel. As automation cut into factory jobs, the industrial unions insisted that their members were capable of doing factory maintenance or building work that traditionally had been farmed out, frequently to building tradesmen. To settle the issue the Federation set down new definitions of job jurisdiction, thus striking another blow against autonomy as well as adding to the centralizing tendencies within the AFL-CIO. The Federation, too, has backed organizing drives among farm workers, hospital employees, teachers and other public employees.

The AFL-CIO has tried a new organizing approach in city-by-city drives to sign up the non-union employees of many small and medium-sized plants throughout the country. Tried first in Rochester, New York, and then in Philadelphia, and the Winston-Salem area of North Carolina by the Industrial Union Department, and in Los Angeles by the Federation, this new approach may further strengthen the central powers of AFL-CIO executive council and the Federation Presidency. "This," declared Meany about the Los Angeles drive, "will be a test of our ability to organize," based on cooperation from "normally competing affiliates." The basis for these drives can also be said to be geographic, or regional, rather than by industry or firm.

The intellectuals of the labor movement suggest that such organizing drives—with their emphasis on the community, joint union action, and central direction—can lead to much more than the mere fattening of union rolls. Solomon Barkin, former director of research for the Textile Workers Union, in a much-discussed pamphlet published by the Center for the Study of Democratic Institutions, *The Decline of the Labor Movement*, declared that "the structure of the labor movement needs revision." He suggested that a new vitality might be found in small communities with a variety of small industrial units in the local union.

The joint organizing drives admittedly are not about to result in just that kind of union. They have, in fact, enjoyed only a modest success. The workers organized were assigned to unions with the proper jurisdiction and not organized in a geographic local union as Barkin suggests. This kind of organizing has given somewhat more strength to the power of central labor councils within the AFL-CIO. Barkin also suggested that the national center of the labor movement needs strengthening. Both of these moves, he argued, will bypass the present inhibiting power structure of the international unions. What has happened, however, has been a striking of a balance between the real power of the international unions and of the Federation.

Richard A. Lester, in his book *As Unions Mature*, wonders if it will stop there. "Will the centralizing tendencies," he asks, "begin to jump the sharp dividing line between the national unions and the AFL-CIO not only with respect to the issue of ethical practices but also with respect to union wage policy, along the lines of developments in England, Sweden and other European countries?"

The answer indicated by trends within the federation seems to be affirmative. The unions, for example, may have to take a new position in regard to the possible inflationary effects of wage raises. This may involve some "code of collective bargaining," within which wage policy would be determined in relation to the overall interest of the whole labor movement rather than in the interest of a narrow sector. Or it may involve acceptance of wage/price controls in some form.

The centralizing functions will reinforce still another tendency within the AFL-CIO—the push into broader fields of economic and social policy. Along with institutional security and respectability, says Lester, "interests broaden, focus widens and activities become generalized." This is already apparent in the formalized

committee structure provided for in the AFL-CIO constitution—in sharp contrast to both the old AFL and the CIO. Under the direction of the AFL-CIO president, a variety of standing committees function in outlining labor's position in relation to almost every aspect of public policy.

Meany, and he could not have done the job without Reuther's cooperation, has laid the foundation for the AFL-CIO's future. It is true, of course, that he has hesitated to use the new powers of his office on issues other than racketeering. He has not cracked down on the building trades–industrial unions jurisdictional fight, nor has he pushed the struggle against discriminatory practices within the unions as hard as some observers believe he should, although he has worked harder in resolving these problems than most give him credit for. Partly, this is a question of priorities and partly it is the absence, until very recently, of an equivalent public pressure to that engendered by the McClellan exposures. Nonetheless, the powers and precedents are there for Meany or any subsequent president of the AFL-CIO to use. This is the legacy of George Meany.

# XIX

## THE BLACK WORKER

FOR MANY IMMIGRANTS THE AMERICAN LABOR MOVEMENT WAS a vehicle for Americanization. Their unions not only protected their jobs but also paved their way to citizenship. The independence Jefferson thought people could gain by owning land was in fact achieved by most immigrants through their unions. It is not too fanciful to think of many of the early strikes for union recognition as bids by this or that ethnic group for a place in the American sun. But this was not the case for the American Negro.

As a slave, he was unable to carve out a piece of economic territory he could call his own, as the Irish were able to do in transportation, the Italians in construction, the Jews in the needle trades. The economic position of the free Negroes in the North before the Civil War was so precarious that in 1837, for example, Philadelphia Negroes comprised 14 percent of the poorhouse population although they comprised only seven percent of the total population. "This dusty statistic," as A. Philip Randolph, the noted Negro trade-union leader, points out, "is an early example of a two-to-one relationship that has shown remarkable persistence down to the present."

Actually, before the Civil War free Negroes in Southern cities were appreciably better off than their Northern compatriots because they often had a monopoly of mechanical skills. But the war to free the slaves changed this situation for the worse. The war, first of all, liberated an industrial impulse that by and large had bypassed the South. The industrial North ignored the freedmen as a potential source for labor, turning to Europe instead to recruit the mass of workmen needed for the new railroads, steel mills, and factories springing up in America's industrial heartland. The freed, unskilled field hands were left to shift for themselves in a deteriorating agricultural economy. Lacking capital and/or land, they were easily frozen out as independent farmers and quickly reduced to the near-serfdom of tenant farming and sharecropping. In Southern cities, whites began to compete with Negro craftsmen for available jobs, with predictable results. At the end of the Civil War, 100,000 of the 120,000 artisans in the South were Negroes. By 1890, the skilled Negro artisan had virtually ceased to exist. What happened? Historian W. E. B. Du Bois cited the weak economic position of the freedmen in the postwar South. Slavery-trained artisans were jacks-of-all-trades. For the most part, Du Bois wrote in his famous study of the Negro artisan, "they were careless and inefficient. Only in exceptional cases were they first-class mechanics." Given the near-frontier condition of much of the ante-bellum South the same no doubt could be said of the handful of white artisans. But the freedmen, unlike their white counterparts, faced what Du Bois described as the difficulty of moving from "doing" work to "getting" work. Slave owners had performed the latter task, and when the masters' help was suddenly withdrawn with emancipation, there were few contractors available to secure work for skilled freedmen. Black energies, too, were absorbed in the tremendous task of building a *safe* body politic in which integrated economic and social institutions might flourish. By and large few of their white allies saw any need for economic development or land reform. Northern radicals, as an instance, were unable to secure the passage of necessary congressional legislation to ensure freedmen the "40 acres and a mule" that might have guaranteed an economic base on which to build a new South. The betrayal of 1877, which returned the South to the unreconstructed Southern Bourbons, destroyed that opportunity altogether.

The political power that might have shielded the development of economic power never got off the ground. As Du Bois pointed out, the Negro's refuge became the low wage and the drive against the low wage became a drive against black workers. Naturally black workers sought to protect their jobs as best they might. Isaac Myers, one of the nine black delegates to the National Labor Union Convention in 1869, for example, broke an 1865 strike of white workers against Negro mechanics and longshoremen in Baltimore by organizing the purchase of a shipyard and railway. His cooperative, the Chesapeake Marine Railway and Dry Dock Company, secured a government contract and employed black and white mechanics. This compelled the ship caulkers' union to admit black workmen, an arrangement that lasted over ten years. But the coming of steel ships killed the trade, the cooperative business venture and the integrated local union.

Southern employers exploited racial antagonisms to their advantage. When white firemen struck the Louisville and Nashville railroad in 1893, the railroad retaliated by turning almost all the brakemen, switchmen and firemen jobs over to nonunion black workers. The textile mills and tobacco factories that dotted the Piedmont at the turn of the century deliberately recruited among poor whites only. The threat of black labor was a useful damper on worker aspirations for higher wages and decent working conditions. The mills would remain nonunion and low-paying well into the present century.

Racial antagonism was there to be exploited. White cotton-mill workers in Walker County, Alabama, drove black workmen out of town when they began work around the factory. Birmingham's white bricklayers, carpenters, machinists and telephone linemen repeatedly struck against the employment of Negroes between 1899 and 1901. When Richard L. Davis, a Negro member of the United Mine Workers Executive Board, arrived in Birmingham in the winter of 1897–98 to encourage unionization of miners, he reported, "The one great drawback is the division between white and colored. . . . While white and colored miners worked in the same mines, and maybe even in adjoining rooms, they will not ride even on a work-train with their dirty mining clothes on together."

Negro spokesmen at the time often looked to white employers and upper-class whites not only for jobs but also for protection against the assaults of white workingmen. Booker T. Washington in 1908 urged Birmingham's black workers to "maintain peaceful and friendly relations with the best white people in the community . . . who give our race employment and pay their wages." The Reverend William McGill, editor of the Birmingham *Hot Shots,* urged: "Every colored laborer [should] strive to make friends with his employer." If a dispute should arise, McGill advised, "Take whatever wages the company offered." The black worker, he continued, who "puts in full time, saves his money, puts it to good use, has no cause to strike, nor sympathize with those that do strike."

Still black workers did not always heed the advice of black ministers, nor white workers fall into divisive traps set by employers. Shortly after the Civil War black bricklayers were successfully used in New Orleans to break a strike of white ones, but this led to a united front of black and white bricklayers that became, as historian Ray Marshall put it, "one of the most successful histories of racial harmony on an integrated basis of any union in the South." Despite considerable racial tension, black and white workingmen worked out work-sharing agreements on the docks in many Southern ports. The Knights of Labor made a valiant effort to organize both Negro and white workers as did the AFL carpenters and bricklayers throughout the South. When white carpenters in Birmingham refused to organize blacks, the

Brotherhood of Carpenters in 1903 sent an organizer to do the job. He had to organize a separate black local, but black carpenters earned the union scale and participated in the Carpenters' District Council. Davis, Silas Brooks, black vice-president of the Alabama United Mine Workers, and his successor, B. L. Greer, were able to unionize both black and white miners in the Birmingham district.

Exploitation of the rich coal and iron reserves of northern Alabama transformed an old cornfield into a booming industrial city. As a recent study in *Labor History* (Summer, 1969) by Professor Paul B. Worthman of Wellesley College, "Black workers and Labor Unions in Birmingham, Alabama, 1897–1904," shows, the growth of the labor movement in Birmingham "stimulated new efforts at interracial workingmen's cooperation and the organization of black workers." The city's labor newspaper, *Labor Advocate*, urged, "Obliterate the Color Line" and cried out, "The common cause of labor is more important than racial differences." Black workers not only joined unions with whites but also became union delegates, organizers and officials. In 1900 some 30 to 40 percent of the 6,500 UMW members in Alabama were black and by 1904 over one-half. The UMW was the strongest union in the state and its integrationist policies became that of the state AFL, which had 235 local unions and some 33,000 members by 1904. The Alabama State Federation of Labor was founded in 1900. A year later a state constitutional convention disfranchised black voters, and at the second state AFL convention delegates elected Brooks as first vice-president and J. H. Bean, a Selma black carpenter, second vice-president. When Selma city officials in 1902 refused a hall to the state AFL convention because of the presence of black delegates, a Birmingham typographer expressed the sentiments of the unionists: "Rather than see one accredited delegate, black or white, thrown out of this convention, I would go to the woods and hold this meeting." But both the city's streetcar company and the United Confederate

Veterans offered the use of their halls and enabled the delegates to remain in Selma.

In the steel mills, however, the craft structure of the AFL tended to set off the unskilled black workers from the skilled whites. The Federation devoted perhaps more attention to organizing Birmingham's semiskilled and unskilled, mostly black labor force than it did to the skilled trades. Its Southern organizer helped found locals of coke workers, ore miners, furnace laborers and draymen among others—some 16 black local unions in all. When the black laborers at the Republic Iron and Steel Mill in Birmingham struck in 1904 for union recognition and a ten-cent-an-hour wage increase, Samuel Gompers, AFL organizer Henry Randall, and leaders of the Alabama and Birmingham labor councils backed the strike and rallied the support of the skilled men. After the company offered a 15-cent wage increase—but not union recognition—it was able to recruit replacements for the laborers, call back the skilled workers and reopen the mill. The predominantly white state federation at its convention that year condemned the return of the white skilled workers as strikebreaking and urged the Federation and the Amalgamated Association of Iron and Steel Workers to organize the unskilled laborers. When the Amalgamated's president, T. J. Shaffer, repeated the appeal to his union's 1905 convention, the delegates ignored him. As professor Worthman notes, "The Amalgamated's animosity toward black laborers in Birmingham, however, cannot be understood solely in terms of racial prejudice. In steel mills in other sections of the country the Association remained just as adamant about not cooperating with unskilled immigrants." The decision to ignore the unskilled was nonetheless disastrous for trade unionism in Birmingham—and elsewhere for that matter.

Tragically Birmingham's small beginning in interracial cooperation did not survive the 1904 recession and a mounting employer counteroffensive against the trade unions. In 1904 the Birmingham furnace companies, which operated about 60 percent of Alabama's coal mines, refused to renew their contracts with the UMW. Some 9,000 miners, probably half of them black, struck. The employers imported blacks and Southern European immigrants as strikebreakers, many of whom promptly joined their fellows out on strike. Conceivably the union might have survived, but the production of coal in convict mines and by strikebreakers enabled the operators to outlast the strikers. A second strike was smashed in 1908 with the active support of the state militia, and the UMW, mainstay of interracial unionism in the state, suffered; its membership fell from 18,000 to 700.

Nationally the Federation and its affiliates were also hurt by the 1904 recession and the employer counteroffensive. They were unable to devote any of their limited resources to salvage the badly crippled local unions in Alabama or elsewhere.

Birmingham was an exception, although one that might have paved the way for a different South. By and large, however, industrialism bypassed much of the South, and as the South was excluded from industrial progress, so was the black worker excluded. Despite the decided shift from agrarianism to industrialism during the last half of the eighteenth century, 88 percent of all Negroes in 1890 were in agriculture and domestic service. By 1900, the figure dropped slightly to 86.7 percent. The Negro held no economic territory—or skills—that he could call his own. The all-Negro locals of AFL unions did not possess the strength of the all-Italian, or -Irish, or -German locals of the various AFL craft unions. The economic alienation of the Negro paralleled a social and political alienation that troubles us to this day.

The journey from agrarianism to urbanism posed its own special hazards for American blacks. Often they were brought North as strikebreakers. During the Chicago 1904 meatpackers' strike, for example, almost 1,400 arrived in one trainload, and angry outbreaks between strikers and strikebreakers soon developed the overtones of a race riot. White workers viewed them as "nigger scabs," but the bewildered blacks were enticed North by promises of work, with nothing said about strikes, and the bitter economic struggles of Northern workers must have often appeared no more than vicious attempts to keep them out of desirable jobs. As the unions made headway in the Chicago stockyards during the early years of the century, observers reported that fully 90 percent of the Northern-born black workers in the yard wore union buttons while few of the migrants did.

World War I cut off the supply of immigrant labor, and Negroes began to leave the land in greater number for the factory. Sterling D. Spero and Abram L. Harris in their pioneer work, *The Black Worker*, calculated that of 825,000 Negroes employed in manufacturing industries in 1920 over 16.6 percent were skilled; 67.9 percent were laborers; and 15.5 percent were semiskilled. For whites the percentages were 32.4 percent skilled, 19.1 percent semiskilled and 48.5 percent laborers. However, in 1926, a reasonably prosperous year in Detroit, Negroes constituted only five percent of the auto city's male work force, but 16 percent of them were unemployed. In 1931, when depression wracked Detroit along with most of industrial America, 60 percent of the city's black workers were unemployed as against 32 percent of the white workers.

The leaving of the land accelerated greatly after World War II. Until 1940, 75 percent of Negro Americans lived in the South, predominantly in rural areas. Wartime manpower shortages and the postwar periods of prosperity created new job opportunities. The migration, however, was a pull-push process. Factory jobs with the promise of higher wages lured young blacks off the land while the mechanization of cotton picking drove others into the cities to seek work. By 1965, 73 percent of the 20.4 million black Americans were living in cities, and 40 percent of that number were in the North and West.

In World War II, the Negro factory worker secured a somewhat stronger beachhead within American industry as a result of the wartime Fair Employment Practices Commission, and the successes of the new industrial unions of the CIO. In 1940, 4.4 percent of Negro male workers were skilled; four years later, the percentage rose to 7.3 percent. The figure for semiskilled Negro workers also rose from 12 percent to 22.4 percent over the same period. A 1902 estimate places 41,000 blacks in the unions with a total membership of 1.2 million. There were an estimated 210,000 black workers enrolled in the CIO of 1940; altogether there were about 600,000 black trade unionists at the time. Many had played a vital part in organizing the new industrial unions. Black workers were essential to the success of many organizing drives—68 percent of the tobacco workers were black; 17 percent of the semiskilled workers in meatpacking, 9.2 percent of coal miners and 8.5 percent of iron and steel workers were black. In 1946 there were 650,000 black members of the AFL, of whom 450,000 were in the South. By the time of the merger of the AFL and the CIO in 1955, there were about 1.5 million black workers in American unions. During the 1940s, there were 26 AFL affiliates whose constitutions barred Negroes from membership. In 1963, the Brotherhood of Locomotive Firemen and Enginemen, the last union to explicitly exclude Negroes, dropped the Jim Crow clause from its constitution. Twenty-six international unions and 17 state central bodies have established civil-rights committees, similar to the civil-rights committee of the AFL-CIO. "The AFL-CIO," declared the 1961 Federation convention, "is in the forefront of the civil-rights revolution in our land. It is a foremost force in the drive to eliminate and prevent every form of race discrimination and race injustice in the American community."

The AFL-CIO, to its credit, has played a significant though not widely recognized role in the civil-rights struggle. It gave important backing to the youthful leaders of the Southern sit-ins when few others were willing to do so. Without its lobbying efforts, present-day civil-rights legislation would not be on the books. Voter-registration drives in the South—and in Northern cities—rely on organized labor for their success.

Much of the civil-rights progress in the unions—and in the country—came about through the efforts of one man, A. Philip

Randolph, and his union, the Brotherhood of Sleeping Car Porters. On the job the porter may have been the invisible man who responded to the call, "George." But in his community he was a figure of some importance. He held a steady job, no small thing in the community of the oppressed, often managed to save a little something and to buy his own home. He was ambitious for his children; the porters put more youngsters through college than any other single group of Negro workers.

Automation and the shift from train to air travel soon will eliminate his job. The union membership is down to 6,000 from a World War II peak of 14–16,000. But the sleeping car porter has long since destroyed his faceless persona and made himself a man. He did so not only by organizing a union and lifting himself by his own bootstraps but also through his unvarying support of Randolph, "a one-man freedom operation." As Murray Kempton put it in his book *Part of Our Time*, "As an individual [the porter] offered dollar upon dollar to campaigns which could bring him no personal profit because he understood, from his own life, what Randolph meant when he said that 'the Negro must supply the money and pay the price, make the sacrifices and endure the suffering to break down his barriers.'"

Randolph's causes have had a way of changing the lives of millions. He not only pulled the porters together into a union recognized by the powerful railroads but forced a President to order an end to discriminatory hiring in World War II defense plants, tossed Jim Crow out of the United States Army and launched the March on Washington that led to the passage of the civil-rights acts of 1964 and subsequent years.

Courteous, grave, deep-voiced, with coffee-brown skin and well over six feet in height, Randolph was once dubbed "a wild-eyed uppity Negro hustler who never made up a Pullman berth in his life." This hustler—an odd epithet for so austere a man—was born on April 15, 1889, in Crescent City, Florida, where his father was a circuit-riding African-Methodist-Episcopal minister. The elder Randolph was apparently a man of iron will. He once forestalled a lynching by organizing an all-night vigil of the men in his parish outside the county jail. "My home," Randolph told me, "was almost Calvinistic. It was rigidly moralistic and rigidly supervised. I never saw a bottle of whiskey, nobody used profanity and there was no playing on Sunday." Many years later, when Randolph as a result of his participation in "Ye Friends of Shakespeare," a Harlem off-Broadway theater group, toyed with the idea of going on the stage, he was dissuaded by the stern admonitions of his father, who considered the stage a sin only one remove from drink.

Randolph attended the Cookman Institute in Jacksonville, a Methodist school now called the Bethune-Cookman College, where he learned Latin, math and the moral code of the New Englanders who made up half the staff. As Randolph has said, it was a time when "the white South feared education for the Negro as they fear the ballot today."

Young Philip came North while still in his teens to work as a hall boy for a cousin who was a janitor in an apartment house. Restless and intellectually curious, Randolph read widely and deeply, heard Eugene V. Debs speak and joined the Socialist party in 1911. (He is a member to this day.) He started City College nights and began work at odd jobs. He also organized his fellow workers wherever he went, which was easier than one might expect, for his employers kept helping him on his way. He had a job as an elevator operator and got fired for organizing; he became a maintenance man, got fired for organizing; and then found a job as a waiter on a pleasure boat and got fired for organizing.

While at City College, Randolph met a young Columbia law student, Chandler Owen. The two men decided to open a job bureau in Harlem with an improvised training program on the side for untutored Negroes from the South. The business did not last very long, but its proximity to the beauty salon of Madame Lilia Walker introduced Randolph to its manager, Lillian Green. Miss Green, a graduate of Howard University, shared Randolph's interests in Shakespeare, socialism and the world. They were married in 1913. "For our honeymoon," Mrs. Randolph once said, "we took an open streetcar to South Ferry, and back."

Mrs. Randolph was a good speaker and once ran for the state legislature on the Socialist ticket. Their relationship was a close one and lasted until her death in 1964. The Randolphs had no children. During the last few years of her life Mrs. Randolph was ill and her husband would come home each evening, cook supper for the two of them and spend the evening reading Shakespeare aloud to his wife.

In 1915 Randolph founded *The Messenger*, "the most danger-ous of all Negro publications." When W. E. B. Du Bois wrote an editorial in the NAACP publication *The Crisis*, calling on Ne-groes to support World War I, Randolph blasted back in *The Messenger*: "Lynching, Jim Crow, segregation and discrimination in the armed forces and out, disenfranchisement of millions of black souls in the South—all these things make your cry of mak-ing the world safe for democracy a sham, a mockery, a rape on decency and a travesty on common justice." After the war, when Marcus Garvey came to Harlem from his native West Indies and moved the people as no one else ever had with his vision of a black empire across the seas, Randolph won a certain uneasy eminence as the only Negro of stature openly to attack Garvey.

Among those who listened to Randolph in the 1920s were a handful of sleeping car porters trying to organize a union. They needed a front man, a leader the Pullman Company could not reach. Ashley L. Totten, eventually the secretary-treasurer of the Brotherhood of Sleeping Car Porters, had just been fired for at-tending a meeting. Totten, along with Milton Webster, a Chicago Republican wardman who had been fired in 1918, and four others met with Randolph, urging him to head the drive to organize the 10,000 porters. *The Messenger* soon evolved into the union publication, *The Black Worker*. Porters pawned their watches to pay union-hall rent; Mrs. Randolph's salary as a hairdresser met household bills and not a few of the union's. William Green, president of the AFL, helped and Roger Baldwin, the civil libertarian, came through with a grant of $10,000 from the Garland Fund. In 1937, after 12 years of struggle, the railroads finally did what they said they would never do: signed a contract with the Brotherhood that quadrupled the income of the porters in a few short years.

Neither Randolph nor the porters allowed matters to rest with that one victory. When Randolph organized the first March on Washington and forced fair employment practices upon a reluctant defense establishment, the porters contributed $50,000 to the campaign. They also helped to keep alive March on Washington committees around the country as watchdogs over the enforcement of wartime FEPC measures. After the war their vigilance resulted in the passage of similar legislation in a number of Northern states. The porters also rallied to Randolph's crusade against Jim Crow in the Army, a campaign that ended when President Harry S Truman issued Executive Order 9981, abolishing segregation in the armed forces. When Mrs. Rosa Parks refused to sit at the back of a Montgomery bus, it was E. D. Nixon, a Pullman porter, who called a young minister, Martin Luther King, and said, "The time has come to boycott the buses." When civil rights became focused on the need for national legislation, it was Randolph who sent out the call once again to march on Washington. He called for 100,000, and while the AFL-CIO did not officially endorse the march, many unions did support it. And on August 28, 1963, 200,000 Americans, white and black, converged on the capital. It was, said *The New York Times* a day later "a high-water mark in mass decency."

Randolph became a vice-president of the AFL-CIO at the merger convention in 1955. Four years later he organized the Negro American Labor Council. "We felt a need for an organization that would give Negro trade unionists a sense of unity, both among themselves and with their white brothers." Seeking to further the civil-rights revolution within the labor movement, the NALC sought to organize black trade unionists not so much as a caucus within unions but as a national pressure group. The initial call proclaimed: "We resent Jim Crow locals; we deplore the freeze-out against Negroes in labor apprenticeship and training programs; we disclaim the lack of upgrading and promotional opportunities for Negroes; we repudiate the lockout against Negroes by some unions; we, above all, reject 'tokenism,' that thin veneer of acceptance masquerading as democracy. Since hundreds of thousands of Negroes are victims of this hypocrisy, we ourselves must seek the cure, in terms of hundreds of thousands, in the dimensions of a mass organization."

The NALC remained pretty much an organization of trade-union staffers. It scored its major success within the United Auto Workers, where its activities led to the election of two black members of the union's executive board, Nelson Jack Edwards and Marcellius Ivory. Now headed by Cleveland Robinson, president of the National Council of Distributive Workers, the NALC has active chapters in New York City, Philadelphia and Detroit.

Economists in the early 1960s were given to treating unemployment in the United States as troublesome "pockets" in an expanding economy. But to Negro workers, these "pockets" were a sea of quicksand sucking them down to extinction. According to official Labor Department figures, non-whites comprised a full 20 percent of all the then unemployed. This figure included Puerto Ricans as well as Negroes, but the department's statistics for 1962 (the same ratio has persisted although the level of employment has fluctuated) also showed that the Negro unemployment rate was almost twice as high as the rate of white unemployment—11 percent as against 4.9 percent for whites. Further, an Urban League survey of unemployment (in 1961) among Negroes in 50 cities revealed that the "percentage of the Negro work force unemployed is frequently twice to three times that of the total unemployment rate." Thus in Chicago, where the total unemployment rate was 5.7 percent, the percentage of Negro jobless was 17.3; in Louisville, Kentucky, the total rate was 8.3 percent while the corresponding figure for Negroes was 39.8 percent; in Pittsburgh, the figures were 11.6 as against 24 percent; in New York City, 6.4 as against ten percent. These statistics also suggested why unemployment was viewed with much less urgency by the white American community than by the Negro; in St. Louis, there were 35,000 unemployed Negroes out of a total of 72,700 jobless; in Gary, Indiana—more strikingly—18,000 out of a total of 20,200; in Detroit, 112,000 out of a total of 185,000. The mid-1960s boom improved the picture somewhat. Still the black workers' economic position remains precarious.

Even when he has a job, the black worker's position is far from enviable. In 1958 the median wage of the Negro male worker was only 59 percent as much as that of the white worker —$2,652 as against $4,569. As Randolph commented wryly: "When a Negro worker goes into the market as a consumer he cannot presume to pay only 58 percent for comparable goods and services . . . purchased by white workers. The fact is, Negroes pay relatively much higher prices." Similarly, white women averaged $2,364 a year, while Negro women—who, it should be added, are more often the breadwinners of the family—only earned $1,055.

Actually, the American Negro stands in somewhat two different relationships to the trade unions, differences that correspond roughly with that between craft and industrial unions. By and large, most industrial unions are integrated though there are exceptions. The work force in the oil industry until recently was largely white because for years the oil companies followed the practice of hiring only white high school graduates. Inside the factory, Negroes may be forced into separate—and unequal— lines of seniority and promotions. Nonetheless, the Negro is *inside* the industrial union. He therefore is a political force to be reckoned with. Negroes can—and do—use this leverage to improve their lot. Black caucuses carry the greatest weight within such industrial unions as the auto workers and the steel workers. In Detroit, an NALC affiliate, the Trade Union Leadership Council, plays a key role both within the United Auto Workers and

Detroit city politics. The old rule—the black worker is the last hired, first fired—no longer retains its original force in much of basic industry as a result.

But the Negro's position *vis-a-vis* the craft unions is something else again. Here he frequently remains an outsider, though there are exceptions. The craft unions are more likely to be ethnically based than the industrial unions. Joining a craft union calls for years of apprenticeship and openings are frequently limited to sons and other relations of full-fledged journeymen. The craft unions consciously limit the supply of labor in their respective crafts. This has meant actual labor shortages in many areas of the building and construction industries when jobs elsewhere go glimmering. The industry benefits greatly from the pumping of public funds into the economy. This sort of activity is likely to expand in the near future, offering attractive jobs to those qualified. (In the other great job-expanding area—the service industry —jobs are by no means as attractive or as well paying though there are many more of them.)

Building has boomed. New construction put in place rose in value from about $72 billion in 1966 to well over $84 billion in 1968. Construction employment rose from 2.8 million in 1960 to 3.2 million in 1968. Congress has promised 26 million new housing units over the next decade. Nearly 150 cities have qualified for Model City planning grants from the Department of Housing and Urban Development. Housing starts, however, did drop in early 1970, and the Nixon recession may dampen building expectations in the immediate period ahead. Nonetheless, construction experts predict that the industry will experience the largest and most rapid growth outside of state and local government and service-industry employment. Department of Labor experts have estimated that if "we are to fulfill our needs in the construction field during the next ten years, we will have to produce about 2.3 million additional skilled craftsmen." The growth and replacement needs for carpenters, for example, are estimated at 32,000 a year, and for plumbers and steamfitters, at 16,000 a year.

This should mean greater opportunities for black workmen and for black youth. Yet until recently they were all but barred from the skilled craft jobs. The NAACP estimated in 1963 that less than one percent of the apprentices in the construction industry throughout the United States were black. As of 1968 only three percent of registered apprentices (including a large number of industrial apprentices) were black. The past performance of the building and construction industry and trades unions is far from promising.

The composition of the building trades varies greatly from city to city, and there are cities where laborers or bricklayers, say, remain largely Italian. Black workers, however, are well represented in the so-called trowel trades, constituting roughly 26 percent of construction laborers, 26 percent of the cement and concrete finishers, roughly 16 percent of the plasterers and about 12 percent of the nation's bricklayers. The pay is good—anywhere from $4 to $6 an hour—for these are union jobs and require a high order of skills. But the work depends upon the weather, though less and less so as technology changes, lacks status and remains dirty, hard and hazardous. Laborers may be hired off the street but not electricians, elevator constructors, iron workers, plumbers or steamfitters to mention only a few trades.

Each craft is a zealously guarded domain where none may enter except those passed upon by its practitioners. There is virtually no way for a laborer, as an instance, to work his way into the cleaner, better-paid and steadier mechanical crafts—electricians, plumbers, steamfitters, iron workers, and sheet-metal workers. Laborers cannot become carpenters even though some of their work appears identical. In clean-work, if the lumber is to be reused, it's carpenters' work; if not, laborers'. Steel door frames are placed by carpenters while steel window frames are placed by ornamental-iron workers. To an outsider there seems little difference between the joining of various sizes of pipes. But if the pipe is used in heating or ventilating, the work belongs to steamfitters, but if it "touches the water you drink," it belongs to the plumbers even though both belong to the same international union.

These jurisdictional complexities are enforced by an intricate system of apprenticeship rules and exclusionary practices. The Scot's burr of the stonesetter in New York City is as thick as one hears in Edinburgh and the accent of the terrazzo worker is touched by the dialect of Friuli, a small town in northern Italy. The local unions of the Painters' Council of New York City are ostensibly organized by craft, but they also were ethnic enclaves —Irish, Italian or Jewish. In 1967, according to the Equal Employment Opportunity Commission, blacks comprised roughly 8.4 percent of all construction workers, somewhat under the overall percentage of black participation in the work force or about 12 percent. But blacks are only 0.8 percent of the mechanical trades. That is, 0.6 percent of electricians, 0.4 percent of elevator constructors, 1.7 percent of iron workers, 0.2 percent of the plumbers, and 0.3 percent of the sheet-metal workers. Until recently, in New York City there were no black journeymen or apprentices in the elevator constructors', iron workers', metal lathers', sheet-metal or steamfitter trades. There were a few in the electricians', operating engineers', and plumbers' unions. In Philadelphia, with a city population roughly 40 percent black, there were only two black plumber apprentices among 111 in 1966, none among 48 electrician apprentices and 34 iron workers. In St. Louis, there were only eight blacks among 179 carpenters, and none among 121 electricians, 60 iron workers and 93 plumbers' apprentices. And so it went from city to city across this broad land.

Demonstrations in New York City in 1963, and elsewhere since, notably in Pittsburgh and Chicago in 1969, built up pressures for change in the building-trades recruiting practices. Legal suits brought by the NAACP broke down formal barriers and opened entrance requirements to all who could qualify. In Detroit, Cleveland and New York there were attempts at integrating building-trades locals, but initially these were sporadic and filled few openings. Opening doors was not sufficient, somebody had to be invited in. The first and most successful effort to do just that was the Joint Apprenticeship Program of the Workers' Defense League and the A. Philip Randolph Educational Fund. With a staff of 63 and branches in a dozen cities, JAP has served as a model for similar apprenticeship recruitment, tutoring and placement operations in at least 40 other cities. These outreach programs have enrolled 5,000 black youths in apprenticeship programs (4,000 in the building trades) over 1968 and 1969. Given the obstacles, it is no mean achievement.

The measurements of success in the job-training field are hard to come by. Graduation certificates are meaningless if there are no jobs. The major strength of JAP is the direct tie between training on the job at a good rate of pay and admission to the union upon attaining journeymen's status. It helps, too, that the staff is mostly young and all black. The dropout rate among apprentices, black or white, is very high, ranging from 30 percent to 80 percent. But the dropout rate of JAP placements so far has averaged six percent. Many of those who do drop out, go on to college. As Ernest Green, the ebullient JAP director, put it, "I'd say that is pretty good when you consider these are the working poor. Most of the guys we get are stock boys and mail clerks who've kept a clean nose while growing up. These are the kinds of kids who are going to become foremen, estimators, draftsmen, even contractors." This, incidentally, is one reason JAP chose the apprenticeship route initially. Apprenticed workers have done better in future careers than those who became journeymen in other ways. A 1956 survey shows that of those who graduated from apprenticeship programs in 1950, 19 percent became supervisors, and eight percent went into the contracting business for themselves.

The so-called Chicago Plan worked out between spokesmen for the black community and leaders of the construction industry and unions after a series of hard-hitting demonstrations shows great promise of a final breakthrough. It has the backing of the AFL-CIO and is being carefully watched by the black community.

Following the demonstrations organized by the Black Coalition of Chicago in the summer of 1969, the craft unions initially offered to open up several thousand jobs. When the proposal was turned down by the Coalition, the unions opened an office to recruit black journeymen in downtown Chicago on the fringe of the Southside. In less than a year that office recruited roughly 300 black journeymen, mostly carpenters, bricklayers, operating engineers and a few electricians. Very few mechanical tradesmen were recruited, however.

Nonetheless, it was something and perhaps contributed to the ultimate settlement that called for 4,000 jobs in 1970 and some 18,000 jobs for blacks over the next five years. The Chicago Plan provided for the immediate employment and union membership for 1,000 journeymen; on-the-job training for another 1,000 workers with some skills but already too old for standard apprenticeships; another 1,000 apprenticeship openings; and still another 1,000 places for preapprenticeship training. Three or four recruiting centers were to be opened in black communities and a full-time staff of outreach experts hired.

New York, Boston and Philadelphia among several other cities are working out similar programs. Much, of course, depends on the continued good health of the building and construction industry as well as continued policing of the agreements by the interested parties. Significantly the Chicago plan, and a similar one in effect in Pittsburgh, allow for this. A supervisory committee with representatives from the black community, the unions and the industry will oversee the implementation of the plan.

# XX

## *AUTOMATION*

WILL SCHUMACHER IS AN OLD-TIME MACHINIST WHO TAKES CON-siderable pride in his craft. Although now nearing retirement, he still follows the latest developments in his field with avid inter-est—and some dismay. Recently he witnessed a demonstration of a robot machinist—a little computer device hooked up to a turret lathe. When a button is pressed, the lathe carriage hisses forward under pneumatic power, the head rotates, gripping a small cylin-der as tools position themselves and set to work one after another. Finished, the turret carriage withdraws, ejects the part, and the machine is ready for the next cycle. The robot can be operated over long distance by teletype, and it can perform a wide variety of jobs by simple changes of instruction on tape. The old crafts-man, who watched the performance without a word, finally said, "There's either the six-hour day or one whopping big depres-sion."

His simple view of automation is widely shared among workers and trade-union leaders. Automation, using the word in its broad-est sense, lurked behind the major strikes of the early 1960s. In 1963 some two million workers were caught up in bitter strikes and prolonged negotiations involving disputes arising from the introduction of new machines and new methods. Wages and, to a lesser extent, fringe benefits were not issues in collective bargaining, although they became so again in the economic high of 1966–69. With the recession of 1970, automation-related issues once again came to the fore. The quickness with which the auto companies and the United Auto Workers, in 1961, reached agreement on so-called national issues is a case in point. As one auto worker put it, "If a guy isn't happy on the job, the money he's making doesn't mean much to him." Underlying the discontent that, in the case of auto workers, expressed itself in walkouts over shift preferences, production standards, and overtime policies is the fear of automation, truly an "automation trauma." One has to go back to the Luddites, the English workingmen who in 1811–16 tried to prevent the introduction of labor-saving machinery by destroying it, to find comparably widespread worry over the displacement of labor by machinery. While American workers as yet have not taken to breaking up the new machinery now being introduced, they have dragged their feet at every opportunity. This created some unusual difficulties for union leaders. As a local union officer of the International Union of Electrical Workers told me, "Workers are scared. In taking a moderate position, I'm not sure we represent the emotions of our people. We're constantly urging them that we must all be realistic."

Though the story may be apocryphal, it illustrates the difficulties that confront union leaders. When the General Motors locals of the UAW went out on strike after the union and the company had arrived at an agreement in 1961, Lou Seaton, GM's vice-president then in charge of labor relations, is supposed to have asked Walter Reuther: "What's going on, Walter? Can't you control your people?" Reuther is said to have replied, "Well, if I can't lead them, I'm sure going to race to get out in front of them."

The pressures on union leaders in the age of automation show up in the strangest places—on picket lines not in front of factory gates but outside union halls. "Some toolmakers with 1937 seniority are on layoff. We want jobs," read one sign carried by a picket. It was aimed not at the auto companies but at Walter Reuther.

We are all familiar by now with the machine miracles that do so much with so little labor. They range from an automatic frankfurter machine that uses four or five workers to do work formerly performed by 50 or 60 to a Raytheon assembly line manned by two employees who test 11,000 radio tubes a day where the same job done manually would require 200 people. Many goods (synthetics, for example) are already produced under automatic or near-automatic conditions. One person sitting at the console of a closed television circuit operates a machine that handles the entire wing of a passenger jet, drilling, countersinking, riveting and smoothing off the finished job. One man with a crane unloads a container the size of a railroad car from a siding onto a ship, performing the work of several 21-man gangs. One-armed robots are welding panels on Detroit's minicars, doing the work of 52 men over two work turns a day.

One of the unsettling things about automation is that very little is known about its real dimensions as a problem. In over a thousand pages of testimony before the House Subcommittee on Unemployment and the Impact of Automation not one of the hundreds of experts testifying could say how many unemployed are out of work directly as a result of automation. However, most could—and did—cite numerous disturbing examples of the displacement of workers by machines. For example, a Bureau of Labor Statistics survey of the results of a shutdown of a steel-car manufacturing plant in Mt. Vernon, Illinois, showed that of the nearly 2,000 laid off, 12 percent were still unemployed two years later, 11 percent were underemployed, and nine percent had left the labor force. A local union official reported that in General Electric's Ontario, California, electric-iron plant, some 600–700 workers now produce 102,000 irons a week, whereas in 1946 1100–1200 had produced 50,000 a week. David J. McDonald, the silver-haired and silver-tongued president of the United

Steelworkers, in 1961, testified, "It seems clear that the industry [steel], operating at capacity, could produce 100 million tons of steel in seven or eight months and could shut down completely for the rest of the year." More recently, in 1963, Leon Greenberg, chief productivity expert for the Bureau of Labor Statistics, testified before the Senate Labor Committee that rising productivity, an outcome of automation, was eliminating a minimum of 200.000 factory jobs yearly.

Concern over automation peaked in the early 1960s when unemployment ran at six to seven percent of the work force. But by the end of the decade unemployment had dropped to below four percent, dissipating the anxiety over automation. Until the Nixon recession began to take hold, there was little concern about the displacement of men by the computer and automated machinery. Its impact has been disguised in recent years by the economic effect of the Vietnam war, which has taken millions of young men out of the labor market and created heavy manpower demands upon American industry, and by the economic lift afforded by the coming of age of the babies born in the post-World War II baby boom, which resulted in a higher than normal rate of new family formations and household consumer expenditures in the late 1960s, and by a highly favorable (though by 1970 rapidly diminishing) postwar balance of trade between the United States and other nations. The United States has been spending roughly $80 billion a year—43 percent of our total national budget—for military purposes, and $5 billion a year to put a man on the moon. Together these expenditures generate jobs for more than one out of every ten workers in the country. As P. L. Siemiller, who retired as president of the International Association of Machinists in 1969, reminds us, "So long as the economy is going full blast there is no real need to cut back that part of the work force that is essentially nonproductive. When a drastic economic downturn comes—and there are now signs of such a downturn in the U. S. economy—a lot of large corporations are going to start analyzing their operations and weeding out all of the jobs that are not absolutely productive or essential. The search for greater economy—the need to reduce labor costs—will also stimulate more computerization."

Employers, it ought to be noted, are much more optimistic than are trade unionists about the long-run impact of automation. Elmer T. Klassen, U.S. deputy postmaster and former president of the American Can Company, stresses the growth that accompanied technological change: "While our country and my company were accepting all the new technology that was available to them, both Mr. Siemiller's union and my company grew substantially. In 1928 Mr. Siemiller's union had 70,000 members, today [1968] they have in excess of 1,000,000 members. In 1928 the machinists' pay rate in the United States was between 60 and 65 cents an hour; forty years later a machinist in the United States earns in excess of $4 per hour. In contrast, my company's sales in 1928 were $100 million; in 1968 they were in excess of $1,500 million. In 1928 we had 16,000 employees; in 1968 we had 56,000 employees."

But in 1970 unemployment began to rise again, sliding upward past five percent of the labor force. In the critical auto negotiations, for example, employers gave notice that something had to be done about "lack of cooperation with technological advances." Organized labor's experience with the automation crisis of the early 1960s remains all too relevant.

Even more alarming to union officials worried about the possible decline in the power prestige of their organizations are the long-run trends in manufacturing that presage a decline in union membership and dues income. (This assumes that unions will not make up the difference by organizing the white-collar workers—a safe assumption based on the record so far.) The average number of workers engaged in manufacturing in 1948 and in 1961 was 15.5 million. But the number of production workers—where the bulk of union membership is concentrated—declined by 1.5 million, while supervisory and clerical workers increased by 1.5 million over the period.

The growth in plant and equipment investment per employee is another indication of the growth of automation. According to the First National City Bank of New York, this investment has just about doubled over 1950–60, rising from $5,400 per employee to $10,100.

Taking a look at the overall economy, there is widespread agreement on the indices of trouble: unemployment persisted at roughly five percent over 1958–63. Long-term unemployment has increased. The number of people unemployed for 15 weeks or longer in September, 1963, was 1,303,000 as against 805,000 in 1960; those unemployed for 27 weeks or longer numbered 619,000 in February 1963 as against 417,000 in 1960.

These figures reflected the open sores of our economy. Labor Department "profiles" of the unemployed showed that they tend to be either young or past middle age, unskilled or semiskilled, and often members of America's minority groups, especially Negroes. These were the immediate victims of the changes being wrought by automation. Many, as "constituents" of unions, have put added pressure on labor to "do something" about automation.

Labor fears that this is only a beginning. Few people, say the union technicians studying automation, can expect to escape its impact. Take the small businessman who, if he can't afford to automate, may be forced to the wall by large competitors who can. The resulting unemployment will be attributed to "business failure" and not to automation, small comfort to the people involved. Union economists also cite estimates that each year it will be possible to reach today's production levels with 1.8 million fewer workers. They also note that Congressman Elmer Holland (Democrat, Pennsylvania), chairman of the House Subcommittee on Automation, had estimated after his 1961 hearings that four million office and clerical jobs will be eliminated by automation within the next ten years. Economist Robert Theobald foresees a future in which only five to ten percent of the population will be usefully employed while the rest exist idly and aimlessly on some form of dole. The prediction of Herb Simon of Carnegie Tech offers only a note of irony, not consolation, to union automation experts. Simon says that all of middle management can expect to be automated out of existence in the near future.

Union automation experts are skeptical of predictions that the service industries will expand sufficiently to absorb labor displaced by machinery in manufacturing. Stanley Ruttenberg, the AFL-CIO's chief economist, says, "Will this grow enough to provide job opportunities? In my judgment, no." Automation, the union men say, is also taking place in the service industries. For example, in New York City alone there were 30,000 fewer elevator operators in 1962 than four years earlier. "When bowling began to expand," says one union economist, "it was predicted that thousands of jobs would be opened up. Well, in my neighborhood there's a brand-new forty-lane alley, operated by one electrician. And at that, he hasn't much to do."

"Our general conclusion," James Wishert, research director of the Meat Cutters and Butcher Workmen, says rather gloomily, "is that the demand for skilled labor is very much overestimated, that the whole trend of automation, as a matter of fact, is to wash out the skill content in most jobs, and the illusion that there is going to be a heavy demand for additional skills on the part of the average blue-collar worker is one that the facts will not support."

Nonetheless, it must be stressed that organized labor is not against automation. As AFL-CIO president George Meany has said, "We do not say the answer is to do away with 'machine production.' We have never said that. We are in favor of technological progress, better methods, more efficiency. All we say . . . is that you have to bring the people along with the machine."

Automation may be a long-run blessing. Yet the displacement of tiresome human labor by wires, relays, and transistors is no comfort to a worker fired because he was "automated" out of a job. On the other hand, make-work is no comfort to a manufacturer who must increase production if he is to remain in business. This is one of the dilemmas of automation. Another, one might add, is the confusion attendant on its introduction. One of the nation's top management consultants gives the example of what he considers prime confusion over automation. He recently visited two companies that were using two identical "consoles" or automation control panels. These huge electronic panels with their dial and warning-light systems, control the flow of production. All the operator has to do is watch for something to go wrong. One company has reached the point where it no longer penalizes the operator if he falls asleep; the various alarms, it has found, are loud enough to awaken the operator should the need arise. But the other company requires that its console operator file reports every 15 minutes, and it sets pressure tolerances at a half pound where ten pounds would do as well. All this is done in an effort to keep the operator interested and awake. "You figure it out," says my consultant friend.

Although automation is often viewed as Dr. Frankenstein's monster, it is also a boon. For example, sociologists have discovered significant changes in attitudes on the part of workers reassigned from manual assembly lines to automated lines. On the manual line the workers desired subconsciously, and sometimes consciously, to stop the line, to interrupt production somehow. At times this resulted in inadvertent sabotage. But on the automated assembly line a team spirit developed that worked to keep production going. The difference, sociologists explain, is quite simple: On the manual assembly line a breakdown afforded the employees a breather, time for a cigarette; but on the automated line, the breather could be taken almost at will, but not at a time of breakdown when all hands were required to get the line moving again.

Automation, however, also leads to conflict. Sol Barkin, the genial former research director of the Textile Workers Union of America, is fond of this illustration: A textile concern introduced six machines for dyeing cloth. Each machine is some 500 feet long, with an operator at each end who communicates with his fellow employees by walkie-talkie and who sees what goes on within the machine by closed circuit television. "Previously," says Barkin, "there were smells, there was heat, there was color, there was feel." The old workmen who did the work the old way were skilled but lacked schooling, so the engineers who installed the new equipment declared that they could not handle the new operation. A man without a diploma could not read was the reasoning. The union demurred; a fight developed.

Fortunately for the old-timers, the union was able to persuade the company that a man who once had the physical experience of performing the job was better able to interpret the dials than a new man with a college diploma. The company agreed to a trial period, and the experiment was a success.

Sometimes displacement is inevitable, though many firms have found that through careful planning layoffs can be avoided by the curtailment of hiring, pooling arrangements, and transfers of employees. This allows a reduction of the workforce to take place through attrition—resignations, retirements, and deaths. The New York City Transit Authority, for example, in just this fashion reduced its work force by 7,658 over five years. The Authority reached a verbal agreement with the union representing its employees, the Transport Workers Union, that adjustment to technological change would be made through normal attrition rather than dismissal. However, the reduction in the TA work force wasn't achieved entirely without tension. A four-day tie-up of the city's transit system by a wildcat strike of motormen and conductors can be traced to a failure to carry out this policy of attrition without adequately informing—or educating—employees.

America's industrial giants take painstaking care when it comes to handling some of the problems that arise when automation is in the offing. United States Steel, for example, makes extensive surveys of the employees about to be affected by a technological change; it confers with union representatives and with the individual employee. The procedure is elaborate and thorough; every man is given a chance to exercise one of several options offered by the union contract—pensions, vacations, insurance coverage, severance pay, supplementary unemployment benefits, "bumping rights" to other jobs, and so on. The results vary, reports a company spokesman, "in relation to the circum-stances surrounding each specific case of technological improve-ment. The range is from cases completely successful in alleviating the abruptness of change to those where there simply is no way within our control to obviate the impact upon some of the em-ployees involved."

As a result of the 1959 steel strike, the steel companies and the USW agreed to establish a Human Relations Research Committee that would oversee studies and recommend solutions of mutual problems in various areas where automation or technological change is likely to cause difficulties. The Kaiser Steel–USW com-mittee, in December, 1962, reported a far-reaching plan for shar-ing the savings from increased automation and productivity. Basically the plan provides that no employee will be discharged because of technological advances. Layoffs may be made because of poor business conditions, but if a worker is no longer needed on a job because of automation or new technology, he will go into an "employment pool" and be continued at full wages. While in the pool, he may be retrained for a new job or be given a job vacated as a result of attrition—death, resignation, or retirement.

The cost of producing a ton of steel in 1961 will be calculated. All savings made on the base-year cost will go into a special fund, and Kaiser workers will get 32.5 percent of the money accumu-lated, which will be distributed on a monthly basis. The company will get the rest of the savings. Kaiser workers are also guaran-teed that their wages and fringe benefits will not fall below those negotiated by the union with the rest of the industry. (Supple-mentary unemployment benefits exist to ease the burden of layoffs due to business conditions.) The first payment of shared-savings, March, 1963, enabled some 3,930 Kaiser employees to split $312,000—their third of $962,000—for an average "bonus" of $75 for the month.

Armour and Company and the packinghouse unions have worked out another approach. Armour agreed to finance a

$500,000 fund for the purpose of studying the problems arising from mechanization and for making recommendations for their solution, including training employees to perform new and changed jobs and promoting employment opportunities within the company for those affected. Similar funds have since been set up elsewhere, notably in the West Coast docking industry.

Automation has also stirred labor to demand a shorter work week. "We cannot," reads a 1962 AFL-CIO resolution, "close our eyes to the evidence of the new technology's impact, the coming of youngsters into the labor market, and the inability of existing economic policies to achieve full employment. We believe attention must be directed now to obtaining a substantial reduction of standard working hours in the 1960s." When the choice is between "cutting employment or cutting hours," the AFL-CIO resolution declares, "the reduction of hours without a loss of pay must be an ingredient of our attack on unemployment."

The catch, of course, is the phrase "without loss of pay," for in steel and a great many other industries workers are already working short weeks and averaging over the year less than the standard 40 hours a week. "We don't mind a shorter work week," one steel executive says, "but what the union wants is 40 hours' pay for 32 hours' work." It is at this addition to employment costs that management balks. Industry spokesmen no longer protest, as National Association of Manufacturers president John E. Edgerton did in 1926, that the shorter work week is immoral, "an unworthy ideal." They concede that a short work week is inevitable in the future. But as an NAM statement on the shorter work week warns, "It is well to remember that even a gradual and moderate reduction in the work week has its price."

The unions vigorously dispute this. Productivity born of automation makes the short week both feasible and a necessity, they argue. The AFL-CIO estimates that up to 15 percent of its twelve and a half million members now put in a contractual, work week of less than 40 hours. About 97 percent of the International

Ladies' Garment Workers Union membership is on a 35-hour week; the printing unions work 37 hours and in many cases 35 hours; a good number of brewery workers, building craftsmen, bakers, newspaper publishing employees, office workers, and municipal administrative and clerical employees enjoy a work week shorter than 40 hours. A six-hour day, 36-hour week has been in effect in Akron's rubber plants since the thirties, when management introduced it as a philanthropic gesture to spread whatever work was available during the depression.

Actually, many millions not covered by shorter-work-week clauses in labor contracts work less than the standard 40-hour work week. Steel workers have not averaged 40 hours of work a week over a year for 30 years, except in 1951, when they hit 40.2, and during the three wartime years of 1943, 1944, and 1945, when they averaged 43.0, 46.7, and 44.2 respectively. According to the Bureau of Labor Statistics, some 11.9 million workers in October, 1961, worked less than 34 hours a week, averaging 24 hours a week. The shorter work week is a reality, possibly a harsh one, for many.

Nonetheless, management is adamant in its opposition to a cut in the work week, especially if take-home pay is to be maintained. Both the Kennedy and Johnson Administrations were on management's side. This seriously inhibited the unions' case for the shorter work week.

In past struggles for a shorter work week, labor won widespread public support for it by arguing that working "sunup to sundown" or, later, ten hours a day was too arduous, allowed little or no time for "improvement." Ira Steward, an energetic Boston machinist who agitated for the ten-hour day in the 1830s, introduced the notion that if hours went down, employment would go up. Today, however, Steward's argument is almost the only one. "We aren't fighting for more leisure," Walter P. Reuther once said, "we are fighting for more jobs." But the public so far appears to be unconcerned. "Labor," argued the president of the

United Auto Workers, "ought to fight to reduce the level of the work week until every American who is willing and able to work has a job in the American economy." To achieve this, Mr. Reuther proposed a national fund financed by a one-percent tax of payroll. Whenever national unemployment rises above a "normal" level, the work week is automatically dropped until full employment is reached. Employers would draw out of the national fund money to maintain 40 hours' pay at the new workweek level. Since Reuther did not expect the Johnson Administration to take up this proposition, he also suggested that similar funds could be set up industry by industry through collective bargaining.

There has been, of course, a decided shortening of work time— a development that may be accelerated without cutting the work week. In aircraft, for example, the third-shift workers are on a 6½ hour schedule but are paid for a full eight hours. A similar system is in operation in the telephone industry and others. Auto workers on a short work week get 65 percent of their regular pay for the time lost. This is another step in the direction of a shorter work week and can be a face-saving solution for union leaders committed to the shorter work week.

Construction workers' call-in time—that is, pay for a half day or a full day if they are called in to work but find no work available because of bad weather or other reasons—and the mine workers' portal-to-portal pay also fall into this category. Longer vacations and more holidays are other ways of shortening work time on an annual basis. Supplementary unemployment benefits, too, help maintain annual income in the face of cutbacks in working time.

Pensions, too, may be said to fall into this category by reducing a worker's life-work time. Lowering the retirement age cuts work time and may create jobs more effectively than shortening the work week. And industry helps pay for this device through union-negotiated pensions.

Labor clearly intends to push for the shorter work week and for other cuts in working time as best it can. However—at least in bargaining—these cuts are more likely to follow the pattern set by the 1962 Steelworkers' can-industry settlement rather than that set by the 30-hour work week won by Local 3 of the International Brotherhood of Electrical Workers in its 1962 walkout. The can agreement provides for extended three-month paid leaves every five years for employees with 15 or more years of service. Similar agreements were reached in basic steel and the aluminum industry in 1963. Longer regular vacations and higher terminal payments to encourage early retirement were also secured. Since the average factory worker has ten or more years of seniority, these gains are not negligible. And they do point to the future. Neither the unions nor management obviously has had the last word about contract clauses as they relate to the changes wrought by automation. One British union, for example, has demanded "lonesome pay" for workers handling automatic processes. Management, for its part, has no generalized program for coping with the industrial-relations problems generated by automation. The unions, however, have gone to considerable trouble to spell out what they want. The International Association of Machinists (a good example, for it is neither a one-skill nor a one-industry union) formulated in 1963 the following collective-bargaining program for the age of automation:

A comprehensive program to deal with the problems of technological change should include: (1) advance notice and consultation whenever employers plan major changes; (2) the right to transfer not only to other jobs within a plant but to jobs in other plants as well, with adequate moving allowances (covering, among other things, necessary living expenses and losses resulting from the sale of homes); (3) training for new new jobs (or for old jobs that have not been eliminated) at full pay and no expense to the worker; (4) preservation of the previous rates of pay of workers who have been downgraded and of a substantial part of the income of those who have been laid off (either through supplemental unemployment benefits, severance payments, or some other device); (5) provision for early retirement with assurance of an adequate pension; (6) continuation of insurance coverage and other fringe benefits during periods of layoffs; (7) negotiations of new job classification and rates of pay wherever automation has increased

# XXI

## *BLEACHING THE BLUE COLLAR*

A NEW BREED OF WORKER IS SHOWING UP WITH INCREASING frequency in U. S. industry. He is called the "automation console operator." He turned up first in oil refineries, and chemical and utility plants. Now he is appearing in steel mills, automobile factories and metal-working plants. To managements and labor unions—and to the whole fabric of U. S. society—he will soon pose a problem.

On the surface the problem may seem small; it appears at first to be nothing more than deciding what uniform this new breed of worker will wear. In one chemical plant the console operators wear green coveralls—not because their jobs are dirty, but so that they will not stand out among the plant's other employees who *do* wear coveralls to keep clean. In another chemical plant the console operators wear suits, white shirts, and ties to work—and they are virtually indistinguishable from the salaried office staff. At a textile dye works, the console operators are upgraded blue-collar workmen with barely eight years of schooling. But at an oil refinery the same kind of button-pushing jobs are performed only by college-educated technicians.

Who are these workers of tomorrow? Are they blue-collar men, with the attitudes, work habits, and labor-union loyalties of today's factory work forces? Or are they white-collar workers with the wholly different attitudes, habits, and anxieties of that group? Is automation bleaching the blue collar? Or is it bluing the white collar? Or does it make any practical difference?

These may all seem like wholly hypothetical, impractical questions. But as automation spreads through industry, they are bound to become questions of great significance, for they will reflect a major change in the relationships of management to labor and of employees to unions. And these changes may eventually affect the political allegiances of millions of people and alter the whole shape of the American society. How these questions are answered will determine, for example, how workers will be paid in the coming age of automation—by the hour, day, or week. Whether the U. S. has a white-collar or a blue-collar work force will determine the working conditions and benefits that workers in tomorrow's industries will seek and demand.

Already some of the old distinctions between blue- and white-collar jobs are disappearing. Muscular fatigue was once an almost inevitable condition of factory work, while mental fatigue was limited to white-collar employees. Now, as more and more factory processes become automated, industrial workers too are discovering the burden of mental fatigue. Says one steel worker who controls automated equipment: "On my old job my muscles got tired. So when I got home I rested a while, and that was that—I wasn't tired any more. On this new job your muscles don't get tired. But you keep on thinking about the job when you get home. It's not so easy to rest any more. And that's something that never bothered me before." Management has long recognized the old factory problem of muscular fatigue and has assigned its factory workers rest time to combat it. Now, as a result of automation, does management have to assign rest time for mental fatigue for its automation console operators?

But this is only the most obvious of the problems that arise as the character of the nation's work force begins to change. Deeper shifts that will force changes in labor and management attitudes are on the way. Two examples give a hint of their extent. High over the hot rolling mills of U. S. Steel's Chicago South Works' 120-million-dollar rolling mill, a cloth-capped, grey-jacketed workman sits in an air-conditioned cab. He is a master roller. Before automation he controlled, by sensitive manipulation of levers, the pressure of the giant rollers squeezing out hot steel. Today, all he has to do is decide the sequence in which the rollers should be used. He punches this information on a card and feeds it to a computer that has already been programmed to control the pressure and speed of the mill's rollers. It is the computer that takes charge and that soon has the steel spinning through the rollers at 1,500 feet per second.

The master roller is still a blue-collar worker, proud of his skills and loyal to his union. His job has changed, but he has not been reclassified and still holds his old pay and rating in the mill. But when he retires, will his replacement have the old skills—or even need them? It is most likely that his replacement will be a member of a new class of "semiskilled engineers," whose coming is feared by today's machinists and metallurgists.

At Boeing Airplane Co.'s huge Wichita plant, dozens of men work side by side preparing punched-tape programs for batteries of numerically controlled machine tools. This work does not require advanced mathematics; high school mathematics is usually sufficient. However, the programmers must know, or learn, the idiosyncrasies of many different types of numerically controlled machine tools. In its Wichita plant, Boeing has found that machinists with no more than a high school education can be made into good programmers. But college graduates, too—men with training similiar to manufacturing engineers—are among Boeing's programmers. Blue-collar and white-collar men work side by side; their jobs are indistinguishable. Only the manner of their payment—hourly *versus* monthly—marks the difference between them.

Daniel Bell, a Columbia University sociologist, has pointed out that automation makes it impossible to measure the individual worker's output. Therefore, Bell claims, the hourly rate has become obsolete; automation will create a "salariat" instead of a proletariat. A foreman in a seamless-pipe mill puts it this way: "As the key men in a semiautomatic mill, my workmen are really technicians—not workmen as we used to think of workmen."

Ever since World War II, collective bargaining has worked to bring the blue-collar worker more and more within the corporate family. Vacations, pensions, sick benefits—all commonplace white-collar–executive prerequisites—have been secured. Automation is already pushing this development further. Even the old distinction between wages and salaries is beginning to fade. International Business Machines, which has done so much to spread automation through industry, has itself eliminated the hourly wage and all its employees are on salaries. Few other companies have yet followed IBM's suit, but soon the difference between salaries and wages may be nothing more than a matter of semantics. For instance, the United Auto Workers made it a goal of their 1961 collective bargaining with the auto companies to demand replacement of wages by salaries (a demand repeated in 1964). This provoked more than one auto company executive to say: "The auto workers are virtually on salary now." The reasoning behind this is that supplementary unemployment benefits guarantee that, if an auto worker is laid off, he receives about 75% of his normal 40-hour-week take-home pay. If he works a short week, he receives about 65% of his base pay for every hour less than 40 a week that he does not work. "In effect," says the industry men, "this is a salary." How much of these union gains should be chalked up to the UAW's hard bargaining and how much should be allotted to the effect of automation is a question that is almost impossible to assess. But there is little doubt that as the auto industry moves deeper into automated production, it will come closer to a full salary system.

The ramifications of this change spread far beyond the mere

details of labor-management agreements. Already there is turmoil in some unions over time-honored seniority rules. Several UAW locals have asked that seniority rules be dropped when it comes to short-term layoffs. Older workers, they argue, should be given the choice between working full time at full pay or taking time off at 75% of base pay. These senior men, often in their late fifties or early sixties, would probably prefer time off, the younger workers say, for their children are grown up, their expenses are smaller, and they are more likely to appreciate free time than the younger workers whose need for full pay is greater. So far, there has been no resolution of these calls for change, and they are likely to cause more and more pulling and hauling in union locals.

Turmoil is brewing, too, in the whole area of incentive pay, and again automation and its effects are responsible. Says one union official: "You don't have to put a machine on incentives. When a company automates, it has one of two choices. It can put its workers on some kind of phony bonus system based on the output of the new machines, or it can raise wages to compensate for the 20% to 30% extra earnings that incentives used to provide."

The management view is more cautious. General Electric's top methods and time-standards analyst, William T. Short, says: "Automation makes it difficult to establish incentive-payment systems—and in some cases doesn't seem to justify incentives at all." Productivity is, in effect, engineered into industry's new automated equipment. A plant manager does not want his work force interfering with the speed of the equipment, because the only effect of their interference will be to decrease production. There is nothing that an automation console operator can do to speed up the production process. Yet, it is precisely because of the cost, capacity, and complexity of automated manufacturing systems that there is now far greater emphasis than ever before on careful maintenance and quick repair of the new equipment. When the cost of an automated production system runs into many millions of dollars, each moment of unscheduled idle time represents a staggering expense for a manufacturer. And getting the full productive capacity out of an automated line is at least as much the responsibility of the maintenance workers as it is of the production workers.

In this context, how can the old systems of incentive payments for higher output be adapted to these new industrial methods? Says one leading industrial engineer: "We just don't know how to handle this problem." Some management consultants believe there can be no answer to the question. One of them says flatly: "Automation makes it impossible to measure an individual worker's output—and it also makes a production-incentive system equally impossible." It is the view of Charles R. Walker, director of research in technology and industrial relations at Yale University's Institute of Human Relations, that automation challenges three main tenets of management philosophy: that the work process can be broken down into its smallest possible components; that jobs can be fitted into rigid structures that emphasize individual duties rather than the whole production process; that everyone in the plant can be put on individual or small-group incentive systems that gear pay to output. "As industries become more automated," says Walker, "the tendency will grow to recognize the cooperative and interrelated character of every man's contribution to production, rather than meticulously to isolate and pay for segments of individual effort."

Walker discovered this process at work when he studied the effect of automation on the men in a seamless-pipe mill. Right after the automated equipment had been installed, only the 27 members of the hot-mill crew were included in the plant's incentive system. The hot-mill workers complained that the system's coverage was too narrow. They wanted the maintenance men—mechanics and electricians—to share in the plan. The reason for this, Walker found, was partly because they thought it was just. But they also recognized the vital point that the attitude and competence of the maintenance men had a big bearing on the production team's bonuses. If the maintenance crew also had a stake in the incentives, they felt, repairs would be faster and better.

It is from such cases as this that difficulties are compounded in attempts to establish incentive systems in automated plants. This is why more managements are taking a new look at the so-called Scanlon Plan. This was devised in the 1930s for the steel industry by Joseph Scanlon, professor of industrial management at the Massachusetts Institute of Technology. It seeks to give workers an incentive in this way: The company determines the share of labor cost in the total costs of production; then, if labor costs are cut below this proportion, management shares the gains with its employees. This puts the emphasis on labor-management coopera- tion, gives the workers a chance to participate in sólving produc- tion problems. But to the plan's present-day advocates, its biggest advantages are that it gives both blue- and white-collar workers a common incentive system and eliminates one more difference be- tween the two groups. "As industry automates," says one indus- trial engineer, "employee bonus systems will come to look more and more like those designed for management."

Thus, it seems, the nation's blue-collar workers are steadily encroaching on more of the prerogatives that were not so long ago limited to management and white-collar staffs. This is, of course, a process that started a couple of decades ago. It was in the late 1930s that plant workers began pushing for—and getting—paid vacations, sick benefits, and pensions. Now automation is forcing a new push by blue-collar workers into white-collar territory. Even a couple of years ago it was strictly a management privilege to be given transfer rights and moving expenses when a company closed one plant and moved elsewhere in the country to a new one. Today, as automation speeds the relocation of industry, unions, too, are demanding—and sometimes getting—the same rights. The transfer of executives, with the company picking up the tab, has long been the practice among management. Signifi- cantly, since the introduction of automation, which has meant in many cases the closing down of obsolete facilities and the opening of new plants elsewhere, the unions are demanding roughly the same rights of transfer for workers—and at the expense of the owners of the company. The implications of this development are far-reaching, even revolutionary. For example, take what happened when Chrysler closed down its Evansville operation and moved the work to its St. Louis plant. Management agreed to allow Evansville employees to transfer job rights to St. Louis and offered some help towards moving. But a hitch soon developed. Many of the Evansville employees had worked there since World War II, had bought homes and had their mortgages almost paid off. But when it came time to make the move to St. Louis, the Evansville workers discovered that no one wanted to buy their homes. True, there was a new plant opening in town, but it was "automated" and wasn't creating any great demand for labor, certainly not enough to offset the attraction of moving with the auto plant, to draw to Evansville additional workers who need new homes.

Many unionists now believe that the company ought to make up the loss entailed when a worker moves. Management, of course, balks at the added expense. There are after all more workers than executives, even at the dawn of automation. But continued automation may bring the economy to the point where management will be able to take such expense in its stride.

Labor mobility, in any event, is likely to increase. "In this age," Secretary of Labor W. Willard Wirtz says, "a man's job is the uncertain product of unpredictable but almost certain change." The number of times a worker will change his job in a lifetime is bound to increase as the nation automates. Retraining, and possibly some sort of retraining allowance, will, in the future, become as much a part of a worker's life as unemployment insurance already is for many.

Automation is also having a solid impact on the structure of trade unions. It is shrinking their membership rolls, and if present trends continue the unions of the future will be smaller (though they may also have a much higher-paid—and in some cases, higher-skilled—membership). Union rolls have already diminished sharply. The United Auto Workers had a peak membership of about 1.4 million in 1953. Now it stands only near the one-million mark. The United Steelworkers' membership dropped from about one million in 1953 to some 843,000 last year. The Machinists union has slid from a 1959 high of 992,000 to 646,000 today.

As automation blends blue collar into white collar, some unions may seek to add to their strength by drives to organize white-collar workers. And the white-collar group may be more receptive, for as office work is automated many of these workers are facing the same problems—layoff and insecurity—that blue-collar workers have lived with. Again, the distinctions between white collar and blue collar are blurring.

The American worker, the U. S. often proudly boasts, is a member of the middle class with attitudes quite unlike those of most European workers. This has long been true of his living and consuming habits, and on this fact have been built the mass markets in housing, appliances, and automobiles. But now automation has stirred other ambitions in the blue-collar work force. The worker wants to be middle class in the factory as well as at home. "Production workers," says sociologist B. J. Widick, "want their coffee breaks, too." And coffee breaks are by no means the end of it. What more and more of the blue-collar work force seeks now is a share in the greater security that salaried white-collar workers have long enjoyed. More and more workers believe that automation makes it possible for them to win white-collar privileges in the factory. An assembly line paced the worker and kept him tied to its movement. But an automated production process is a very different kind of operation. The worker is not bound to the movement of the automated line. Indeed, so long as it keeps moving, the worker is, in a sense, free. In a few extreme cases he has nothing to do but watch and stay alert to call the maintenance crew if anything goes wrong.

The master roller in the steel industry rides in an air-conditioned cab where his predecessors sweltered. The automation console operator in the textile dye works now sits at ease in officelike surroundings where a short time ago he sweated among the steaming vats. Steadily the old distinctions between the front office and the plant are disappearing. The white laboratory jacket, rather than today's wilted blue and white collars, may be the symbol for tomorrow's work force.

# XXII

## *PRESIDENT KENNEDY AND THE UNIONS*

THE AIR OF EXPECTANCY THAT SURROUNDED THE BEGINNINGS OF
the Kennedy Administration had a decided piquancy for organized labor. For eight years the unions had longed for a friend in
the White House. Harassed by the renewed recalcitrance of management and apprehensive over the economic downturn, they
worked very hard to elect John F. Kennedy, whose bona fides as a
friend of labor were exemplary. But the fruits of victory are not
always of an unmixed sweetness. The alliance between organized
labor and the Kennedy Administration was an uneasy one indeed.

For the last four of five years of the Eisenhower Administration the unions had floundered in a morass of self-pity and frustration. It was not possible, they argued, to increase their membership when the National Labor Relations Board was loaded
against labor, when union resolutions welcoming the Supreme
Court decision on school desegregation hampered their activities
in the South, and when white-collar workers were being scared off
by the exposures of the Senate Select Committee on Improper
Activities in the Labor or Management Field, headed by Senator
John F. McClellan. But whatever the causes, the blunt fact was

that the high expectations of great activity and even greater achievements raised by the merger of the American Federation of Labor and the Congress of Industrial Organizations in 1955 were never realized.

Although the unions, as a result of the McClellan hearings, adopted a Code of Ethical Practices and cleansed themselves of much of labor racketeering, they were unable to avoid Congressional action. In 1959, Congress passed the Landrum-Griffin Act, which embodied recommendations developed out of the Senate Select Committee's findings. The act, among other things, barred known criminals from union office; required filing of reports disclosing union financial activity and the operation of welfare funds; and spelled out a "Bill of Rights" for union members, protecting their rights to freedom of expression, assembly and to a hearing in disciplinary proceedings. The passage of the act was appropriately symbolic of labor's fall from grace.

The blame, until the 1960 election, could be lodged at President Eisenhower's door. But the election of John F. Kennedy placed the responsibility squarely on the shoulders of labor itself. President Kennedy was without question a friend of the unions, and he also knew more about labor—its strengths as well as its weaknesses—than any other current elected public official and certainly more than any previous President. Franklin D. Roosevelt was intuitively sympathetic to the workers and supported their efforts to organize, but he did not have Kennedy's detailed knowledge of unions. Harry S Truman received his labor education, so to speak, in office. Kennedy, by contrast, came to the Presidency after twelve years of intensive legislative experience in labor affairs—including an instructive term of service on the McClellan Committee.

This knowledgeability lay behind the caution that President Kennedy exercised in his appointment of Arthur J. Goldberg as Secretary of Labor. In December, AFL-CIO president George Meany had arrived at Kennedy's Georgetown residence with the names of five elected union officials, all of whom had the Federation's approval as candidates for the cabinet post. Kennedy, however, in the light of his experience on the McClellan Committee, well knew that he could not appoint a labor executive to administer the reform provisions of the Landrum-Griffin Act; he chose, instead, a man who was *from* the unions but not *of* them. As special counsel to the AFL-CIO's Ethical Practices Committee, Arthur J. Goldberg had won recognition and respect—both from the public and from the Kennedy brothers—for his independence of union bossism. To be sure, many union officials would have liked to disown Goldberg altogether for his part in the cleaning up of corruption inside the labor movement and in the expulsion of the Teamsters from the AFL-CIO. But they dared not do so. Goldberg was the perfect appointee for an administration basically friendly to the unions but only too aware of their failings and vices.

When the President appointed Goldberg to the Supreme Court, the unions did not bother to press the suit of a favored candidate. President Kennedy appointed W. Willard Wirtz, Goldberg's Undersecretary of Labor, to the Cabinet post. It was an appointment more in keeping with the Administration's relationship with the unions. Wirtz is an attorney specialist in labor arbitration. With the Government's greater imvolvement in collective bargaining as a third party, Wirtz' expertise made him a natural for the post. Actually, unionists were much relieved by his appointment. There is a decided feeling that organized labor can do better with a Labor Secretary from outside union ranks. "We can put pressure on a Wirtz," an AFL-CIO official declared, "that we could never bring to bear on a Goldberg!"

However unhappy the unions were over these developments, their feelings were assuaged by the efforts of the Democrats to make the labor law less burdensome to the unions—particularly such weaker unions as the Textile Workers—and so help organized labor rather than obstruct it. The Republican 3 2 majority on the National Labor Relations Board was upset by President Kennedy early in his Administration. This, of course, is the name of the political game. President Nixon, in turn, shifted the balance to one more in keeping with his politics.

The Kennedy board, naturally, could not set aside the law; it could have been, and was, considerably more liberal in its interpretations. In doing so, it relied heavily upon the original idea behind the Wagner Act that the public interest is served by strengthening weak unions *vis-à-vis* strong employers until a more or less even balance is achieved. This, for example, is what the board had in mind in the Deering, Milliken, Inc.–Darlington Case decided in 1962. One of the nation's largest textile chains was ordered to pay back wages to 500 workers who had lost their jobs when an affiliated mill shut down in 1956 after its workers had voted to be represented by the United Textile Workers. In previous cases, the NLRB had held that it is an unfair labor practice for a company to shut down to avoid dealing with a union. The question in the Deering case was whether or not a chain could be held accountable for such an action on the part of a subsidiary. The NLRB not only held the chain responsible for back pay but also required it to reinstate the discharged workers if it should reopen the Darlington operation. The company also must offer them first crack at available jobs at other mills in the area and pay travel and moving expenses. Although the close 3-to-2 NLRB decision was immediately challenged by the company and remained before the courts for several years until finally upheld by the Supreme Court in 1970, the union welcomed it as an aid to organizing in textiles and in the South. "It is a breakthrough," said a United Textile Workers spokesman, "as far as fear among Southern textile workers is concerned. We can now tell the guys in the mill that Uncle Sam is behind him."

The tragic death of President Kennedy did not change the fundamental relationship between the unions and the Democratic Administration in Washington. Union leaders quickly rallied to the support of President Lyndon B. Johnson. Economically and politically the Johnson Administration was a revival of the Rooseveltian New Deal. The passage of civil-rights legislation, the war on poverty, Medicare and Medicaid, improvements in the minimum wage and Social Security benefits, educational aid, the Model Cities program and other social legislation were of importance to working people. Moreover, these gains accompanied an improvement in the economic climate. During 1961 to 1966 the rate of real economic growth averaged annually 5.1 percent. The rate of unemployment, as officially measured, fell from seven percent to 3.5 percent. The money supply was expanded relatively liberally and the upward spiral of interest rates was restrained. Prices were amazingly stable; the average annual increase in consumer prices was only 1.6 percent.

Throughout the latter part of the Eisenhower Administration and the early Kennedy years, automation coupled with an economic downturn and an unemployment rate greater than five percent posed a threat to the unions. Overall union membership fell from a 1956 peak of 17.49 million to a low of 16.3 million in 1961. Blue-collar, industrial unions suffered the most. The United Auto Workers, with a peak membership of about 1.4 million in 1953, fell to the million mark in 1961; the Steel Workers fell from well over 1.2 million in 1959 to about 850,000 in 1961; and the Machinists slid from a million-member high in 1958 to 800,000 members in 1963.

The economic downturn of the early 1960s gave management the weapons it needed to hold down labor costs and to retain control over the allocation of returns on recent investment in automation. To secure these goals, management was willing to "invest"—the word is General Electric's—in strikes. Strike action, in the period running roughly from the 1959 steel strike to 1964, became a method by which management could dispose of inventories and gain the upper hand in running factories. Strikes had to do with job rights—the question of whether the employer has the right to abolish a job without the specific consent of the workers involved. Or, to put it another way, does the worker have the right to a specific job regardless of technological change, because he has invested a certain number of years of his life in it?

This question—brought dramatically to the fore by automation —aroused greater passion than any issue in labor-management struggles since the sit-down strikes of the 1930s. The sit-downs established the bare essential fact of a job right; the employer could no longer fire a worker because of his interest in organizing a union. Once having won recognition, the unions turned from the issue of the worker's property right in his job to the benefits surrounding the job—higher wages, vacations, ajudication of grievances and so on. In the late 1950s the fundamental job right was challenged anew as a result of automation; management, however, saw an opportunity to reassert old prerogatives.

Union howls of anguish to the contrary notwithstanding, management has no desire to destroy the unions; it finds them much too useful as a disciplinary force. It did, however, want the power to determine the new conditions of work in automated plants and to do this it challenged the definition of job rights embodied in the extensive grievance procedures, seniority rules, work practices, etc., which had developed in the prosperous postwar years. It should be recognized that, despite management's argument, work practices (which, of course, include featherbedding) did not spring up in a wholly arbitrary or irrational fashion. Some did, but many more came into being as a result of union victories in countless subterranean battles fought out from day to day in the shop. Management lost these battles in part because it did not pay to push employees to the striking point during periods of prosperity. The recession and a continuing level of unemployment above five percent of the work force, however, provided management with an opportunity to reopen the struggle.

As is often the case, no one won a complete victory. Collective bargaining, however, survived the automation crisis by demonstrating that it is a viable instrument for the resolution of industrial problems. On the Atlantic and Gulf Coast docks, for example, containerization (the bulk loading of cargo in ready-packed trailer-truck bodies or containers) threatened the abolition of longshoring jobs. Two hard-fought strikes—four weeks in 1965 and 57 days in 1968–69—saved jobs *and* paved the way for containerization. The 1966 contract capped the remarkable reform of the ILA, a ten-year progression from a collection of racket-ridden baronies to modern unionism. It was expected that Walter P. Reuther and the socially conscious United Auto Workers would make the initial breakthrough that would bring the working class to the safe haven of the salaried. The UAW did so with its guaranteed annual wage in the form of supplementary unemployment benefits. But the racket-tarnished ILA went the distance. The 1965 agreement provided that a dock worker with 700 hours of work to his credit (two-thirds of the 20,000 men working on Port of New York docks then averaged 1,200 hours of work a year) would be guaranteed 1,600 hours of work a year, the equivalent of a salary of $5,800 a year. The 1969 pact upped the guarantee to 2,080 hours of work; at the then hourly rate of $3.62 an hour, a salary of $7,529.60. At the end of the three-year agreement longshoremen will earn $4.60 an hour and have a guarantee of $9,568 a year. The dockers also secured the right to load and unload shipments in containers consolidated from more than one shipper, within a radius of 50 miles from the port. In exchange for these job-saving concessions, the union has allowed the industry to introduce containers as the basic packaging of shipping. Their use, no doubt, will be expanded as port facilities allow and at a pace determined by collective bargaining. This should permit the gradual phasing out—rather than an abrupt termination of the waterfront labor force. Dockside employers secured the right to make certain job assignments hitherto the prerogative of the longshoremen and won a reduction in the work gang, from 20 to 17. The reduction, however, is to take place through attrition.

This essentially was the bargain struck between unions and management in most negotiations during the early 1960s. Management won the right to make job assignments within the factory, subject, of course, to the normal grievance procedure. In return the unions won various protections against mass layoffs.

Reductions in the work force were to take place through attrition. Automation funds were set up to help pay for early retirement and otherwise cushion the impact of technological change. Conceivably management might have pushed the unions harder than it in fact did. But a massive tax reduction in 1964 cushioned the cost of such settlements. And the Democratic presence in Washington took the edge off managements' willingness to take on the unions.

President Kennedy sought a stable economy. As John Kenneth Galbraith reports in *The New Industrial State*, "In the earliest days of the Administration, it was agreed among those concerned with economic policy that some special mechanism for restraint would be required were there to be a close approach to full employment." Consequently President Kennedy in September, 1961, requested the steel companies and the steel union, then engaged in contract negotiations, to hold their demands within what could come from productivity gains. In the winter of 1962 the President's Council of Economic Advisors declared: "The general guide for noninflationary wage behavior is that the rate of increase in wage rates (including fringe benefits) in each industry be equal to the trend rate of overall productivity increase." This figure was set at 3.2 percent a year. As a guide to noninflationary "private behavior," the Advisors felt that prices should be reduced if a company's productivity was higher than the average rate of growth, raised if the company rate was below average, and unchanged if the company was right on the productivity button. Exceptions were noted to cover the need to attract capital or labor. Enforcement of the guideposts was to be "voluntary compliance" backed by public awareness.

The guideposts were established in a period of relative economic stability, and for a time both prices and wages rose in accord with the general rise in productivity. The guideposts were enforceable because there was no strong disposition on the part of the unions to make large wage demands—the emphasis was on "improvements" and job security—and because business was not in a position to raise prices. In the spring of 1962 an agreement that provided for no wage increases was reached in the steel industry, and President Kennedy repelled an industry attempt to upset the guideposts by what he regarded as an untoward price increase. In 1963 the steel industry adopted an extended vacation plan—13 weeks off for the top fifth of the work force each year for five years—that was reckoned well within the guideposts. This was the pattern in a majority of labor settlements during the guideposts' first two years.

However, the economic theorists of President Kennedy's "thousand days" had not reckoned on high profits and their temptations. Corporate earnings rose to an all-time peak. American Telephone and Telegraph, as an instance, reported net earnings of $1,479,517,000 in 1963, $1,658,606,000 in 1964, and $1,796,-094,000 in 1965. General Motors' earnings rose from $1,591,-823,000 in 1963 to $2,126,000,000 in 1965. To ask workers to practice restraint in the light of these figures was to ask the impossible. Sensing even greater profits ahead, industry, for its part, was anxious to return to the wage-settlement-*cum*-price-rise cycle so recently abandoned. In 1964 auto-union president Reuther charged that company profits were so high that the industry could easily meet the union's demand for a "whopping package" and even cut prices. President Johnson and his Council of Economic Advisors urged restraint—"The most constructive private policy would be to arrive at price decisions and wage bargains consistent with the general guideposts." But the auto companies chose not to defend the line and with scarcely a scrimmage Chrysler led off for the companies with a 39-cent offer said to be at the guidepost figure. Then, with what some businessmen considered indecent haste, Chrysler acceded to the UAW's demand for 15 cents more in "hard money." By hitting first at Chrysler, which was especially anxious to avoid a strike and hang on to the larger share of the auto market secured by its recent comeback, Reuther scored something of a coup. With the leverage gained in the Chrysler settlement, the union soon pressured the other auto companies into line. Before Reuther was through, sizable gains, notably in improved pensions and early-retirement provisions, were all neatly wrapped in separate packages with varying price tags at Chrysler, Ford and General Motors. The increase averaged about 4.9 percent of the industry's labor costs. The wage guideposts had been exceeded by 1.7 percent and with the industry's blessing.

Though breached, the guideposts remained standing. The companies agreed to absorb the immediate inflationary consequences of the negotiations by holding the line on 1965 car prices. Malcolm L. Denise, Ford vice-president for labor relations, told the press after his firm settled with the union, "We've gulped it down and we are going to try and digest it." Political considerations may have dictated the industry's decision. To raise prices in the middle of a Presidential election campaign without first contesting the union's economic demands meant running the risk of drawing public attention to the industry's pricing system. For its part, the White House viewed the auto settlement as a "unique" case to be judged in the context of "very high profits." The wage and benefit record for 1964, a White House statement said, "will show an average increase reasonably close to the guidepost levels." Close perhaps, but an exception had obviously been made.

Since the auto industry could not—or chose not—to pass on to consumers its increases in labor costs, it turned inward, seeking savings that would maintain its pricing formula. Chrysler remained open—both the union and the management had a stake in Chrysler's comeback—but General Motors was shut down for 31 days and Ford, 20, as a result of a struggle over work rules.

In the eyes of management, control over work assignments, production standards and similar matters means greater efficiency and savings in costs; for the worker, control over the job means greater ease at work, personal dignity and possibly a larger measure of security in an age of automation. Workers at GM, who were expected to push for more money in a traditional trade-union fashion in response to rising profits, balked instead at the company's attempts to tighten up work practices and to increase the work load. The company was ready enough to put up the cash to meet the union's requests for improvements in health and welfare benefits, to increase the annual improvement factor in the third year of the agreement from 2.5 percent to 2.8 percent and to continue the cost-of-living allowance expected to add ten cents over three years to the then basic hourly wage of $3.01. If the companies had their way, these changes would be more than made up for by technological changes and tighter work practices.

The union, on its part, sought changes or to retain work rules that tended to reduce productivity at the same time the company hoped to tighten things up. The 1964 auto walkouts, too, reflected membership dissatisfaction with the union's lack of power to solve in-plant job problems. The same dissatisfaction was reflected in an almost complete turnover in leadership of the union's General Motors locals over the preceding several years. The walkout probably eased the situation by letting off steam and by eliminating a backlog of 24,000 grievances ranging from excessive overtime to the ratio of relief men to the assembly-line work force.

The 1964 auto settlement left the guideposts askew. Profits pushed them over with an assist from subsequent big-package settlements in steel, the electrical-goods industry and others. Corporate profits after taxes had risen almost twice as fast as the Gross National Product and about twice as fast as the compensation of all employees. For the six years 1961 to 1966, the total compensation of all employees in the private economy *fell* more than $50 billion—over $8 billion a year—short of the amount it would have been if the incomes of all employees had risen sufficiently to provide them with real hourly increases of 3.2 percent a year, the guideposts' formula for maintaining proportional shares of labor and nonlabor income. Real hourly income for all employees rose by only 2.6 percent. Shortchanged, workers through their unions began to push for equity.

Belatedly Presidential economic advisors came to realize that the great rise in profits and the lag in worker income created an imbalance. "Now that profits after taxes," Gardner Ackley, then chairman of the Council of Economic Advisors, intoned in 1966, "are providing the highest sustained rate of return on owner's equity in our modern history, it is time to ask whether a further rise in the *share* of profits in the national income is in the interest either of the health of the nation's economy or in the interest of business itself."

The unions were quick with an answer. General Electric made a vain attempt to hold its offer in the 1966 negotiations to the guideposts' 3.2 percent. But 11 GE unions banded together for the first time and won a five-percent annual wage increase over a three-year period. GE's average hourly rate, as a result, rose from $2.84 to $3.12. That for all practical purposes was the end of the guideposts. In 1967 the United Auto Workers declared, "Both as a matter of equity for workers and their families, and as a necessity for the nation's economy, it is essential that the UAW make a maximum contribution" toward establishing "a healthier balance in the distribution of our national income through the winning of substantial wage increases for all its members." Wage gains that year came to an immediate 20 cents an hour more for workers on auto assembly lines and an extra 30 cents for skilled workers. Wages, then at an average of $3.40 an hour, went up three percent in the second year of the contract. Pensions were boosted from $4.25 a month for each year of service to $5.25 in 1968 and to $6 in 1969.

Unions prospered under the Kennedy and Johnson Administrations. Total union membership rose from the 1961 low of 16.3 million to 17.9 million in 1966, reflecting the growth in the total labor force from 73 million to 78 million and the decline in unemployment to below four-percent levels. The Teamsters rose to

1.6 million members; Auto Workers, to 1.4 million; and the Steel Workers, to 1.06 million. The AFL-CIO unions managed to grow by seven percent—but the real lift came from the growth of public-employee unions, which doubled or trebled their membership.

# XXIII

## PUBLIC EMPLOYEES GO UNION

ON NOVEMBER 3, 1965, THE DAY AFTER NEW YORK'S MAYORALTY election, Mayor-elect John V. Lindsay received a telegram, one among many, of "sincere congratulations" from the late Michael J. Quill, president of the Transport Workers Union, AFL-CIO. Along with the telegram Quill sent a copy of the 76 proposals his union planned to submit to the New York Transit Authority for a new contract covering the roughly 35,000 workers who operate the city's buses and subways. Included among the 76 were demands for a four-day (32-hour) work week, a 30-percent wage increase, a half-pay pension after 25 years of service, and six weeks of vacation after a year on the job. ("We wished to remind him of our very modest requirements," Quill said upon release of the telegram to the press.) The mayor-elect was also informed of the union's "long-standing commitment with the membership to live up to our traditional slogan of no contract, no work" on January 1, 1966, and he was invited to name a representative to sit in on the negotiations between the union and the Transit Authority, "an autonomous operating agency" established by the state legislature. The mayor-elect did not reply. The next day the union presented its proposals to the Transit Authority. The then chairman Joseph O'Grady, declaring himself "flabbergasted," estimated that these demands would cost $250 million over two years. "There isn't enough gold in Fort Knox to pay this bill," O'Grady told reporters.

Thus far, the pattern was in perfect accord with what New Yorkers had come to accept as standard transit repertoire. "The script," as knowing New Yorkers were wont to call the biennial go-around between the TWU and the Transit Authority, with City Hall as a backdrop, was distressingly familiar—so much so that many hoped that the new mayor would tear it up or at least refuse to play his assigned role; some even hoped that Lindsay would call "Quill's bluff," no matter the cost (secretly believing, of course, that there would be no strike). Indeed, as November wore on with Lindsay still silent, it appeared that the mayor-elect was writing a new part for himself. When he proferred a list of ten possible mediators for the TA-TWU negotiations, Mayor-elect was writing a new part for himself. When he proffered a list Ignoring Kheel's very real ability as a mediator and the trust he had built up over the years with both parties, Lindsay chose to see in him only the fixer or, as he later termed it, a "power broker," who could not be allowed "to dictate to this city the terms under which it will exist."

After considerable backing and filling by all the parties involved, including the issuance of an injunction, the strike began at 5:00 A.M. on a dreary Saturday morning, January 1, 1966. It took three hours and two minutes for the last train, the IRT Seventh Avenue express, to roll into the 241st Street station. Later that morning inaugural ceremonies for the 103rd mayor of New York were held on the City Hall steps beneath a gray sky, before a crowd of 2,500 people. Mayor Lindsay, in his inaugural address, blasted the walkout as "an unlawful strike against the public interest . . . an act of defiance against eight million people."

At the time a good many people believed that Irish Mike Quill merely sought to embarrass the Waspish new mayor. "Let them flex their muscles a little," an aide reportedly advised the mayor. Many thought that the strike would evaporate over the weekend. What they overlooked, as did nearly everyone *vis-à-vis* public employees generally, was the economic interests of the transit workers. The then "modest but adequate" budget of the United States Bureau of Labor Statistics called for $6,900 in annual earnings for a family of four living in New York City. It allowed the husband a coat every five years, a bottle of beer every other day, a new hat for the wife once every two years, two movies a month, and less than one egg a day per person. As consumer consultant Sidney Margolius said, it might more accurately be described as "shabby and respectable." The average basic annual earnings before taxes of all hourly-rated Transit Authority employees for fiscal 1965 was $6,299, or about eight percent below the "modest" budget. Railroad clerks, car cleaners, porters and platform men—who compromised roughly 32 percent of the TA work force—averaged $5,500 a year, well below the budget. Bus operators—17.6 percent of the work force—averaged $6,071 a year, not a munificent sum for a skilled worker. As one bus driver told me, "Look, I drive a 20-ton vehicle for $129 a week after seven years. Most men who are driving a one-ton or a one-and-a-half-ton truck get more than that. And I carry people, not boxes."

So on Monday morning New Yorkers almost literally "crawled" to work, doubling up for rides, walking or hitchhiking to their jobs. Back at the hotel negotiations site, around tables covered with green felt, men doodled—a skull and crossbones, a neatly delineated ice-cream cone, a fat X. Tuesday opened with the announcement, heard by many over car radios as they inched their way into the city, that Quill and eight other strike leaders had been found guilty of civil contempt and had been ordered imprisoned until such time as they called off the strike. Quill, an Irish revolutionary from County Kerry, rose to the occasion as if the whole city had become the stage of the Abbey Theater. "We will continue in mediation until we are dragged from our seats," he declared. "Then we will throw in our second line of leader-ship." Bundled in a dark overcoat, a blackthorn shillelagh hooked over a shaky arm, with bloodless lips and drawn face, Quill ar-rived before the TV cameras for his confrontation with the city marshal. "The judge can drop dead in his black robes. . . . I don't care if I rot in jail, I will not call off the strike." Once alone in the prison front office, Quill collapsed from exhaustion, in-correct use of the medication that had been prescribed for his physical condition, and heart congestion. On January 28, 1966, 15 days after the end of the strike, Michael J. Quill died of heart failure in his sleep.

Before his death, however, he had the satisfaction of seeing his old script, calling for a cliff-hanging wrap-up, dusted off and freshened by a fat settlement package for his faithful followers. It included a 15-percent wage increase over three years, raising the top hourly rate to $4 an hour as of July 1, 1967. A $500 pension supplement, tossed in at the last minute by a nervous Lindsay aide (much to the surprise of everyone concerned) be-came the basis for improvements negotiated in 1968—half-pay retirement at age 50 with 20 or more years of service. Two years later the union secured—again in strikeless negotiations—a new contract worth 24 percent in gains. Top-rated Transit Authority employees earned $4.81 an hour in 1970 and will get $5.30 an hour on July 1, 1971. (The 1970 hourly average was $4.17 an hour.) The 1967 transit settlement not only provided a platform for subsequent TA-TWU negotiations but did so as well for other city employees.

Indeed, Mike Quill's last hurrah was a curtain raiser for emerging unionism among public employees. New York City was wracked by sanitation, school and welfare employee strikes in 1968–69, and Martin Luther King, shortly before his murder in 1968, marched with striking sanitationmen in Memphis, Tennessee. The end of the 1960s' spectrum in public employee militancy ranged, as in Memphis, from hard-fought strikes for union recognition, to, as in New York City, the angry eruptions of the already organized against the demeaning terms of public employment.

The meek public servant is no more. "I am *not* a public servant," Joseph La Penta, head of the West Hartford police affiliate of the American Federation of State, County and Municipal Employees Union, AFL-CIO, angrily snapped at me in a debate. Sanitationmen in communities as far apart as Scranton, Pennsylvania, and Shreveport, Louisiana, walked off the job, demanding the union shop in Scranton and union recognition in Shreveport. In an action reminiscent of the labor troubles of the 1930s, Roanoke, Virginia, sanitation men sat down on their jobs for a day. Welfare workers in Lake County, Indiana, quit work to protest the firing of their local union president as a result of his participation and leadership in demonstrations over contract talks. In Bloomington, Indiana, municipal workers ignored an injunction and the pleas of their leaders that they return to work. Firemen in Rockford, Illinois, struck over pay demands, and all but one member of the Indiana, Pennsylvania, police force walked out because the city council would not meet their request for a pay hike.

Nurses in Philadelphia carried on with "informational" picketing and threatened to strike over wages and working conditions. Hospital employees in Charleston, South Carolina, struck for recognition and won through the united backing of the labor and civil-rights movement. Teachers struck in city after city despite jailing of union leaders, including Albert Shanker, president of the 40,000-member United Federation of Teachers' New York local of the American Federation of Teachers, AFL-CIO, and AFT President David Selden, jailed for 40 days following his marching on a Newark teachers' picket line in the fall of 1969. In 1966 there were more teacher strikes (33) than in the entire preceding decade (26). While the yearly number of public-employee strikes in the entire nation never exceeded 50 before 1966, there was a fivefold increase in 1967 alone. Clearly a new mood existed.

What occasioned it? Three factors, I believe. First, the growth in the sheer number of public employees; second, a change in their economic position and status in the community; and, third, acceptance of trade unionism as respectable and of collective bargaining as a means for resolving personnel and political problems in the rapidly expanding public sector.

Public employment is by far the fastest-growing segment of the labor force. Between 1947 and 1967 the number of public employees at all levels—federal, state and local governments—increased by over 110 percent, from 5,474,000 to 11,616,000. During the same period private nonagricultural employment increased by only 42 percent. Most of the growth in public employment occurred among the 80,000 units of state and local government. Federal employment rose from 1.8 million in 1947 to 2.7 million in 1967, while state and local government employment rose from 3.5 million to 8.8 million. By 1970 state and local government employment exceeded 9 million and is expected by U.S. Department of Labor experts to rise to 11 million or more by 1975. Labor Department projections show state and local government employment rising by an additional 49 percent between 1965 and 1975 while total private employment will grow only by some 24 percent.

The great and growing number of governmental employees have problems of wages, hours and working conditions similar to those of employees in private industry. At one time being a civil servant was a prestigious matter. The pay was comparable to that in private employment and the work steadier than in the private sector throughout the long, grim years of depression. Pensions and vacations were established in public employment long before becoming commonplace in private employment. Postmen were envied because of their job security and teachers, for their three months off in the summer. One of the shocks of the 1970 postal walkout was the discovery of how little our faithful mailmen earned. It wasn't the minimum so much, which was low enough indeed at $6,176 a year, but the fact that it took 21 years of slogging through slush, snow and sweltering summers to reach the maximum of $8,442 a year. Truck drivers in the 1960s earned more than teachers with fewer headaches, namely classes chockablock full, with too many youngsters for any single teacher to handle. The long vacations became a nightmare that had to be filled with a second job; moonlighting, too, became commonplace among teachers. As union statisticians pointed out, public employees earned from ten to 30 percent less than workers in private industry. Contributory pensions became obsolete in private employment as employers assumed the costs of a growing range of welfare benefits but continued on in public employment. According to an American Federation of State, County and Municipal Employees (AFSCME) study, city laborers in Boston averaged $737 a year less than manufacturing laborers, while in Detroit a city stock clerk averaged (in 1967) $1,085 a year less than automobile company stock clerks. And there were examples close at hand underscoring for the unorganized public employee the strengths of unionization. According to a 1966 survey of the National League of Cities, white-collar workers in government lagged in pay scales behind government blue-collar workers who have been organized and have won "prevailing rates," that is, wage scales comparable to those paid their crafts in private industry. A journeyman electrician working for the city of San Francisco earned $12,979 a year while the librarian with a M.A. received a top salary of $12,150. A municipal draftsman in Detroit could earn only $8,795 a year as compared to the plumber's $10,088.

Along with these niggling differences there developed a loss in status for the public employee. The vast growth in public employment assured an increase in bureaucratization and depersonalization of employee-employer relationships. As Arnold Zander, former president of AFSCME, pointed out, "A detached central personnel agency is less apt to secure satisfactory settlement of employee's grievances" than an ongoing, union-established grievance procedure. The trend toward larger, more central school systems, for example, entailed a greater centralization of decision making, a greater distance between administrator and teacher, and more bureaucracy. No one listened to the teacher, neither child nor parent, administrator nor community. Tough kids believed "teach" a "softy"; that is, until the teachers fought back. My neighborhood school, P.S. 29, is 75 percent black and Puerto Rican, mostly Puerto Rican. The youngsters are a tough lot, coming from tenements off Columbia Street, which runs south from Atlantic Avenue along Brooklyn's waterfront into Red Hook. Shortly after the 1962 teachers' strike, which won the United Federation of Teachers its first contract in the New York City school system, Bill Pyles, one of the three men teaching in P.S. 29, was saying what a pleasure it was to teach. He was asked why that year was so special. "I think it was the strike," he answered. "The kids saw teachers on television, fighting. We were tough like truck drivers and Jimmy Hoffa. We won the strike and won the kids' respect. So now they listen when we teach."

Of course, the mood did not last, but the point made did. In union there is strength. As de Tocqueville noted, "The most natural privilege of man, next to the right of acting for himself, is that of combining his exertions with those of his fellow creatures and of acting with them." By the 1960s trade unions had won acceptance and collective bargaining was widely recognized as an appropriate way to settle wages and work-related issues. Unionists became respectable. Union leaders have been named to innumerable Presidential commissions and other public and quasi-public bodies. Public-opinion surveys show that union officers registered significant gains in occupational prestige between 1947 and the present. And, as Professor Everett M. Kassalow of the University of Wisconsin noted, "This legitimacy is being transferred to public employees" and has acted as a spur to organization. Acceptance of trade unionism, however, has broader ramifications than mere respectability among members or would-be members. Union recognition entails acceptance of collective bargaining by employers, in this instance, the managers of public agencies, departments and other bodies or enterprises. The public, too, must accept collective bargaining and its consequences else unions could not survive in the public sector.

Acceptance has been grudging; numerous hard-fought strikes attest to this unwillingness on the part of public management to recognize the unions of their employees' choosing. Still the evidence is overwhelming that acceptance is on the increase. The Massachusetts Legislative Research Bureau in a 1968 study found that 38 states granted the right, at least to *some* employees at the state or local level, to organize and bargain collectively. (Three states, as of 1968, prohibited public-employee unions—North Carolina, Georgia and Virginia.) Nine states, all but one since 1965, have enacted comprehensive labor-relations statutes affecting public employees. (Wisconsin enacted its statute in 1962; the remaining eight states are Connecticut, Massachusetts, Michigan, Missouri, New York, Oregon, Rhode Island and Washington.) No two states treat the subject in exactly the same fashion, though the broad provisions for allowing union representation and for collective bargaining share some similarities in those states with comprehensive statutes. With one exception, California, which has been silent on the question, all states but Hawaii prohibit strikes by public employees. In 1970 the fiftieth state adopted a law granting all state and city employees the right to strike provided the walkout does not endanger public health. Nonetheless, the degree of acceptance, given recent conflicts, is remarkable.

This suggests that public employers have learned from those in the private sector that collective bargaining has its uses—for setting the wage bargain, resolving grievances and as justification for the size of the budget. As John Kenneth Galbraith repeatedly has reminded us, the public sector is a poor relation within our affluent society. Desperate public managers ever short of funds for necessary public services encounter what Galbraith calls "negative discrimination," an unwillingness on the part of the industrial system to invest in that which does not serve its immediate needs or produce profit.

Those who believe government ought to do less for less, or even more for less, have reason to fear, or worry over, the rise of public-employee trade unionism with its constant demand for "more" and consequent upward thrust on costs in the public and quasi-public sector. Yet school superintendents are learning what police commissioners have long since discovered—that the unions are the best lobbyists for next year's budget. The heads of government agencies want "more," too, more policemen, teachers, nurses, social workers, firemen and park attendants. The need is often real enough but the means of raising the money just as frequently tenuous. Legislators must be convinced to loosen public purse strings; taxpayers must be won over. This takes some doing, as any public-works chief will attest. The skillful presentation of any governmental budget calls for adroit lobbying, and the most effective lobbies in state legislature after state legislature are frequently those of police and teacher organizations. If the head of a sanitation or parks department can get the unions to exert their influence on the state legislatures or city council, he may well feel that union recognition is well worth the price. State legislators, too, may come to accept collective bargaining and its settlements as justification for "inevitable" increases in taxes, and so on. This process of "justification" is a factor in the growing acceptance of trade unionism within the public sector.

Public employees have been organized longer than the current upsurge in public-employee unionism suggests. Civil-service organizations, benefit societies and unions have existed in public employment since the adoption of the civil-service merit system in 1883. Postal workers have been organized since the 1880s and the 115,000-member International Association of Fire Fighters was chartered by the AFL in 1918. Police and teacher organizations go back to just before World War I in a number of major municipalities, especially in the East. The Boston police strike occurred, after all, in 1919. The chief difference between these older organizations and the new ones, and between the way the old unions operated and the way they function now, lies in the development of collective bargaining in public employment. By and large, before the current upsurge, which began in the early 1960s, civil-service organizations and the public-employee unions lobbied in the legislatures and did not bargain directly with their employers, the respective governmental agencies. AFSCME, for example, did not mention "collective bargaining" in its traditional resolution lauding the merit system until its 1954 convention. It was only after that convention, according to Leo Kramer, a former AFSCME staff member and author of a Harvard study of the union, that "the union gave increasing emphasis to collective bargaining, union representation, recognition, checkoff of union dues, and signed agreements." Lobbying, though it still remains important, had become an elephantine process, a slow and unrewarding way of improving wages and working conditions. Legislators and administrators caught between conflicting and sometimes contradictory demands for additional public services, balanced budgets and tax cuts and for increased pay and benefits for public employees simply stalled. Aggressive bargaining backed by strike threats—and strikes—promised to short-circuit administrative and legislative procrastination. Collective bargaining, moreover, appears to assure the periodic resolution of employee requests for improvements of all kinds.

As a consequence of this realization, collective bargaining spread as unions flourished in the public sector. In the mid-1950s AFSCME established city-wide bargaining in Philadelphia, which became a model for other municipalities. In 1958 New York City adopted a system of labor relations designed to promote the type of "collective bargaining prevailing in industry." Others followed suit, and by 1966 state and local governments had entered into more than 1,000 separate agreements with employee organizations. AFSCME won what amounted to exclusive bargaining rights for city employees in such cities as Boston, Cincinnati, Detroit as well as New York. Founded in 1937, AFSCME hovered in membership below the 100,000 mark for decades. Between 1953 and 1960, when the union began to pursue collective bargaining aggressively as a goal, it doubled its membership from 87,090 to 182,504; by 1967 AFSCME hit 350,000 and was growing at the rate of a 1,000 new members a week. At its 1970 convention the union reported a membership of 460,000, making it the fastest-growing union within the AFL-CIO and placing it among the ten largest unions in the country. AFSCME has organized architects and zookeepers in some 1,900 locals throughout 45 states, the District of Columbia, Puerto Rico and the Canal Zone. Nurses and dietitians, street cleaners and gravediggers, psychiatrists and librarians all carry AFSCME cards. The union even has a vice-president who is a Catholic priest, Father Albert Blatz, a chaplain at a state hospital in St. Peter, Minnesota. Union officials estimate that roughly 70 percent of the members are white and 30 percent black and that 70 percent are blue-collar and 30 percent white-collar workers. AFSCME's pugnacious president, Jerry Wurf, estimated in 1969 that the "reasonable potential of the union in the near future was somewhere between one million and two million members. Some believe that it may outstrip the giant Teamsters Union as the country's largest trade union.

Other unions in the public-employment field have shown phenomenal growth. President John F. Kennedy's Executive Order 10988, issued in January, 1962, stimulated unionism among federal employees. Up until then the overwhelming majority were unorganized with the exception of postal employees. The Kennedy order, which had a spillover effect in legitimizing unionism in state and local public service, declared that "the efficient administration of the government and the well-being of employees require that orderly and constructive relationships be maintained between employee organizations and management." The direct consequence of the Kennedy order was the rise in membership of the American Federation of Government Employees, AFL-CIO, from 68,000 in 1961 to 196,000 in 1967. By the end of 1969 AFGE membership had jumped to 482,000.

Teachers, too, unionized. On November 7, 1960, 6,000 New York City teachers struck for a day to secure a representation election. The United Federation of Teachers won the election and the right to represent the city's 44,000 teachers in bargaining. Some foot-dragging over money matters on the part of the Board of Education led to a second strike, on April 11, 1962, which pulled out 20,000 teachers and won the UFT its first contract. New York City became the first major metropolitan school district in the country to engage in formal collective bargaining. The UFT grew in membership from 7,500 in 1960 to its 1970 strength of 44,000. The American Federation of Teachers, AFL-CIO, the UFT parent organization, which had been dawdling along for years with a membership of 40,000–50,000, began to win bargaining elections in other big cities: Cleveland with 5,200 teachers, Detroit with 9,700, and Philadelphia with 11,000, as well as in a number of smaller cities, bringing the AFT membership to 170,000 in 1969.

Taking note of this "resurgence in militancy" among teachers, *The New York Times* editorialized: "There was mounting evidence that teachers are no longer content to rule only the classroom to which they are assigned. They want a hand in the assignment and a voice in the policy that controls their professional lives. They are not asking to run the schools, but they want their views heard and heeded."

AFT organizing campaigns along with those of the hospital workers and AFSCME in Memphis and elsewhere became one of the few instances of real cooperation between the civil-rights and labor movements. In Philadelphia, as an instance, the 500-member AFT local found it could not win collective-bargaining rights without the support of Philadelphia's more than 3,000 black school teachers. Bayard Rustin was brought to Philadelphia to speak and help organize; Martin Luther King, A. Philip Randolph and James Farmer were also involved in winning Philadelphia for the AFT. This civil rights–labor coalition for a time was effective both ways. For several summers in the middle 1960s the AFT sent teacher volunteers to staff Southern Freedom Schools.

The New York success led to a change in the leadership of the AFT. At the 1964 convention in Chicago militants ousted a moribund leadership and elected New York's UFT head Charles Cogen president. Cogen, a veteran teacher-unionist, was chairman of the social-studies department at Bay Ridge High School in Brooklyn at the time of his election to the AFT post. First elected head of the UFT in 1951, Cogen developed a young and vigorous secondary leadership within the UFT, including the then 36-year-old Albert Shanker, now UFT president, and David Selden, Cogen's assistant and successor in the AFT. This group led the New York local in its stunning 1960 and 1962 victories and has shaped the character of the AFT since.

The militancy of the AFT sparked a similar aggressiveness within its rival teacher organization, the larger National Education Association. Traditionally the NEA eschewed affiliation with any labor organization, collective bargaining or strike action. But under pressure from its members and in the face of competition from the AFT, the NEA moved into collective bargaining with a growing number of school boards or administrations. In 1962 the NEA convention adopted a resolution declaring that the "NEA insists on the right of professional associations . . . to participate with boards of education in the determination of policies of common concern, including salary and other conditions of employment." The NEA persisted until recently in condemning strikes as "unprofessional," preferring the use of what it calls "sanctions" to bring recalcitrant school systems into line. Where the NEA finds "sub-minimal" educational conditions, it puts sanctions into effect. NEA members are not supposed to apply for jobs within such blackballed school systems. Those members working within such a system are encouraged to find jobs elsewhere as soon as their contracts run out. In 1964, as an instance, the NEA imposed a state-wide sanction against Utah schools which began with a two-day walkout. The sanction was lifted when the state legislature granted an additional $24.6 million in state aid to the schools over a two-year period.

The NEA had in 1970 a membership of about 1,086,000; over 90 percent of the nation's 1.5 million or more teachers are either directly enrolled in the NEA or in state and local organizations affiliated with the national body. The two-to-one membership ratio between the NEA and the AFT has been steady for more than a decade and has not been changed appreciably by the AFT's late 1960s gains. NEA's national budget runs almost $10 million a year. Of this, about $400,000 is earmarked for "federal relations" and "legislation"—euphemisms for lobbying that gives the NEA considerable strength in Washington on educational matters. Significantly the 1969 federal aid-to-education bill was saved by a liberal-labor education coalition, with both the AFL-CIO and NEA playing leading roles.

The AFT-NEA rivalry gave way in 1969–70 to a grudging cooperation. Some 1,800 teachers in Flint, Michigan, merged their AFT and NEA chapters. The members of the Los Angeles Association of Classroom Teachers, NEA, and of Local 1021 AFT, consolidated their organizations with the blessings of the respective national groups. AFT president Selden termed the LA merger "a promising experiment in teacher unity." NEA president that year, George D. Fischer, added, "There can be no doubt that one day soon all teachers in America will have one organizational voice." The Los Angeles teachers struck for union recognition in May, 1970, waiving a five-percent pay increase to get it and smaller classes and a reading program. Whether or not the two organizations will ultimately merge, there is no question but that their approach to teacher problems has converged. As UFT president Albert Shanker once told me, "We may not end up organizing all teachers, but the teachers are going to end up with a union-like movement."

Much the same might be said for the other major independent organization on the public and quasi-public scene, the American

Nurses Association. Again, the late 1960s saw a well-organized profession slowly taking on the appurtenances of trade unionism. Except in recruiting literature, which often sounds desperate, the ANA rarely talks of service to humanity, the joys of tending the ill and other laudable attributes of the profession but does a good deal of complaining about heavy patient loads, mountains of paper work and the frustrations of having to rely on unsound equipment and hastily circulating doctors. Their complaints are justified. Throughout most of the 1960s chronic shortages of nurses existed in most major hospitals, roughly 20 percent across the nation. Salaries were increasingly low, next to lowest of all professional and technological occupations. Secretaries averaged $10 a week more than nurses while teachers earned almost $1,500 a year more.

Like the profession-oriented NEA, the nurses' association has been slow to develop clout in the form of strikes or strike threats. Yet the ANA for two decades had assisted local units to organize for collective bargaining, offered legal counsel, economic and labor-relations advice and worked for favorable state legislation. From 1960 to 1965, however, nurses participated in only one work stoppage; in 1966 nurses engaged in six—San Francisco, Minneapolis, New York, Seattle, Chicago, and in Richmond, California, where nurses actually walked a picket line. In May, 1968, the ANA biennial convention voted to terminate its 18-year voluntary no-strike policy. As one nurse put it, "When hospitals buy equipment, do the profit-making companies quail before the fact that the hospital is a charitable institution? They do not. The equipment is paid for or the hospital doesn't get it. If money can be found for equipment, it can be found for adequate service." Significantly the ANA's collective-bargaining program calls for not only increased salaries and shorter hours but also increased participation by nurses in the planning and administration of nursing services.

Police benevolent associations have worked for decades in tandem with the unionized firemen to secure wage increases and improved working conditions. AFSCME has a dozen or so police locals, mostly in various Connecticut cities and towns. Policemen otherwise have shown little interest in national trade-union affiliation. But in 1969 the leaders of the New York City Patrolmen's Benevolent Association expressed an interest in launching a new police union and in seeking an AFL-CIO charter. John J. Cassese, the New York PBA head, retired to take on the task of organization. A 1970 conference, representing some 10,000 policemen and held in Omaha, drafted a constitution for a new International Brotherhood of Police Officers, elected Cassese president and Robert Bragg, a retired detective sergeant from Omaha, secretary-treasurer. Affiliation with the AFL-CIO, however, remained uncertain. The International Conference of Police Associations and the Fraternal Order of Police, both independents, countered the new Brotherhood by creating a joint council with a combined membership of 300,000. The council has adopted a resolution *not to affiliate* with the AFL-CIO.

When workers are in the mood to organize, they are likely to sign up with whosoever is at hand. Auto workers during the frenzied upheaval of the 1930s sought membership in the bartenders' union—that being the union with a card-holder closest to many an auto plant. One finds today municipal employees joining the Teamsters, the Laborers and Building Service Employee unions among others. Hospital workers in New York City's quasi-public "voluntary hospitals" joined a union of druggists largely, though not entirely, because it was the union at hand at the right moment. Municipal employees, who may feel weak and much put upon, seek out the Teamsters because of that union's great power and also because the Teamsters are well organized and are found literally "everywhere." These unions, too, are aggressively organizing. The Teamsters outside the AFL-CIO possess the added advantage of not having to observe jurisdictional lines. As a result, the truck drivers' union has several hundred thousand members in public service.

The 474,529 member Laborers' International Union and the

350,000-member Building Service Employees' International Union both possess jurisdictions that allow them to enter the public field, especially within their respective job categories. The BSEIU has shown a 35-percent increase in the public-employee sector—both local and state and among federal employees. Most are elevator operators, building repair and service employees, but the union has new strength in some municipal and quasi-public hospitals and among such professionals as nurses and school custodians. The Laborers' membership in public service has jumped from 7,500 in 1960 to some 30,000 in 1970, and the union is actively organizing. The Machinists, which for many years had an active federal employee group, has more than doubled its government-employee membership since the advent of the Kennedy order. The Amalgamated Transit Union and the Transport Workers Union, between them, have some 150,000 public or quasi-public employees organized in mass transit.

Although the unions have made major excursions among professionals and white-collar workers in public employment, the major thrust has been among blue-collar workers. Roughly two-thirds of AFSCME's membership, for example, remains blue-collar. Unionization in all likelihood will drive up wages, improve working conditions and benefits and result in the upgrading of many public employees. This will substantially benefit the black and white working poor, many of whom are to be found working for state and local governments. The number of blacks employed by municipal governments, for example, is high in proportion to the black population in many cities. Exact figures are hard to come by since few cities have conducted ethnic surveys of civil-service personnel. Most observers, however, agree that blacks and other minorities are filling lower-echelon civil-service jobs in most of our major cities. In Philadelphia, for example, over half the membership of the AFSCME District Council, which represents a majority of the city's employees, are black. Sanitation and street-cleaning departments in several major cities—Cincinnati, Philadelphia and Memphis are examples—are mostly black.

AFSCME relies on black organizers in many areas of the South in its drive to organize municipal employees below the Mason-Dixon Line. The 65-day strike of 1,375 predominantly black sanitationmen of Memphis in 1968 illustrates the ties that exist between public-employee trade unionism and metropolitan minorities.

As a special report of the Southern Regional Council pointed out, the Memphis sanitationmen's walkout was "More Than a Garbage Strike"; in truth, it began as both a simple workers' grievance and a race issue. On January 31, 1968, 22 employees in the Memphis sewer department were sent home when it began to rain. White employees, however, were not, and when the rain stopped after an hour or so, they were put to work and paid for the full day. When the black workers complained, they were paid two hours' "call-up" pay. After seeing what their pay envelopes contained at the end of the week, they called a meeting of Memphis AFSCME Local 1733 and went out on strike the following Monday, February 12.

Mayor Henry Loeb held that the strike was illegal and that the strikers had to return to work before their grievances could be discussed. The mayor also added that he would never sign a contract with the union since it was against city policy to do so. Memphis had no formal agreement with any one of several organizations representing its 20,000 public employees. The objective of the strike soon became union recognition and a contract with the city. The workers insisted on an effective grievance procedure, the dues checkoff, merit promotions "without regard to race," equal treatment in the retirement system, payment of overtime, and a 15-cent boost over the $1.60 hourly rate. During a series of confrontations—they could hardly be called "negotiations"—the city offered a ten-cent wage boost, concessions on all other demands except union recognition and the dues checkoff.

The strike then centered on union recognition. As Jesse Epps, a black Mississippian and AFSCME organizer assigned to Memphis, put it, "The basic issue is not pay, but recognition of the union. There has never been the unity in the Negro community of Memphis that there is now, and the reason is that recognition of the union involves recognition of the workers *as men*. The mayor wants to say, 'Go on back to work and then we'll do right about your complaints; you know our word is as good as our bond.' Just as if Memphis were a Delta plantation."

The police broke up a sit-in at City Hall with billy clubs and Mace, an action that rallied the black community in Memphis solidly behind the strikers. Over 90 percent of the sanitation workers were black; roughly 38 to 40 percent of Memphis, with a total population of 527,492, is black. As the union-community alliance developed, economic and political pressures began to build up with boycotts of downtown businesses and periodic marches on City Hall. The city countered with a far-reaching injunction prohibiting both the strike and all forms of picketing. Dr. Martin Luther King was drawn to the struggle and his presence dramatized its urgency to the nation. His tragic murder precipitated a settlement of the walkout favorable to the union.

Since Memphis, public-employee unions have become increasingly involved with minority-group workers. Black and Puerto Rican workers, for example, are holding jobs in many metropolitan hospitals. And just as the building trades many years ago drew on ethnic bonds and a common language to strengthen union solidarity and to organize, so do hospital-worker organizers. Drug and Hospital Local 1199 of New York City is slowly on the way to becoming a national hospital union through such efforts. Spanish-speaking organizers have fanned out through Connecticut toward Massachusetts following the movement of Puerto Ricans out of New York City into hospital jobs in New Haven, Hartford and Boston. Black organizers work among black hospital workers in Baltimore and Charleston—and so the union grows. Local 1199 is an integrated union as are all the unions in the public sector, but, as do the rest, it takes advantage of roots struck into the black, Puerto Rican and other minority communities by the labor movement. In Charleston, South Carolina, Local 1199 enlisted the support of the civil-rights movement to win recognition for hospital workers seeking to build a union there. Mrs. Coretta King spoke repeatedly at rallies, and the Reverend Ralph E. Abernathy, Dr. King's successor as head of the Southern Christian Leadership Conference, went to jail during the organizing campaign.

Obviously relations between the labor and civil-rights movements are not all sweetness and light and brotherly love. Trade unions often want to concentrate on the bread-and-butter issues around which collective bargaining turns and on which black and white workers most readily agree. Black civil-rights activists and black ministers often seek to broaden the struggle to encompass all the grave concerns that worry the black community. Sometimes these fit together easily as they did in Memphis and Charleston, but at other times they become a source of conflict. The unionized professionals' insistence on "standards" may seem discriminatory to blacks. "Community control," and/or "decentralization," may appear to organized public employees as threats to hard-won job rights.

The unhappy 1968 New York teachers' strike illustrates the point. It began over the dismissal of 19 teachers by an experimental school district in Ocean Hill–Brownsville, a grim, rundown corner of Brooklyn. The United Federation of Teachers struck in the fall of 1968 to enforce its contract with the Board of Education, and two short strikes appeared to settle the matter with a commitment from the Board of Education to enforce the contract and one from Mayor John V. Lindsay to back that commitment. But the city administration undermined the agreements and a much longer strike ensued. In all, the three strikes kept 50,000 teachers and one million pupils out of school for 36 days of the first 48 days of the 1968 fall term.

The union won the narrow issue of contract enforcement (admittedly important to the teachers), but the strike seemingly created a deep-running hostility between the black community and the UFT. Reconciliation seemed impossible, and many white liberals hastily condemned the union for alleged "racism." Significantly, however, not two years later, when black workers were asked to make a choice in a representation election between the allegedly "racist" UFT and another union, the predominantly black paraprofessionals chose the UFT. And in nearby Newark black and white teachers struck together to win important contract gains in the fall of 1969. While one hesitates to read reconciliation into these developments, nonetheless they do point up the fundamental attraction of trade unionism to exploited workers—black or white.

Collective bargaining is sure to grow in the 1970s within the public sector. Strikes, too, will increase despite legal bans. If the history of collective bargaining in the private sector provides any guide, however, walkouts in time will decrease in number and intensity. We have come a long way since Governor Calvin Coolidge sent his terse telegram to AFL president Gompers in response to the Boston police strike in 1919: "There is no right to strike against the public safety by anybody, anywhere, anytime." We are beginning to recognize that the public sector is not sacrosanct and that the distinctions between the private and public sectors are often moot. The park attendant performs a socially useful function, yet one cannot pretend that social catastrophe is imminent should he withdraw his services in a conflict with his immediate employer, the public-parks department.

Some private services, provision of heating fuels, say, are eminently more critical than many public services, yet we do not ban strikes in such areas. How essential, for example, is the mail as compared to telephone service or firemen? The 1970 postal strike pinched more people a good deal harder than any other recent strike. But it did not cripple the country, and we could have survived easily a full-scale strike. Where one draws the line is increasingly difficult in our complex society. AFSCME's constitution recognizes that law-enforcement groups cannot be allowed the right to strike. In fact, however, there have been police strikes without any noticeable collapse of society. Collective bargaining is a process which transforms pleading into negotiation, a form of participatory democracy. But as AFSCME president Jerry Wurf has pointed out, it must take place among equals. Strike prohibitions Wurf added, "are not simply ineffectual, though they are undeniably that. What is far more serious, they warp this vital process. They bring employees to the bargaining table, but as inferiors. Simultaneously they provide false reassurance to management representatives and induce less than genuine negotiations. Ironically they create the very tensions, exacerbate the very situations, provoke the very strikes they were allegedly formulated to prevent."

We may take the 1970 postal walkout, which brought federal troops rolling into New York City, as a sign that the old way of doing things in public employment are at an end. Lobbying truly is no way to set wages and the conditions of work. The advantage to an employer of the right to strike is that he knows where he stands right off, and there does not seem to be any public gain in denying this awareness to government as an employer. In truth, the traditions of service in public employment —and especially so in such critical areas as police, fire, teaching, nursing—are such that it takes a good deal to provoke a strike. We'd be far better off to rely on these traditions than on meaningless strike bans.

Collective bargaining has worked fairly well in the private sector and it is sheer idiocy to believe that the same techniques are inadequate for the public sector. As Theodore W. Kheel wisely has warned, "No one should be misled in the belief that there is a single, all-pervasive solution to strikes. There is no panacea." Still some form of labor legislation governing public employees is politically inescapable, and a law that encourages voluntary methods for reaching an agreement is perhaps the best of possible legislation. Mediation can be encouraged, and fact-finding in some instances has much to recommend it. But fact-finding has disadvantages; it delays a settlement, and it may underscore the financial woes of public agencies in such a way as to reinforce their refusal to concede to their employees' requests for improvements.

Former Secretary of Labor George Schultz has suggested that, under appropriate circumstances, the parties ought to be compelled to make a "last offer," which then would be submitted to a third party who must select one or the other "offer" without modifying it. Such a gimmick might force both sides to be realistic and might be a practical alternative to strike action. In general, however, whatever pressures may be applied through the law should be on the parties to negotiate. They should not be encouraged to postpone the inevitable, which is the chief result of extended cooling-off periods and emergency hearing boards. Nor should they be encouraged to pass the buck, which is the chief weakness of arbitration. Arbitration is also ineffective as a strike deterrent; instead of official strikes, one gets wildcats (at least this has been the experience in New Zealand, where some form of compulsory arbitration has existed for nearly half a century). All in all, the trouble with putting the techniques for resolving labor disputes into the law is that the machinery becomes so inflexible and predictable that it discourages voluntary settlements.

Whatever laws are adopted, the 1970s promise to be a decade of expansion for public-service unionism.

# XXIV

## *BLACK UPSURGE IN THE UNIONS*

BLACK UNION ACTIVITY IS ON THE INCREASE. BLACKS ARE ORGAN-
izing new locals among hospital workers, municipal employees
and in the retail and service trades. Black caucuses form at union
conventions, and there are national black caucuses within the
United Auto Workers, the United Steel Workers and the American Federation of Teachers, and black rank-and-file rebellions
have erupted in the New York and Chicago transit unions. Black
pride provides the thrust for black representation within the labor
movement as it does in all our institutions.

This thrust gains a lift from a continuing ground swell of black
employment in unionized industries and industries ripe for unionization. The number of black workers with seniority and trade-
union experience has grown, and blacks are no longer automatically last hired and first fired. In 1954, according to the
Bureau of Labor Statistics, out of a total nonwhite work force of
6.3 million, there were 316,000 craftsmen, foremen and kindred
workers; a million nonfarm laborers; 1.3 million operatives and
kindred workers. Between 1965 and 1969 the total nonwhite

force rose from slightly over 7.7 million to almost 8.6 million, while the number of black laborers dipped from 985,000 to 859,000, the number of black craftsmen rose from 520,000 to 752,576, and that of black operatives from 1.6 million to 2.1 million. As workers gain seniority, they tend to move upward, out of the ranks of the unskilled into those of the semiskilled and skilled. As the figures above indicate, this is happening to an increasing number of black workers.

There are, unfortunately, no precise figures on black trade-union membership. AFL-CIO spokesmen estimate that two million out of a total membership of almost 14 million are black. There are another 500,000 or perhaps 750,000 blacks in unions affiliated with the three-million-member teamsters', auto and chemical workers' union, the Alliance for Labor Action. Where black workers are to be found in concentrated numbers still remains a guess. Two small unions, the 6,000-member Brotherhood of Sleeping Car Porters and the 3,000-member United Transport Service Employees, are virtually all black. The powerful 450,000-member Laborers' International Union and the 50,000-member International Longshoremen's Association are about 40 percent black. Some 45 AFL-CIO unions have "substantial" black memberships—that is, a larger percentage of black members than the 11–12 percent rate of black participation in the labor force.

To give a few examples: the State, County and Municipal Employees (450,000), the merged Meatcutters-Packinghouse Union (488,000), Letter Carriers (189,000), Postal Clerks (143,000), International Ladies' Garment Workers Union (455,000), Building Service Employees International Union (350,000), the Laundry Workers (25,000), possibly the Steel Workers (1.1 million), and the American Federation of Teachers (140,000) are among unions with 20 percent or more black memberships. Of the 1.7-million UAW members, about 25 percent, or 400,000, are black. As is the case with many unions, the black membership tends to be concentrated in urban areas. Of the 350,000 auto workers in the Detroit area, which encompasses a good number of predominantly white suburbs, it is estimated that upwards of 40 percent are black. Most of these live and work in Detroit.

So far, between-convention black caucuses exist in only three major unions—those of the auto workers, the steel workers and the teachers. This may reflect the state of accommodation to rising black memberships with the unions. Blacks have been active since the founding of the Packinghouse Workers, and three blacks sit on the executive board of the Meatcutters, now merged with them. There are two blacks on the UAW's 27-man executive board. The Longshoremen have had black vice-presidents for some time now, and the Laborers' union, as several other unions, now also has a black vice-president. Two black labor leaders, A. Philip Randolph of the Sleeping Car Porters and Frederick O'Neal, president of Actors' Equity, sit on the AFL-CIO executive council.

Another key activity among black trade unionists is a growing involvement in political action. Norman Hill, associate director of the A. Philip Randolph Institute, says that the response among black trade-union activists to the institute's political-education programs has been "tremendous." The institute has set up a new regional office in Chicago, with Maida Springer Kemp as field director, and it now plans to open offices in other black trade-union centers around the country. "We're not a caucus in the sense of engaging in internal union politics," Hill told me. "Our main focus is on COPE [Committee on Political Education] activity, but we also recognize the thrust toward black representation. The black-labor alliance will only work politically if there is black representation on all levels of the COPE decision-making apparatus." The institute probably reaches more black unionists than any other single national organization.

The relative absence of widespread black-caucus activity at the national level reflects the present level of black power or consciousness, the absence of a dramatic issue to pull people together and the difficulty of doing so when memberships are widely scattered. Within the Building Service Employees International Union, for example, blacks participate within the local unions as local leaders and on local organizing and service staffs. In 1969 several ex-BSEIU staff members joined a rival Teamsters-sponsored organizing drive, drew up a bill of complaint against the BSEIU and circulated it among BSEIU activists as "black demands." This brief flyer at black-caucus activity did not take root, partly because of the difficulty in pulling together a diffuse rank and file.

Black caucuses in the trade unions are still a new development. They cannot be understood apart from a specific industry, union, and in some instances a specific city in which they are found. Within the American Federation of Teachers, which has a tradition of caucus activity, the Black Caucus enjoys the quasi-official standing afforded each of the other three major caucuses in the union—the majority, pro-administration Progressive Caucus, the conservative National Caucus, and the New Caucus, which considers itself to the left of the other two. Perhaps because all these older caucuses are integrated, or because the New Caucus had preempted the role of black spokesmen, it was not until the 1969 AFT convention in New Orleans that a caucus was formed on the basis that "everybody black ought to belong." Chaired by Zeline Richard of Detroit, the AFT Black Caucus draws its chief strength from black teacher activists in Chicago, Detroit and New York.

At the 1969 AFT convention the Black Caucus drew up a list of questions, which was considered at a hastily summoned executive council meeting. "We recognize that blacks, by virtue of their history, have legitimate and special concerns," AFT president David Selden told delegates. "The AFT leadership will respond calmly and in good faith." On the whole, the union leadership seems to have done so. The Black Caucus, angered by a refusal of two bars to serve black delegates, wanted to know: "Why, instead of taking some affirmative action in protest, did the AFT set up a study commission to evaluate the indignities suffered in New Orleans by many black delegates to this convention?" After hearing the commission's findings, the convention picketed the two bars and the executive council of the AFT maintained an all-night vigil.

The Black Caucus raised questions about such issues as community control of schools, employment opportunities on the AFT staff, minority representation on policy-making bodies in big-city locals and AFT support for black teachers punitively transferred following the 1969 strike in New Orleans. The caucus further asked for a special meeting with the AFT executive council, which took place in December, 1969.

*The American Teacher*, in its October, 1969, and January, 1970, issues, carried full accounts of convention developments and of the special meeting. The AFT provided airfare and hotel and living expenses for a five-member Black Caucus delegation to the December meeting. Some of the council's answers to the Black Caucus may be of interest: in the New Orleans matter, the council reported full support of the penalized strikers and cited the assumption of two-thirds of the $5,367 in legal costs incurred so far. As to staff, there are three blacks among the 12 persons employed in the organizing department—a director of field services, a national representative and an apprentice organizer. The last vacancy on the national representatives' staff was filled by a black. The AFT council is considering guidelines in order to guarantee minority representation on big-city locals, and it has reaffirmed its commitment to the AFT's 1968 decentralization resolution, which urged AFT assistance to communities that are seeking responsibility for educational decision making, keeping in mind teacher tenure and due process.

While in the AFT relations between the leadership and the Black Caucus appeared amicable, as of early 1970, this cannot be said of their counterparts in the Steel Workers. Black steel workers picketed the 1968 steel-union convention in Chicago, and there was a sharp debate on the convention floor over black representation on the union's executive board, which consists of three executive officers and 30 district directors—all white. All

these officers are elected every four years by a membership referendum. At the convention the Ad Hoc Committee, the black
caucus within the Steel Workers, proposed the institution of a
second vice-presidency, to be held by a black.

The proposal was overwhelmingly defeated, largely on the
grounds that such a post would be "appointive" rather than elec-
tive. The Steel Workers' president, I. W. Abel, drew applause
when he declared, "I didn't hold office all these years as a Welshman, but as a steel worker elected to office." Vice-President
Joseph P. Molony summed up the prevailing view: "We are
opposed to any procedure that would establish an office in our
union based on race, national origin, religion or color. This
would be a form of Jim Crowism in reverse and contrary to our
rigidly enforced policy of nondiscrimination." So it would be—
yet this view ignored certain realities. As one member of the
National Ad Hoc Committee put it, "Sure, it's best for a Negro to
be elected, but there's not much chance of that. Since there isn't,
one should be appointed." Balanced tickets are not exactly unheard of in American politics, nor within the steel union, where
ethnic politics often play a lively role at local and district levels.
As I read the 1968 convention debate, black delegates were
simply asking recognition of that political fact—a demand echoed
in other unions, incidentally. "Create a new office and name a
black to fill it on the administration slate," was, in essence, what
they said. Black steel worker Raymond Freeman said:

"We can understand what you are talking about when you
say run for the office, but you also understand . . . that you
control the circle from which we have to run, and in order to
break this crust, there must be a place for us to run. In order to
run we are asking you now to give us the second place on the
ticket and we will assure you that we will put a Negro in office."

There is some question as to black strength within the steel
union. The Ad Hoc Committee claims that 20–25 percent of the
union's 1.1 million members are black; union spokesmen cite
industry figures that suggest that 16 percent, or roughly 200,000

members, are black. According to Richard L. Rowan's study of Negro employment in the *basic* steel industry in the October, 1969, issue of *Industrial and Labor Relations Review,* out of a total blue-collar work force of 361,995 in 1966, 58,273 or 16.1 percent were black. Operatives—that is, semiskilled workers—comprised 37.1 percent of all employees in basic steel. Of these 172,683 workers, 30,719, or 17.8 percent, were black in 1966. Out of 69,807 laborers or unskilled workers, 19,356, or 27.7 percent, were black. Of 111,047 craftsmen in the industry, 6,586, or 5.9 percent, are black. Yet while heavy concentrations of black steel workers exist in Baltimore, Birmingham, Chicago, Detroit and elsewhere, there are no predominantly black steel-union districts.

Conceivably the union might carve out a new district, as the UAW has done, to expand its executive board and ensure the election of a black. But this, so far, has not seemed politically feasible. Such a division would cut into the power of the district director affected, and the blacks in the union simply did not, as of 1970, have the political muscle to move the leadership in that direction. However, the Abel-Burke-Molony administration has shown some awareness of the need for black representation at top policy levels of the union. When the director of the Baltimore District 8 retired in 1969, they saw an opportunity. There are 38,000 steel workers in this district; most of them work for Bethlehem Steel, and 35–37 percent are black. Leander Sims, a black Steel Worker union representative, ran against Edward Plato with the full backing of the Abel administration. Sims lost, by a bit more than 1,500 votes. Fewer than 10,000 members voted, even though there was both a district and a national union contest. Abel himself barely won the district, and it is clear that Sims lost because black steel workers didn't come out to vote for him in the expected numbers. Since then, Sims has been appointed assistant director of the district.

The National Ad Hoc Committee played only a small role in

the Sims-Plato contest: it had no rank-and-file backing in the district. The committee, founded in 1964, has a simple, three-point program that does not seem to have broad mass appeal. Drafted by Aaron H. Jackson of Detroit and Rayfield Mooty of Chicago, the program calls for: (1) Negroes on the Executive Board; (2) full integration at all levels within the various districts and national offices as department heads and in policy-making; (3) reorganization of the Civil Rights Department.

In sharp contrast to the Dodge Revolutionary Movement, a black faction within the UAW, whose members are under thirty and fresh to employment in the auto industry, the Steel Workers' Ad Hoc Committee consists largely of older men with considerable trade-union experience. Jackson has been active as a negotiator, shop steward and local officer for over 20 years, Mooty was a charter member of his aluminum local union, and has been shop steward and president during his 30-odd years of union service. The Ad Hoc Committee meets twice a year; it drew 350 to its last meeting, at Gary, Indiana, in July, 1969.

The committee supported Abel against David McDonald in the 1965 steel-union elections and as a result secured a commitment from Abel to make changes in the union's hiring and promotional policies. Mooty grumbled to me about a lack of meetings with leaders of the union, but conceded that there had been some changes. The Ad Hoc Committee, he said, won point three, the reorganization of the union's Civil Rights Department, now headed by a black, Alex Fuller, and some gains under point two. Although Mooty retains his militancy, the Ad Hoc Committee, I would judge, has lost some of its zest. A number of its key activists are now on the union staff, and there doesn't seem to be any sizable steam building up behind the one remaining point demanded in the Ad Hoc Committee's program. This, I suspect, reflected the 1970 political realities in the union: the officers had until 1973 to go before elections; a constitutional amendment that would open a spot for a black had little chance of success in the interim; all that remained was to wait for a director to retire in a district where a black would have a reasonable shot at election.

Black activity within the United Auto Workers is a good deal more lively and varied than within the steel union. It reflects a broader spectrum of tendencies within the black community, from dedicated integrationists to feisty black nationalists. The League of Revolutionary Black Workers is a sect with factions in several auto plants. The Trade Union Leadership Committee, headed by Horace Sheffield, has been in existence for over ten years and has successfully fought for black representation in the top councils of the auto union. It has some 3,000 members, who come from all unions in Detroit but chiefly from the UAW. At its peak the TULC had over 7,000 members and helped elect Mayor Jerome Cavanaugh despite opposition from the UAW's top leadership. Strictly speaking, the TULC is not a caucus, but its impact on the union may be measured in terms of 80 black international representatives on a staff of 1,050 and the growing number of black local union officers. At UAW conventions, as in other unions, blacks are probably proportionately represented, and perhaps even more so among officers in most locals where black workers exist in any number. Brendan Sexton, the UAW leadership-program director, is not far off the mark when he asserts, "I don't claim that black workers are equally represented at all levels in the union, but blacks have done better in the UAW than in any nonblack national organization."

Dodge Main, an ungainly collection of four- and six-story, 1920s-style factory buildings, occupies roughly a square mile of Hamtramck just across the Detroit city line. It is the home of DRUM (Dodge Revolutionary Union Movement), the founding contingent of the League of Revolutionary Black Workers. "There isn't a more likely place in Detroit for the DRUM phenomenon," I was told by an auto-union official, who readily conceded that this surfacing of black militancy in the Detroit-area auto plants had "somewhat surprised Solidarity House," Detroit shorthand for the top leadership of the UAW. Conditions at Dodge were affected by economic developments within Chrysler and the auto industry as a whole. Managerially incompetent and scandal-ridden, Chrysler seemed headed for the junkyards by 1960–61. The subsequent auto-sales boom and the skills of Lynn Townsend, in 1970 chief executive of the corporation, saved Chrysler, and the company raised its share of the market from ten percent in 1962 to 18 percent in 1969. Record earnings in 1968 amounted to $290.7 million, or $6.23 a share on sales of $7.4 million. Chrysler employment rose from roughly 75,000 in 1962 to slightly over 133,114 in 1966. The 1960s were boom years for the industry. Domestic employment among the big three—General Motors, Ford and Chrysler—rose from 693,186 in 1961 to 953,585 in 1966.

With four big plants in the Detroit area, Chrysler is a major inner-city employer. Chrysler emerged from World War II with the largest percentage of black employees in the industry. In 1946, 17 percent of Chrysler's 71,000 employees were black; 20 years later, 23.1 percent of its 133,114 employees were black. The rise and fall of Chrysler employment, therefore, is fairly crucial to Detroit's black community. For example, back in 1957 employment at four Chrysler Detroit plants was 45,584, including 9,242 blacks, or 20.3 percent. After a layoff, these plants employed in 1958 some 22,776 workers, of whom 3,345, or 14.7 percent, were black. Over the last six years black employment in Detroit's auto plants has risen sharply. At Chrysler Local 7, roughly 65 to 70 percent of 7,638 members are black; 65 percent of the 4,012 UAW members at the Chrysler Eldon Gear and Axle plant are black; and roughly 60 percent of the production workers at Dodge Main are black.

Just seven years ago a worker had to have 20 years' seniority to work at Chrysler; today roughly 65 percent at Dodge Main have less than six years' seniority. Turnover is very high, especially among the young, unmarried workers. According to industry estimates, some 46,000 new hires passed in and out of

Detroit-area auto plants in 1968. According to one UAW chief steward at Dodge, representing some 400 workers, "Two hundred guys must've passed through my department since August." Some quit " 'cause the work is too hard," or on account of the "speedup," as older workers put it. Others are fired because they haven't caught on for a variety of reasons. One youth fired for absenteeism complained, "How could they miss me in a plant with 6,000 guys workin' in there?" In what amounts to an almost full-employment economy, some blue-collar youths are dropping in and out of industry pretty much the way their middle-class peers do at college—in reponse to mood, the need for "bread" and parental push. The consequence of this new youthfulness within worker ranks is a dash of volatility to what is a Detroit mixture—black militancy, revolutionary adventurism and working-class politics.

Detroit is a high-octane town. If the mixture is right, it doesn't take much to spark a wildcat walkout at its auto or supply-parts plants. Despite automation, the assembly line has not changed its essential character as an engineered, mechanical pacer of man. Although I've been told that the auto companies find it more economical, even efficient, to add an hour or two of overtime rather than constantly fiddle with the speed of the line to get out the production, the assembly line remains the chief irritant in auto-labor relations. William Gilbert, newly elected president of Chrysler Local 7, put it as well as anyone I talked with: "Production is up 63 percent over '49–'53, when there were 14,500 people in the plant. Now we've got 6,500. They call it 'advanced technology,' I call it speedup." The line may move at 65 jobs an hour, he explained, "but a guy gets different work assignments two or three times a model. The engineers are constantly in there. They take away one task, and put two back." The assembly line is why auto workers retain the right to strike over work standards. This right is hedged in, a necessary precaution against constant disruption. Aggrieved workers must request permission from the local union for strike action on unresolved grievances, and the strike vote must be carried by a two-thirds majority. After such a vote, the international sends to the company "a five-day letter," giving the company five days to settle the grievance or else face a strike. Such strikes are a barometer of tension within the industry, and significantly strikes shoot up in number each negotiations year.

Grievances pile up, and often a group of workers will take matters into its own hands by simply walking out when conditions have become intolerable and the settlement machinery seems to move too slowly. Chrysler was out to make 1968 a big year and the pressures at Dodge Main had intensified to near breaking by spring. The line was edged up from 49 units to 58 units an hour. The workers were in a feisty mood, and the local-union leadership was away, at the UAW convention in Atlantic City, when there was some trouble in the bumper room on May 2, 1968. Workers there decided not to return to work after lunch. "White women led that walkout," a black shop steward at Dodge Main told me. Nonetheless, when everybody went back to work, Dodge fired two white women and five black men.

DRUM began agitation for the return of the black workers, distributing a four-page weekly outside the plant to black workers. In early July DRUM, backed by "militant community elements," picketed Dodge Main, halting only black workers. The three-day demonstration crippled Dodge by a production loss of some 1,900 cars. Meanwhile, the union had secured the reinstatement of five of the seven discharged in May. The remaining two were members of DRUM. No one was fired for the July "disturbances."

The agitation at Dodge got attention elsewhere. Other black workers began forming similar groups in auto plants around Detroit, each demonstrating, if nothing else, the American fascination for alphabetizing—FRUM (Ford Revolutionary Union Movement); ELRUM (Eldon, Chrysler's only gear and axle plant); JARUM (Jefferson Avenue); MARUM (Mack Avenue); and even CRUM (Chrysler Revolutionary Union Movement).

This does not exhaust the list. There is GRUM (General Motors Revolutionary Union Movement) and HRUM, in Chicago, is for Harvester what DRUM is for Dodge. John Watson, 26, and Mike Hamlin, 28, pulled these groups together in the League of Revolutionary Black Workers and became League functionaries. Both had worked on the *Detroit News* loading dock earlier and had been active in CORE. They seem to have been influenced by several of the radical splinter groups one still finds in Detroit, among them the followers of author C. L. R. James. Watson, then at Wayne University, had been elected editor of the student paper, the *south end*. Emblazoned with the slogan "One Class-Conscious Worker Is Worth 100 Students," the paper was enlisted in the revolutionary struggle of black workers as embodied in DRUM, hailed as the "Vanguard of the Black Revolution."

In the plants, however, the "vanguard" elements did not fare so well. At least within the UAW, black caucuses did much better in a series of local elections held since DRUM appeared on the scene. Black auto workers were elected as presidents of Local 900 (Ford's Wayne plant), Local 47 (Chrysler Detroit Forge), Local 961 (Chrysler Eldon Gear), Local 7 (Chrysler), Local 51 (Plymouth) and at Local 1248 (Chrysler Mopar), where 80 percent of the plant's 989 workers are white. A black was elected vice-president of Briggs Local 212, the first time a black has held a top-level office in that local union. Within the plants there is a noticeable trend toward black representation; predominantly black districts, or departments, tend to elect black committeemen and black shop stewards.

Solidarity House naturally hailed these election results as a setback for DRUM and a victory for UAW internal democracy. The union leadership is divided on how best to handle DRUM and like developments. As spokesman for a hard line, UAW secretary-treasurer Emil Mazey blasted DRUM as "a handful of fanatics, who are nothing but black fascists . . . whose actions are an attempt to destroy this union." Last March the union executive board in a four-page letter to Detroit-area members warned: "The UAW . . . will not protect workers who resort to violence and intimidation with the conscious purpose of dividing our Union along racial lines." Mazey, who argues that no union has done more for black workers than the UAW, insists, "We can no longer tolerate the tactics of these young militants." Douglas A. Fraser, head of the UAW Chrysler Department, and Paul Schrade, director of West Coast Region 6, among others, however, believe in keeping lines open and acknowledge that blacks in the union have suffered inequities and indignities. The UAW has cracked down, at least verbally, on "militant violence" while in practice opening up staff jobs and political advancement to moderately militant blacks.

"The most potent argument you can use against extremists is that the system works," said Fraser, in talking about the 1969 local elections. "The victories by Negro candidates show that the democratic way allows for change." Some among the newly elected blacks, however, are not at all happy about being touted as the UAW answer to black extremism. When I asked William Gilbert, president of Local 7, if he wanted to talk about developments within his local, he said, rather sharply, "There was no publicity given to the fact that Negroes were kept out of the movement, in part due to caucuses backed by the International. If no coverage before, why now? Somebody must be feeling guilty."

In Local 7, as I found out later and as Leon England, another black officer of the local, put it, "It took seven years to get what we got." "Back in 1963," England told me, "we recognized that, if black workers don't move, the labor movement doesn't move." As far as I can tell from talking with a number of black UAW members, the caucuses building on this fundamental notion have been the successful ones. And it has not been easy. Aside from the arduous in-plant political work and the plugging away at grievances and the like, there is the impatience of the young. England estimates that 60 percent of his local membership is under 35. "They face much higher work standards than when we came in," he told me. "Because they're young, they're restless. It's a hard question to answer, when a young man says, 'You've been here 30 years and a white guy's here four and he's down at Solidarity House.' What kind of answer can I give that youngster? That I've just started to move this last year?"

DRUM indeed exercised considerable appeal among young black workers. When DRUM's "support cadre" picketed Chrysler's Eldon Gear and Axle plant, causing a shutdown, the company discharged 26 of the workers involved. Of these, according to Watson, four had at least 20 years of seniority. But the rest had only a year or less. Their youthfulness in part, may explain DRUM's shrugging off the importance of local union elections. As Hamlin told me, "Our thrust is not getting workers to vote in union elections *per se*." Both Watson and Hamlin, however, possess a pragmatic as well as a chiliastic bent. They readily concede the necessity of obtaining "relief" for black workers. And, in this instance, Hamlin quickly added, "We participated [in elections] as an organizal technique and as a possible way of having some impact, because there are things stewards can do that benefit workers on the line."

The League of Revolutionary Black Workers, in fact, figured as an organized caucus in only two 1969 elections—at Eldon Gear and Axle Local 961 and at Dodge Local 3. ELRUM endorsed three of the eight black winners in the election for the ten top Local 961 offices. Four ELRUM candidates lost, however, and Fred Halsey, ELRUM chairman, seeking a trusteeship, was the poorest vote-getter among the candidates. At Dodge Local 3, where presently four out of six full-time officers are black as well as 56 percent of the elected shop stewards, DRUM lost in two special elections, one for a trusteeship, won by a popular white worker, and the second for the vice-presidency, won by Andy Hardy, dubbed a "Tom" by DRUM, who defeated a white candidate in a runoff election by roughly 2,800 to 1,200.

DRUM seems to have forsaken electoral "reformist" activity altogether. According to the January 23, 1969 issue of the *south end,* "The election [for trustee in Local 3] was still a significant victory for the black workers. It was their contention that the unions are inherently undemocratic, and that even with the overwhelming support of the workers, the union bureaucracy cannot be broken through peaceful, democratic methods. As a result, thousands of black workers have gained practical experience in a reform movement, they have seen that reform is impossible and are therefore rapidly joining the revolutionary caucuses being set up by DRUM."

But in fact, *DRUM,* the weekly distributed at Dodge Main, ceased publication. Watson and Hamlin became community organizers and have taken up other, additional causes. HRUM and other League groups, however, have continued, often sporadically. The last Detroit-wide Revolutionary Black Worker demonstration aimed at the UAW, on November 9, 1969, drew roughly a hundred persons, some from the plants, some from Wayne University and some from the black community.

This does not quite fit in with the claim for a black revolutionary upsurge. Numerically my estimate is that the League's hard core hovered around a hundred young blacks, the majority of whom are either community people or students at Wayne. Followers fluctuate, of course. One League-summoned "mass meeting" drew seven people, while another shut down Dodge Main. It may yet recruit a real cadre, or even build a constituency among young black auto workers in Detroit. The labor market has been tight, but President Nixon's war on inflation has created unemployment in Detroit, and Chrysler has laid off workers. Some of those hard-core unemployed so eagerly sought by the auto companies over the last year have been let go. If auto production is pared back, young auto workers will be hit hardest. Conceivably the League might develop a program and a thrust that would appeal to these workers. Exactly what it might do is unclear—attack the UAW and/or the motor companies, disrupt production by mass picketing, hit at high-seniority workers, march on city hall for jobs? The last recession did not exactly produce a revolutionary mood in Detroit or the country at large. It is true, however, that the temper of the black community is radically different, edgier and more political. At the same time, more black workers have the seniority entitling them to union-won benefits—both as cushions against layoffs and as guarantees of jobs. They aren't likely to take attacks on their union lightly. How this will ultimately affect the kinds of agitation the League can carry on is a question. Significantly DRUM's setbacks in this last period came, in the main, from the older and more stable groups of black workers. At Dodge Main, I was repeatedly told, DRUM's unqualified attack on *all* the black stewards and committeemen as "Uncle Toms" put off a considerable number of workers who might otherwise have been more receptive to its message.

The League no doubt suffers from those internal contradictions which plague all parties dedicated to "revolution" while agitating for "relief" from present wrongs. Programmatically DRUM has been criticized by some UAW people for raising so-called middle-class demands. At Dodge, after pointing out that 90 percent of all the foremen, 99 percent of the general foremen and 100 percent of all plant superintendents were white, DRUM demanded 50 black foremen, ten black general foremen and three black superintendents. This may have amounted to a demand that all white supervision must go, but it also reflected DRUM's immediate goals—"relief" for black workers—and related to their ultimate revolutionary aim of a workers' state. "He [the black foreman] would have to be accountable to us," Hamlin told me in discussing this point. "Realistically I know he wouldn't, but at least the verbal racist shit would stop."

Hamlin, at least, envisages "a workers' state [where] workers have control over management," and, I gather, on the Chinese rather than the Yugoslavian model. Presumably, since demands are also "educational," such DRUM demands as the appointment of "a black brother as head of the board of directors of Chrysler Corporation" are related to its view of what ought to be. Most of the original demands naturally relate to the Dodge situation—for "all black doctors and 50 percent black nurses" in the medical center; that all plant protection guards be black; that "every time a black worker is removed from plant premises he be led by a black brother"; that black workers "fired on trumped-up racist charges" be rehired with back pay; that a rank-and-file committee investigate grievances, etc. Others point a direction—that "all black workers immediately stop paying union dues" and that "the two hours' pay that goes into union dues be levied to the black community to aid in self-determination for black people."

The League of Revolutionary Black Workers enlarged DRUM demands to urge the firing of Walter P. Reuther and for the election of a black UAW president, a 50-percent black executive board and staff. It wanted a cut in union dues and an end to the checkoff—"Progressive in the 1930s, today it prevents workers from disciplining poor union leadership." At the same time, the UAW "must" fight against speed-up, for a five-hour day and a four-day week, and for a doubling of the wages of all production workers. Last but not least, the UAW should call a general strike to end the Vietnam war, to end all taxes imposed on workers, to boost taxes on industrial profits to make up the difference and to force the reallocation of all federal monies spent on defense "to meet the pressing needs of the black and poor populations of America."

There is some Black Panther activity within the UAW and other unions. Panther chief of staff David Hilliard, in the April 24, 1969, *Black Panther*, claimed that a majority within DRUM and FRUM are Panther party members. Under the new line of "a united front against fascism," the Panthers, to quote their paper again, "after having concentrated previously on community affairs" are turning "toward an alliance with labor." As Kenny Horsten, director of the Black Panther caucus at the Fremont GM plant, put it, "We've got two enemies; the union and the corporation, in that order, and only when we recognize that the enemy is within can we effectively combat the corporation, the power structure. We can't at this time, combat the corporation because the union leadership is like a brick wall between the workers and the corporation. . . . So we have to form more caucuses and a revolutionary movement, so that we can break down this wall and then we can proceed to move against the corporation with the might of the union behind us—and not in front of us."

There are about 5,000 workers in the Fremont GM plant, of whom 30 to 35 percent are black and Mexican-American in equal proportions. Horston, who has worked in the plant six years and formed his caucus in late 1968, ran for board member at large in the 1969 local elections, getting about 500 votes where he needed 800–900 to win.

Not surprisingly there have been meetings between the DRUM people and the Panthers. As a party, the Panthers possess the ideology, however rudimentary, that could sustain in-plant DRUM-type agitators. The Panther-Communist Party alliance, in the places where old-time Communist workers are still to be found, might provide certain kinds of know-how. But as of 1970 nothing much developed out of this alliance, perhaps because the Panthers were occupied with court cases and campaigns to save their leaders from jail.

Black caucuses in the auto, steel and teachers' unions are a consequence of the overall rise in the level of black consciousness—but, so to speak, at one remove. For an insight into the relationship between developments in the black community and within the unions, one must look to the cities, where black workers live and work. The spectrum of black involvement in the labor movement ranges from black agitation aimed at opening jobs in the construction industry to the organization of hospital and municipal employees. Without black-community pressure, for example, there would be no offer from the Chicago building trades of 4,000 jobs over 1970, including apprenticeships, journeyman status and openings for training; nor would the recent trade-union successes among hospital workers in Charleston or among municipal employees in Memphis have been possible without black-community support. Black-caucus activity in such cities as Detroit, Chicago and New York fall somewhere between these two forms of community involvement.

Developments in Chicago are radically different from anything currently observable in New York, and somewhat different from what goes on in Detroit. Chicago politics sets the scene, and one should keep in mind that black politics in Chicago differ in style from black politics elsewhere. The Daley machine and its black counterpart, the machine of Congressman William L. Dawson, cast a long shadow. But as James Q. Wilson perceptively pointed out in *Negro Politics* (1960): "The Dawson machine is not a simple replica—albeit a highly successful one—of any political machine; it is a *Negro* [current parlance, *black*] machine, and many of the incentives and constraints to which it responds can only be understood by the fact of its being Negro." This is also profoundly true of the black opposition to Dawson. The black liberal challenge to the Dawson machine creates a black community conflict; it is not a simple reflection of the labor/liberal *vs.* Daley struggles. Actually the latter are a pale reflection of the former.

Like the black community, black-organized labor divides politically into various components, notably the old AFL and some CIO unions, strongly tied to the Daley/Dawson machines, while the UAW, Packinghouse Workers and other liberal unions support reform efforts. Significantly the latter endeavors have been rooted in Chicago's black precincts, ever since Willoughby Abner, now a vice-president of the American Arbitration Association and formerly of the UAW staff, challenged the Democratic Party machine in the 1950 primary election to decide the party's candidate for state senator. Abner lost, but the UAW has been engaged in precinct work in the black community ever since, sometimes supporting Democratic regulars and at other times white and black dissidents.

The machine-reform constellation not only dominates Chicago politics; it also influences the current rise in black-worker activism in the community and among the unions. As in Detroit and other urban areas in the North, Chicago unions are experiencing, on one hand, a sharp rise in black rank and file and, on the other, the continuation in leadership of the preceding white, often ethnically conscious, generation of unionists. Unlike other cities, however, Chicago is the best example of the new black community involvement in trade-union affairs.

Black-community leaders, however tentatively, have given advice to black workers and have been drawn into the internal affairs of several key unions. Moreover, a fair number of black trade-union activists have been drawn into orbit, so to speak, around the charismatic Reverend Jesse Jackson and his Operation Breadbasket.

Operation Breadbasket was launched in the late 1960s, following the late Martin Luther King's frustrating Chicago summer. As an arm of the Southern Christian Leadership Conference, Operation Breadbasket feeds the hungry, boycotts for jobs, encourages black self-help and engages in a variety of antipoverty endeavors. In Chicago, Operation Breadbasket has become an institution and enjoys a *succès d'estime*—largely through the dynamism of the Reverend Jackson. Two or three thousand people turn out every weekend to hear him preach, and at times to boycott or march at his behest. Understandably black workers frequently turn to him when in need of advice or support.

To a trade unionist the consequences often seem contradictory. Operation Breadbasket, for example, supported a group of Cook County hospital workers, members of AFSCME (American Federation of State, County and Municipal Employees), who walked out in the course of a jurisdictional fight with the BSEIU (Building Service Employees' International Union). Earlier, Operation Breadbasket leaders had urged black teachers not to support an AFT strike and subsequently urged them to withdraw from the union altogether. (In Chicago suburbs black teachers are among the most militant supporters of AFT organizing drives.) Like many black activists, Operation Breadbasket ministers see the unions as a mixed blessing. The UAW, after all, is a heavy supporter of Operation Breadbasket. Teachers, too, black and white, contribute as individuals to Operation Breadbasket. Significantly the Breadbasket teachers dropped their withdrawal plea, and their current anti-unionism has an old-fashioned schoolmarm ring. As one young lady told me, "We get all the benefits anyway." Their current interest is in improving education for black children. As the Reverend Calvin Morris, shepherd of Operation Breadbasket's trade-union flock, told striking hospital workers, "Much of the labor movement is obese, fat and tired. . . . Yet the Lord never leaves us comfortless; even in the midst of fat-cat unions we still see some light shining."

Operation Breadbasket is community-oriented, and though political in black-powerish fashion (the Reverend Jackson is said to have political ambitions), it has not injected itself into the unions, as would-be radicals often dream of doing, and as such politicals as the DRUMites and Black Panthers are doing in a small way. Rather, Operation Breadbasket is drawn in when dissidents are in trouble and need outside support. This, at least, seems to have been the case with Chicago's rebel bus drivers.

Back in early 1968 a group of black bus drivers decided to challenge the white leadership of the local union, the 12,000-member (3,500 retirees and 8,500 working members) Division 241 of the Amalgamated Transit Union, AFL-CIO. In the streetcar era, the local was almost entirely white but in recent years the Chicago Transit Authority has hired more and more blacks. Now roughly 72 percent of the 6,800 bus drivers are black, but on taking into account the other CTA workers represented by the local, the racial breakdown is roughly 60 percent black, 40 percent white. The leadership of the local, however, continued predominantly white. All the top officers were white—president, two vice-presidents, a recording secretary and a financial secretary— and out of 26 executive-board members only four were black.

At first, the Concerned Transit Workers concentrated on the issue of representation. As one spokesman, Wayman Benson, put it, "This is nothing different than the old plantation system. Here you have a union with about 65–70 percent blacks and the leadership is virtually all white. How long do you think we can stand for this?" Black workers turned up in growing numbers to protest a union rule that allows pensioners to vote, only to be ruled constantly out of order. The provision is in the international union's constitution; but this did nothing to ease black suspicions that the nearly all-white pensioners tended to vote as a bloc for the present administration. With negotiations in the offing, the CTW also began agitating about the mishandling of grievances and demanded cleaner and safer buses, uniform allowances and improved sick leave and hospitalization plans.

The insurgent blacks called two walkouts in 1968—a four-day one in July and a 20-day, knock-down drag-out affair beginning the day before the Democratic convention and lasting until mid-September. Operation Breadbasket provided counsel and office space for the strikers. An injunction helped break the strike; over 140 drivers were suspended, and 42 were fired. At this point, the CTW changed its goal. As Wayman Benson put it, "We felt we had run into a stone wall and so we decided to try and form an independent union." Robert Cavins, 31, a driver with five and a half years' experience, was named temporary president of the regrouped CTW, Operation Breadbasket pledged its continuing support and a drive was launched for signatures demanding a representative election.

Soon, however, everything bogged down. Illinois has no state labor-relations system, and the National Labor Relations Board has no jurisdiction over local transportation systems. There is no legal mechanism for calling a representation election, and any other way of gaining representation rights is forestalled by circumstances. For one thing, Division 241 did not simply sit back. "We have not been in the union business all these years for nothing," said one officer. "There are a lot of problems to be considered when people try to pull out and start their own union. We have no intention of giving up without a fight." Division 241 president James J. Hill named blacks as second vice-president, assistant recording secretary, assistant financial secretary-treasurer, and to four board posts. The militants greeted the appointments with customary derision—"tokenism," "Uncle Toms," etc. Yet the appointments were not without effect, and a number of black drivers believe it is a matter of time before they take over anyway. As one driver told me, "Why throw away all that's been built up all these years?" Moreover, the CTW, in attempting to take black bus drivers from Division 241, opposed what nearly everyone conceded would be the sure ratification of a new contract in 1969. Quite legitimately the CTW might have claimed credit for the $4-an-hour settlement—after all, wildcats are an index of militancy—while pointing out inadequacies in the new agreement. But by blasting what the workers by and large saw as gains, the CTW began to lose its following.

Several black trade-union leaders told me privately that they blamed "the ministers" for the CTW loss. (In fairness, I would credit the understandable impatience—and lack of experience—among the CTW rank and file and leadership, too.) "They had a case," one black leader told me, "but they blew it." He thought the second wildcat a serious mistake and the decision to break away catastrophic. "The struggle for black representation within 241," he added, "had the support of other trade unionists, and could have been won." Charles Hayes, a vice-president of the merged Butcher Workmen, Meatcutters and Packinghouse unions and chairman of the newly formed Operation Breadbasket Black Labor Leaders of Chicago, felt he had to support the CTW strike. "I'm still hopeful that the leadership situation can be cleared from within," he told me.

Those who hold this view cite the December, 1969, elections within a sister local, Division 308 of the Amalgamated Transit Union, which represents 3,800 rapid-transit workers in Chicago. Leonard Beatty, 45, a black motorman with 18 years on the job,

348

defeated John A. Burns, a 63-year-old motorman and former president of the local, by a vote of 1,124 to 1,098. Four other black men were elected to the division's nine-man executive board. However, Hugh Hegarty defeated black candidate Clarence Knox for secretary-treasurer, the only other full-time office. As Beatty told reporters, "It was two Irishmen against two blacks; one each was elected." Neither Beatty nor Burns is certain whether blacks comprise a majority of Division 308's membership. There is, however, a parallel with the racial balance within Division 241 of the Amalgamated Transit Union, and it seems likely that a majority of the working members are black while a majority of the retirees are white. Burns, who returned to his job as a motorman, attributes his defeat to the generation gap. "They wanted a young man and so I'm on the way out." He also said that race was not voiced during the campaign, "although I'm sure it was on peoples' minds."

Beatty's victory, in a way, is one of the consequences of the bus drivers' wildcat strike. Beatty and his supporters decided to challenge Burns at the time of the wildcat in August, 1968. "We've been preparing a long time to assert ourselves legally," Beatty said. "I never believed in wildcat strikes. But I would like to think this was a victory not just for blacks but for younger workers, for a better deal."

Both in transit and among teachers, Operation Breadbasket adherents did try for a time to pull their black fellow workers out of long-established unions, but both efforts have pretty much subsided. CTW's case for an election and for reinstatement of those fired landed in the courts. Some of those fired have formed a bus company of their own, doing charter work. Others have found, as one told me, "better jobs."

As a consequence of the rise in black consciousness, some black trade unionists of some 25–30 unions formed the Black Labor Leaders of Chicago under the aegis of Operation Breadbasket. Most of them are local union officers, and a number are black staff people. They meet regularly and are still in the process of formulating concrete programs and goals. "We do try to help Operation Breadbasket," Charles Hayes, chairman of the group, told me, "but our prime concern is to move the trade-union movement into some positive direction, some implementation of the things we've talked about over the years in terms both of employment and of leadership within the union movement itself."

Hayes, at least, takes a dim view of a break-away-from-the-unions tendency among black workers, though he believes the tactic may have some validity in specific situations. "We think that you work within, fight within the unions to bring about the kind of change that you want, rather than to try going off and form a counterforce." Hayes also indicated that his group intended to get deeper into political action. While he expressed a willingness to work with COPE on voter-registration drives and the like, he pointedly declared, "We have reached a point of maturity where we as black people can no longer rubber-stamp for COPE necessarily. I think we must support candidates based on their commitments to the needs of the total community, not just on the basis of political expediency."

Is the Chicago experience *sui generis* or a harbinger of things to come? A little of both. There is only one Reverend Jackson, a human dynamo. He holds together much that might otherwise fly apart. Then, there are the Chicago political machines, refusing to die in the face of liberal onslaughts.

What happens, of course, depends in part on white reaction. Racism exists among white trade unionists, but I would not say that the efforts of white union officers to continue in office despite significant shifts in the racial composition of their locals are simply racist or a manifestation of white backlash. Some of the response is just an ordinary political wish to hold power.

White workers, it is true, are often resentful of the change; they don't react politely to being called "Honkie," and the surfacing of subterranean racism is not unknown. I have a leaflet distributed by the National Socialist White People's [Nazi] party at a Harvester plant, which says, among other things: "Not content to take our jobs away, these Black savages have beaten our kids in school, terrorized our women on the street and run us out of our own neighborhoods where we grew up and raised our families." There's no denying some think like this, but in fact few heed the call of this hate sheet. The membership of the NSWPP is probably smaller than that of HRUM at Harvester (Harvester Revolutionary Union Movement), and both are tiny indeed.

Polarization has occurred, but blue-collar Wallaceism is a response to developments outside the plant or the union. The Flint UAW local that endorsed Wallace in the 1968 Presidential election (and later rescinded the endorsement) did not go on to adopt resolutions favoring the exclusion of black workers from the plant or the union. A black UAW representative who was elected a shop steward in that same local told Brendan Sexton that several of his strongest white supporters wore Wallace buttons. When Sexton asked if they were still friends and supporters, he said, "Hell, yes." There will be more "two Irishmen against two blacks" contests within the unions, but if blue-collar Wallaceism grows, it will be because of social and economic developments outside the unions and not because of hotly fought elections within. By and large, most union officers continue in office because they do a job, and not because of their ethnic origin or color. These factors play a role, but ordinarily not to the exclusion of all others. Human passions being what they are, one ought to add a cautionary note. The unions have not been hit so hard by black militancy as have the churches, the poverty programs and the universities. When and if they are, there may well be an intensification of racial hostilities. (My feeling that this won't happen is based on two things. First, it hasn't happened, although there are more black trade unionists than black parishioners in the churches under attack or black students in assaulted universities. Second, white workers just aren't loaded with the guilt feelings of white ministers and other middle-class types who are, for good or bad, vulnerable to supermilitancy.)

Militancy obviously has its uses. DRUM was a panic button, and both the union and the company reacted. More blacks are now on the staffs of both institutions than before DRUM made its appearance. When you are seeking representation within existing institutions, it is sometimes useful to threaten the building of a separate, new institution—especially if someone else raises that specter for you, so that if convenient you can repudiate it later.

At a time when black workers are going through an awakening of ethnic class-consciousness, it is unreasonable to expect the emergence of only moderate expressions of their essential demand—recognition. During the 1930s, workers played off the CIO against the AFL, and radical parties and sects flourished at the fringes of the mainstream of the unions. It is a tribute to these workers—and one should remember black and white workers did build together—that their institutions are now absorbing, not without pain or conflict, aggressively militant black caucuses. No less than white, black workers want what Samuel Gompers so tersely described as "more." It doesn't seem likely that they are going to jettison existing ways—collective bargaining for one—or existing institutions—unions, for another—just in order to satisfy an abstract ideology of black expressionism. Especially since it appears that they are now making their own mark within the unions.

What will the impact be of increasing black representation in the unions? Progress, of course, but first some skepticism. I am sure that some of the black youngsters now entering building-trades apprenticeships will end up running local unions—or become contractors. The building trades may swing a little as a result, but I doubt very much that the inherently conservative character of those unions will change. Black craftsmen will find, as white craftsmen did before them, that a tight rein on jobs, on entry and craft structure pays off. And they, too, will want buildings built, a feeling shared with the dominant real-estate interests of every city. More blacks, perhaps, will add weight to the discernible sea change already underway among building tradesmen, away from the Republican Party to the Democrats. Beyond this, however, there's likely to be little enough change within the building trades, excepting those which come through changes in technology.

Nonetheless, greater black participation in the unions will re-invigorate social unionism. Many white workers, especially those in powerful unions and in well-organized industries, are content to leave job questions to the unions, while seeking solutions to social and economic problems elsewhere. This, as much as anything, explains blue-collar Wallaceism and conservative voting of home-owning workers on local tax-supported issues. Black workers are no more exempt from the pulls of class solidarity in the plant—and the pride of home-ownership—than white workers. But, on balance, they do want more government action along a broader front than their blue-collar white fellows. Black workers live in communities with drastic problems that cry out for radical solutions. And they are going to use all the resources at their command to get answers to their problems. Local union leadership is a power base, and if that base can be mobilized for action to solve community problems, black labor leaders are going to act. It will be worth watching.

# XXV

## *THE POLITICAL IMPERATIVE*

MOST STRIKES OF ANY CONSEQUENCE MAKE HEADLINES, BUT FEW truly set off a decade or mark a major turn in labor relations. The 102-day General Electric strike, which began on October 27, 1969, and involved 147,000 workers as well as the cooperation of 13 unions and all but shut down the fourth largest corporation in the United States, was such a strike. Along with the 113-day General Motors strike of 1946 and the 116-day steel strike of 1959, it was one of the key strikes of our time. Each strike posed issues that get to the guts of any real attempt at achieving industrial democracy or democratic planning. The 1946 auto strike turned on the opening of corporate books, which is the first step toward public involvement in key pricing decisions. The crux of the 1959 steel strike was an attempt by management to curb workers' rights through the leverage of automation. GE sought the same goal by using the whip of inflation. The strike pointed up the whole debate over wage or price inflation and raised the question of economic controls.

Initially, however, the strike was a test of General Electric's approach to labor relations and of its applicability to the new corporate conglomerates. For over 20 years General Electric played one group of workers against another. The unions representing GE's employees were unable to pursue common goals. None had the majority and the divisions among them were those among the unions generally—craft *vs.* industrial unions, AFL *vs.* CIO, as well as a major struggle over the Stalinist leadership of the then largest union, the old CIO United Electrical Workers. On the whole, relations between the corporation and the CIO union had been amicable from recognition in the mid-1930s through the war years. But when the internal fight over Communist control of the union broke out at the end of World War II and was followed by a long series of contests between the expelled UE and a new CIO union, the International Union of Electrical Workers, the company apparently saw in these developments an opportunity for a more aggressively management-oriented employee-relations policy. In 1947 the company unilaterally dropped a profit-sharing plan that had existed since 1915. Its employees and their unions were not asked their opinion, and by this simple arrogance the company marked the beginning of a new style. A new man was in charge, Charles E. Wilson, and he requested Lemuel R. Boulware, GE vice-president in charge of "affiliated" companies, to review GE's employee relations.

Boulware was an imaginative man and came up with the first truly new anti-union formula since James H. Rand, Jr., devised his famous Mohawk Valley formula in 1936. As is the case with most innovations, the new contained a good deal of what was in the old. The basic ingredients called for the labeling of union leaders as "outside agitators," "radicals" and "creeping socialists"; economic pressure on the community by threats to move plants (a cornerstone of GE's application of the formula which dovetailed neatly into the corporation's decision to decentralize productive facilities as much as possible in the post-World War II period); the organization of a back-to-work movement whenever strikes occurred; a show of police and "Citizen's Committee" force; and a grandstand opening of struck plants. Boulware added a dash of Madison Avenue sophistication and applied the formula on a continuing basis rather than simply confining it to a crisis, a strike or union organizing drive. "Communications" was the rubric under which GE carried out one of the most intricate and long-lasting anti-union campaigns in corporate history.

"This program, of course," Boulware once wrote, "is a job-marketing program. It is an adaptation from the consumer-marketing process. . . . The job marketers and the product marketers deal with the same people and the same considerations." In short, GE set out to "merchandise" its employees. The late Professor Benjamin Selekman, a distinguished industrial-relations scholar, in 1958 termed Boulwareism "an outstanding example of cynicism. [It] denies workers adequate and competent representation. . . . It denies a human institution of the opportunity to grow in maturity and responsibility."

GE sought to put an end to what Boulware termed "Eastern bazaar haggling" by making what he called "truthful offers," or what were really disguised ultimata. The bargaining table became just another flat surface for tossing on a take-it-or-leave-it package all dressed up in the best interest of the workers as seen by their bosses. The unions were viewed as the enemy and negotiations, as a means of doing away with them. Like all good generals, GE management recognized that on occasion one loses a battle. When times were propitious for workers, the company was always prepared to bend a little, flex the formula and even bargain. But it was ever ready to spring back to the attack, as it did in 1960 when it went all out against the unions. A three-week strike was a near disaster for IUE, the majority union within the company. In the period following that strike, GE management fought the union, plant by plant, IUE won several elections but at tiny locations with a total membership of scarcely above a hundred. It lost ten important elections, affecting several thousand workers all told.

The union countered by filing unfair-labor-practice charges, hitting at the fundamentals of Boulwareism. The NLRB agreed that the company had violated the Taft-Hartley Act, which requires good-faith bargaining on the part of employers and unions alike. The company appealed the decision, and a United States Court of Appeals upheld the NLRB decision. Ultimately, in 1970, the United States Supreme Court denied GE's appeal of the lower-court decision. Economic conditions—a tight labor market and good business prospects—modified the company's conduct in 1966. The unions, too, tried a new strategy, coordinated bargaining, which pulled together the AFL-CIO unions (but not the independent UE) representing different groups of GE workers. The company walked out, refusing to meet with a joint committee of the unions. The issue went to the courts, but meanwhile the company and each of the unions managed to reach a settlement without a strike.

Coordinated bargaining was the unions' response to the rise in conglomerates, new corporate umbrellas for diversified companies. Conglomerates often critically change collective-bargaining practices developed by individual unions and their respective firms before acquisition. On merger or acquisition, the corporate master may insist on the shutdown of "nonprofitable" plants or even ignore the pension commitments of acquired companies. Joseph P. Molony, vice-president of the United Steel Workers, charged at Senate hearings on conglomerates in 1970, for example, that the conglomerates often converted money marked for pension benefits into quick profits. "When a union tries to obtain assurances of continued payment of pensions," Molony said, "it is often told by the conglomerate that it should not protest until it has been hurt." To protect themselves from such sharp practices and other changes, the unions have banded together in joint bargaining committees. As of January 1, 1970, there were some 80 different AFL-CIO coordinated bargaining committees covering workers employed by most of the nation's major conglomerates. In the court challenges originating in the 1966 GE negotiations, the court ruled that companies were not compelled by law to negotiate with a coordinated bargaining committee, but by the same token they could not dictate the composition of committees representing their employees. (Joint bargaining is legal if the company agrees to it.) So, as in GE in 1970, members from other unions could sit in, but not bargain for their respective members, while the company bargained with a particular union. It doesn't sound like much of a gain, but it meant a greater unity among the many unions confronting a single powerful employer. By sitting together, though not actively bargaining, the various unions are able to keep their members informed at all times of all developments. The GE strike of 1970 was a test of the court ruling and a major test of coordinated bargaining as a technique.

Coordinated bargaining was perceived by GE executives as a threat. The company refused to engage in joint bargaining, and reluctantly bowed before the court ruling that it could not dictate the composition of committees representing GE employees. For clout, however, the company relied on changing economic and political conditions. Nixon was in the White House and inflation was rampant in the land. The conservative climate in Washington, it was believed, would be favorable to GE's stand that the unions' demands were inflationary. A huge advertising campaign was launched to prove this to the public. The company also counted on "communicating" the righteousness of its war against inflation to its employees. Boulwareism was dusted off, refurbished and enlisted in President Nixon's war against inflation.

The Coordinated Bargaining Committee, encompassing ten AFL-CIO affiliates, the independent UE, UAW and Teamsters unions, sought to avoid crisis bargaining even though that is often the easy way to whip up membership militancy. IUE, the largest union within GE, led off the negotiations, with members of the other unions present, a full two months before the contract expired in an effort to avoid a strike. As Paul Jennings, IUE president and spokesman for the Coordinated Bargaining Committee, stressed, "We have established reasonable bargaining objectives based on the needs of the men and women we represent and the affluence of the company." The unions proposed an across-the-board increase of 35 cents an hour, effective immediately; another 30 cents an hour in October 1970; and 25 cents more a year later. Various contract improvements were also advanced, including a cost-of-living formula. In all, some 122 economic and noneconomic proposals were placed upon the collective-bargaining table by the unions.

The impetus for this thrust for "more" rose out of the inflation of the late 1960s. Soaring living costs had eroded the 12.4 percent 1966 GE wage-benefit package. The average 9.5-cents-per-year increase since 1960 for GE workers was 7.5 cents below steel, 11.2 cents below auto and 11.7 cents below wage gains in aerospace. GE hourly rates ranged from $1.81 an hour to $5.76 and averaged $3.25. There wasn't much question about GE's ability to pay. Since 1960, GE sales increased 80.8 percent. GE profits, after taxes plus depreciation allowances (together called "cash flow"), zoomed almost 200 percent. GE's average rate of return on stockholders' investment rose to over 15 percent. In 1968 its profit rate was 22 percent higher than in manufacturing as a whole. And in midstrike GE announced further price increases on its products.

The unions' attempt to get an early start on negotiations came to naught. GE negotiators politely informed the union men, "We can't negotiate until we are in formal negotiations." Later they said, "Wait until we get the whole ball of wax." In an effort to secure real bargaining, the union proposed a "moratorium" while both sides examined each other's proposals. The following day, as John Shambo, head of the IUE's General Electric negotiating team, told me, the union negotiators entered the GE boardroom and "they had their slides and projectors, saying, 'We're telling you now what it is.' I knew then we were in for a battle for sure." Phillip Moore, GE's man in charge of negotiations, had already circulated a memo among the corporation's top management predicting a strike and saying, "At the end of three weeks they will be straggling back."

Both the manner and the content of the offer left the unions little choice, although they tried. With six days to go before the expiration of the contract, the unions modified their proposals in an effort to get bargaining started and to avoid a crippling walk-out. But the company insisted on what IUE president Jennings termed "a horrible example of deceptive packaging" with "a skimpy eight-dollar-a-week pay raise" in a three-year contract with no other increases. Moreover, the company demanded the removal of what little cost-of-living protection the old agreement contained, rejected all union efforts to set up machinery for the peaceful resolution of worker grievances while seeking to limit the unions' right to strike over grievances. Management, too, de-manded the unilateral right to cut wages of any worker under the guise of adjusting job rates downward. As local union after local union voted down the company's offer, GE persisted in its take-it-or-leave-it line. As Shambo told me after the strike ended, "They misread the whole thing; they just didn't believe there would be a strike this long."

What happened was a Boulware backlash. GE invested years —and a good deal of money—in cultivating an image of benign interest in the welfare of its employees. But all that effort blew up during the course of the 102-day strike. When the strike began running beyond the predicted three weeks, GE trotted out another offer, adding a three-percent wage increase for each of two suc-ceeding years. It also proposed a cost-of-living formula, which union economists quickly demonstrated would actually cost GE workers money. The formula was to apply to wage rates *before* the three-percent increase so, should the cost-of-living rise by, say, three percent, GE workers would lose two percent. Moreover, the new offer ignored the unions' request for arbitration and retained the company's right to cut wages at will. It soon became apparent that the new offer was a sugarplum in a holiday-season package designed to coax the workers back into the plants. Between December 7, when GE made its second offer, and December 22, a strategic three days before Christmas, GE management launched a flood of letters and telephone calls to individual workers' homes, placed radio and newspaper advertisements harping on the "in plant by Christmas" theme. The plan, as outlined in a confidential memo sent to all GE plant locations, called for at least nine letters to each striker and a series of telephone calls from foremen and plant managers. In Pittsfield, Massachusetts, alone company officials made over 800 telephone calls. But GE blandishments fell flat. As one GE worker explained, "Most of us do not like being manipulated, and we certainly don't care for alleged superiors claiming that they know what is good for us."

The strike remained better than 90 percent effective to the end. At one location the local management felt so hopeless—the strike was so evidently solid—that it did not comply with the headquarters directive. By December 19 a company spokesman ruefully conceded, "There has been no great return [to work]." The unity of the GE strikers was all the more remarkable when one considers the diversity of the corporation's operation and the range of skills employed. GE plants are scattered around the country, manufacturing a broad range of goods from giant dynamos to electric toasters. IUE local unions, for example, range in size from 15,000 at Louisville, Kentucky, "Appliance Park" to 20-man appliance-repair shops. Some IUE members, such as those in Schenectady (12,000 making heavy electrical equipment) or in Lynn, Massachusetts (9,000—jet turbines, etc.), are sophisticated unionists with a long history of militance. These are factory workers, mostly men and with a high degree of skill and earning what workers call "good money." Other union members are new to the union—young workers, many women, and the unskilled and semiskilled. Local 805, Tell City, Iowa, for example, comprises about 1,000 workers, of whom about 80 percent are women manufacturing motors and tubes. "The largest wage increase they ever got in a single year was 20 cents," a union representative told me. So the company's first and second offers must have appeared pretty good to them, or so one would think. Yet, according to one of the strikers, "We didn't have but two scabs, and they came out after a couple days and we never had another."

The labor movement, too, helped sustain the strike. AFL-CIO contributions to the GE strike fund reached $2 million. The United Auto Workers gave a million dollars in support of the strike. An AFL-CIO–sponsored boycott of GE products helped crimp the corporation's profits during the strike. GE has claimed that the boycott was ineffective—and it is true that generally speaking boycotts are a weapon of last ineffectual resort—but it scored modest success where unions are politically strong and where GE workers live. At the height of the strike GE chairman Fred J. Borch went before the New York Society of Analysts to announce that the company's third-quarter earnings had been wiped out. So the company did feel an economic squeeze. Before the strike, in many product lines GE was having trouble keeping up with demand. Back orders, in many instances, were actually unfilled and GE was unable to stockpile in preparation for the strike. The general level of prosperity and a continuing shortage of skilled workers, too, helped the union. In Lynn, and in several other GE centers, some of the highly skilled workers were able to pick up temporary jobs to carry them through the long days of the strike. Others dug into savings or depended on their wives' earnings to see them through. Altogether, the unions spent over $12 million in strike benefits to help those whose needs were greatest.

The strike was won when GE consented to bargaining in early January. Chief federal mediator J. Curtis Counts entered the picture on January 7. "At that point," Shambo told me, "at his request, with no fanfares of publicity, we did what we wanted to do from the first. That is, go through this thing issue by issue. We had the cost of living wrapped up almost two weeks before the final settlement."

The contract, ending the strike on February 5, 1970, was ratified by a vote of 56,553 to 19,470 among IUE members. The vote was roughly of the same proportion among the other unions, although there was some dissatisfaction; a majority of the 12,000-member Schenectady local voted against ratification as did some

International Association of Machinists local unions. Union economists calculated the total value of the GE settlement terms at 98 cents an hour over the full contract period of three years plus 14 cents in the "roll-up" value of benefits such as vacation pay, for a total of $1.12 an hour. This includes an immediate pay hike of 23 cents an hour, 15 cents more in 1970 and the year after; up to 21 cents in cost-of-living adjustments, and 12.8 cents in insurance and vacation improvements, paid days off, hospitalization and other benefit gains.

The modern labor contract is complex and wide-ranging, covering many facets of a worker's life. So victory isn't always a matter of dollars and cents. One of the changes secured by the unions in the GE contract provides automatic progression to the top of the job rate on all jobs instead of the former "merit award" system. Doesn't sound like much, but for GE workers it means an end to demeaning favoritism. The workers did not win every issue. Union negotiators were unable to secure a completely satisfactory grievance procedure, especially the arbitration of unresolved complaints. GE workers, however, retained the right to strike over such grievances and in such a way as to give them some edge. The company wanted the right to shut down the entire plant if, say, a department of even ten people walked out over a worker's beef. This lockout power was denied GE by the unions.

Throughout the negotiations the corporation fought for a provision in the new contract that would break up IUE's national bargaining unit of 90,000 into 126 or more separate units. "Balkanization" is a key to successful Boulwareism. It would enable the company to decertify the union at its weakest points, forcing it to expend resources in a never-ending battle over representation rights at its fringes. An NLRB decision rejected company-supported petitions to decertify IUE at two service shops, involving 20 workers. As it happened, the decision came at a critical moment. Its effect is to prevent future GE attempts to decertify a single unit or groups of units within the IUE jurisdiction. From such victories, the unions hope, will come a defeat of Boulwareism

—in General Electric and among its followers in other corporate managements. But GE is a tough outfit, ever practical. Virgil Day, GE's vice-president for industrial relations and Lemuel Boulware's successor, has blandly shrugged off the past. "In my opinion, Boulwareism never existed." But as he went on to spell out management's goals for the 1970s, one sensed the iron beneath the velvet. Day warned that the decade could be "a disaster for the American worker—in part self-inflicted with the acquiescence and misleadership of those officials who seem to be overly responsive to the membership and their very real fear of inflation." With the economy weakened by a "pinch" on profits, unions should lower their wage demands, Day suggested. As for management, he added, it should show a "tougher backbone" at the bargaining table. Moreover, there is need for "labor-law reform" to restore "management rights." Day called upon corporate management to get "more involved in politics," pointing out that "labor's legislative program is an adjunct of its economic program. Its occupational-safety bill would aid strikes . . . by permitting federally ordered shutdowns. Raising the minimum wage affects negotiated rates. Pension changes and higher Social Security taxes impose costs without bargaining."

Boulwareism, or some variant, is, in truth, as much a part of management's response to organized labor as Gomper's dictum, "More," is of labor's to capital. General Electric is perhaps more energetic, even imaginative than most corporations in this particular area of corporate endeavor. Still, GE is not all that much different in character from General Motors, U.S. Steel or any other major business firm. So we may take the GE strike as a paradigm of labor relations in our time even though they may be better or worse in any other given situation or at any other given moment. If one examines the GE settlement, one can see how the terms both conformed to and reinforced existing trends in collective bargaining.

Major contract negotiations in 1970 affected about five million workers. It was a big year in the cycle of contract negotiations (a turn of two to three years on the average), with roughly twice as many workers affected as in 1969. Wages were in first position as an issue, according to an analysis prepared by AFL-CIO economist Rudolph Oswald for *The American Federationist* of March, 1970, with job security coming up fast behind and improvements in benefits of all kinds running strong in third place. With inflation eroding past gains, many unions sought the added protection of cost-of-living or escalator clauses in new contracts, continuing a thrust started in 1969. Most typically, union negotiators sought a clause specifying that wages must be adjusted at regular intervals based on changes in the government's Consumer Price Index. Contract negotiations in 1969 raised the total number of workers covered by some sort of escalator clause to the highest level since 1961. According to the Bureau of Labor Statistics, cost-of-living provisions in 1970 covered some 3.4 million workers.

Wage settlements in 1969 edged higher at annual rate of increase of 8.2 percent the first year of the contract and at 7.1 percent when averaged over the lifetime of the settlement. (The average is based on agreements covering a 1,000 or more workers.) The GE and other 1970 settlements were in line with a rising trend that began with a 1966 average first-year-of-contract increase of 4.8 percent, rising to 5.6 percent in 1967 and jumping to 7.2 percent in 1968. Construction workers, as a class, continued to do better financially than those in manufacturing, scoring an average first-year wage increase of 14 percent. However, when averaged over the life of the agreement, this gain amounted to 13 percent a year. The New York Typographers' 1970 settlement providing a 41.7-percent wage hike over three years was in keeping with the construction-industry pattern as was the trucking-industry settlement that followed an 85-day strike of Chicago drivers who had rejected a previous pact worked out nationally providing for a 28-percent hike. But these were exceptions to the general rule of contract agreements worked out in 1970. The United Rubber Workers, for example, ended a seven-week Goodyear strike in early June with a $15-million package, providing wage and fringe benefits totaling $1.30 an hour over a three-year contract. According to a company spokesman, this was an eight-percent increase over the previous settlement, an ambiguous phrasing. The average hourly rate at Goodyear before the 1970 agreement was $3.87 and the strike settlement provides for a 30-cent increase the first year and 26 cents an hour more in each of the other two years. The Rubber Workers also secured a major 1970 objective—a joint occupational-health study financed by company payments of one-half cent per man-hour.

Fringe-benefit improvements negotiated in 1969, according to economist Oswald, "usually meant better pensions and greater health protection." Holiday and vacation provisions were liberalized with some gains in shorter hours and other job-security provisions. Over the past 30 years the amount of fringe benefits paid to all workers in the private, nonfarm sector has soared from five percent of total compensation to 19.6 percent. This is a direct consequence of unionization and a fruit of collective bargaining. Paid holidays, as an instance, were once the rare privilege of a few, mostly salaried white-collar employees. Today more than 90 percent of all factory workers enjoy paid holidays, and over 40 percent received eight or more in 1968. Paid vacations and holidays were among the first fringe benefits won by workers through their unions; health and welfare benefits are more recent gains, being largely a product of post-World War II bargaining. The breakthroughs of the 1950s became solid, rising trends in the 1960s. According to Labor Department surveys, fringe benefits grew more than twice as fast as straight-time pay over the decade. At the start of the 1970s, however, there were no startling departures or significant new directions. Most of the changes were refinements of existing benefit structures. For example, in the steel industry the basic supplementary unemployment-benefits plan provides for basic weekly supplementary-unemployment benefits of 65 percent of average straight-time hourly earnings, with a maximum of $52.50 for laid-off workers receiving state unemployment benefits and $80 a week for those whose benefits are exhausted. Under the terms of the 1968 contract, a joint committee was set up to establish an Earnings Protection Plan, which is designed to cushion the impact on income of workers whose pay is reduced because of automation, technological change or other economic factors. The new plan became effective in 1969. In any quarter in which earnings are adversely affected, workers with two years' service will automatically receive 85 percent of their average hourly earnings in the previous four quarters. The plan is financed by a two-cent company contribution derived from the contingent liability funds set aside for supplementary unemployment benefits and is clearly a refinement of that program and of the guaranteed annual wage.

The same process of refinement is observable in the shortening of the work week. No one has matched the broad jump made by the electricians of New York City to the 20-hour week, but a growing number of workers are shaving off two and three hours from their work week. Plumbers in Saratoga Springs, New York, for example, recently brought their work week down to 37 hours, and the Service Employees Union in New York City reduced weekly hours in the private hospitals from 37½ to 35. A few firms have successfully introduced the four day week, working their employees nine even 10 hours a day. The National Industrial Conference Board, incidentally, has predicted that the average week actually worked by private, nonfarm employees, which was 37.7 hours in 1970, will drop to 36.8 hours by 1980. A recession might intensify labor's drive for a shorter work week, however, and a downward drift might become a decided plunge. In April, 1970, some 490 delegates representing white-collar office and technical employees of the steelmakers voted to recommend that the Steel Workers Union take up the four-day week as a bargaining goal in 1971. As I. W. Abel, president of the union, noted, "When there's a shortage of labor and lots of overtime, there's not too much interest in the short work week. But when unemployment rises and layoffs increase, you get people thinking more about sharing the available work." And he added, "If we ever should get around to a peace economy—and I hope we do—we better get around to a four-day work week pretty fast." Any break of this magnitude by workers in a major industry such as steel would go a long way toward bringing on shorter hours for millions.

Trade unions, as Michael Harrington has said, are the most effective antipoverty agencies in the country—both in terms of benefits, wages and working conditions won and in terms of constant political pressure for a full-employment economy. White middle-class liberals wring their hands over the plight of the black poor; the working poor, black, Spanish-speaking and white, organize unions. The dramatic rise of Local 1199, the Drug and Hospital Union affiliated with the Retail, Wholesale and Department Store Union, AFL-CIO, illustrates the process. When hospital workers in New York City began to organize in the late 1950s, they were earning roughly $35 a week. A strike in the spring of 1959 won recognition for their union, Local 1199. It was a victory wrested through their own strength but one that might not have been possible without the backing of a united labor movement, which strikingly included solid support from New York's allegedly conservative building tradesmen. That victory doubled the hospital workers' weekly wage to a $75-a-week minimum, a gain for the poor as yet unmatched by any antipoverty or community-action program. By 1968 the hospital union had established a $100-a-week minimum in New York City's 34 nonprofit private institutions. Negotiations in 1970 increased the minimum to $130 a week and established a two-percent-of-payroll contribution to the union's benefit fund to finance dental and drug prescription plans among other benefits. The New York pattern ultimately will affect hospital workers elsewhere as well as act as a spur for unionization.

Agricultural workers, too, are taking the first step into the working class. Attempts to organize farm workers were made by the IWW before World War I, by the Southern Tenant Farmers

Union during the grim depression years when black and white sharecroppers fought Delta plantation owners, and by the National Farm Labor Union in the late 1940s. None succeeded and all were ultimately broken by terror and violence.

When black sharecroppers formed a union in eastern Arkansas in 1919, over 100 were murdered in the "Elaine Massacre." One of the survivors was among the 20 black and white sharecroppers who met in an abandoned schoolhouse on a cotton plantation near Tyronza, Arkansas, in July, 1934, to form the Southern Tenant Farmers Union. Many such continuities are buried in the history of labor. One senses the desperation and the courage that brought blacks and whites together in the Delta country of the 1930s in the recollections of H. L. Mitchell, the president of their union: "I remember one old white man [at the Tyronza meeting] who got up and said that he'd once been a member of the Ku Klux Klan, but that everybody was in the same boat in this fight here. Negroes were on the plantations . . . and the union should include both white and colored and fight for the rights of everyone." This solidarity withstood the machine-gunning of sharecroppers' homes and the flight of STFU's leaders and many members across the river into Memphis when the union first struck the Arkansas delta plantations. In 1935, 4,000 cotton pickers struck for ten days and forced a raise in wages to 75 cents a hundred pounds picked. But as Mitchell pointedly put it, "There weren't any negotiations. There never have been." And in the spring of 1936, at the height of the cotton-chopping season, the governor sent in the National Guard to break an SFTU strike, and the union never really recovered. Without protection in the law, the sharecroppers were literally beaten out of their union.

The only success scored by agricultural workers was in Hawaii. The International Longshoremen's and Warehousemen's Union unionized the island's dock workers and gained a substantial measure of political power as a consequence. In 1945 the union secured passage of an Employment Relations Act, which established collective-bargaining rights for agricultural workers.

Within a year the ILWU had unionized Hawaii's sugar and pine-apple plantations. Significantly the Hawaiian Pineapple Company, the largest producer on the islands, chose not to combat the union. But this was not the case on the mainland, where the continuing difficulties faced by agricultural workers is perhaps best illustrated by the fateful 1947 NFLU strike against the Di-Giorgio Fruit Corporation of Kern County, California.

With 4,600 acres, DiGiorgio is one of the country's largest "factories in the field," in Carey McWilliam's descriptive phrase. As a popular strike ballad put it:

> God Almighty made the Valley
> For a land of milk and honey,
> But a Corporation's got it
> For to turn it into money.

Wages were depressed by the importation of cheap labor from Mexico, the braceros. One worker testified in 1962 before a government commission, "I remember in 1948, when they didn't have any braceros, we got $1.10 a bucket [cherries]. Then— after they ran the [Mexican] Nationals in—the price went down to 85 cents a bucket and even lower. Just the last couple of seasons, it finally got back up where it was 14 years ago: $1.10 a bucket. And the only reason it did was because the union put the heat on the government and made them take out the Nationals." The importation of braceros played a crucial role in the DiGiorgio strike. Twenty-mile picket lines were maintained for nine months by the strikers despite harassment from local law-enforcement officials and the shooting of strike leader James Price. But the workers could not withstand the importation of strikebreakers under the aegis of the federal government. The strike was broken and with it a major effort at organizing 200,000 California farm workers.

In 1959 the AFL-CIO created an Agricultural Workers Organizing Committee and by June, 1963, had spent over $500,000 in organizing drives centered in California and extending up the Pacific Coast. Congress, in 1964, after pressure from the AFL-CIO as well as from religious and civil organizations, including the National Advisory Committee on Farm Labor, founded by Norman Thomas, Frank P. Graham, A. Philip Randolph and Mrs. Franklin D. Roosevelt, secured a ban on the importation of braceros. A year later the new union zeroed in on the grape harvest, a strategic move with far-reaching consequences. The grape industry is not typical of agriculture. It is a highly skilled, 12-month-a-year operation, entailing the hand pruning and cultivation of the invaluable vines. There is a large resident labor force which is supplemented by additional thousands of workers for the summer harvest. During May, 1965, members of the AFL-CIO union successfully struck in the Coachella Valley, increasing wages from $1.20 to $1.40 an hour, and the box incentive from 15 to 25 cents. Meanwhile, the independent National Farm Workers Association succeeded in winning a fight against a rent increase for the 20-year-old metal shacks, without windows or running water, which constituted housing for Delano-area grape workers. The leader of this fight was a remarkable young man, Cesar Chavez. It was his decision—and that of his fellow Mexican-Americans in Delano—to join the predominantly Filipino members of AWOC in a strike against the Delano grape growers that precipitated a national boycott of nonunion grapes and hopefully the ultimate organization of California's agricultural workers.

Chavez, whose father had come from Mexico, was born in 1927 on his grandfather's farm in Yuma, Arizona. During the depression the farm was foreclosed and the family moved to California and began moving with the crops. Over the years Chavez attended more than 30 schools only to drop out completely in the eighth grade to help support the family. He first worked in Delano in 1937, when he was ten. One fall the family picked grapes near Fresno. Each week the labor contractor said he could not pay them since he had not yet been paid himself. "At the end of the seventh week," Chavez recalls, "we went to the contractor's house and it was empty—he owed us for seven weeks' pay, and we haven't seen him to this day."

Out of such experiences Chavez developed a devotion to his people and an understanding of their needs. During the 1949 NFLU cotton strike Chavez led one of several caravans of automobiles that toured the cotton fields of California, calling out to pickers that a strike was on and that the union was seeking an increase in wages. After spending roughly a decade working with Saul Alinsky's Community Service Organization, Chavez moved with his wife and children to Delano. "I had some idea on what should be done," he has said of the move. "No great plans; just that it would take an awful lot of work to organize farm workers. It was a gamble. I went around for about 11 months and I went to about 87 communities and labor camps and in each place I'd find a few people who were committed to doing something; something had happened in their lives and they were ready for it." When about 600 to 800 AWOC workers struck 34 ranches in the Delano area in 1965 for a $1.40 minimum and improved working conditions, Chavez's group of some 1,100 members joined the walkout. *"Huelga!"* (Strike!) became the rallying cry that brought the two organizations together in the United Farm Workers' Organizing Committee, AFL-CIO.

Recognition, as in past trade-union struggles, became the key issue, second only to improvements in working conditions and wages. On one farm in the Delano area, 67 workers had to drink water from a single beer can. Lacking state-required portable toilets, workers relieved themselves in the fields. Without water, workers ate their meals with hands dusted by "hard pesticides," DDT and like poisons. Only the large ranches were struck initially—Schenley, the Sierra Vista Ranch of DiGiorgio, and others that employed thousands of workers to harvest the grapes. Strikebreakers were hired, trucks and tractors were driven alongside union picket lines, choking the strikers with dust. Picket signs were riddled with bullets, sprayed with insecticide. Workers who had lived for years on grower property were evicted.

The strike dragged on and a boycott was mounted against Schenley products. Following a march of 8,000 on the state capital at Sacramento, Schenley agreed to a contract providing for a $1.75-an-hour minimum wage, fringe benefits and a union shop and hiring hall. The spring, 1966, Schenley victory was followed by the capitulation of DiGiorgio later in the year to the union's demand for arbitration. The DiGiorgio arbitration award, in 1967, was in line with the settlement reached with Schenley, but it also included an employer contribution to a union health and welfare fund—an unprecedented development for farm labor. But the strike continued against some 30 growers for another two years, supplemented by a national boycott of nonunion table grapes. The boycott cost the growers 20 percent or more of the market for table grapes, according to the union. Governor Ronald Reagan warned that the boycott could destroy the industry, despite growers' protestations to the contrary.

In 1970 the growers began to topple before the union's persistence. A committee of Catholic bishops, chaired by Bishop Joseph Donnelly of Hartford, Connecticut, became interested in the struggle and successfully intervened. Within three months the United Farm Workers Organization signed contracts with 25 California growers, bringing about 25 percent of the state's 78,000 vineyard acres under union contract. A key contract with a farm corporation that grows 46,000 acres of citrus, nuts, wine grapes and other fruits, has been secured and another with a company that produces 98 percent of the dates grown in the United States. The producer of ten percent of California's $11-million melon crop has also signed a union agreement. A new union label—a black Aztec eagle in a white circle on a red background—proudly promised a brighter future for the downtrodden farm worker.

Farm and hospital workers are among the latest groups of working men and women to rise through their own efforts and with the support of their fellow workers out of what Marx caustically termed the *lumpenproletariat* into the unionized working classes. What the American labor movement has succeeded in accomplishing was portrayed in a survey of union members conducted for the AFL-CIO by the John Kraft polling organization. The results were carried in the August, 1967, issue of *The Federationist* and its findings have not been significantly eroded by the subsequent inflation. The profile of the unionized is:

> 46 percent of union families are in the $7,500–$15,000-a-year income range;
> 32 percent are in the $5,000–$7,500 range;
> nearly 50 percent are less than 40 years old, 25 percent are less than 30 years old;
> nearly 75 percent of members under 40 live in suburbs, nearly 50 percent of all members now live in suburbs;
> about 20 percent of union members are women, about 13 percent are black, and four percent Mexican or Oriental;
> 54 percent have belonged to their union for ten years or more, 25 percent have belonged for five years or less;
> 58 percent identify themselves as Democrats, 16 percent as Republicans, 17 percent as independents, nine percent uncertain.

Some have seen in the above statistics what an editor of *The Public Interest*, Winter, 1968, termed the *embourgeoisement* of American workers. To bolster this view, other findings of the Kraft poll were cited as proving "the conservatism of the group and its middle-class concerns." The Kraft poll, as an instance, asked union members, "What are the big problems on your mind—the things that bother you and should be getting attention?" Fifty-three percent spontaneously mentioned economic issues, 42 percent discussed Vietnam and 33 percent mentioned civil rights and law enforcement. Of those concerned with economic issues, the most pressing problem was taxes, and the second was the high cost of living. The significant difference was between those under 30 and those between 30 and 49. Of the latter group 55 percent mentioned economic issues, and of these the single largest mention was taxes (about 28 percent), the high cost of living was mentioned by 13 percent in this group. Of those under thirty 61 percent named economic questions as pressing, and of these 20 percent named the high cost of living and 13 percent said taxes. Where civil-rights and law-enforcement problems were raised, a significant proportion mentioned juvenile delinquency as a relevant concern. On Vietnam the single largest group (about one-third) said that President Johnson was doing the best he could, the second largest wanted to escalate the war, while a smaller number wanted an immediate end to the war.

Why the sum of these findings evidence "middle-class concerns" is something of a mystery. In 1967 Vietnam, for instance, as a *hot* issue was a middle-class, and not a working-class, issue. Workers' sons were fighting there, and not the children of the rich or those of the comfortable middle class. Since, by and large, most workers believed that their country's cause was right and deserving of support, this was reflected in their backing of President Johnson. Since then, incidentally, a growing number have questioned whether or not their country's course was correct. By 1970 trade unionists were as deeply divided as most of the country over the issue. While the federation's top leadership continued to support the country's Vietnam policy, emphasizing the need for a just and honorable peace and not, as some would have it, an all-out escalation of the war, other important union leaders differed strongly. The 1970 conventions of the State, County and Municipal Employees Union and of the Amalgamated Clothing Workers condemned the Vietnam and Cambodian war policies of the Nixon Administration. The United Auto Workers, the Teamsters and the United Distributive Workers in the Alliance for Labor Action supported the 1969 antiwar moratorium campaign as did other unions. Nonetheless, as a class issue, Vietnam remained until recently a source of middle-class agitation.

One of the major differences between American workers and those in class-conscious Europe has been the high incidence of home-ownership. In Detroit, a working-class city, a majority of workers own their own homes. This fact of ownership leads to the anomaly of the militant worker in the plant who returns home to

vote conservatively as a property owner, on local tax-related issues, school-bond issues and the like. He exists, but the tax rebellion of the late 1960s also contained a deep class resentment
over a tax structure that inherently favors the rich. In general, the
rate of taxation declines as income rises. Some individuals and
corporations pay little or no tax at all, though their incomes may
exceed $5 million annually. Estimates of total tax loads indicate
that 33 percent of the income of those earning $3,000 to $5,000
goes to taxes, and only 28 percent of those earning $15,000 or
more. Tax loopholes yawn for the rich and are as the eye of a
needle for the workingman and workingwoman. Most workers are
perfectly aware of these imbalances. Small wonder then that they
rebel or list taxes as a pressing economic problem when taxes
begin to prick under the rise of civic costs. Economic issues and
the high cost of living affect the affluent only peripherally but
are prime issues of the deepest concern to American workers.
Forty-six percent of union *families* (note, not individual workers)
may fall into the $7,500–$15,000-a-year income range, but they
do so at a time when the U.S. Department of Labor reports that
an income of $9,191 a year enables a city family of four to
maintain "a moderate standard of living." Only about a third
of all American families reach that standard, one quickly out-
dated by a profit-prompted inflation. As Brendan Sexton has
pointed out, "Certainly, the typical production worker is much
better off than a Mississippi farm tractor driver or a city mother
living on welfare, but he hardly lives opulently. He treads water,
financially and psychically."

The 1970s may see the development of a true working class
in the United States. Until recently, ethnic and religious animosi-
ties often outweighed class solidarity among working people in
this country. Ethnic and religious differences help account for
the lack of a working-class or labor-oriented party in American
politics. There are signs, however, of change. In 1964 the
Republican candidacy of the conservative Arizonian Senator
Barry M. Goldwater was seen as a threat to the moderate welfare-

ism of the New Deal, Fair Deal and Great Society, and was so rejected by a great majority of Americans. In the 1968 elections, largely because of the Vietnam war and a startling inflation, the differences between candidates did not seem so clear-cut to many middle-class Americans. (Black Americans living somewhat closer to the harsh realities of American life recognized the difference, and 90 percent voted for the Democratic candidate, Vice-President Hubert H. Humphrey.) The liberal, labor and minorities coalition, in Gus Tyler's perceptive phrase, "became unglued." Many workers, as much as 24 percent of union members, according to a Lou Harris poll in August, 1967, leaned to the third party of George Wallace. While there were racialist and racist overtones to this attraction, there were also powerful class undertones. This was recognized by Senator Edward Kennedy in his appeal to the supporters of his murdered brother to reject the "extremist" Wallace. "Most of these people," Senator Kennedy said of working-class Wallace supporters, "are not motivated by racial hostility or prejudice. They feel that their needs and their problems have been passed over by the tide of recent events. They bear the burden of an unfair system of Selective Service. They lose out because higher education costs so much. They are the ones who feel most threatened at the security of their jobs, the safety of their families, the value of their property and the burden of their taxes. They feel the established system has not been sympathetic to them in their problems of everyday life and in a large measure they are right." Significantly it was a class attack mounted by the unions against Wallace stressing his anti-labor record that changed the minds of Wallace-prone workers. The 24-percent preference for Wallace slid to 12 percent by election day.

American workers are not, nor are they likely to be, class-conscious in the apocalyptic Marxist sense. As Sexton points out, "Unionists have learned a hard lesson after almost a century of fierce bloodletting on the picket line: *that combat is the last, not the first resort.*" Their antagonists, he adds, "are the employer and the conservative legislator, not the 'capitalist system.'"

Moreover, most workers have scored their major gains through collective bargaining, or so it seems at first glance, for being human, they tend to forget what lies at one remove beyond the struggles on the picket line, that is, a large body of protective legislation secured by trade-union political action. And until recently much of trade-union visible effort was expended on organizing and in collective bargaining. Instead of seeking improved pensions through the Social Security system, the unions have secured supplementary pension benefits under contracts with private firms. Instead of seeking medical-care benefits through some variant of socialized medicine, they have secured coverage through negotiated insurance plans. Instead of seeking higher unemployment compensation through the federal-state system, they have gone all out for supplementary unemployment benefits (SUB) paid by industry. The result—as Daniel Bell demonstrated in a *Commentary* article, "The Subversion of Collective Bargaining"—has been a heavy imbalance favoring workers in the larger, better-organized industries. The giant unions worked out a *quid pro quo* with their industrial counterparts: collective bargaining became a means of justifying price increases, and in return, industry granted major wage gains and substantial improvements in fringe benefits. But it was usually difficult to extend similar gains to the weaker unions, whose members, moreover, had to bear the additional burden of higher prices.

This is only one of the many indications that collective bargaining of the traditional kind is no longer an effective instrument for achieving the major social goals of the labor movement. As the economic situation worsens, management gets tougher. A long strike, in their view, becomes another, more advantageous form of layoff: you cut back on production that otherwise might flood the market and gain a little clout for pressuring workers into line. Historically, when unions have been confronted by stiffening employer resistance to bargaining demands, they have sought relief in legislative and political action. This is perhaps the lesson learned from the GE strike, the UAW strike against General